THE
GREAT DUKE

OR

THE INVINCIBLE GENERAL

Arthur Bryant

COLLINS
St James's Place, London
1971

William Collins Sons & Co Ltd
London · Glasgow · Sydney · Auckland
Toronto · Johannesburg

First published 1971
© Arthur Bryant 1971
ISBN 0 00 211936 6
Set in Monotype Fontana
Made and Printed in Great Britain by
William Collins Sons & Co Ltd Glasgow

"If England should require the service of her Army again, and I should be with it, let me have 'Old Nosey' to command. Our interests would be sure to be looked into; we should never have occasion to fear an enemy. There are two things we should be certain of. First, we should always be as well supplied with rations as the nature of the service should admit. The second is we should be sure to give the enemy a damned good thrashing. What can a soldier desire more!"

PRIVATE WHEELER OF THE 51ST FOOT

"Dormir avec Napoleon, dormir avec le vainqueur du monde! Mais M. le Duc était de beaucoup le plus fort!"

ATTRIBUTED TO MLLE. GEORGES
OF THE COMÉDIE FRANÇAISE

"Great in council and great in war,
Foremost captain of his time,
Rich in saving common sense,
And, as the greatest only are,
In his simplicity sublime"

TENNYSON

CONTENTS

MAPS

INTRODUCTION

ENCOURAGED by the reception of my short life of Nelson, I have followed it with a companion study of his great contemporary, Wellington. This necessarily is a far larger book, for his military life in high command lasted much longer than Nelson's and covered a more crowded field. As the only criticism of my *Nelson* was that it was too short, I hope this may be forgiven.

This book is not intended to take the place of the fine full-length biography on which my friend, Elizabeth Longford, is engaged, and of which the second volume has still to be published. It is primarily a study of Wellington as a soldier and commander, the greatest, I think, this country - or perhaps any other - has produced. He proved, in fact, invincible, or "bahadur" as his Indian soldiers called him. As it was in India, between his twenty-eighth and thirty-sixth years that he made himself master of his profession and learnt to organise, supply and command armies, and where he won his earliest and most daring victories, I have described these years in greater detail than has usually been accorded them. The latter part of the book, covering his better-known European campaigns, is based on the ten years' research I did in the 'forties on the period of our history covered by Wellington's military service and public life, and throughout the greater part of which he was a dominating national and international figure. Here I have drawn on descriptions of his Peninsular and Waterloo campaigns and battles from my *Years of Victory* and *Age of Elegance*. Where I have done so I have revised, rewritten and expanded them to form part of a comprehensive portrait of the man and his achievements.

As Wellington was a very plain and direct man, I have tried to make my account of him match his character. Wherever possible, I have allowed him to speak for himself for, as his voluminous letters and dispatches show, no one, on questions of fact, ever expressed himself better. "There is nothing in life," he said, "like a clear definition," and he was a great definer. Throughout I have tried to set him in the context of the terrible events with which, during the years

11

covered by this book, he and his country were faced, and which, more than any other man of his time, he learnt to master. I have described, too, the human instruments - the officers and soldiers, without whom his career would be meaningless and through whom he did his work.

Tennyson, in his Funeral Ode, called him "the Great Duke" and "England's greatest son"; his senior officers "Old Chin"; the rough, untutored soldiers who fought under him "the long nosed b— who beat the French" or "Old Nosey". It was under this last unflattering, but just, pseudonym—and he cared little for flattery but much for justice—that he did his greatest service to his country and was remembered by his men. The sub-title of my book is inspired by Mr Jac Weller's description of him in his careful study, *Wellington in the Peninsula*, as "the only undefeated first-rank general in history". Whatever may be said for or against him, unlike Napoleon he proved invincible. "The Duke of Wellington," wrote the great German historian, Niebuhr, "is, I believe, the only general in whose conduct of war we cannot discover any important mistake." Once, asked how many guns he had captured, he replied he did not know but guessed about three thousand, adding as an afterthought that what was more extraordinary was that he had never lost, except temporarily for a few days or hours, a single gun.

ARTHUR BRYANT

ENGLAND'S GREATEST SON

In the middle of the last century, in the lifetime of men and women with whom the author has spoken, there was to be seen, walking or riding the London streets, a most distinguished-looking old man. Wherever he went, everyone stopped and saluted him as though he were a king. As men uncovered, he would lift a stiff forefinger to the brim of a tall grey hat. The gesture was never omitted and never varied. He was always immaculately dressed, in spotless white trousers and a skin-tight, single-breasted blue frock-coat. His hair was silvery, his eyes bright and piercing, his figure lithe and upright as a boy's, save for the shoulders which were bent with age, his finely chiselled features and long Roman beak like an eagle's. To the early Victorians he seemed as much a landmark as St Paul's or his own gigantic statue - cocked-hat, cloak, world-famous charger - riding above the triumphal arch opposite his house at Hyde Park Corner. Everyone called him the Duke, as though, in a country with two dozen of the richest dukes in the world, there was only one. For, so long as Wellington lived, for most Englishmen there was only one.

Yet he was a simple man - bleak, frugal, unsparing of himself. As his contemporary, Greville, wrote, he was without a particle of vanity or conceit. Though surrounded by admiring crowds whenever he appeared, he never seemed aware of the universal adulation. He did whatever he was asked to do by the Government of his country: took, as Greville said, "more pride in obeying than in commanding, and never for a moment considered that his great position and elevation above all other subjects released him from the same obligation which the humblest of them acknowledged. An ever-abiding sense of duty and obligation made him the humblest of citizens and the most obedient of servants. The Crown never possessed a more faithful, devoted and disinterested subject."

Thirty and more years before, at the age of forty-six, he had performed the greatest miracle of the age. For ten hours, until the arrival of the Prussians, he had held the ridge at Waterloo with a largely raw, untrained and uncoordinated international army against a veteran French force nearly twice its size in real effectives and commanded by the greatest military conqueror of all time. His allies, badly beaten at Ligny two days before, were a day's march away, and Napoleon had staked everything on forcing a victory before they could reach the field. But for the Duke there is no doubt he would have done so. It was Wellington's calm, inflexible will, his brilliant disposition and control of his slender forces, above all the tremendous prestige of his past victories, as he rode, immaculate and unperturbed, along the stricken ridge, that kept his young troops to the sticking-point until, as night fell, the furious French attacks weakened and collapsed and the Prussians came up.

Yet the Duke had not always seemed a hero to his countrymen. Fifteen years after Waterloo, the hated champion of a lost political cause, he had been booed by the rough mob of the unpoliced capital whenever he appeared in the streets. His house in Piccadilly still carried the iron shutters - it does to this day - which he had had installed in front of the gaping windows the populace had smashed while his dead wife lay inside. This time he had been unable to hold the political ridge with his handful of peers and Tory diehards, and the forces of Reform had swept victorious across it. Yet in defeat and retreat his calm greatness had become once more apparent. The principle on which he acted, then as always, was his own undeviating ideal of duty. The King's government, he said, must be carried on; civil war - the worst of all evils - avoided; the public served. For this end he was ready to sacrifice everything: Party consistency, reputation, his own pride. The only thing he never broke was his word and his honour. He led his forces off the field and continued to serve the State in subordinate, as in supreme office, and with the same unsparing devotion. He was the greatest public servant - and soldier - Britain had ever known.

Chapter One

THE REJECTED BEAU

The rare old Duke of York,
He had ten thousand men;
He marched 'em up a great high hill,
Then marched 'em down again.

OLD SONG

ARTHUR WESLEY, as his family name – later changed to Wellesley – was then spelt, was born probably on May 1st 1769, in his parents' town house in Merrion Street, Dublin. His father was the first Earl of, and second Baron, Mornington in the Irish peerage – an artistic, music-loving, but rather feckless Anglo-Irish landowner who, having made a somewhat sensational start in life as an infant prodigy, had been honoured for his madrigals, glees and sacred compositions with an honorary Doctorate and Professorship of Music by Trinity College, Dublin.

Arthur was the third of five surviving sons and a daughter, all of whom in youth outshone him. His earliest years were spent in Dublin and among the green hunting fields of County Meath where his father's pretentious but slightly ramshackle seat, Castle Dangan, was situated. Ireland at that time, in contrast to England – then in the high noon of aristocratic good fortune and splendour – was an uneasy polity where Palladian mansions stood in a wild, romantic and mournful landscape peopled by ragged, half-tragic, half-reckless Catholic peasants. The Wesley family, whose real patronymic was Cowley or Colley—Wesley they had inherited with their estates through the distaff—was part of a ruling caste of English descent and Protestant faith, who, dispossessing the native Catholic peasantry, had monopolised all wealth and power in the country. It was a convivial, hard-living, pugnacious and, where its political and religious supremacy was threatened, unyielding minority. It governed Ireland through Dublin Castle – the glittering seat of British authority – and, after 1782 until the Act of Union of 1801, through a

15

highly corrupt, Protestant and, being Irish, eloquent Parliament representing only a minute fraction of the population.

Arthur's childhood does not seem to have been very happy. By his mother—a strong-minded but rather imperceptive and conventional society woman, the daughter of an Irish banker, Viscount Dungannon—he was regarded as the dunce of the family: "my ugly boy, Arthur," she called him. He had light blue, rather dreamy poetic eyes, a sensitive mouth and fair brown hair. The craving for affection, which in the years of his fame and public acclaim often broke through his somewhat gruff and chilling reserve, had little scope in the rigorous rough and tumble of early family life. It was the spartan rather than the tender that his mother sought to inculcate in her brilliant brood; the practice, which she strictly enforced, of regular cold-morning bathing* became a lifelong habit with him, as was the curb he was taught to place on his strong, perhaps overstrong, feelings. The nearest he came to receiving indulgence in his rather lonely youth seems to have been from his grandmother, Lady Dungannon, whom he used to stay with at her home, Brynkinalt, in North Wales, on his journeys between Holyhead and London.

Because his happy-go-lucky, extravagant father lived beyond his means and preferred London to Ireland, he passed at the age of seven from a gay country-house in Meath to lodgings in Knightsbridge and a private school in Chelsea, where he described himself as having been "a dreamy, idle and shy lad," undistinguished both at work and play. His chief interests were the fiddle and a passionate love of music which he inherited from his father. His career at Eton, a rough place where a lad had to sink or swim and where he once won a fight against a bigger boy, ended prematurely when, three years after his father's death in 1781, his mother, to save money, took him, at the age of fifteen, to board with an advocate's family at Brussels. When she returned to England, not knowing what to do with her "awkward son", she sent him to the fashionable academy of equitation at Angers in France to study the military sciences of horsemanship, fencing, fortification, mathematics and—since it was still the France of the *ancien régime*—dancing, deportment and graceful manners.

Here under its stately deputy-governor, M. de Pignerolle, the fifth of his dynasty, the till now callow youth learnt to respect the absol-

* Muriel Wellesley, 82.

ute rectitude, antique courtesy and high sense of honour of the old royal France,* so soon to perish, with its corrupt court, stagnant administration and over-privileged and idle *noblesse*, in the fires of revolution. About the same time another aspirant to a military career, born in the same year as himself - the son of a poor Corsican widow named Bonaparte - after serving a hungry apprenticeship at a much less aristocratic French military establishment, received his first commission as a gunnery officer in the French Army.

From his year at Angers, where he was chiefly remembered by his companions for his delicate constitution and his affection for a small and inseparable terrier named Vic, and where he seems to have known some happiness,† Arthur Wesley returned to England shortly before his eighteenth birthday, a polished young gentleman with a perfect command of French. "He really is a very charming young man," wrote his gratified mother, "never did I see such a change for the better in anyone." One of the celebrated Ladies of Llangollen, whom he visited while staying with his grandmother, described him in her diary as "a charming young man, handsome, fashioned, tall and elegant." Yet, by the standards of the extravagant social world into which he had been born, he was an embarrassingly impecunious one. His eldest brother, Lord Mornington, now a rising young politician and junior Lord of the Treasury, bought him an ensign's commission in the 73rd Regiment, then serving in India, and secured him an aide-de-camp's appointment at ten shillings a day on the staff of the Lord Lieutenant of Ireland, the Marquis of Buckingham. For the next five years - while across the English Channel the first high hopes of reform in a bankrupt and disintegrating

* A century later another British soldier, Major-General Sir Edward Spears, growing up in the Château de Voutenoy in Burgundy, learnt from his kinsman, Gaston Rafinesque, "what a French gentleman can be like, a perfect example of rectitude and honour". The latter loved to quote Boileau's lines:
" *L'honneur est comme une île escarpée et sans bords,*
L'on n'y peut plus rentrer dès que l'on est dehors."
Sir Edward Spears, *The Picnic Basket*, 28.

† At a reception at the Tuileries after Waterloo, Lady Shelley, leaning on the Duke's arm, described how he suddenly dropped it "to greet and kiss with reverence the hand of the most charming old lady of the *vieille cour* that I ever met. The Duke introduced her to me as the Duchesse de Serant" - her husband had been the hereditary Governor of the College - "in whose society he had passed the happiest part of his life, and to whose matronly kindness he owed more gratitude than he could ever repay. . . . The Duchesse de Serant spoke to me of the noble qualities of mind and heart which had, in those early days, endeared Wellington to the Duc de Serant and herself." Lady Shelley, Vol. I, 119/20.

France turned to horror as the Paris mob, tasting noble blood, drove from excess to excess and, throughout that wide and beautiful land, castle after castle went up in flames - the young soldier lived the gilded, fashionable social life of Dublin Castle, dancing attendance on two successive vicereines, Lady Buckingham and Lady Westmorland, and engaged in a continuous round of dinner parties, dances, picnics and amateur theatricals. And though, by a series of exchanges and purchases, he was able - as was then normal for a young man with aristocratic connections - to rise by the time he was twenty-two to the rank of captain, his pay was quite insufficient to defray the mounting bills for fine clothes, horses, wine and gambling which the life of a Dublin Castle aide-de-camp made obligatory.

To these circumstances, only aggravated by his election—with the appropriate and necessary bribery—to the family seat for Trim in the Irish Parliament, he owed a humiliating and deeply-felt disappointment in love. The girl, the Hon Catherine, or Kitty, Pakenham, three years younger than himself, was the daughter of a country neighbour, Lord Longford—a pretty brunette with a fascinating figure and bookish tastes, who in a demure Jane Austenish way, returned his affection. But as he completely lacked the means to support her, and, as the embarrassed state of the Wesley's fortunes were well known, the romance was frowned on by the girl's family and the offer of his hand rejected.

Yet for all his lack of worldly prospects, and though to superficial observers he seemed "a shallow, saucy stripling,"* there was something unusual about young Captain Wesley. The long aquiline nose and curved eyebrows ran to a mighty brow and jutting chin which hinted at hidden powers of brain and resolution. In 1793, when through further regimental exchanges and purchases with money advanced by his brother Mornington, he became a major and, shortly afterwards, lieutenant-colonel in command of the 33rd Regiment of Foot - the future Duke of Wellington's West Riding Regiment - these became more apparent. He had something of his own to work for at last. Into the detailed care of his men, provision for their feeding, health and clothing, training, discipline and *esprit de corps*, he threw his mind and heart. Within a year he had made his regiment the best drilled on the Irish station. And qualities which

* Charles Napier, I, 52.

had passed unnoticed in the butterfly life of a Dublin Castle ADC were now seen - thoroughness, exactitude, and a capacity for accurately weighing up facts and figures and putting them to practical, common-sense use. It was now that he learnt the basis of his profession—"the actual handling of troops, the mechanical process of bringing them into play"—at the lowest level which he defined as the knowledge on which all successful command in the field depends. "One must understand the mechanism and power of the individual soldier," he told his friend, Croker, after Waterloo; "then that of a company, a battalion, a brigade and so on, before one can venture to group divisions and move an army. I believe I owe most of my success to the attention I always paid to the inferior part of tactics as a regimental officer. There were few men in the Army who knew these details better than I did; it is the foundation of all military knowledge." It was this which caused an experienced officer, Colonel George Napier - father of the famous fighting family - to remark at the time: "Those who think lightly of that lad are unwise in their generation; he has the makings of a great general."*

*   *   *

The year which first saw Arthur Wesley in charge of men saw something more momentous. For Britain, whose reforming Prime Minister, William Pitt, had a few months before declared her to be on the threshold of a long spell of peace, was reluctantly drawn into war with Revolutionary France, whose brash, ruthless leaders were showing the same contemptuous disregard for international frontiers and treaties as they had done for the lives and property of their own former rulers. Half-pay Captain Nelson, eating his heart out on his father's glebe amid the Norfolk sand dunes, was given a ship and sailed for the Mediterranean; presently Lieutenant-Colonel Wesley was ordered with his regiment to Flanders.

It had not been expected that the war, into which Great Britain had been forced in defence of her treaty obligations, would last long. The excited hordes of Revolutionary France, proclaiming death to all aristocrats and established Governments, would, it was felt, be soon driven back to their fields and cobbled slums by the meticulous, pipe-clayed, professional armies of monarchical Europe, now banded

* *Croker Papers*, I, 337; Charles Napier, I, 52.

against her by her outrageous excesses. Yet, after a few initial reverses, the opposite happened. Disregarding every established rule of war, the French rabble in arms, disciplined by terror and the guillotine, began to sweep all before it and, in the flush of successive victories, became such an army as the world had never seen.

For in their blue jackets and wooden sabots - "the blue earthenware" of the émigré aristocrats' contemptuous phrase - the men encamped to defend the French frontiers were learning how to put the Marseillaise into action. Among those whom they elected as colonels were seven future Napoleonic marshals and a quarter of the Imperial Generals of Division. "We lived," wrote one of them long afterwards, "in an atmosphere of light; I feel its heat and power now at 55, just as I felt it on the first day." For them and their political masters in Paris success was the only criterion; those who failed in battle went to the guillotine. Every man not crippled by age or infirmity was pressed into the armies - a force purged by desperation of fear and pity. The party tyrants, posted at the headquarters of every command, terrified generals and soldiers alike into unquestioning obedience to the dictates of the all-powerful Committee of Public Safety in Paris.*

Yet this amalgam of enthusiasm and terror could not have been transformed into the irresistible force it became without organising genius. Two days before the *levée en masse* was ordered for the entire manhood of France—a new conception of war which blended the modern nation-state with the embattled tribe of the remote past—a forty-year-old captain of Engineers, Lazare Carnot, was appointed to the Committee of Public Safety. Austere, unsparing, a student of history and theology with Roman virtues and Calvinistic ideals, the tall ungainly republican captain, stretched out on the floor of his office among his maps and green portfolios, forged the weapon of the future Napoleon. He revolutionised the formation, discipline and training of every unit, chose the officers, set the armies in motion according to a single daring and methodical plan, organised the

---

* Wellington's own views on the triumph of Revolutionary enthusiasm were set out in a letter of October 6th 1809, to Sir John Anstruther. "I fancy that, upon reflection, it will be discovered that what was deemed enthusiasm among the French, which enabled them successfully to resist all Europe at the commencement of the revolution, was force acting through the medium of popular societies and assuming the name of enthusiasm, and that force, in a different shape, has completed the conquest of Europe and keeps the continent in subjection." Brett-James, 171. See *idem* 224.

transport and commissariat, and mobilised the intellect of the nation to devise weapons of war. Far away on the frontiers, and in the great confused camps of the interior, the ragged armies responded to that unseen touch, while, in the sun-drenched squares and narrow, evil-smelling streets of the cities, the gangs went about their business of terror and the guillotine rose and fell.

Using the interior lines which France's central position gave her, Carnot and his Revolutionary armies struck at the encircling cordon of enemies - weak at every point and strong at none - with the shock of concentrated hammer-blows. They attacked in the new tactical order that "the organiser of victory" prescribed for them: the picked men - the natural fighters - going ahead in clouds of sharpshooters, the remainder massed in columns whose density made up for lack of training and whose superior numbers, launched in endless waves, and accompanied by fast-moving horse artillery, enabled them to break the rigid, professional lines of their foes.

Among those who suffered under the impact of this new technique of war was the little British Expeditionary Force which for the past year had been serving in Flanders under the Duke of York with the Austrian and Prussian armies on the northern frontiers of France. In June 1794, on Carnot's orders, General Jourdan and the reconstituted Army of Sambre-et-Meuse crossed the Sambre and captured the key town of Charleroi, whence a generation later Napoleon was to strike at the armies of Wellington and Blücher. The speed and fury of its attack broke the overstretched cordon of the professional monarchical armies. As a result, the British, their flank exposed by the Austrian retreat, were compelled to fall back in haste, abandoning Tournai, Oudenarde and Ghent without a shot. On July 5th, at an allied council on the future field of Waterloo, the Duke of York pleaded with the Allied commander, the Prince of Coburg, for a stand on the ridge of Mont St Jean. Yet, scarcely had a decision to fight been reached, than the Austrians, fearful for their communications, once more abandoned their allies and retreated eastwards towards their bases on the Rhine, leaving the road to Brussels open. By doing so they not only exposed the expeditionary force's flank but forced it to fall back, in isolation, northwards on its own base at Antwerp. "The opinion which the British nation must have on the subject," wrote the indignant Duke of York to Coburg, "is that we are betrayed and sold to the enemy."

In this witches' cauldron of disaster, Arthur Wesley served his first apprenticeship in war. It proved hard and discouraging. He landed at Ostend at the end of June 1794 with his regiment as part of a force hastily sent out from England under Major-General Lord Moira to save that indefensible port, and which only just escaped encirclement by a brilliant march across the French front to join the Duke of York's army as it retreated towards Holland. At Boxtel on September 15th 1794, the twenty-five-year-old former Dublin Castle ADC received his baptism of fire when the enemy, crossing the Dommel in overwhelming force, drove the British from their positions. A counter-attack under cover of darkness failed disastrously, largely owing to faulty command and the lack of training of newly-promoted youthful regimental commanders fresh from England. But Lieutenant-Colonel Wesley's 33rd regiment proved an exception and, by its discipline and steady musketry, plugged a dangerous breach in the line and, when others were failing, firing company volleys in extended line beat off a strong attack by a French column.

Sullenly the army retreated beyond the Waal. It felt neglected and forgotten. Its boots were worn out and its uniforms stained and ragged; the new recruits who filled its ranks arrived in thin linen jackets and trousers without waistcoats, drawers and stockings. The Wagon Corps, founded to supply its needs, seemed to have been raised from the thieves' kitchens of Blackfriars and Seven Dials, and was known to the troops as the "Newgate Blues"; and the military hospitals proved shortcuts to the next world. A Dutch observer counted 42 bodies flung out of one barge of 500 sick, who had been left untended on the open deck without even straw to lie on. The surgeons' mates allowed the sick and wounded to starve, and spent the sums they claimed from Government in drinking and debauchery.

From top to bottom the military administration, tested by adversity, was rotten. "I learnt more by seeing our own faults and the defects of our system in the campaign of Holland, than anywhere else," the future Duke of Wellington recalled. "I was left there to myself with my regiment, the 33rd, on the Waal, thirty miles from headquarters, which latter were a scene of jollification, and I do not think that I was once visited by the Commander-in-Chief. The infantry regiments, taken individually, were as good in proper hands as they are now, but the system was wretched." Everything which

could make an efficient fighting force was lacking except courage.
"We want artillerymen," wrote the Duke of York's ADC, Captain
Calvert, "we want a general officer at the head of the artillery, we
want drivers and smiths; . . . we want a commanding engineer of
rank and experience; . . . we want, at least, two out of the four
brigades of mounted artillery with which his Grace of Richmond is
amusing himself in England. We want a total stop put to that per-
nicious mode of bestowing rank on officers without even the form of
recommendation, merely for raising (by means of crimps) a certain
number of men, to restore to the Army those independent and disinterested feelings and high principles which should actuate a soldier
and form the basis of the military discipline of a free country." The
new Secretary at War, when he visited the front, commented bitterly
on the shortage of artillery drivers. "One sits at home quietly and
overlooks such particulars," he wrote, "but the fate of armies and of
kingdoms is decided often by nothing else."*

With more than half its 21,000 infantry down with typhus,
wounds and exposure, and with Dutch traitors and French agents
swarming through its lines, the army had only one hope - winter.
The floods of November turned the Waal into an impassable barrier
of desolate waters. Behind it a forlorn handful of redcoats preserved
the last foothold of the *ancien régime* in the Low Countries, guarding
the banks of Amsterdam and the Dutch fleet and naval stores. In a
letter written that December, Arthur Wesley, already a veteran
campaigner, drew a picture of their plight. "The French keep us in a
perpetual state of alarm; we turn out once, sometimes twice, every
night; the officers and men are harassed to death, and, if we are not
relieved, I believe there will be few of the latter remaining shortly.
I have not had my clothes off my back for a long time and generally
spend the greatest part of the night upon the banks of the river." He
described how the enemy, who kept him and his men continually on
the *qui vive* at night, would chatter to them by day across the river
and even show off before them by dancing the *carmagnole*, occasionally scattering the spectators with a cannon-ball.

A week before Christmas the floating ice in the Waal began to pack.
By the new year the frozen flood had ceased to be a barrier. Breaking
every canon of eighteenth-century warfare and trusting for supplies to a barren and ice-gripped countryside, the French poured

* *Windham Papers*, I, 224; Calvert, 338, 359-60; Ellesmere, 161; Fortescue, IV, 315.

across the river. To avoid annihilation the outnumbered British and Hanoverians fell back hastily towards the Ysel.

The cold of that January was something which old men remembered fifty years afterwards. The retreat of the army across the icy wastes of Gelderland had the quality of a nightmare. There was no shelter against the arctic wind. Discipline vanished, and even the Brigade of Guards engaged in pitched battle round the bread wagons with their traditional foes, the Hessians. "Those who woke on the morning of the 17th of January, 1795," wrote Sir John Fortescue in his *History of the British Army*, "saw about them such a sight as they never forgot. Far as the eye could reach over the whitened plain were scattered gun-limbers, wagons full of baggage, stores or sick men, sutlers' carts and private carriages. Beside them lay the horses, dead; here a straggler who had staggered on to the bivouac and dropped to sleep in the arms of the frost; there a group of British and Germans round an empty rum cask; here forty English Guardsmen huddled together about a plundered wagon; there a pack-horse with a woman lying alongside it, and a baby swaddled in rags peering out of the pack with its mother's milk turned to ice upon its lips - one and all stark, frozen, dead. Had the retreat lasted but three or four days longer, not a man would have escaped."* As it was, more than six thousand - a third of the expeditionary force - perished in four days.

The retreat completed the disintegration of Holland. The mob rose, set up trees of Liberty and flaunted the tricolour. On January 20th the French entered Amsterdam and proclaimed a revolutionary Republic. There was not even time to remove the fleet. A few smaller vessels got away to England, but a flying body of French horse and artillery galloped across the frozen Zuyder Zee and surprised the Dutch battleships ice-bound in the Texel.

All hope of any further stand now vanished. The starving and demoralised survivors of the British Expeditionary Force fell back into North Germany. That a remnant returned to England at all was largely due to young Lieutenant-Colonel Wesley. In temporary command of a brigade covering the retreat, he was always on the spot, saw everything for himself, did everything. That his men were without overcoats in a freezing winter, that the commissariat on which their food depended failed utterly to function, was not his fault. Whatever he could do to remedy these defects, he did. Not that

* Fortescue, IV, 320-1.

it brought him credit with the higher command, for those who do work their superiors leave undone are seldom thanked. But he saw how war should not be waged, and it was a valuable lesson. "I learnt," he said afterwards, "what one ought not to do, and that is always something."

Early in March, 1795, the Government sent transports to the Weser to evacuate the survivors. On April 13th the infantry embarked at Bremen and Arthur Wesley returned to Ireland, a depressed and disillusioned man. Before leaving for Flanders he had written a farewell letter from barracks to his unattainable love, telling her that, if ever an improvement in his circumstances should cause her and her family to change their minds, his would still be the same. So hopeless did his prospects in a hide-bound, incompetent Service now seem that he thought of resigning his commission and, still with hopes of Kitty Pakenham, vainly applied for a post in the Revenue Department and, when this failed, for other appointments on the Irish Establishment.

But the days of easy patronage were past, both in Dublin and London. Ireland, the grievances of her oppressed Catholic majority inflamed by French Jacobin agents, was on the verge of revolution, while England, her continental allies defeated, was facing challenges straining all her resources. In May, 1795, the new Dutch or Batavian Republic concluded an alliance with France, granting her the use of its fleet against Britain, an annual tribute and the permanent maintenance of a French army in Holland. Luxembourg surrendered in June, and Sweden made peace in the same month. In July Spain withdrew from the Coalition, secretly undertaking to use her influence to turn Portugal against England. Only Austria, little Piedmont, and the kingdom of the Two Sicilies remained languidly faithful to the Grand Alliance. All were far away from Britain. Between her and them lay a victorious France set on her destruction, with its population swollen by conquests from twenty-six to thirty-five millions, or three times as great as hers. "Dread and terrible times," wrote Parson Woodforde of Norfolk in his diary, "appear to be near at hand."

Under the leadership of men prepared to stop at nothing, France was seeking to impose a new order on the world by naked force. With the entire coastline of western Europe from the Elbe to Biscay dominated by foes, Britain was at war with the most dangerous force in the world: a spontaneous explosion of human energy exploited by men consumed with the lust for tyrannic power. Compared with the French Republic with more than half a million men in arms, she maintained at home a peacetime establishment of less than 15,000 troops, with another 30,000 scattered about the world, mostly in remote and unhealthy stations like the West Indian sugar islands which constantly called for new drafts to replace the inroads of yellow fever. She was now trying by every means open to a libertarian and parliamentary Government to raise more troops, and every regular unit of her Army was needed for immediate service overseas.

In the autumn of 1795, six months after their return from Germany, Lieutenant-Colonel Wesley and his regiment therefore sailed again from Southampton as part of an expedition under Lieutenant-General Sir Ralph Abercromby against the French islands in the Caribbean, where 12,000 British troops had been lost in the past year through sickness. The convoy and its escorting fleet left Southampton on November 16th and was at once overwhelmed by a terrific storm off Portland which drove it back to port, wrecking seven of its transports on the dreaded Chesil beach. When it put to sea again in December it was dispersed by a second gale, and little more than half its ships and men ever reached the West Indies. The remainder, after seven desperate weeks at sea, were driven back to England, including the 33rd Regiment, whose young colonel thus twice narrowly escaped death by drowning and the even greater likelihood, had his ship reached Barbados, of death from the dreaded "black vomit".

He did not return unscathed. His health was gravely impaired by the cumulative effects of those terrible weeks at sea and the hardships of the retreat through flood and ice of the previous winter. At one time, suffering from recurrent bouts of fever and rheumatism, his life was despaired of. When, after recuperating at Poole, his regiment was ordered in April 1796 to India, he was still too ill to accompany it. While that spring he slowly convalesced, winding up the affairs of his Irish constituency and struggling to adjust his debts before sailing for the Cape to rejoin his regiment, his contemporary, General Bonaparte, having won the approval of his political masters by repressing a mob in Paris with a "whiff of grapeshot", had embarked on a campaign of glory. Appointed at 26 to command the so-called Army of Italy in the Alpes Maritimes, he had arrived at Nice on March 26th, to find his command starving, despondent and in rags. Believing that to the daring everything was possible, and that "he who stays in his entrenchments is beaten," within a few days he had inspired it with something of his own dazzling faith and vitality. He had immense will-power, genius of the highest quality and unbounded ambition. On April 10th the young eagle struck. For just under a fortnight the struggle against the Austrians and Piedmontese in the mountain passes continued. In six battles against forces twice his strength, Bonaparte drove a wedge between his enemies. Then, with the Alps turned and Turin threatened, the terrified House of Savoy sought an armistice. The victor gave it a few hours to accept terms which reduced Piedmont to impotence. Then, with his flank secured, he poured into Lombardy. On May 9th he flung back a bewildered Austrian army from the bridge of Lodi and drove on to Milan. On the 15th he entered the Lombard capital, its inhabitants, gleeful at the defeat of their Teutonic masters, strewing his path with flowers. A new phenomenon, startling as the French Revolution itself, had appeared in the disintegrating 18th century world.

If Napoleon Bonaparte's star was in a dazzling ascendant, Arthur Wesley's seemed anything but bright. He was now in his twenty-eighth year, heavily troubled with debt and bound on a six months' voyage to a remote land far from the scene of the great struggle on which his country was engaged. Promotion in the higher ranks of the Army was notoriously slow and only to be obtained by seniority. He had given his heart and offered his hand to a woman who was not pledged to him and who had rejected him. When he sailed from Portsmouth that June it cannot have seemed to him that the future had much to offer.*

* Yet one person at least seems to have believed he had a great future – the doctor who treated him in his illness. "I have been attending a young man," he told a friend, "whose conversation is the most extraordinary I have ever listened to. . . . If this young man lives he must one day be Prime Minister." Ellesmere 161.

Chapter Two

APPRENTICESHIP TO COMMAND

If Arthur has good luck he will be called to act on a greater
stage than dear Dublin.
                                              LORD MORNINGTON

Running like a golden thread throughout Arthur Wellesley's
Indian career – as indeed it runs through the whole fabric of
his life – is the deep love of peace he held in his heart. Peace not
only between nation and nation, but between man and man.
Again and again in his Indian correspondence, one finds him
acting as peacemaker.
                                              MURIEL WELLESLEY

IF success in his chosen profession seemed elusive, during the eight
months' voyage to the Cape and India, which restored his health and
spirits, Arthur Wesley did his best to deserve it. Like the young
Winston Churchill on a similar voyage a century later, he used the
time to increase his knowledge of his profession and of the distant
world to which he was travelling. To make himself a fuller man by
study, he took with him a carefully chosen library of two hundred
volumes, half of them bought from a Bond Street bookseller at a
cost of £58 - a considerable sum at that time for a financially embarrassed man with little to live on but his pay. A large proportion
were books on India and Indian campaigns, laws and customs,
including Persian, Arabic and Bengali grammars and dictionaries
from which to gain a working knowledge of the peninsula's principal languages. Others were Caesar's *Commentaries*, military works by
Marshal Saxe, Frederick the Great and General Dumouriez, the
French Revolutionary general, Plutarch's lives, Adam Smith's
Wealth of Nations, Blackstone's legal *Commentaries*, and Hume's,
Smollett's and Robertson's histories. Locke, Paley, Voltaire, Rousseau
and Swift, too, were represented. The only light reading were *The
Woman of Pleasure*, Louvet's *Adventures du Chevalier de Faublas*, and
a translation of a new German romance called *Leonora*. There was

28

also - useful for a regimental commander in the East - Chapman's *Venereal Disease.*

Many years later when his friend, Lady Shelley, consulted him about a young kinsman embarking on his career, the Duke of Wellington replied, "There is nothing like never having an idle moment. If he has only one quarter of an hour to employ, it is better to employ it in some fixed pursuit of improvement of mind than to pass it in idleness or listlessness. . . . There is nothing learnt but by study and application. I study and apply more, probably, than any man in England."* It was true of this long voyage in wind and sunshine when he was laying the foundations of the military and administrative knowledge and lore which he was to apply with such far-reaching results in the years ahead.

After rejoining his regiment at the Cape—the half-way house to India, captured from the Dutch a year earlier—where he spent several pleasant and health-giving weeks, Arthur Wesley landed at Calcutta in February 1797. His first impressions of the strange oriental world in which he found himself were not favourable and did no more than reflect the conventional views of the expatriate society of the Bengal capital. "It is a miserable country to live in," he wrote to his brother. "There is more perjury in the town of Calcutta alone than in all Europe taken together. . . . I have not yet met with a Hindoo who had one good quality, and the Mussulmans are worse. Their meekness and mildness do not exist. It is true that the feats which have been performed by Europeans have made them objects of fear, but, wherever the disproportion of numbers is greater than usual, they uniformly destroy them if they can, and in their dealings and conduct among themselves they are the most atrociously cruel people I ever heard of."† Among those he met at this time was the last survivor of the Black Hole of Calcutta - the grandmother of one of his brother's political colleagues who, as Lord Liverpool, was to be his own chief many years later, first as Secretary of State for War and then as Prime Minister. He also visited the battlefield of Plassey where Clive forty years earlier had avenged that monstrous event.

A fellow officer described him at this time as "all life and spirits, . . . with a large aquiline nose, clear blue eyes, . . . speaking remarkably

* *Lady Shelley*, II, 128.
† *Supplementary Despatches*, I, 12-17.

29

quickly."* Though, as colonel of a newly arrived regiment, he took part, as was expected of him, in the convivial hospitalities of Calcutta – much impressing the diarist William Hickey, no bad judge in such matters, by the exceptional strength of his head – he had not come to the Orient for its social pleasures. He quickly realised that, if he was to make something of a military career in India, he must avoid the self-indulgence which brought so many of his countrymen there to an early grave. The prescription for a healthy life which he adopted for himself was regular exercise, a sparing diet, largely of rice, and little or no wine. The first Indian lesson he mastered was to command himself in the conditions of a semi-tropical climate.

Before he had been many weeks in the country his regiment was ordered on an expedition under Major-General Sir James Craig to capture Manila, the capital of the Spanish Philippines. Though her army had been driven from the Continent, and the coasts of western Europe were barred to her by the triumphant French, Britain was still able to retaliate in the outer oceans by using sea-power against the colonial possessions of her enemies, including those of her former allies who had yielded to them. With a chance of active service and the possibility of distinction in the field, the young colonel's hopes rose. On the voyage to Penang, where the expedition was to assemble, he showed his habitual meticulous care for his regiment's health and hygiene. All spirits – a quart daily between every eight men – were to be diluted with three parts water, every man's hammock was to be scrubbed regularly, and, in accordance with his own regimen of bathing every day in cold water, where total immersion was not possible, feet and legs were to be washed every morning and evening.†

The attack on Manila, however, never took place, for events in Europe had become so threatening that all available troops had to be recalled for the defence of India itself. In October, 1796, while Wesley had been at the Cape with his regiment awaiting transport to the Ganges, Spain – still the second naval power on the Continent – had declared war on England. With the French, Dutch and

* Elers, 46-7.
† Brett-James, 110. Captain George Elers, who met him on a voyage to India, noted that he was "remarkably clean in his person". Forty years later, in early Victorian England, the Duke was considered remarkable for taking a daily bath. Elers., 46-7; *Early Victorian England*, I, 87.

Spanish fleets aligned against her, it became necessary for Britain to withdraw from the Mediterranean to protect her own shores. Though she had been saved from invasion by a victory won in February, 1797, by Admiral Sir John Jervis and Commodore Nelson off Cape St Vincent, the early summer of that year had seen the country brought almost to the brink of ruin. First the Channel Fleet and then the North Sea Fleet had mutinied, and only the firmness of Pitt and the innate patriotism of the ordinary Englishman had averted defeat and revolution.

All this Arthur Wesley, who received no letter from England until a year after his departure, learnt when he returned to Calcutta at the beginning of 1798. He also learnt that his brother, Lord Mornington, who had earlier been nominated for the Governorship of Madras, had been appointed Governor-General of India in place of the veteran Lord Cornwallis, who, with a French landing and a national rising imminent, could not be spared from Ireland.

Mornington's arrival at Calcutta that May proved the turning-point in the young colonel's career. It coincided with a change in the spelling of the family name, the new Governor-General having, before leaving England, adopted the older and grander version of Wellesley, which all five brothers henceforward used. It was his ambition to make his appointment—"the most distinguished situation in the British Empire after that of the Prime Minister of England," he called it—the start of a new era which should see his country established for all time as the paramount power in the peninsula. At that time, with its three Presidencies, Bengal, Madras and Bombay—half a century earlier minute trading stations dependent on the precarious goodwill of native princes and competing on equal terms with other European factories, French, Dutch and Portuguese—the East India Company controlled two wide stretches of the east coast of India and a narrow one on the west. But the heart of its wealth and power was the great alluvial province at the mouth of the Ganges - the richest in all Hindustan - which had been won for it forty years earlier by the genius of Clive. Since then there had flowed into England from this oriental El Dorado an ever-growing stream of spices, indigo, ivory, sugar, tea, ebony, sandalwood, saltpetre, cotton, silks and calicoes and of fabulously rich merchants who bought up estates and pocket boroughs, married their children into the aristocracy and received from their less fortunate countrymen the envious name of nabob. It was due to them and their excesses that Britain had recently become conscious of its eastern possession and had assumed responsibility for its government, Pitt's East India Act of 1784 subordinating the till then untrammelled political power of the Company's Directors inLeadenhall Street to a Board of Control appointed by the Crown. But in matters of finance, with its vast wealth controlled by money-minded merchants, the Company was still all - or all but all - powerful.

Outside its thriving Presidencies anarchy prevailed throughout the peninsula, in the whole of which there was no such thing, as Arthur Wellesley was to discover, as a stable frontier. The Moslem empire of the Moguls from the North, who had ruled most of the sub-continent in the sixteenth and seventeenth centuries, had long disintegrated before the attacks of marauding armies of Mahratta horsemen who, under a series of usurping adventurers, kept all eastern and central Hindustan in a state of perpetual turmoil, and one of whose greater chieftains, Madajee Scindia, had occupied Delhi itself - the old imperial capital - holding the heir of the Moguls a puppet captive there. With their clouds of fierce irregular cavalry and their infantry and artillery officered and trained by European mercenaries, the Mahrattas, when united, were a match even for the East India Company's disciplined Sepoys, if not for the handful of Regular English and Scottish regiments which the British Government loaned to the Company. By their perpetual plundering they had reduced vast areas to starvation and ruin and made the life of the Indian cultivator a misery.

The only other power capable of withstanding them—for the ancient kingdoms of Oudh and Hyderabad could no longer defend themselves from these martial plunderers without aid from their British neighbours—was the great southern empire of Mysore where another soldier of fortune, a rough Moslem adventurer of genius named Hyder Ali, had displaced the ruling dynasty of a Hindu state and established a highly aggressive military satrapy in its place. At the time of the American War of Independence, when all the maritime powers of Europe had coalesced against Britain, aided by officers and arms from the nearby French trading, naval and military station of Pondicherry this formidable warrior had come near to overrunning the Madras Presidency. Only the fortitude of the East India Company's last independent Governor-General, Warren

Hastings, had enabled the British to retain their hold on Fort St George and their rich coastal settlement until the Royal Navy, battling against odds, regained command of the threatened trade-routes through the Atlantic and Indian oceans. Since Hyder Ali's death in 1782, his equally fierce and aggressive son, Tipoo Sultan—known and feared by the British commercial community of Madras as the "tiger of Mysore"—ruled in his place and was for ever restlessly intriguing with the French, and with the warlike Moslem kingdom of Afghanistan beyond India's northern mountain range, both against the East India Company and the Mahrattas, hoping by loosing new wars to overthrow these infidels and restore Moslem dominion over all Hindustan.

Now, still in his thirties, the new Anglo-Irish proconsul—ambitious, brilliant, imaginative, a friend and confidant of the Prime Minister, Pitt—was resolved to make an end of French threats to India by a direct extension of British rule, regardless of his parsimonious paymasters, the East India merchants, whose interest was in profits, not empire. He saw the French Revolutionary attempt to proselytise and overthrow established authority everywhere as an impending threat to Britain's position in the East. He was confirmed in this belief by the arrival on the Malabar coast, at Tipoo Sultan's invitation and at his capital, Seringapatam, of a small contingent of French revolutionary incendiaries from Mauritius, and by a flamboyant proclamation by the Jacobin Governor of that island calling for a liberating war to drive the British – "those oppressors of the human race" – out of India. Nor was this threat to the Company's rule wholly imaginary, for at that moment—as yet unknown both to the Governor-General and the British Government at home—the conqueror of northern Italy, General Bonaparte, was preparing to sail for Egypt with an army of 40,000 men and thirteen ships of the line, there to establish a base from which to "hunt the English out of all their eastern possessions" and make himself master of the Orient.

Having no official military adviser, Lord Mornington used his brother as an unofficial one. He could not have chosen a better. The real danger to British India, as the latter had earlier pointed out in a letter to the Governor-General, was, not so much a French invasion, as that Frenchmen from Mauritius,* serving in the armies of native

* *To the Earl of Mornington, July 12th 1797.* "As long as the French have an establishment there, Great Britain cannot call herself safe in India."

princes, should teach them the new tactics which had proved so successful in Europe, of attacks, under cover of intense preliminary bombardment, in densely massed columns, "than which," he wrote, "nothing could be more formidable to the small body of fighting men of which the Company's armies in gereral consist. In the end they would force us to increase our armies and, of course, our expense to such a degree that the country could not be kept, or, indeed would not be worth keeping."

For though Arthur Wellesley did not share his brother's imperial ambitions, he had already a clear idea of what was necessary for Indian campaigning. He was the brain behind the coming operations against Tipoo's inaccessible capital, Seringapatam, and his French-trained army. And it was a brain which looked far ahead and left nothing to chance. "It is better," he told the Governor-General, "to see and communicate the difficulties and dangers of an enterprise, and to endeavour to overcome them, than to be blind to everything but success till the moment of difficulty comes, and then to despond."*

On August 19th 1798, taking his regiment with him, he sailed from Calcutta for Madras, which he reached four weeks later, after narrowly escaping shipwreck when his ship struck a reef at the mouth of the Hooghly. He and his men also suffered on the voyage from dysentery caused by tainted water casks supplied by a careless contractor. His mission, which naturally aroused a good deal of jealousy, was to act as an intermediary between his brother and the Governor of Madras, Lord Clive, whose first instinct and that of his Council, was to do nothing and wait, in the hope that it might never happen, till Tipoo and his French advisers struck. With his charm and quiet good sense—what his brother, in the days when he represented his Irish parliamentary constituency, had described as his "excellent judgment," amiable manners, admirable temper and firmness—he won the Governor's confidence while simultaneously checking Lord Mornington's eagerness to precipitate an appeal to arms before the army was ready. "If it be possible," he wrote, "to adopt a line of conduct which would not immediately lead to war, provided it can be done with honour - which I think indispensable in this Government - it ought to be adopted." "Your propositions to Tipoo," he advised the impatient proconsul a little later, "ought to be moderate at least as much as to make it probable that he will acquiesce in

* Supplementary Despatches, I, 195-6.

them." At the same time he co-operated with the Commander-in-Chief of the Madras Presidency, Lieutenant-General Harris* - a veteran of Bunker's Hill and the American War - in preparing lines of communication between the coast and the Mysore uplands. From the start he grasped that a campaign, which involved marching a force of 50,000 men, its siege-train and 100,000 camp followers, across two hundred miles of roadless jungle, must primarily be a matter of forecasting the precise quantities of food, fodder and munitions needed at every point of the advance. "I have prevailed upon Lord Clive," he reported, "to appoint a Commissary of Stores ... Matters can then be brought into some shape and we shall know what we are about, instead of trusting to the vague calculations of a parcel of blockheads who know nothing and have no data." He made meticulous estimates of the number of bullocks which the collectors of the districts under the Company's rule could assemble without doing injury to the cultivation of the country. "It is impossible," he wrote, "to carry on a war in India without bullocks,"† and it was bullocks in tens of thousands that he had to find.

All through the autumn and early winter of 1798, while the Governor-General and Tipoo both waited for news of Bonaparte's Egyptian venture, Arthur Wellesley was busy at the army's advance base on the frontier preparing for the campaign ahead. It was a formidable assignment for a twenty-nine-year-old lieutenant-colonel who had never commanded anything larger than a brigade, and that only for a few weeks. "When I left Madras to take command of the troops," he wrote to his younger brother, Henry, who was acting as the Governor-General's secretary, "I had not even a servant with me, and I came away at an hour's notice. There was not a grain of rice to be got in the bazaar at Arcot, and, after bullying day and night, I have now got plenty in my camp and have been able to go on for a fortnight without drawing upon the public stores, contrary to the expectation of everybody, and without putting the public to the expense of a single shilling."

This achievement—a victory over what he called "that cursed institution," the Madras Military Board—won him the growing trust of the Commander-in-Chief, General Harris, who, like everyone

* Afterwards 1st Lord Harris of Seringapatam (1746-1829).
† *Supplementary Despatches*, I, 57.

else, had not at first been well-disposed towards the Governor-General's emissary. But the young colonel was so unfailingly obliging and helpful, and so efficient in whatever he undertook, that it was impossible to resent or resist him for long. And when Lord Mornington proposed to join General Harris's headquarters for the campaign, like a loyal subordinate he used his influence to dissuade him, telling him that his presence, far from giving confidence to the general, would virtually deprive him of his command and adding that, were he in Harris's situation and his brother were to descend on the army, he himself would quit it.

An essential preliminary to the campaign was to gain the co-operation of the half-senile Nizam of Hyderabad whose dominions bordered Mysore to the north and who, though bound to Britain by treaty, had 14,000 troops in his service trained and officered by Frenchmen. After firm action by the British Resident had induced the Nizam to replace these by British officers and admit into his country 6000 of the Company's Sepoys, Colonel Wellesley was rewarded for his remarkable organising skill and the happy relations he had established with the native trading community, by being given command of the Hyderabad contingent. This was to form the right flank of the army on its march to Tipoo's capital. So great was his resource in overcoming, in the teeth of time and shortages of arms and money,* all the immense difficulties of mobilising and supplying so large a force, and so great was the tact, good sense and tireless energy with which he worked to do so, that the Commander-in-Chief risked the disapproval of the military authorities in England - rigid sticklers for seniority - by appointing him to this coveted command over the head of his senior by twelve years, Major-General David Baird, a veteran of an earlier campaign against Mysore. In a letter to the Governor-General Harris testified in glowing terms to the services of his young assistant. "The very handsome appearance and perfect discipline of the troops do honour to themselves and to him, while the judicious and masterly arrangements in respect to supplies, which opened an abundant free market and inspired confidence in dealers

---

* At one moment the supply of ready money in his camp at Vellore was so short that he told his brother that he was obliged to borrow from the officers of the army and sell his own horses to equip and send off two detachments. *Supplementary Despatches*, I, 192.

of every description, were no less creditable to Colonel Wellesley than advantageous to the public service and deservedly entitle him to my thanks and approbation."*

The command thus conferred on a mere lieutenant-colonel was equivalent in size to what in England would have been given to a lieutenant-general of twice his age—a circumstance little calculated to win favour for him with bureaucratic minds at the Horse Guards, the administrative headquarters of the British Army—or at the Court of St James where a monarch with a retentive memory jealously guarded the rights of senior officers against jumped-up juniors. His force consisted, in its gratified recipient's words, of "six excellent battalions of the Company's Sepoys, four rapscallion battalions of the Nizam's, which, however, behaved well, and really about 10,000 (which they called 25,000) cavalry of all nations, some good and some bad, and twenty-six pieces of cannon." To it was added his own fine English regiment, the 33rd, bringing the total under his command to some 16,000 fighting men and an even larger number of camp followers.

By the turn of the year it had become known to the Governor-General that Tipoo's hopes of French aid from Egypt were at an end. Bonaparte's army, notwithstanding its victory of the Pyramids and occupation of Cairo, had been marooned in that country by Nelson's annihilation of his fleet at the battle of the Nile. Lord Mornington, therefore, delayed no longer, and, at the beginning of February, 1799, as the Sultan of Mysore continued to procrastinate, gave the order for the army to advance on Seringapatam. For the next seven weeks the whole "monstrous equipment", as Arthur Wellesley called it—a huge perambulating oriental town of pavilions, huts and booths, covering an area of seven miles by three—moved slowly forward at about five miles a day, with its 120,000 bullocks, vast trains of camels and elephants, 47 giant siege-guns and a horde of camp followers. It was a race against time before the coming of the monsoon made the hill rivers impassable, and only Wellesley's careful and far-seeing preparations enabled the immense caravanserai to supply itself on its long laborious march through mountain and jungle. It was supported from the other side of the peninsula by a much smaller force of 6000 men of the Bombay Army, operating from Cannamore on the Malabar coast under Lieutenant-

* Lushington, 250.

General James Stuart, who on March 2nd, having reached a point fifty miles to the west of the Mysore capital, was unsuccessfully attacked by Tipoo's army. On the 27th, operating from interior lines, Tipoo's cavalry, with strong infantry support, struck again, this time at Harris's slowly advancing columns at Mallaveley, but again was driven off by the steady musketry of Wellesley's Sepoys and a bayonet charge by the 33rd. Ten days later, after crossing the Cauvery river – no inconsiderable feat – the army reached Seringapatam and laid siege to its formidable fortifications. "We are here," Wellesley wrote to his brother, "with a strong, healthy and brave army, with plenty of stores, guns, etc etc, and we shall be masters of the place before much time passes over our heads."

Before they were, this intensely able, industrious and seemingly supremely self-confident – but beneath the surface deeply sensitive – young aristocrat suffered a setback which revealed for a moment another side of his character. Set to clear a dense bamboo wood called the Sultanpettah Tope on a pitch-black night, his small task-force stumbled on a strongly-held enemy position and was badly shot up. In the ensuing confusion, in which several of his men were killed or taken prisoner, his nerve, undermined by a bout of dysentery, seems for a moment to have failed, and, losing part of his force in the darkness, he called off the attack and arrived at midnight in a state of considerable agitation at General Harris's tent to report his failure.* Though next day he redeemed himself by driving the enemy out of their position, the episode, which was much magnified by jealous tongues, taught him a lesson he never forgot: to keep his quick imagination—the quality which made him so perceptive and intuitive a commander—under an iron control, one which, with the years, became second nature. "The only thing I am afraid of," he once said long afterwards, "is fear."† That moment of failure taught him, too, as he wrote at the time, "never to suffer an attack to be made by night upon an enemy who is prepared and strongly posted, whose posts have not been reconnoitred by daylight."

On May 4th 1799, after the formal siege-works had been completed

---

* Fortescue, IV, 735-7; Muriel Wellesley, 49-51. Twelve of his men were taken prisoner and subsequently found buried with nails driven into their skulls. Another, the brother of a great friend of his, was killed. A. Wellesley to Knight of Kerry, April 18th 1799. *National Library of Ireland*, cit. Longford, 63.   † Stanhope, 12. See also Greville, I, 67

and a breach made in the walls, Seringapatam was taken by storm. Tipoo himself fell in the fighting. Wellesley was in charge of the reserve in the trenches and took no part in the actual assault. But he was given the task of restoring order in the sacked city, and, because of the skill he had shown in obtaining the co-operation of Indians of all classes while building up the expedition's supply-lines and in leading the Nizam's army, he was subsequently appointed by General Harris as Military Governor of Seringapatam. That he was entrusted with such a charge over the head of Major-General Baird, who had heroically led the storming parties, was a bitter disappointment to that officer and the subject of his as bitter complaint. Yet, having formerly been Tipoo's prisoner and kept in irons for three years by him and his father, Hyder Ali, Baird - a man, though of great nobility and courage, of exceedingly hasty temper - was naturally prejudiced against the people at whose hands he had suffered, whereas Wellesley, despite his first unfavourable impressions of India, had, with his clear sense of realities, grasped the nature of the problems confronting human nature in a land where life and personal security were so precarious. Understanding these, he was able to make allowances and to sympathise with and respect native customs, beliefs and prejudices.* So scrupulous was he in his respect for these that, though Mysore was predominantly Hindu, including its former royal house—whose representative, a boy of five, was now restored to his dispossessed forbears' throne under British protection—having assumed responsibility for the safety and happiness of Tipoo Sahib's Moslem family, Wellesley did his best to prevent the dead sultan's harem from being searched for hidden treasure.† He even, for fear of offending Moslem beliefs and customs, forbade the return of its inmates to their former husbands. "The company having taken this family under its protection," he told a protesting Christian missionary, "it is not proper that anything should be done which can disgrace it in the eyes of the Indian world, or which can, in the most remote degree,

---

* Long afterwards, with his complete freedom from sham modesty, Wellington told John Wilson Croker that he was the right person to have been selected for the post. "I had commanded the Nizam's army during the campaign and had given universal satisfaction. I was liked by the natives." *Croker Papers*, II, 102-3.

† "I had nothing to do with it except that I obeyed the General's order and . . . took every precaution to render the search as decent and as little injurious to the feelings of the ladies as possible." *Supplementary Despatches*, I, 278, and also 419-21, 440.

cast a shade upon the dead or violate the feelings of those who are alive."

*   *   *

Colonel Wellesley's first task was to restore order and stop the looting which followed the storm of the city. "Scarcely a house," he told the Governor-General, "was left unplundered. . . . I came to take command on the morning of the 5th, and by the greatest exertion, by hanging, flogging, etc. etc., in the course of the day I restored order among the troops, and I hope I have gained the confidence of the people."* "Plunder is stopped," he reported next day to General Harris; "the fires are all extinguished, and the inhabitants are returning to their houses fast." Thereafter he re-opened the bazaars, and supervised the rebuilding of the city.† Its former government having been overthrown, he had to re-establish courts of justice, with separate tribunals for Moslem and Hindu laws and rules for pleading and arbitration – matters with which his study of Blackstone and oriental law during the voyage to India had made him familiar. The supreme object he set himself in everything he did was to "gain the confidence of the people." For this, he saw, two things were essential: respect for their religious creeds and observances, and regard for their possessions, whether it were a poor cultivator's holding, a merchant's stock or a hill rajah's domain. In a letter to the able native who, as Dewan to its youthful Rajah, co-operated with him in the administration of Mysore for six fruitful years, he defined the principles which always guided him in his work. "Protect the ryots and traders, and allow no man, whether vested with authority or otherwise, to oppress them with impunity."‡ Justice according to accepted native beliefs and customs, scrupulous observance of every pledge given, and security for life and property were his recipes for good government. Provided these were assured, it mattered little who ruled. "As for the wishes of the people," he wrote, "I put them out of the question; they are the only philosophers about their governors that I ever met with – if indifference constitutes that character."§

* *Supplementary Despatches*, I, 212.

† "This morning I was there at half-past ten, and the people who mix up the chunam were then coming to work, in number about twelve, and there were no other persons near the work." *Supplementary Despatches*, I, 226.

‡ To Purneah, Dewan of the Rajah of Mysore, March 2nd 1804.

§ To Major Munro, August 20th 1800.

For he was coming to understand India and its problems. It was a country utterly different to that to which Englishmen were accustomed: in which, outside the main British preserve in Bengal, there was no power except that of the sword and, in which, as a result, plunder had become the chief, indeed, almost the sole, means of advancement for any man of enterprise and spirit, and in which, despite the relics and wealth of past civilisations, society - for lack of rule and law - was sinking fast into the brutal condition in which war was the natural state of mankind.* The crying need of the cultivator, craftsman, merchant, landowner—of all who, if left to themselves, could create wealth instead of merely filching or, in trying to do so, destroying it—was public order and justice. It was not the function of the soldier to govern, but to suppress lawless violence. It was his business, in Virgil's words, to impose the way of peace, spare the subject and battle down the proud. On the army's ability to do this for India and its people of all creeds, castes and classes, British rule must rest. "It depends," he said, "on justice, freedom from corruption, and unswerving truth to one's word and to every obligation one has undertaken."

In everything he did this wise young administrator sought to create, not destroy. He held that Mysore - restored now to the family of its former Hindu rajahs - should, under British protection, retain its identity, and that any extension of the Company's territories should be limited to what could be effectively administered and held. In a letter written in the summer of 1800 he set out his views on the problems of political stability in a still anarchical sub-continent.

"In my opinion the extension of our territory has been greater than our means . . . We have added to the number . . . of our enemies by depriving of employment those who heretofore found it in the service of Tipoo and of the Nizam. Wherever we spread ourselves . . . we increase this evil. We throw out of employment and means of subsistence, all who have hitherto managed the revenue, commanded or served in the armies, or have plundered the country. These people become additional enemies at the

---

* In June 1841, in conversation with Francis Egerton, afterwards Lord Ellesmere, he cited as an example of this, two hill forts in India within gunshot of one another. "They used to be perpetually and without reason firing on each other. I was obliged to tell them I would take them both." Ellesmere, 171.

41

same time that, by the extension of our territory, our means of supporting our government and of defending ourselves are proportionately decreased."*

In particular, he urged that the Company should not extend its frontiers into Mahratta territory, for, as he warned his brother, "it is impossible to expect to alter the nature of the Mahrattas; they will plunder their neighbours, be they ever so powerful. . . . It will be better to put one of the Powers in dependence upon the Company on the frontier, who, if plundered, are accustomed to it, know how to bear it and to retaliate, which we do not."

While Arthur Wellesley was mastering the administrative problems of pacifying a land where anarchy was endemic, he was learning, though still only a colonel, how to lead armies in battle. After General Harris's forces had returned home, he was appointed to command all the troops remaining in Mysore and south-west India. For though the country was now under the Company's protection, it was still far from pacified. There were the lawless Polygars in the east and south, the martial Nairs in Malabar, and the tribal Arab Moplahs on the coast, all of them challenging authority. And among those who escaped from the prisons of Seringapatam during the siege was a notorious freebooter named Dhoondiah Waugh, who, grandiloquently calling himself "King of the Two Worlds", attracted an army of malcontents and disbanded soldiers and, seizing several abandoned fortresses, started to harry and plunder far and wide. It was Wellesley's task to pursue, corner and destroy him. And this proved no easy matter, for, living on the countryside, his adversary needed no transport or supply-lines to impede his movements, while the pursuing forces depended on both. When Waugh's chief stronghold at Chitteldroog was captured and his principal roving band worsted, the elusive brigand merely withdrew into Mahratta territory. Here during the winter he recruited a still larger army and, after routing a large force of Mahratta cavalry, he returned in the spring of 1800 to harry the Carnatic and Mysore.

Once more Wellesley took the field, spending a second summer in the saddle and under canvas while he coped with the problem of keeping his troops fed and supplied in a bridgeless countryside.

* To Major Munro, August 20th 1800.

"What a pity it is," he wrote after failing by one day to ford a river before the monsoon broke, "that I cannot move on for want of grain! My troops are in high health, order and spirits, but the unfortunate defect of arrangement . . . previous to my arrival has ruined everything. . . . If I had been able to reach the river one day sooner I should have been across before it filled. . . . How true it is that in military operations time is everything!"* In the end, after he had chased his quarry from one side of the Deccan to the other, by dividing his forces into two – one to hold and the other to pursue – he caught up with him at Conahgull near the borders of Mysore and Hyderabad on September 10th 1800. Charging at the head of two British and two native cavalry regiments, he routed a force of 5000 men in a stoutly contested encounter in which Waugh was killed. "The troops behaved admirably," he reported; "if they had not done so, not a man of us would have quitted the field."

It was Wellesley's first victory in sole command.† It had been founded on foresight and meticulous organisation of commissariat and transport. By it he had proved – something new in Indian warfare – that it was possible for regular, disciplined troops not living on plunder to hunt down the lightest-footed and most rapid armies, instead of only being able, as in the past, to win pitched battles or storm fortifications.

Just before taking the field against Dhoondiah Waugh for the second time, Wellesley received from his brother, the Governor-General, a most tempting offer – the military command of an expedition intended against the French island of Mauritius. He had reluctantly refused it on the grounds that the destruction of the brigand forces harrying the Deccan was essential for the tranquillity of southern India and that, unless they could be quickly rounded up and destroyed, there could be a general insurrection of the discontented and disaffected. Now that Dhoondiah Waugh was dead, the offer

---

* To Lieut-Colonel Close, June 30th 1800.

† Nearly a quarter of a century later Harriet Arbuthnot, the woman who seems to have come nearer than any other to capturing and holding Wellington's rather lonely heart, recorded in her diary: "I received this day (it being my birthday) a present from the Duke of Wellington of some strung emeralds and pearls as a bracelet. They were given him by a Mahratta chief for the first battle fought by him in which he commanded in chief. They were part of an ornament to a sword and he says he cannot employ them better than in sending them to me as token of his regard and affection." September 10th 1800. Arbuthnot, I, 185.

was renewed and accepted. "If you should succeed in taking the Isles of France and Bourbon," his brother wrote, "I mean to appoint you to the government of them with the chief military command annexed." But after taking up his post at Trincomalee in Ceylon, where the expedition had assembled, and making all arrangements for its equipment and supply, its young commander learnt, first, that it was to be sent instead to the Red Sea to take part in a combined operation against Bonaparte's abandoned army in Egypt—at which, on his own responsibility, receiving the news from England, as he did, some time before it would reach the Governor-General at Calcutta, he ordered it to sail for Bombay instead of Madras—and, then, when his troops were already embarked for the former port, on the pretext that the command was now too important for a mere colonel, that it had been given over his head to the hero of Seringapatam, Major-General Baird, whose claims on the grounds of seniority had been stronger than Lord Mornington could resist.

It was for Arthur Wellesley a bitter disappointment and humiliation, so much so that he felt that he had been deliberately slighted by his brother and that his military career was permanently blighted. So strongly did he protest at what he regarded as his brother's bad faith that for a time communication between the two ceased. The blow was softened a little by what he called "the kind, candid and handsome manner" in which he was treated by Baird, who found it impossible to harbour any resentment against the younger man who had formerly been preferred over his head but now, as his second-in-command, carried out, despite his disappointment, every duty with such conscientious industry, dispatch and sound military judgment. But shortly before he was due to sail for the coming operation against the French in Egypt—on which he had prepared for his chief a most lucid and detailed memorandum— he was stricken down by a fever.* It was fortunate that he was, for the ship in which he was to have embarked, foundered with all hands.

---

* It was accompanied by acute infection, the Malabar itch – caught on shipboard through sleeping in a victim's bed – for which he had to undergo a prolonged course of nitrous baths under Dr Scott, the inventor of nitric acid. Stanhope, 102-3; Gurwood, 20-4.

Chapter Three

WELLESLEY BAHADUR

He looks to India with filial affection as the cradle of his
military glory.

Mrs Arbuthnot's Diary, October 8th 1825

It is a proud phrase for us to use but a true one, that we have
bestowed blessings upon millions, and the ploughman is again
in every quarter turning up a soil which had for many seasons
never been stirred, except by the hoofs of predatory cavalry.

Lord Hastings, 1819

WELLINGTON returned in the summer of 1801 to his old command
in Mysore, a disappointed man. Yet once back in saddle and at desk,
he had no time for repining. As always, he was tirelessly occupied
by the task of reducing all things, both military and civil, to good
sense and order. And, in his wide domain, which stretched from the
Malabar coast to the Madras and Hyderabad borders of Mysore,
there was no end to what needed doing to replace anarchy, chaos,
and corruption by sound rule, efficiency and just dealing. Reading,
when he was old and famous, through the dispatches written during
his crowded Mysore years, he said that doing so brought back "the
enterprise and excitement of the time," making him feel young
again. "They are as good," he said, "as I could write now. They
show the same attention to details - to the pursuit of all means,
however small, that could promote success."* As a result, almost
everything he did for himself, and which did not depend on others,
succeeded.

Nor was the setback to his military career permanent, as he had
feared. For though, in 1802, a peace was concluded between the
British Government and Bonaparte—now, after a brilliant campaign

---

* *Gascoygne Heiress.* . . . "They are valuable," Wellington told George Chad in 1836,
"as a professional book, more so than Caesar's *Commentaries* because Caesar wrote afterwards for effect. These are a collection of instruments used at the time. They were all
written in my own hand." Chad, 19. See Stanhope, 49, 57; Fraser, 12.

45

against the Austrians, First Consul and absolute master of France—and disarmament and economy were the order of the day, the lull in the long struggle between the two countries proved only temporary. Even before war broke out again in the following spring, the French dictator had dispatched emissaries to Pondicherry—which by the terms of the peace treaty was to have been restored to France—with secret offers to the Mahrattas of men and arms for the expulsion of the British from India. But the Governor-General - now Lord Wellesley as a result of a marquessate conferred on him after the capture of Seringapatam - was not to be tricked. Anticipating instructions from home to delay the restoration of the French settlements, he took advantage of a quarrel between the principal Mahratta princes to offer British protection to the unpopular titular head of their confederacy, the Peshwah, who had been driven by them from his capital, Poona. On the last day of 1802, by a treaty signed at Bassein in the Bombay Presidency where he had taken refuge, the Peshwah accepted a subsidiary alliance with the East India Company - similar to those with Hyderabad and Mysore - and the admission to his territories of its advisers and troops. This made war sooner or later almost inevitable between the British and the greater Mahratta chieftains who were challenging the Peshwah's authority. For they would never brook any interference with the freedom to raid and plunder on which their wealth and power depended.

It was the Governor-General's policy to bring, as he put it, "the Mahratta power under British protection," so closing the last remaining door to the French and fixing what he called "the peace of India on foundations of the utmost stability." For the next step, that of restoring the Peshwah to his capital, he turned to his soldier brother, now back in favour and commanding the Company's forces in Mysore, Malabar and Canara. During the previous year—at last gazetted a Major-General, on the Indian, though not the British, Army List—the latter had been perfecting his system for maintaining disciplined armies in the field in conditions of eastern warfare. His more recent experience in a forest campaign against the rebellious Rajah of Bullum, had lain mainly in hill and jungle. Now he had to operate in the more open Mahratta country where speed of movement was essential. He had one great asset - the flourishing state of Mysore which he had done so much to create and from which he was able to obtain almost everything needed to supply his troops. Yet to move an army of 10,000 men with their ordnance and supplies for six hundred miles from southern to central India without living on the country called for remarkable organising capacity. He had to transport them and their stores across a bridgeless, anarchical land where there was no law, no civil government and where the cultivator was at the mercy of roaming bands of plunderers who made it impossible to produce anything more than the barest subsistence.

In a war against the greater Mahratta princes—with their European trained infantry and massive artillery a far more formidable enemy than the vast disorganised rabbles of unreliable mercenaries whom Clive had routed forty years before—ample supplies in the field were essential. Otherwise, though incapable of defeating disciplined European and Sepoy troops by themselves, by cutting an adversary's communications and forcing him to retreat to avoid starvation, their hordes of irregular horse could drive him into a position where he could be encircled by superior numbers of infantry and then annihilated by their artillery. "They follow him with their cavalry in his marches," Wellesley wrote, "and surround and attack him with their infantry and cannon when he halts and he can scarcely escape from them. That, therefore, which I consider absolutely necessary in an operation against a Mahratta power . . . is such a quantity of provisions in your camp as will enable you to command your own movements and to be independent of your magazines."*

This was the end to which all his immense organising powers were directed. "If I had rice and bullocks," he recalled long afterwards, "I had men, and if I had men I knew I could beat the enemy."† In past campaigns enormous quantities of hired bullocks had been used; for Harris's advance to Seringapatam 120,000 had been requisitioned, necessitating hordes of attendants and camp followers, all of whom had had to be fed, reducing the army's rate of advance to a bare five miles a day. And the appalling wastage of animals through inefficient handling, shortage of fodder, disease and starvation had meant that, when the siege-train and its heavy guns reached their destination, there were never enough bullocks surviving to bring

---

* To Colonel Thomas Murray, September 14th 1804.
† A. Griffiths, *Wellington, his Comrades and Contemporaries*, 16.

them back, and they had to be left where they were and abandoned.* Arthur Wellesley's answer was to rely on a "public" bullock department whose personnel were employed by the Company under regular supervision and discipline, and only to hire additional draught-cattle when it was necessary and then on monthly contracts - with penalties for failure - based on prompt payments and strict justice, "which ought," he wrote, "to prevail in all the Company's transactions with the natives of this country." As a result, in a country which had been heavily plundered by a marauding Mahratta army, he was able to cover the 600 miles from Seringapatam to Poona in the worst season of the year without the loss of a single draught-animal and to do so at an average rate of thirteen and a half miles a day. Once during the two months' march, his ordnance and provision train travelled sixty miles in thirty hours - something which in past Indian wars would have been impossible. "Rapid movements with guns and carriages," he insisted, "cannot be made without good cattle, well driven and well taken care of. . . . If I had had the service of such cattle only as served Lord Cornwallis and General Harris in former wars, I should never have reached Poona."†

On May 13th 1803, the unpopular Peshwah was accordingly restored to his throne, the insurgent Mahrattas who had expelled him having withdrawn to the north on the British approach. On an alarm that they were about to burn the town, Wellesley covered the last forty miles in a single night at the head of 400 horse. By gaining the confidence and co-operation of the lesser Mahrattas along the line of march, and by the admirable discipline he maintained, with a resultant complete absence of plunder, he had completed the transfer of his army from south to central India without the slightest opposition. The far-reaching political consequences of his great march, a colleague considered, were due to "the admiration which the southern Mahratta chiefs entertained of his military

---

* "In former wars the utmost exertion which it was possible for the army to make was to draw its train of artillery to Seringapatam. It was not possible and never was expected that the guns and carriages which were drawn there should be brought away again. Accordingly . . . it has invariably happened that by far the greater part of the train and carriages have been left behind when the army marched away." To Lieut-General James Stuart, August 2nd 1804.

† "I therefore take the liberty of recommending this establishment of cattle to your protection. It is founded upon the most efficient and most economical principles and will never fail the army so long as it is superintended and conducted as it has been." To Lieut-General James Stuart, August 2nd 1804.

character and the firm reliance the inhabitants placed on his justice and protection."

He had now, however, to deal with the great northern chieftains, Dowlut Rao Scindia, Maharajah of Gwalior, and Ragojee Bhoonslah, the Rajah of Nagpore, styling himself by the grander title of Rajah of Berar - a vast territory including regions filched from Britain's ally, the Nizam of Hyderabad. Together they could put into the field against the joint forces of Wellesley's troops from Mysore and the Company's subsidiary division from Hyderabad some 50,000 men, or more than three times the force opposed to them. Their plundering armies, with those of their fellow Mahratta, Jeswunt Rao Holkar, Maharajah of Indore—who, however, for the moment was glutted with the plunder of the Peshwah's lands —dominated Hindustan. Scindia was not the genius his father had been, but his resources were very great, and he and Ragojee Bhoonslah between them controlled most of central India. General Wellesley still hoped to avoid war with them, believing that, if Britain remained firm but conciliatory, their threats would end in nothing. Holding that India's trouble lay in lack, not excess, of native authority, he had no wish, like his brother, to destroy their independent rule, but merely to make it peaceful and responsible. "In my opinion," he told his political agent and friend, John Malcolm, "we ought to withdraw from Poona, and leave some chance that the principal chiefs may have the power of the State in their hands. We ought to keep up our connexion with the Peshwah so that he might not be trampled upon; at the same time, we ought to increase our influence over the chiefs of the empire, in order that it may preponderate in all possible cases in which the State should be called upon to decide. In short, I would preserve the existence of the State, and guide its actions by the weight of British influence, rather than annihilate it."*

* * *

Yet though he felt it was his duty to avoid war, if at all compatible with his country's honour, it soon became clear that Scindia and the Rajah, with their vast marauding host massed on the northern territories of the Company's ally, Hyderabad, were merely playing

* To Major John Malcolm, June 20th 1803.

for time. Having been given plenary powers by the Governor-General to expel them either by diplomacy or war, after prolonged negotiations and repeated warnings to them to withdraw he delivered a final ultimatum on August 6th. "I offered you peace," he wrote, "on terms of equality honourable to all parties; you have chosen war and are responsible for all consequences."

Nor, having made his preparations, did he doubt his ability to deal with them. "The chiefs of the Mahratta empire," he told his brother, "have been accustomed to look at a confederacy of the greater powers among them as a force which nothing could withstand. They recollect its success against the British Government in former times and they anticipate the same success. . . . They do not compare the strength of the British Government at this time with its former weakness."* It was a strength he had done more than any man to create.

For though he could look for little aid from his allies, the Nizam and Peshwah,† who failed to provide the grain they had promised and refused to admit his troops, even the sick, into their fortresses, he had made his usual careful provision for keeping the field. Every detail down to the minutest point of equipment and transport had been anticipated. Even before leaving Seringapatam, he had arranged for a new depot on the Bombay coast, to which, as he marched towards it, he transferred his maritime base by an imaginative use of sea-power which anticipated by a decade his 1813 Peninsular campaign. Here he established vast supplies: thousands of cattle for slaughter, salted meat, biscuits and arrack for his European troops,‡ rice for his Indian, and grain for his horses, with medical stores of bark, Madeira, mercurial ointment, calomel and nitrous acid. Using his public bullock-train - "good cattle, well driven and well taken care of" - to keep his army provisioned in the field, his plan was to advance north-eastwards into the interior to join the Company's Hyderabad contingent which, under Colonel Stevenson,

* July 24th 1803.

† "The Peshwah's servants are very profuse in promises, but very sparing in performance." To Lieut-General James Stuart, June 19th 1803. In another letter Wellesley described the Peshwah as "a shocking fellow! impossible to get on with and callous to everything but money and revenge." Brett-James, 48 n.

‡ For his 3000 European soldiers, 3000 cattle, 90,000 lbs of salt meat in strong kegs, and a similar quantity of biscuits in round baskets and 10,000 gallons of arrack in six-gallon kegs. To J. Duncan, Governor of Bombay, January 20th 1803.

was trying to prevent the Mahratta army from striking deeper into the Nizam's territories. Then, with the united Army of the Deccan of 15,000 British and Sepoy regulars and several hundred native auxiliary horse, he intended either to force the enemy to battle or keep them so closely on the run as to make it impossible for them to plunder, thus depriving them of the only resource by which so large a body could be kept in the field. And, by equipping his forces with boats and pontoons to enable them to cross rivers in flood during the rainy season, he hoped to steal a march on an enemy dependent at such time on fords. "Keep your infantry in a central situation and let your supplies collect them," he advised Stevenson, who was anxious on account of the width of front he was having to hold till his chief could join him. "Move forward yourself with the cavalry and one battalion, and dash at the first enemy that comes into your neighbourhood. You will either cut them up or drive them off. . . . A long defensive war will ruin us. . . . Dash at the first fellows that make their appearance and the campaign will be your own."*

Wellesley's first step was to secure a firm strategic base for his drive into the interior. Marching from Poona, he laid siege on August 8th to the great Mahratta fortress of Ahmednuggar, a place of immense natural strength which had often been attacked, but never taken. On the first day he carried the town wall or pettah by storm, following it up with the capture of the main fort two days later. "Those English" wrote an astonished eyewitness, "are a strange people and their general a wonderful man. They came here in the morning, looked at the pettah wall, walked over it, killed all the garrison and returned to breakfast! What can withstand them?"

By the capture of the fortress Wellesley had secured an impregnable advanced-depot and communications-centre, cutting the northern chieftains off from all connection with their fellow Mahrattas in the south. "I shall fill Ahmednuggar with provisions," he announced, "and when that is completed all the Mahrattas in India would not be able to drive me from my position."†

Yet he had no intention of standing on the defensive. With a speed and daring comparable to that of Bonaparte in his Italian campaigns,

* *Dispatches*, II, 208, 210, 219; Fortescue, V, 19.
† To Lieut-Colonel John Collins, August 18th 1803.

51

he was out to break the arrogant Mahratta confidence. "We must get the upper hand," he wrote, "and, if once we have that, we shall keep it with ease and shall certainly succeed."* To do so he relied on his British regiments, with whom he believed he could achieve almost anything, so indomitable was their spirit and so great the moral ascendancy they had established. In a report written after the campaign, he paid a remarkable tribute to their qualities:

"They are the main foundation of the British power in Asia. Bravery is the characteristic of the British Army in all quarters of the world, but no other quarter has afforded such striking examples of the existence of this quality in the soldiers as the East Indies. An instance of their misbehaviour in the field has never been known; and particularly those who have been for some time in that country cannot be ordered upon any service, however dangerous or arduous, that they will not effect, not only with bravery but a degree of skill not often witnessed by persons of their description in other parts of the world.

"I attribute these qualities, which are peculiar to them in the East Indies, to the distinctness of their class in that country from all others existing in it. They feel that they are a distinct and superior class to the rest of the world which surrounds them, and their actions correspond with their own notions of their superiority. Add to these qualities that their bodies are inured to climate, hardship and fatigue by long residence, habit and exercise to such a degree that I have seen them for years together in the field without suffering any material sickness; that I have made them march 60 miles in 30 hours and afterwards engage the enemy, and it will not be surprising that they should be respected as they are, throughout India. . . . These qualities are the foundation of the British strength in Asia. . . . They show in what manner nations, consisting of millions, are governed by 30,000 strangers."†

And they were "as orderly and obedient," he added, "as they were brave."

They were now to have an opportunity to show their metal. In his immediate command Wellesley had two Highland regiments –

* To Lieut-Colonel Close, August 17th 1803.
† Memorandum on British Troops in India. Brett-James, 121-2.

the 74th and 78th Foot* - and one English regiment of horse, the 19th Light Dragoons. On August 24th, after a halt at Aurungabad, his Army of the Deccan crossed the swollen Godavery river in basket-boats made of bamboo laths, thorn and leather - a device for campaigning in a bridgeless land which he had copied from Caesar's *Gallic War*. Linking forces with Colonel Stevenson's Hyderabad division, he began to shepherd Scindia's and the Rajah's harrying hordes northwards and eastwards, seeking every opportunity to bring them to battle without giving them a chance to escape the hunter's net and double back to plunder the Nizam's or Peshwah's territories. All the while, marching sometimes by day and sometimes by night, and making a fortified camp at every halt—another lesson learnt from Caesar, whose *Commentaries* and the Bible were the only books he took with him on the campaign†—his men kept up a steady three miles an hour, measuring the day's march by the perambulator or measuring-wheel‡ which always accompanied his Indian marches. "I never was in such marching trim," he told John Malcolm on September 6th. "I marched the other day 23 miles in 7½ hours. . . . It is impossible for troops to be in better order."

On September 22nd he and Stevenson, now more than two hundred miles from his base on the Bombay coast, temporarily separated, each taking a different defile through a range of hills barring their way, both to save time—for the passes were too narrow for both to use at the same time—and lest, by leaving either open, their quarry might slip through and fall to plundering again in their rear. It was arranged that they should join forces again on the 23rd and attack the enemy next day, if he had not by then retreated again.

But when on September 23rd Wellesley emerged from the hills, with Stevenson still ten miles from the rendezvous where they were to camp for the night, he was informed by his native guides that the Mahrattas were starting to retire and that the cavalry had already moved off, leaving the infantry and guns to follow. The opportunity of catching the latter strung out on the march was too good to

---

* After the Cardwell reforms they became respectively the 2nd Battalions of the Highland Light Infantry and the Seaforth Highlanders.

† Carola Oman, *Gascoygne Heiress*, 112.

‡ "The men who had charge of these wheels attained such extraordinary correctness of judging distance that they could be depended upon almost as completely without the wheel as with it." Maxwell, I, 72-3. See also Stanhope, 16, 23.

miss, and he at once decided to attack without waiting for Stevenson.* Owing to the enemy's immense strength in cavalry, it was impossible to confirm the accuracy of the report without using his whole force to reconnoitre. But when, moving forward to attack the, as he thought, retreating foe, he found that he had been grossly misinformed and that the whole Mahratta army of more than 40,000 men was drawn up in battle array on a six mile front immediately in his path, their infantry and artillery on their left behind the steep-banked Kaitna river, and the cavalry on the right and now moving up fast against him.

His position was most precarious. Threatened by an overwhelming deluge of native cavalry, it was impossible to stand where he was and be attacked in an unprepared position by an enemy six times his strength with more than a hundred guns to his own fourteen and eight light pieces. Yet, if he fell back on his fortified camp and waited for Stevenson, he would be harried by the hordes of horsemen already swarming round him and might well lose his baggage-train, already under fire, and, with it, all further mobility of movement and chance of catching his quarry. Without hesitation he decided to do the one thing which could both secure his outnumbered force from destruction and simultaneously enable him, by rolling up the Mahratta infantry from the flank, to achieve the aim of his offensive. For if he could destroy them, the war would be won, since only a hard-core of disciplined infantry and artillery, such as Scindia's French officers had trained, could enable the traditional Mahratta cavalry hordes to subsist in face of the fast-moving, self-contained field-forces he had created for their discomfiture and destruction.

Feeling, therefore, that the opportunity might never recur, he staked everything on being able to traverse the enemy's front and find a passage across the river somewhere beyond their extreme left, from which vantage point to turn back and assail them. He had, he told John Wilson Croker many years later, some of the best native guides that could be had, and he had made every effort to ascertain whether the river was anywhere passable, and all his informants had assured him that it was not. At last, in extreme anxiety, he resolved to see the river for himself, and accordingly, with his most intelligent guides and an escort of cavalry, he pushed forward to a

* "It was so important to our interests at this moment to strike a blow that I thought there was no time to be lost." To Lieut-General Stuart, September 24th 1803.

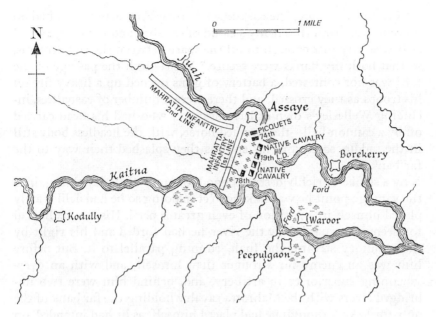

The Battle of Assaye

small eminence in sight of, and opposite the village of Assaye, which stood beyond it and on the bank of another stream, the Juah, running nearly parallel to it. There he again questioned his guides about a passage, which they still asserted not to exist. Yet he could see through his glass, a short way beyond the enemy's left, one village on the near bank of the Kaitna and another exactly opposite it on the other bank. So, the account he gave Croker continued, "I immediately said to myself that men could not have built two villages so close to one another on opposite sides of a stream without some habitual means of communication either by boats or a ford – most probably by the latter. On that conjecture, or rather reasoning, in defiance of all my guides and information, I took the desperate resolution, as it seemed, of marching for the river, and I was right."*

* From the account of the critical preliminaries to the Battle of Assaye which Wellington gave to John Wilson Croker, then Secretary to the Admiralty, while they were staying at the Marquis of Hertford's seat, Sudbourne, in December 1826, and which Croker set down as nearly as possible in the Duke's own words from notes made on the same evening. *Croker Papers*, I, 332, 353-4. "When one is strongly intent on an object," Wellington told Lord Mahon, describing the same occasion, "common sense will usually direct one to the right means." Stanhope, 49.

"I found a passage," he continued, "crossed my army over, had no more to fear from the enemy's cloud of cavalry, and my army, small as it was, was just enough to fill the space between the two streams, so that both my flanks were secure." Yet though the passage of the ford was not contested, a battery of guns opened up a heavy fire on his troops as they crossed, and there were a number of casualties, including Wellesley's own orderly dragoon who had his head carried off by a cannon-ball—the terrified horse, with the headless body still in the saddle, scattering his staff as they splashed their way to the far bank.*

By a stroke of richly deserved good fortune, Wellesley thus gained the vantage-point he was seeking. Yet in doing so he had deliberately placed himself in a position of even greater peril. His left, as he had foreseen, was guarded by the river he had forded and his right by the tributary stream, the Juah, running parallel to it. But before him was an enemy far stronger than himself, and with an overwhelming superiority in artillery, and, behind him were two unbridged rivers with the Mahratta cavalry holding the far bank of the only ford. And, though he had placed himself, as he had intended, on the Mahrattas' flank, they had, with their recently gained skill in manoeuvring, changed front on perceiving his passage of the river, and were now drawn up between the Kaitna and the Juah with more than a hundred cannon and at least fifteen thousand foot, including sixteen battalions of French-trained infantry. His own seven thousand were seemingly doomed.

It is doubtful if in any battle of modern times a responsible commander ever took a more daring calculated risk to achieve victory; in none even of the young Napoleon's battles was there anything quite to equal it. Wellesley had no advantage in weapons such as was enjoyed by British commanders in later Indian wars; in cannon he was hopelessly outnumbered. Except for his three British regiments - a mere 1500 men - there was little to choose in morale and discipline between his fine Sepoys and the valiant Mahratta infantry and gunners. But like the great admiral who five years earlier had shattered the French fleet in Aboukir Bay and was now, at that very moment, once more at his station off Toulon, he had taken every conceivable care to ensure victory, and, now that the chance had come, heavy though the odds might seem, was

* Fortescue, V, 26.

ready to stake everything on it. He knew that in battle with the Mahrattas - the bravest and fiercest fighters in Hindustan - the only safe rule was to attack first and never give them time or opportunity to use their superior numbers to encircle, and then, with their cannon, to annihilate.* He knew, too, that taught by their French instructors the new Revolutionary tactics of using masses in dense columns under cover of intensive artillery bombardment, Scindia's infantry and gunners constituted a more formidable force than any encountered in the Indian battles of the past. A few weeks earlier he had been warned of their new-found fighting skills by the Company's former Resident at Scindia's court, Colonel Collins, then on his way back to Bombay - a little man with a flash of fire in his dark eyes, looking in his antique military coat and black silk hat crowned by an ostrich feather, "not unlike a monkey dressed up for Bartholomew Fair." "I tell you, General," he had said at the end of their interview, "their infantry and guns will astonish you."† The truth of his prediction was now to be proved.

"In all great actions there is risk," Wellesley had written a few weeks earlier to his brother, the Governor-General. The wise course in action, he once said, is to attack your enemy at the moment he is preparing to attack you.‡ In front of the little British-Sepoy force the confined space between the two rivers seemed to one who was present "to be covered by one living mass to which our handful of men . . . was but a drop in the ocean." Preparatory to attacking, Wellesley drew up his infantry in two lines behind a low ridge which partly sheltered it from the enemy, with one of his two British regiments, the 74th Highlanders, on the right, and the other, the 78th Highlanders, on the left, and with the cavalry as reserve in the rear. Yet even in this position the fire of the Mahratta artillery was so intense that to remain exposed to it for long seemed suicide, and, though his troops had already marched twenty miles under a burning sun since dawn, the British commander ordered an immediate advance. Warning the officer commanding the pickets in front of

---

* To Colonel Murray, September 14th 1804, "You must by all means avoid allowing him to attack you with his infantry. There is no position in which you could maintain your camp against such powerful artillery as the Mahrattas have."

† "We little thought how true his words would prove." Major John Blakiston, *Twelve Years Military Adventures*, I, 144-5.

‡ Fraser, 39.

the 74th to avoid the strongly-held village of Assaye on the enemy's left, where their heavy batteries were concentrated, he himself directed the main attack against their right along the banks of the Kaitna through what he described in his dispatches as "a very hot fire from cannon, the execution of which was terrible." "It seemed," wrote Captain Blakiston of the East India Company's Engineers, "as if each individual felt that this was to be the test of discipline against numbers and that nothing but the utmost steadiness and determination could make up for the appalling disparity of force, . . . Not a whisper was heard through the ranks; our nerves were wound up to the proper pitch, and everyone seemed to know that there was no alternative but death or victory."

But while on the one flank Wellesley succeeded in his object, forcing back the enemy's infantry from the Kaitna and driving them, a congested mass, towards the Juah, on the other his little army was faced with disaster. For his brave picket commander, Colonel Orrock, in the storm of smoke and fire, lost his sense of direction and led his men and the 74th Highlanders who were following, straight into the mouth of the batteries massed around Assaye. "In the space of little more than a mile," wrote Blakiston, "a hundred guns, worked with skill and rapidity, vomitted death into our feeble ranks." In one platoon all but seven out of fifty men fell. Reduced from a battalion to little more than a company and still desperately defending its colours, the 74th was simultaneously assailed by the fire of the massed cannon in Assaye, the musketry of Scindia's French-trained infantry, and a fierce charge of Mahratta horse. After losing seventeen officers and nearly four hundred men, the Highland regiment was only saved from annihilation by Wellesley sending in his cavalry reserve to their rescue. In a magnificent charge the 19th Light Dragoons and the Fourth Native Cavalry not only routed the Mahratta horse but drove the enemy's first line of infantry into and across the Juah.

Gradually, in the furious hand-to-hand mêlée of the assault, the tide of battle turned as the British second line came into action. Everyone in Wellesley's little force distinguished himself; in the Eighth Native Infantry, known as "Wellesley's Own," five officers and non-commissioned officers of one famous fighting family all fell. Wellesley himself refused to blame the officer whose mistake in leading his men and the 74th into the hell of fire around Assaye occasioned at least half his casualties. "I lament the consequences of his mistake," he wrote in his dispatches, "but I must acknowledge that it was not possible for a man to lead a body into a hotter fire than he did the picquets on that day against Assaye."*

"Clashed with his fiery few and won." Throughout the engagement the thirty-four-year old commander never weakened in his resolve to break the enemy's will to resist. He himself had one horse shot under him and another piked, while almost every member of his staff was struck down or had his mount killed or wounded. He was described by one young officer of the 78th, Colin Campbell, whom he had made a brigade-major for his gallantry at the storming of Ahmednuggar, as being in the thick of the action the whole time: "I never saw a man so collected as he was," he wrote. Many years later his Spanish aide, Alava, recalled how in battle Wellington became a man transformed - "like an eagle." He can never have seemed more so than on this desperate field. At one moment a havildar of native cavalry, who had captured a Mahratta standard, was brought to him for congratulation, at which—"with that eloquent and correct knowledge in the native language for which he was celebrated," recalled Sir John Malcolm—he promoted him on the spot with the words, "*Acha havildar; jemadar.*" Long afterwards, when the victor of Assaye had become world-famous, at a dinner attended by his old comrades-at-arms to commemorate his victory, the Indian soldier whom he had honoured on the battlefield, and who looked back to it as the greatest moment of his long and honourable life, could not be induced to speak of his former commander as the Duke of Wellington, saying that that was his European name, but that his Indian name was "Wellesley Bahadur" - Wellesley the Invincible!†

The day was finally won in the gathering dusk when the Highlanders carried Assaye with the bayonet, driving the enemy from their guns, ninety-eight of which remained in their hands. It was, the victorious general reported, the most severe battle he had seen or, he believed, that had ever been fought in India; it showed "what a small number of British troops can do". Close on half had fallen, and more than nine hundred of the Sepoys and native auxiliaries. But the enemy's casualties were four times as great, and they had

* Blakiston, I, 156-82; *Dispatches*, II, 323-9, 338, 349; *Supplementary Despatches*, IV, 185-90; Fortescue, V, 19-34; Maxwell, I, 55-60; Hickey, 274-5.

† Malcolm, II, 278-9.

lost almost every gun, while Scindia and the Rajah had fled the field. "I believe such a quantity of cannon and such advantages have seldom been gained by any single victory in any part of the world," Wellesley wrote to his brother. Once, in old age, when he was asked what was the best thing he had ever done in the fighting line, he was silent for a time, then answered, "Assaye." He did not, said his interrogator, add a word.*

* * *

There was no pursuit, for the shattered cavalry was in no state to pursue. The army slept where it had fought, Wellesley himself in a farmyard sitting—a dead officer on one side and one with an amputated leg on the other—with his head between his knees, dreaming fitfully that he had lost everyone he had known in the battle and that he had no friend left alive. Next day Colonel Stevenson, to whom he had sent notice of his intention to attack before making his bold decision, arrived with the Hyderabad division, having been entangled during the night in a nullah. His surgeons helped to dress the wounded, many of whom had to be left on the field until the commanders of the Nizam of Hyderabad's neighbouring forts could be induced to admit them. A similar failure by the Company's allies to provide the grain they had promised prevented Wellesley from following up his victory. "The Nizam's aumils behave very ill," he wrote from Assaye five days after the battle, "and his killadar of Dowlutabad refuses to receive our wounded, so that I have been obliged either to leave our brave fellows exposed in an open town or to send them to Ahmednuggar . . . and to wait till I can get my doolies etc. back again. Thus are all our best plans thwarted, and yet these are the best of our allies!"†

Though the confederates' strength had been broken, and Scindia's and the Rajah's men had fled from the field plundering one another, the survivors were still capable of rallying and resuming their old trade of robbing their neighbours' territories; they had, indeed, no other way to live. For the next two months Wellesley and Stevenson, therefore, operated separately, the latter reducing Scindia's last remaining strongholds in the Deccan - Burhanpore and Asseerghur - while his chief, with his swifter and more mobile force, marched at

* Chad, 20.   † To Lieut-Colonel Close, September 28th 1803.

speed from place to place, countering every attempt of his quick-silver enemies to slip past him into his allies' dominions. "Since the battle of Assaye," he wrote at the end of October, "I have been like a man who fights with one hand and defends himself with the other. With Colonel Stevenson's corps I have acted offensively and have taken Asseerghur; and with my own I have covered his operations and defended the territories of the Nizam and the Peshwah. In doing this I have made some terrible marches, but I have been remarkably fortunate, first in stopping the enemy when they intended to pass to the southward through the Cassebarry ghaut, and afterwards, by a rapid march to the northward in stopping Scindia. I think we are in great style to be able to act on the offensive at all in this quarter; but it is only done by the celerity of our movements."* Once he covered seventy miles between sunrise on one day and midnight on the next.

Though, in the enemy's weakened condition, he left it to his lieutenant to head the advance into Berar, he was careful to advise him how to conduct his operations. "Do not," he wrote,

"attack their positions, because they always take up such as are confoundedly strong and difficult of access, for which the banks of the numerous rivers and nullahs afford them every facility. Do not remain in your own position, however strong it may be or however well you may have intrenched it; but when you shall hear that they are on their march to attack you, secure your baggage and move out of your camp. You will find them in the common disorder of march; they will not have time to form, which, being but half disciplined troops, is necessary for them. At all events, you will have the advantage of making the attack on ground which they will not have chosen for the battle; a part of their troops only will be engaged; and it is possible that you will gain an easy victory. Indeed, according to this mode, you might choose the field of battle yourself some days before, and might meet them upon that very ground.

"There is another mode of avoiding an action, which is to keep constantly in motion; but unless you come towards me, that would not answer. For my part, I am of opinion, that after the beating they received on the 23rd September, they are not likely

---

* To Major Merrick Shawe, October 26th 1803; *Croker Papers*, II, 232; Ellesmere, 184.

to stand for a second; and they will all retire with precipitation. But the natives of this country are rashness personified; and I acknoweldge that I should not like to see again such a loss as I sustained on the 23rd September, even if attended by such a gain."*

While Wellesley, living for weeks in the saddle, sleeping in tents and never entering a house, made war like Alexander with trains of elephants and camels, his brother, the Governor-General, had launched a second war against Scindia's dominions in the north. Marching from Bengal up the Ganges, capturing Agra and Delhi and liberating the puppet Mogul emperor, the Commander-in-Chief, General Lake, on the first day of November defeated the Mahrattas in a desperately fought encounter at Laswaree. Though not commanded as at Assaye by their vanquished chief, Scindia's men fought, as Lake wrote, "like devils or, rather, like heroes; I never was in so severe a business in my life or anything like it." It was a measure of what the Army of the Deccan had accomplished on the banks of the Kaitna five weeks before.

Even before news reached him of the defeat of his northern armies, Scindia, shattered by Assaye, had sued for peace. But, being a Mahratta, he did so intending to squeeze every possible advantage from the negotiations and use them to gain time for further military operations should any favourable opportunity occur. On November 7th a vakeel or envoy arrived at Wellesley's camp with an escort of an elephant, two camels and forty horse. After the customary *gullehmillow* or hugging-scene and the formal presentation of shawls and jewels, the vakeel assured the general that "the Maharajah, his master, wished for nothing so ardently as his friendship and amity." It turned out however that he had no powers to treat or bind his principal. "I cannot account," Wellesley wrote to his brother, "for Jeswunt Rao Goorparah coming unprovided with the usual powers. In proportion, however, as I gain experience of the Mahrattas, I have more reason to be astonished at the low and unaccountable tricks which even the highest classes of them practise, with a view, however remote, to forward their own interest."†

Knowing, however, that such subterfuges were inevitable, the young general did not allow the delay to ruffle either his courtesy

* To Colonel Stevenson, October 12th 1803.
† To the Governor-General, November 11th 1803.

or patience. Aware that Scindia was reduced to great distress, he wished to make peace with him, both to free his hands for the invasion of Berar and lest, by weakening one Mahratta overlord too much, he should merely augment the power of another, the formidable Holkar, who, though not at present at war with the Company, could easily, by acquiring the bulk of his defeated rival's disintegrating army, provide a new threat to the peace of India.

By the terms of the suspension of hostilities which on November 23rd Wellesley concluded with Scindia's vakeels,* the Maharajah was to withdraw his troops at once from the war-zone, thus abandoning his ally, whose principal stronghold of Gawilghur Colonel Stevenson was preparing to beseige. As, however, Scindia's forces showed no sign of carrying out this essential condition but remained in the immediate proximity of the Rajah's army opposing Stevenson's advance on Gawilghur, Wellesley lost no time in reminding him that there was no suspension of arms for his ally and that there could be none for him until he had complied with the terms of the truce.† Warning him that his duty was to attack the enemies of the Company wherever he found them, he marched on November 28th to join Stevenson, summoning him to meet him next day at Paterly near the Purna river. For he was resolved to strike the confederates a crowning blow with his entire army, reunited for the first time since the morrow of Assaye. Resuming his march at six next morning he was joined by Stevenson in the early afternoon of the 29th at Paterly. There he found, as he had anticipated—viewing them through his telescope from a tower in the town—that the forces of the defeated Scindia and the Rajah were once more together, drawn up in battle array some six miles away on the Plain of Argaum.

Though his men had been marching in intense heat since dawn, he decided to attack at once. By the time, however, he was in position to do so, it was already half-past four and only an hour or two of daylight remained. Advancing through shoulder-high corn which covered the plain, his columns came within striking distance of the Mahrattas before they were observed. Greeted by a furious cannonade

* "They seem to have much confidence in me, which, at all events, is a point gained in the negotiations." To Lieut.-General Stuart, November 23rd 1803.

† "If advantage should be taken of the cessation of hostilities to delay the negotiations for peace, your Excellency will observe that I have the power of putting an end to it when I please." To Governor-General. Gurwood, 119.

from their massed guns, though less intense a one than that which they had faced so heroically at Assaye, two Sepoy battalions, exhausted by the long day's march, unexpectedly broke and turned tail. But Wellesley quickly and calmly rallied, reformed and led them back into the attack. An officer, who witnessed the scene, described what he did. "The general, who was then close to the spot under a tree giving orders to the brigadiers, perceiving what had happened, immediately stepped out in front, hoping by his presence to restore the confidence of the troops. But, seeing that this did not produce the desired effect, he mounted his horse, and rode up to the retreating battalions, when, instead of losing his temper, upbraiding them and endeavouring to force them back to the spot from which they had fled, as most people would have done, he quietly ordered the officers to lead their men under cover of the village, and then to rally and get them into order as quickly as possible. This being done, he put the column again in motion and, leading these very same runaways round the other side of the village, formed them on the very spot he originally intended them to occupy. "This," recalled one who was present,

"was at once a masterpiece of generalship and a signal display of the intuitive knowledge of human nature only to be found in great minds. There is not one man in a million who, on seeing the troops turn their backs, would not have endeavoured to bring them again to the spot from which they had retreated. In this attempt it is more than probable that he would have failed, and in that case, the panic would, most likely, have extended down the column, producing the most disastrous consequences. As it was, the retrograde movement was mistaken by all but the troops who actually gave way, for a countermarch. Indeed, it is very probable that, owing to the conduct of the General on this occasion, even the runaways might have flattered themselves into this belief, and thus have been saved from that sense of degradation which might have had a serious effect on their subsequent conduct during the day."*

* "This circumstance produced in my mind the first clear idea of that genius, which has since been so mainly instrumental, by its conduct and example, in achieving the deliverance of Europe. From the first moment I saw General Wellesley I formed a high opinion of him; but from this time forth, I looked up to him with a degree of respect bordering on veneration." Blakiston, 198-200.

Wellesley himself admitted that if he had not been there, the day would have been lost.

While he was bringing the two battalions back into line, he had ordered his troops to lie down to minimise the effects of the intense bombardment to which they were being subjected by the enemies' batteries. "We shall have to take those guns before midnight," he remarked. He had drawn his infantry up in a single line with the cavalry in reserve behind and, with a force of less than 11,000 men, he now advanced, shortly before five o'clock, against the enemy's 30,000. But the Mahrattas' morale had been broken at Assaye, and, faced by that fierce and unrelenting assault, they gave way, leaving thirty-eight cannon and all their ammunition in the victor's hands. But for the fall of darkness, few would have escaped. As it was, the cavalry pursued the survivors by moonlight far into the night, slaying thousands and capturing vast numbers of elephants, camels and baggage. Wellesley's casualties were only 562, or about a twentieth of the troops engaged.

"Our late victory was grand," he wrote to the Company's Resident in Mysore, Colonel Close. "It has made a great impression throughout the country. Indeed, between the destruction there dealt out and the subsequent desertion of troops, the enemy have but few troops left; and I anxiously hope that they will come within reach to allow me to give them a parting blow with our cavalry only. . . . I have succeeded in bringing upon that rascal" - Ragojee Bhoonslah - "the full measure of God's vengeance; and, if I live a month longer, he shall either be at peace with the Company or I shall be at Nagpore with all the armies either with me or about me. We shall take Gawilghur, I hope, with ease."*

The end of the Mahratta war can be told in excerpts from Arthur Wellesley's letters, Dispatches and General Orders of the next three weeks. In that short time he not only forced Scindia and the Rajah to accept terms of peace compensating the Company and its subsidiary allies for the injuries done them and restoring the territories they had usurped, but captured, with the loss of only 14 killed and 112 wounded, the supposedly impregnable mountain fortress of Gawilghur. While he supervised Colonel Stevenson's assault operations on one side of the mountain range on which it stood, he

* To Lieut-Colonel Close, December 6th 1803.

himself blockaded it from the other, daily riding fifty miles between the two camps as he supervised the dual siege.

30 Nov. "I propose to march tomorrow towards Gawilghur, and I shall lose no time in attacking that place."*

2 Dec. "A vakeel has come in from the Rajah of Berar, but nothing very particular has occurred. I have demanded compensation from the Rajah, and I have desired the vakeel to stay at Ellichpoor until he is authorised to grant it. The powers of Scindia's vakeels were not quite so perfect upon this point as I wished; and they shall go away tomorrow unless they can produce them in a more perfect form. There is no dealing with these Mahrattas unless they are treated in this manner, and unless a regular document is brought forward upon every point that may occur.

"The Rajah is much alarmed about Gawilghur, and I think he is sincere; indeed, I think Scindia is so likewise. But every Mahratta chief is so haughty and so prone to delay, that I suspect both these chiefs will be ruined rather than submit to the conditions which I must require from them."†

3 Dec. "I have Gawilghur now in sight and it does not appear to be so strong as many hill forts in Mysore taken by our troops.

"Scindia has ratified the treaty for suspending hostilities and his vakeels say that he is going to the east of Ellichpoor according to the agreement. I have told them that I shall consider it as void on my part if he does not perform all the conditions. We have advanced no farther in the peace than that the vakeels have brought forward a kind of consent to treat upon the basis of giving compensation to the company.

". . . Ragojee Bhoonslah has likewise sent a vakeel here. I have made the same demand from him. . . . They are most terribly alarmed for the loss of Gawilghur etc. On this ground I expect to conclude with Ragojee immediately. His vakeel pressed hard for a suspension of hostilities, which I positively refused."‡

* To the Governor-General, November 30th 1803.
† To Major Merrick Shawe, December 2nd 1803.
‡ To Lieut-General Stuart, December 3rd 1803.

7-13 Dec. "Colonel Stevenson had equipped his corps at Asseerghur for the siege of Gawilghur, for whose service it had long been destined; and I therefore determined that he should make the principal attack by Labada, while I should cover his operations by my own division and all the cavalry and, if possible, assist them by other attacks to the southward and westward. . . . On the 7th both divisions marched from Ellichpoor: Colonel Stevenson into the mountains by Damergaum, and my division towards the southern face of the fort of Gawilghur. From that day till the 12th, on which Colonel Stevenson broke ground near Labada, the troops in his division went through a series of laborious services, such as I never before witnessed, with the utmost cheerfulness and perseverance. The heavy ordnance and stores were dragged by hand over mountains and through ravines, for nearly the whole distance, by roads which it had been previously necessary for the troops to make for themselves.

"On the 12th, at night, Colonel Stevenson erected two batteries in front of the north face of the fort. . . . On the same night the troops of my division constructed a battery . . . on the mountain under the southern gate, with a view, if possible, to breach the wall near that gate; or, at all events, to draw the enemy's attention to that quarter.

"The fire of all these batteries opened on the 13th in the morning."*

14 Dec. "Colonel Stevenson's division is to storm the northern face of the Gawilghur tomorrow morning at 10 o'clock."

15 Dec. "Major-General Wellesley has great satisfaction in congratulating the troops under his command upon the brilliant success of this day."†

17 Dec. "Colonel Barclay informed me that, while detained at one of the gates to allow the troops to pass out, he had amused himself with making some of them lay down their plunder. I have seen many places taken by storm and I never saw one in which so little irregularity was committed and which was so little plundered; and it is but doing justice to the corps to declare that, in an hour after having stormed that large place, they marched out as if they had been only passing through it. . . .

* To the Governor-General, December 15th 1803.
† *General Orders*, December 14th and 15th 1803.

"I am induced to believe that Ragojee is serious and that he will ratify the peace. . . . But there is nothing so likely to produce this desirable result as the continuance of the pressure upon him. I propose, therefore, to continue my march to the eastward, but not with so much celerity as I should have done if there had been no peace."*

23 Dec. "The ratification of a treaty of peace concluded with Ragojee Bhoonslah, Rajah of Berar, is to be delivered to Major-General Wellesley at 12 o'clock today.

"A royal salute is to be held in readiness in the park, to be fired on the delivery of the treaty. . . .

". . . Major-General Wellesley intends riding out to meet Vittel Punt, the Dewan of Dowlat Rao Scindia; he will be glad to see any officers off duty who may wish to be present at the delivery of the treaty or to ride with him to meet the Dewan.

"An extra dram to be issued to the Europeans today, on the occasion of the peace with the Rajah of Berar."†

*　　*　　*

The campaign General Wellesley had planned and directed with such masterly skill was now at an end. By his victories at Assaye and Argaum—and even more, perhaps, by his marches and the genius of his commissariat arrangements—the British Government and East India Company had been placed, as he wrote from his camp on January 16th 1804, "in a most glorious situation. They are the sovereigns of a great part of India, the protectors of the principal Powers, and the mediators, by treaty, of the disputes of all. The sovereignty they possess is greater and their power is settled upon more permanent foundations than any before known in India."‡ All they needed, he added, was popularity which, from the nature of British institutions and justice, was likely to follow as soon as a period of tranquillity had given the people time and opportunity to realise their new security and happiness.

The only remaining danger to the future peace of Hindustan was from the freebooters thrown on the countryside by the defeat of

---

* To Colonel Stevenson, December 17th 1803.
† *General Order*, December 23rd 1803.
‡ To Major Kirkpatrick, January 16th 1804.

the armies in which they had served and whose dissolution spread the germs of anarchy over a wider area. "Conceive a country," the victorious general wrote, "in every village of which there are from twenty to thirty horsemen who have been dismissed from the service of the State and who have no means of living except by plunder. . . . There is no law, no civil government and no army to keep these plunderers in order, and no revenue can be collected – indeed, no inhabitant can, or will, remain to cultivate unless he is protected by an armed force stationed in his village."*

For a few weeks after the peace, Wellesley himself was engaged in hunting down such larger splinter forces from the defeated armies as were still at large. In a letter written in early February 1804, he described how he had destroyed one such roving company which had been raiding villages in northern Hyderabad, where they had beaten up a contingent of the Nizam's troops and captured four guns.

"I marched on the morning of the 4th twenty miles; at night, twenty-four miles, and arrived here at nine o'clock on the morning of the 5th. Some of our faithful allies in my camp had given them intelligence of my march, and they had struck tents and were going off. But I pursued them, cut up many, took all their baggage, bazaars, guns, ammunition, etc, and entirely dispersed them. The 74th regiment, one battalion of native infantry, and five hundred men from the other corps in camp were up in the pursuit. The whole was over by twelve o'clock on the 5th. I think that by that time the troops had marched sixty miles, from six in the morning of the 4th, in which time they halted ten hours, from twelve at noon to ten at night of the 4th. If the night had not been very dark, and the road very bad, I should have been in their camp at daylight and should have taken the whole party.†

"I think," he added with pardonable pride, "we begin to beat the Mahrattas in the celerity of their movements."

* To Major Merrick Shawe, February 26th 1804.
† To Colonel John Murray, February 7th 1804. "The result of this day is the complete defeat of a numerous and formidable band of freebooters who were the terror of the country, were daily increasing in numbers and had already defeated a body of the Soubah's troops. . . . I do not think that they will venture, or indeed that they can collect again, as they have lost everything which could enable them to subsist when collected." To the Governor-General, February 5th 1804.

Because, dedicated soldier though he was, the object of all soldier-ing in his view was to secure justice and a lasting peace, Wellesley was strongly opposed to depriving the greater Mahratta chiefs of more territory or power than was necessary to prevent them again breaking the peace or oppressing their neighbours. "When war is concluded," he wrote, "I am decidedly of opinion that all animosity should be forgotten." He particularly resented the Peshwah's at-tempts to use hard-won British victories to avenge himself on his de-feated rivals. "The war will be eternal," he wrote, "if nobody is ever to be forgiven. When the empire of the Company is so great, little dirty passions must not be suffered to guide its measures."*

Nor was it only the Company's Indian allies who proved grasping in the hour of triumph. Unfortunately some of its own servants, including the Governor-General, out of a well-meaning desire to extend the benefits of British rule took advantage of Scindia's and the Rajah's helplessness to put constructions on the terms of the peace treaties which they were not morally capable of bearing. "I am afraid," General Wellesley wrote sadly at the end of January, "that the moderation of the British Government in India has a strong re-semblance to the ambition of other governments."† "I would sacri-fice Gwalior or every frontier in India ten times over," he told John Malcolm, "in order to preserve our credit for scrupulous good faith and the advantages and honour we gained by the late war and the peace; and we must not fritter them away in arguments drawn from over-strained principles of the laws of nations, which are not under-stood in this country. What brought me through many difficulties in this war and the negotiations for peace? The British good faith and nothing else."‡ So disgusted did he become by what was being done that within three months of his victory he confessed that he would give a large sum to have had nothing to do with the peace treaties. "All parties were delighted with the peace but the demon of ambition appears now to have pervaded all; and each endeavours by forcing constructions to gain as much as he can."§

* To E. Scott Waring, March 12th 1804. To Lieut-Colonel Close, January 22nd 1804.
† To Major Malcolm, January 29th 1804.
‡ To Major Malcolm, March 17th 1804. "No worthwhile progress can be made in any negotiation that is not founded upon respect for the character of the British Government and which is not carried on in cordial and civil language." To the Governor of Bombay, February 22nd 1804.
§ To Major Malcolm, January 29th 1804; April 13th 1804.

Nor was it only on moral grounds that this thirty-four-year-old soldier, so much wiser than his years, opposed his brother's policy of reducing hitherto independent princes to mere ciphers, tied by subsidiary treaties to the Company's apron strings and completely dependent on British arms for the preservation of internal order. "I have always been anxious," he wrote, "to protect the great families of the Mahratta empire, as I am convinced that the peace of the country is more likely to be secured through their means than through any other. We have weakened Scindia more than is politic, and . . . we shall repent having established such a number of these little independent powers in India, every one of whom . . . will occasion a constant demand for employment of troops, a loss of officers and men and a claim of money."† Apart from British Bengal which enjoyed the advantages of a civil government and only required military force for its protection against foreign enemies, "all the other barbarous establishments called governments," he pointed out

"have no power beyond that of the sword. Take from them the exercise of that power and they have no other and can collect no revenue, can give no protection, and can exercise no government. . . . Their territories are overrun by a race of armed men who are ready to enlist with anybody who will lead them to plunder; and there is no power in the country to support the government and give protection to the industrious classes of the inhabitants excepting the British troops. . . . The danger of the evil is increased by the extension of our arms, our influence and our protection: first by the increase of the number of the people who must and will subsist by plunder, and secondly by narrowing the scene in which freebooters may plunder with impunity. . . .

"We have within the last five years extended ourselves by our policy and our bravery over the whole of India except the territories of Holkar and the Rajah of Berar. . . . In this vast extent of country in which the numbers of the people with arms in their hands who have no means of living except by plunder are so much increased, no man can venture to plunder without incurring the risk, at least, of being destroyed by a British army. Habits of industry are out of the question; they must plunder for subsistence or be destroyed or starve. . . . As we have now narrowed

† To E. Scott Waring, January 21st 1805; to Major Malcolm, April 9th 1804.

the scene so much, we must not expect that our own territories will be entirely free from their depredations. . . .

"The Governor-General has never had this picture before him. No man has ever had so many opportunities of contemplating the subject in all its parts as I have. . . . The remedy is clear, viz. to force the allies to keep up their military establishments."*

It was because, against his advice, the Company was pressing too hard on Scindia - stripped of his northern provinces along the Jumna and his western seaports and forced to accept a defensive treaty with a British army in his territories - that by the spring of 1804 everything, against all earlier expectation, was pointing to a new Mahratta war. For, by rendering Scindia powerless, the victors had unwittingly strengthened his rival, Jeswant Rao Holkar, to join whose freebooting hordes, then living at large in Rajputana, disbanded or deserting Mahratta horsemen were now flocking in thousands. And Holkar, as Wellesley knew, was a formidable operator, whose territories he had been particularly careful to avoid during the campaign against his fellow chieftains.† "The consequence of Scindia discharging all his military establishment," he warned his superiors at the time of his surrender,

"will be that all persons discharged must go into Holkar's service in order to gain a livelihood and thereby increase his means of annoying the other Powers of India, every one of whom will be connected with the Company. . . . Scindia's military resources are nearly destroyed; those of Holkar are unimpaired. Scindia has no abilities himself and has no person about him capable of managing his affairs; Holkar has the reputation of being an able man, and has certainly been a successful one."‡

The inevitable consequence, as General Wellesley had foreseen, was that, being a Mahratta and meeting no resistance, Holkar moved with his reinforced army into Scindia's now defenceless

* To Major Merrick Shawe, February 26th 1804.

† "Take care that, in establishing your frontier, you do not interfere with Holkar. He has not hitherto committed hostilities against us, and I have cautiously avoided to touch upon him." To Colonel Murray, October 13th 1803.

‡ Memorandum for Major Malcolm, January 7th 1804.

territories to plunder, regardless of the fact that, by the defensive alliance the latter had concluded with the East India Company, the British were bound to come to his aid. When the Commander-in-Chief, Lord Lake, called on Holkar to withdraw, the great freebooter, true to type, merely went on plundering and forced Lake to take the field against him.

In this new war Wellesley took no part. A drought had caused famine in the Deccan, and, with no fodder for horse or bullock, a 600 mile march from Poona to Indore was out of the question until the monsoon had brought on new grass and crops. All he could contribute to the campaign in the north was the advice, based on five years' experience, which, at the Commander-in-Chief's request, he sent him on his method of coping with a fast-moving host of plundering horsemen. "I have served a good deal against this description of freebooter," he wrote,

"and I think that the best mode of operating is to press him with one or two corps capable of moving with tolerable celerity, and of such strength as to render the result of an action by no means doubtful if he should venture to risk one. The effect . . . is to oblige him to move constantly and with great celerity. When reduced to this necessity, he cannot venture to stop to plunder the country, . . . the subsistence of his army becomes difficult and precarious, the horsemen become dissatisfied, they perceive that their situation is hopeless, and they desert in numbers daily. The freebooter ends by having with him only a few adherents, and he is reduced to such a state as to be liable to be taken by any small body of country horse . . .

"Whenever the largest and most formidable bodies of them are hard pressed by our troops, the village people attack them upon their rear and flanks, cut off stragglers, and will not allow a man to enter their villages. Because their villages being in some degree fortified, they know well that the freebooters dare not wait the time which would be necessary to reduce them. When this is the case, all their means of subsistence vanish, no resource remains excepting to separate; and even this resource is attended by risk, as the village people cut them off on their way to their homes."*

* To Lord Lake, May 27th 1804.

73

Unfortunately, Lake's lieutenant, Colonel William Monson, operating two hundred miles in advance of the main army with a force of 12,000 men and fifteen guns, ignored one of Wellesley's cardinal rules for Indian warfare - to avoid retrograde movements in the face of an enemy.* Finding himself deep in Holkar's country in the presence of an army of 40,000, instead of attacking, as Wellesley had done at Assaye, he lost his nerve and began a retreat which ended in the destruction of his cavalry and transport, the capture of all his guns and the loss, after terrible sufferings, of nine-tenths of his force. To Wellesley, Monson's "retreats, defeats, disgraces and disasters" seemed " the greatest and most disgraceful to our military character that had ever occurred." "It is worth while," he wrote, " to review these transactions in order that we may see to what these misfortunes ought to be attributed, that, in future, if possible they may be avoided.

" First; we should never employ a corps on a service for which it is not fully equal.

"Secondly; against the Mahrattas in particular, but against all enemies, we should take care to be sure of plenty of provisions.

"Thirdly; experience has shown us, that British troops can never depend upon Rajahs or any allies for their supplies. Our own officers must purchase them; and, if we should employ a native in such an important service, we ought to see the supplies before we venture to expose our troops in a situation in which they may want them.

" Fourthly; when we have a fort which can support our operations, ... we should immediately adopt effectual measures to fill it with provisions.

" Fifthly; when we cross a river likely to be full in the rains, we ought to have a post and boats upon it, as I have upon all the rivers south of Poona."

" In respect of a corps in the situation of Monson's, they must be decided and quick; and in all retreats it must be recollected that they

---

* "A retrograde movement is always bad in this country." To Lieut-Colonel Close, June 23rd 1803.

are safe and easy in proportion to the number of attacks made by the retreating corps."*

*   *   *

Since the end of his campaign, Wellesley had been suffering severely from lumbago - "a disorder" he had written, "to which all persons in camp are liable. If I do not go into a house soon I am afraid I shall walk like old Pomeroy for the remainder of my life." For this reason, as for many others, he was anxious to return home. Though the shock to British prestige administered by Monson's disaster - redeemed in November by Lord Lake's defeat of Holkar at Furruck-abad - caused him to postpone his departure for England for a further six months lest his services in the field should again be needed, he was now determined to wind up his Indian affairs as soon as he could be released. "I am anxious," he wrote, "to a degree I cannot express to see my friends again." At thirty-five he felt he had done all he could do in India and that his place was now at home where his country was facing, single-handed, the greatest threat in her history, with all western Europe from the Straits of Gibraltar to the Texel aligned against her and Napoleon and his Grand Army waiting to invade her. "I have served as long in India," he told a friend, "as any man ought who can serve anywhere else; and I think there appears a prospect of service in Europe in which I should be more likely to get forward."

The personal difficulties which had forced him to quit England eight years earlier no longer operated. Thanks to prize money won in Mysore and during the Mahratta war, his debts were all paid and he had accumulated nearly £43,000† - a modest fortune which made him independent. And though, with its rule-of-thumb obsession with seniority and disregard of Indian claims, the Horse Guards had still failed to confirm his appointment to the staff of the Madras Army - a slight he felt severely - recognition from England had come with

---

* To Lieut-Colonel Wallace, September 12th 1804.

† "When I came from India I had 42 or 43 thousand pounds which I made as follows. I got £5000 prize money at Seringapatam; £25,000 prize money in the Mahratta War; the Court of Directors gave me £4000 for having been a commander in Mysore, and the Government paid me about £2000, . . . the arrears of an allowance as Commanding Officer at Seringapatam." To Hon William Wellesley-Pole, September 13th 1809.

a Knighthood of the Bath conferred on him for his victory of Assaye. The presentation by grateful Anglo-Indian friends and admirers of a golden vase worth 2000 guineas, addresses from the inhabitants of Bombay and Seringapatam, a jewelled sword given by the southern Mahratta chiefs and another worth £1000 by the merchants of Calcutta, all testified to the regard in which he was held by members of both the European and native communities.

Yet the greatest thing India had given was what she had taught him. In eight years of serving her he had learnt to be a diplomat, an administrator and a field commander, versed in every art and technique which could create order, trust, stability and peace out of chaos and anarchy. Nor were the lessons learnt in a dissolving land wracked by perpetual war without relevance to the problems of the western civilised world to which he was now to return. For outside island England, the ancient polity of Christian Europe, until lately so seemingly stable, had in the past decade dissolved into recurrent war and anarchy, with its greatest and most populous nation-state, torn by the passions of revolution, turned freebooter under the inspired command of the most formidable military freebooter of all time.

Compared with that man of genius and destiny—born in the same year as himself and now Emperor of the French and the self-proclaimed successor of Charlemagne—Arthur Wellesley was still very small beer. Yet at an age when most of his British military contemporaries had never commanded more than a brigade and had little, if any, experience of fighting, let alone of victory, he had directed forces in war which, before the final disbandment of the Army of the Deccan in the summer of 1804, had numbered up to 50,000 men. He had marched and manoeuvred them, at speeds till then deemed impossible in India, over vast areas of desert, jungle and wasted countryside, winning against odds, with a daring unsurpassed even by the victor of Marengo and Rivoli, battles which, had his countrymen studied their details or been aware of their impact on the next century, would already have entitled him, at thirty-five, to a place among the shapers of human destinies. "I understood as much of military matters," he said in after years of this period of his career, "as I have ever done or do now."*

* Stanhope, 131.

As a soldier his imaginative enterprise, celerity and daring had been matched by the meticulous forethought and industry with which he attended to every detail that could ensure success and safeguard the health, comfort and lives of his men. "I consider nothing in this country so valuable," he wrote in one of his dispatches, "as the life and health of the British soldier."* For those who had been the hard core of his armies - exiles like himself in a strange land - and without whom, for all his meticulous planning and brilliance in command, his victories could not have been won, his praise was unstinted. "Their patience under fatigue and the persevering activity with which they performed all the duties required from them," he told the Governor-General at the conclusion of the Mahratta War, "were equal to their bravery when opposed to the enemy in the field; and the consequence of all those good qualities is that, notwithstanding the distance and difficulties attending our communication with the sources of our supplies, the great bodies of the enemy's horse and the disaffected and disturbed state of the countries under the government of the Company's allies, . . . throughout the campaign we did not lose one convoy nor a particle of the Company's property of any description."†

Nor did the grateful general forget his Indian soldiers. He urged that provision should be made for the wounded of the silladar or irregular native horse, and for the families of those killed. "It is not reasonable," he wrote, "to expect that persons of this description who have no means of subsistence excepting those afforded by military service will risk their lives or will be disabled unless made certain of a provision hereafter. The want of this provision is the great defect of all the native military services, and is the cause of the frequent instances of misbehaviour before an enemy of the country troops. The truth of this observation is proved by the fact that . . . those now in the service of the Rajah of Mysore, for whom provision is made in case they should receive wounds and for their families in case they should be killed, have uniformly behaved better in battle than any other native troops of whom we have a knowledge. I therefore strongly recommend that . . . measures be adopted . . . to submit the claims of those disabled by wounds and of the horsemen who may be killed in the Service to the decision of a committee of officers,

* Stanhope, 131; *Dispatches*, II, 222.
† To the Governor-General, January 17th 1804.

in the same manner as the claims of persons actually in the service of the Honourable Company."*

In the military correspondence of Wellesley's Indian years preserved in his dispatches, one can see the untiring diligence, sound judgment and inspired common sense of this still young but great commander. A decade later in the Peninsula, the Judge-Advocate-General, Francis Larpent, testified how admirable he was in all business, "ready, decisive and civil." He was already so in Mysore and the Deccan. He once told a colleague that, whatever the provocation, letters should never be marred by severity or asperity but should always confine themselves to a plain and short abstract of the fact. He expected others to observe the same restraint. In one of his earliest Indian letters, written in March 1799 to a hot-tempered senior officer of his regiment over-hasty on the epistolary trigger, he made this point very forcefully.

"If I had passed a censure upon your conduct for a circumstance which no exertion of yours could have prevented, I should probably have been as unreasonable as you have represented me in the epithets which you have applied to it; but the fact is, I passed no censure. . . .

". . . I have a right, and it is my duty, to interfere in any matter of detail in which the 33rd are concerned; and that being the case, it was my duty to send to you when I thought something had escaped your notice.

"This is not the first time that I have had occasion to observe that, under the forms of private correspondence, you have written me letters upon public duty, couched in terms to which I have not been accustomed. It is impossible to believe that you mean to use those terms; and yet I cannot but reflect that no sensible man ever writes a letter in passion; that he inquires and considers, and, in the end, finds, as you would have done in this instance, that he had no reason to be displeased. However, it is necessary that I should inform you that the next letter of that kind that I receive I shall send to the Commander-in-Chief, and leave it to him to give such answer to it as he may think fit."†

The climatic conditions of living and working in India were not

* To the Secretary of the Governor of Bombay, June 27th 1804.
† To Major John Shee, March 21st 1799.

easy on men's tempers. So it came about that early in Arthur Wellesley's career he had become accustomed to dealing with human irritability and touchiness. "Captain Mackay is an honest and zealous servant of the public," he wrote to the general officer commanding at Bombay, "and he conducts his own important department in such a manner as always to have the cattle under his charge in a most efficient state for work; but he is the most unaccommodating public officer that I have met with. He has never failed to contrive to quarrel with the head of every other department with which he has been concerned; and I have always had the greatest difficulty in keeping matters between him and others in such a state as that the Service should not be impeded by their disputes. I imagine that the difficulties between Captain Mackay and Major Symons, to which you have alluded, are to be attributed to the state of Captain Mackay's temper; and possibly, in some degree, to a want of accommodation on the part of Major Symons. I make no doubt but that you will have observed that this officer also, although an excellent man, has more of the oak than the willow in his disposition."*

The greatness of Arthur Wellesley's mind lay in the clarity with which it grasped essentials and the force and reasoning power with which he impressed those essentials on others. The first of these for a soldier was discipline and what he called, "regularity" - that perfection of military conduct which riveted every link in the chain of command from the highest to the lowest. An officer to command must be worthy of command: be both a gentleman—honourable, faithful to his trust, truthful, self-controlled and considerate to others—and a soldier dedicated by study and experience to the mastery of his profession. Only so could he deserve and win the confidence which had to exist between men who faced death together and depended on one another utterly." This capacity to generate mutual confidence between leader and led Wellesley saw as the indispensable requisite for victory, creating in the led the determination and desire to obey and in the leader the knowledge that obedience would be forthcoming under all circumstances. "Depend upon it," he told Lord Stanhope, "it requires time for a general to inspire confidence or to feel it; for you will never have confidence in yourself until others have confidence in you."

* To Lieut-General Stuart, May 26th 1803.

79

"The real reason I succeeded in my campaign," he said, "is because I was always on the spot - I saw everything and did everything for myself." And by everything he meant everything. "When preparations are to be made for a great foreign war, such as the late war against the Mahrattas," he told General Stuart after Monson's disaster, "the mere readiness of the troops is nothing in comparison with the preparations required for the departments of the Service. You could march the troops from the most distant garrisons before these could be ready and, therefore. . . . the field force would be no use." Reading the twelve massive volumes of his Indian and Peninsular Dispatches many years later, a friend remarked that, until he read them he had had no idea of the variety necessary for a Commander-in-Chief. Asked how, with so much on his hands, he managed to cope, the Duke replied, "I never should if I had not been very young in command."* It was the fact that he was which enabled him a decade later to defeat one after another of Napoleon's veteran Marshals and supposedly invincible armies, and, in the end, Napoleon himself.

For all his mastery over himself, which grew with the years, being a perfectionist he suffered much over mistakes and miscarriages caused by failure in others to do their duty. "I don't know whether I ought to regret the disposition which I feel to consider nothing impossible," he wrote to the Governor of Bombay, "to suppose that everything can be effected by adequate exertions, and to feel deeply and complain of disappointment. I really believe I may sometimes have complained without much cause."†

Towards corruption and betrayal of trust he was inexorable. "You reproach me," he wrote to one of his officers, "with having withdrawn from you my confidence. A man must have been stout indeed in his confidence in anybody who would continue to repose it after having received such complaints as I have received against you. It is not the fact that you did Major —'s duty without receiving his salary. You received the allowance for the duty you did and your own allowance for the duty done by another person in the field. . . . You have been accused on oath, in a public trial, of having received through your moonshee 1200 rupees on corrupt grounds. The moon-

---

* To Lieut-General Stuart, July 3rd 1804, *The Conversations of the First Duke of Wellington with George William Chad*, 19.
† To Governor of Bombay, January 7th 1804.

shee positively received the money. He must be prosecuted in the Phousdarry and convicted of a breach of trust and duty, otherwise you must resign your office. . . . I cannot go on with a man against whom there will be such a public imputation as there will be against you if the moonshee should not be convicted of having taken and applied this money to his own use."* To another officer to whom a Rajah had offered a bribe of 4000 pagodas to have his State taken under British protection, with a suggested further 10,000 pagodas for himself, Wellesley replied:

"I cannot conceive what can have induced the Rajah of Kittoor to imagine that I was capable of receiving that or any other sum of money. . . . I desire that you will tell them . . . that you have no authority whatever to listen to such proposals. . . . In respect to the bribe offered to you and myself I am surprised that any man in the character of a British officer should not have given the Rajah to understand that the offer would be considered as an insult . . . If he should renew it you will inform him that I and all British officers consider such offers as insults on the part of those by whom they are made."†

Wellesley set himself relentlessly against "dubashery" - the vicious practice under which Europeans in responsible positions used Indian subordinates as a cloak and instrument for rapacious, corrupt and oppressive dealings. During his military administration of Mysore he instituted a systematic investigation of frauds and embezzlements from the Seringapatam arsenal by British officers and officials which ended in the condign punishment of the malefactors and brought to a close a scene of villainy which, he wrote, "would have disgraced the Newgate calendar."

The same virtues of industry, dispatch and attention to the minutest detail which made Wellesley a great commander, made him also a great administrator. Readiness to obey and to take responsibility‡ were the guiding stars by which he steered: that and the subordination of his own interests and desires to those of the public. "I have never had much value for the public spirit of any man," he told his

* To Lieut ————— July 17th 1804.
† To ————— January 20th 1803.
‡ "I am not afraid of responsibility; God knows I am ready to incur any personal risk for the public service." To Colonel Murray, August 29th 1803.

brother, Henry, "who does not sacrifice his private views and convenience when it is necessary."* To an official who sought to absent himself from duty during an emergency for pressing family reasons, he replied that it was essential for a man filling a public situation with great public interests in charge, to lay aside all private considerations. "I am very much distressed on account of the inconveniences which your family suffer in your absence from Madras"; he wrote, "and equally so that it is not in my power to relieve their distress by allowing you to quit your situation. But, under present circumstances, it is not in my power to grant your request to go to Madras consistently with the duty which both you and I owe to the public as public men."† It was this that made him distrust the judgment of every man in a case in which his own wishes were concerned, including, incidentally, his own.

That he should have felt impatient with the delays and vexations of bureaucracy was inevitable. "Every day's experience of the Service," he wrote to General Stuart in May 1803, "shows that the business of every department in the Army has become so complicated from the multiplicity and variety of checks and vouchers, that it is scarcely possible to carry on the duties of any one department exactly in the mode pointed out by the regulations."‡ Yet it was not with administration as such that he quarrelled but only with bad administration. India, which has known so many great British administrators, can seldom if ever have known a better than the young Anglo-Irish colonel who at the age of thirty took over, first the civil, and then the military administration of a conquered and, at that time, anarchical Mysore.

The great end of all his work both as administrator and soldier was to establish civil government in India at all levels which could protect the cultivator, artisan and merchant from lawless rapine and give every man justice and security for peaceful and stable production. The sole *raison d'être* for a British army in Mysore, he told his troops, was to protect the inhabitants, not to oppress them. Never—though at the time, as he saw clearly, all government in India outside Bengal depended on the sword—did he favour military as opposed to civil administration. "On the contrary," he wrote,

* To the Hon Henry Wellesley, March 25th 1801.
† To Major Graham, March 2nd 1804.
‡ To Lieut-General Stuart, May 30th 1803.

"although a soldier myself I am not an advocate for placing extensive civil power in the hands of soldiers." It was one of the points on which he was most insistent when, as the result of his victories, vast new areas were brought through subsidiary treaties under the Company's control, that its troops should take no part in the collection of revenue or the day-by-day enforcement of public order, but should be concentrated in military cantonments for purely military purposes, leaving government and the enforcement of law to the native rulers with the advice of their British civilian Residents.* In a reply to an Address from the native inhabitants of Seringapatam, he defined his duty as being always to conduct the public affairs entrusted to his management according to the orders and intentions of the Government he was serving and under whose protection they themselves were living. It was a position from which, through his long life, he never swerved; he held his sword at the commandment of the magistrate.

His view of India and Indians was a realist one. "Asiatic governments," he wrote, "are arbitrary, the objects of their policy are always shifting. They have no regular established system the effect of which is to protect the weak against the strong; on the contrary, the object of each of them separately, and all of them taken collectively, is to destroy the weak. And if by chance they should, by a sense of common danger, be induced for a season to combine their efforts for their mutual defence, the combination lasts only so long as it is attended with success; the first reverse dissolves it."† "Conciliate them as much as possible," he advised a fellow administrator on his dealings with Mahratta dignitaries and functionaries during the war against Holkar. "To treat them with the greatest kindness and attention is the only way of drawing from them any assistance. At the same time you must not lose sight of the fact that they are Mahrattas; that there is not one of them who can be implicitly trusted; and that, most probably, all are in correspondence with the enemy's camp. You must not allow them to perceive that you distrust them."‡

* At the time of the Afghan War of 1842 he referred to one of its causes as "the breach of a fundamental rule universally established in our own intercourse with the native powers that no troops should be employed in the collection of revenue." *Greville Memoirs*, Pt. II, II, 138-9.
† Memorandum on the Treaty of Bassein. Gurwood, 189.
‡ To Colonel Murray, May 22nd 1804.

Where an Indian showed himself worthy of trust, he gave it unreservedly. One such was the Rajah of Mysore's Dewan or chief minister, Purneah. "Purneah," he wrote, "like other men, has his faults. He is particularly jealous of the intercourse between the servants of his Government and European gentlemen and the favours which the former may receive from the Company. This jealousy arises . . . partly from being insensible of the strong impressions in his own favour which his conduct, his character and his abilities have made upon all the persons who have at present any power in India."* To Purneah himself he wrote before he left the country:

"I part with you with the greatest regret, and I shall ever continue to feel the most lively interest for the honour and prosperity of the Government of the Rajah of Mysore over which you preside. . . . Every principle of gratitude, therefore, for many acts of personal kindness to myself, and a strong sense of the public benefits which have been derived from your administration, render me anxious for its continuance and for its increasing prosperity; and in every situation in which I may be placed you may depend upon it that I shall not fail to bear testimony of my sense of your merits upon every occasion that may offer, and that I shall suffer no opportunity to pass which I may think favourable for rendering you services."†

Such feelings were reciprocated by those he served and defended. "We, the native inhabitants of Seringapatam," ran an Address of July 1804, nine months before Arthur Wellesley left India, "have reposed for five auspicious years under the shadow of your protection. . . . May you long continue personally to dispense to us that full stream of security and happiness which we first received with wonder, . . . and, when greater affairs shall call you from us, may the God of all castes and nations deign to hear with favour our humble and constant prayers for your health, your glory and your happiness!"‡

*   *   *

* To Captain Wilks, September 9th 1804.
† To Purneah, Dewan of the Rajah of Mysore, March 2nd 1805.
‡ Longford, 97.

Besides experience, India had given Wellesley the blessing of a physical stamina to match his moral. The two grew together; he once said that the recipe for health in that country was to live moderately, take exercise and keep the mind employed and in good humour with the world. Asked by his old tutor, who remembered his delicacy in youth, what enabled him to perform such feats of endurance during the long day at Waterloo, he replied, "Ah, that is all India." It was there, under its strong suns, that it became habitual for him to live for months at a time in the saddle and under canvas; to be, like the Mahratta freebooters he hunted, almost a centaur. Many years later, when in the crisis before Ligny he rode over from Quatre Bras to take counsel with Blücher, the Prussians were astonished at the way he used his horse as a travelling field-headquarters, with a change of clothes strapped behind the saddle and a portable desk with pen, ink and paper at his side. It was a way of command he had acquired in his campaigns against Dhoondiah Waugh and Scindia when, often for months at a time, the invariable address at the head of his letters was the single word, "Camp."

At the time he left India he was a spare, well-knit, muscular man of medium height with long face and narrow jawbones, an aquiline patrician nose and firm chin, sunburnt complexion, close-cropped, light brown hair already faintly streaked with grey, and clear blue eyes of a strange intensity. He had a quick abrupt way of speaking with a slight occasional lisp, and, save when roused by iniquity or gross dereliction of duty, a calm, equable temper and good humour. With those he liked, especially with the young officers of his military household, he could be gay and merry, and, when free from the almost continuous pressure of work and responsibility, he much enjoyed amateur theatricals, dinner parties and dances. "There is excellent galloping ground in the neighbourhood of the camp," he wrote to one of his Bombay lady friends after the end of the Mahratta War, "and the floor of my tent is in a fine state for dancing, and the fiddlers of the Dragoons and bagpipes of the 74th and 78th play delightfully." Though five years after his rejection by Kitty Pakenham he could still write to a mutual friend that, notwithstanding his good fortune and the continuous activity of his life, the disappointment he had suffered was as fresh in his mind as if it had happened yesterday,* he was a great favourite of the ladies, to

* "How much more would they bear upon me if I was to return to the inactivity of a

whose charms he was very susceptible, particularly, wrote a fellow officer, married ladies. His liking for one of them, the wife of a captain in the Madras Artillery who, in 1801, became Commissary of Stores at Seringapatam, caused quite a scandal. For "little Mrs Freese," - "the little lady," as his correspondents called her - whose charms are still commemorated in a portrait at Stratfield Saye, he seems to have felt a genuine love, standing godfather to her son, Arthur, and later giving him a home in England when his parents sent him home to be educated. His delight in children was a rather unexpected facet of his character; after the defeat and death of Dhoondiah Waugh, he took under his protection his four-year-old son, Salabut Khan, settling on him a sum for his education before he left India.

He did so on March 10th 1805, sailing from Madras in *HMS Trident*, the flagship of Vice-Admiral Peter Rainier, the retiring Commander-in-Chief of the East India station. The voyage, like that to India eight years before, took six months, including a month's wait at St Helena which he recalled as having the most healthy climate in which he had ever lived, "a charming climate," he called it. Here he stayed in a house which, ten years later, was to become for a short time the home of the fallen titan whom his victory at Waterloo was to consign to that remote island. Then, with the *Trident* escorting a rich convoy of China and India merchantmen, he sailed for "England, home and beauty," through waters made perilous by Napoleon's roaming fleets, who all that summer were desperately attempting to evade her pursuing squadrons as they criss-crossed the Atlantic in a vain endeavour to win for their imperious master that forty-eight hours' command of the Channel on which depended his hopes of subjugating the defiant island shopkeepers and, by doing so, winning the mastery of the world.

---

home life? Upon the whole I think that for many reasons preferable as well to another person as to me, I am better away. . . . Fortune has favoured me upon every occasion and, if I could forget that which has borne so heavily upon me for the last eight years, I should have as little care as you appear to have." To the Hon Mrs Olivia Sparrow, August 1801. Longford, 103-4.

Chapter Four

NIMMUKWALLAH

I am nimmukwallah, as we say in the East, that is, I have eaten
of the King's salt and, therefore, conceive it to be my duty to
serve with unhesitating zeal and cheerfulness where and whenever the King and his Government may think proper to employ
me.

ARTHUR WELLESLEY

ARTHUR WELLESLEY returned to England at a most dramatic
moment. Shortly before he landed at Deal it became known that
Napoleon, whose Grand Army of invasion had been waiting for
nearly two years on the heights above Boulogne, had broken his
"camp beside the ocean" and marched eastwards towards the Danube
to counter the threatening Austrian and Russian coalition which the
British Prime Minister had been secretly building against him. And
on the day after his arrival in London and on the very day before
Nelson left the capital for the last time to take command of the
Combined Fleet off Cadiz, the unknown major-general, who was
destined to succeed him as Britain's chief champion against Napoleon,
had a chance encounter with the great admiral whose pursuit of
Villeneuve that summer had been the decisive factor in defeating the
Emperor's maritime designs. Having an appointment in the old
Colonial Office in Downing Street to discuss Indian affairs with the
new Secretary of State for War, Lord Castlereagh—who had been
detained in a cabinet meeting—he found sitting in the waiting-room,
as he afterwards recalled, "a gentleman who had lost an eye and his
arm. We entered into conversation, neither of us being at all aware
of who the other might be, and I was struck with the clearness and
decision of his language, and guessed from the topics which he
selected that he must be a seaman. He was called in first, and had his
interview; I followed, and after settling our business, was asked
whether I knew who it was that preceded me. I answered no, but that
I was pretty sure from his manner of expressing himself that he was
no common man. 'You are quite right,' was the answer, 'and let me

add that he expressed exactly the same of you. That was Lord Nelson.' " According to another account of this meeting, which Wellington also gave in old age to John Wilson Croker, Nelson had begun by talking about himself in a manner so vain and silly as to surprise and disgust him. But, after ascertaining that the young soldier was the victor of Assaye, he became a different man and talked of the state of the country and of affairs on the Continent with rare sense and knowledge. "In fact," Wellington recalled, "I don't know that I ever had a conversation that interested me more."*

At that time outside the circle of his own and his brother's political associates of Dublin Castle days Arthur Wellesley was almost unknown in England - a sallow stranger from the Orient. He was under no illusion as to how military experience gained there was regarded at home, and, above all, at the Horse Guards; a book on the European war which he had been reading on the voyage, compared an English general returning from India to "an admiral who has been navigating the Lake of Geneva." Yet one Englishman in high place was quick to realise the young "Sepoy general's" quality. Soon after his return, the latter received an invitation from the Prime Minister, William Pitt, whose appointment of his brother as Governor-General of India had given him his first chance in life. Because of the precarious state of his health, Pitt was spending the parliamentary recess at a house in Wimbledon where, at his request, Sir Arthur visited him, subsequently riding with him up to London. "We rode very slowly," he reported to Richard, "and I had a full opportunity of discussing with him and explaining all the points in our late system in India, to which objections had been made, which were likely to make any impressions upon him."

Pitt's mind at that time was full of the Coalition he had created to raise the siege of his country and of the great battles now pending for the liberation of Europe. His hope was to send a British army to North Germany to encourage Prussia to throw in her lot with Austria and Russia against Napoleon, and, despite Sir Arthur's lack of seniority, he seems to have asked his advice and to have led him to think that he might be employed in the forthcoming expedition. He afterwards told his niece, Lady Hester Stanhope, that the young general had given him such a clear idea of affairs in India, speaking of them as though he had been a mere regimental surgeon and had

* Gleig, 46-7; Croker Papers, II, 233-4. See also History Today, February 1958.

had no part in them, that he did not know which to admire most, his modesty or his talents, on which, in fact, as he saw, the fate of India had clearly depended.

So it came about that when, shortly afterwards, Sir Arthur travelled to Cheltenham to take the cure for rheumatism - a legacy of his campaigning days - the thought of seeing active service was much in his mind. It happened that he had another and more romantic reason for visiting the fashionable Gloucestershire spa. Though in his Indian years his fancies had strayed far from the un-attainable Irish girl he had vainly loved when he was a penniless Dublin Castle ADC, Kitty Pakenham's friend, the Honourable Mrs Sparrow, had let him know on his arrival in England that she was still unmarried and not forgetful of him. Nor had he forgotten the promise made in his farewell letter to her eleven years before, that if his circumstances ever changed, as they had now done, his mind would "still remain the same." For though, as an eligible, handsome and well-connected bachelor with an aura of heroic deeds and victories in a distant land, the newly-returned general was quite a matrimonial prize in the London drawing-rooms and though he was far from unresponsive to female charms and flattery,* he was a man to whom fidelity to his word was a matter of honour. On September 24th, in reply to a letter received a week earlier from his old love's match-making friend, rebuking him for not having communicated with Kitty, he had written:

"I see evidently that you imagine that I am unworthy of your friend. . . . All that I can say is that, if I could consider myself unworthy of neglecting such a woman, I would endeavour to think of her no more. I hope that you will find that I am not quite so bad as you imagine I am."

At the end of his letter he added,

"You have not told me what is to become of your friend in the winter. Does she remain in Ireland? Shall I go over to see her? . . .

---

* "Sir Arthur is handsome, very brown, quite bald and has a hooked nose." According to Kitty's niece, Mrs Foster, in a letter written long afterwards, many ladies "flocked admiringly round the gallant and attractive young officer, and rumour even linked his name with one particular one. *Wellington MSS*. cit. Longford, 112n.

I am very apprehensive that, after having come from India for one purpose only, I shall not accomplish it; and I think it not impossible that, if the troops under orders for embarkation should be sent to the Continent, I shall be ordered to go with them and possibly never see you or her again."*

For, if Arthur Wellesley, by his own principle of honour, was a wooer, he was by the same principle even more, a soldier.

When, after a two days' visit to his former chief, the Marquis of Buckingham, at Stowe—where a fellow guest noted that he still retained his old feelings for his friends of Dublin Castle days—he reached Cheltenham, he found that Mrs Sparrow had already communicated the contents of his letter to Kitty in Ireland, with the implication that he had authorised her to renew his proposal of earlier years. Her reply, written on October 8th, while showing where her heart lay, expressed a well-founded doubt as to her old admirer's real wishes.

"I have in vain sought in his letter for one word expressive of a wish that the proposition should be accepted. It is quite impossible for me to express the apprehension that prays upon my heart. . . . I think he wishes to be ordered abroad and perhaps he is right, for I am very much changed. . . . Read his letter again, my dear Olivia; is there one expression implying that 'Yes' would gratify or that 'No' would disappoint?" †

Sir Arthur's reaction upon being shown this missive was not dissimilar to that with which, before Assaye, he had taken the news that the entire Mahratta army lay immediately in front of him. He at once went into the attack, renewing his offer. In those critical October days, while Nelson waited off Cadiz for the sight of Villeneuve's sails and Napoleon's encircling columns moved round the flanks of Mack's army at Ulm, the future Duke of Wellington sealed his marital destinies amid the elegant social activities of Cheltenham Spa. Without having seen his intended bride for eleven years, he sent her a formal proposal and was duly, though hesitantly, accepted.

* To Hon Mrs Sparrow, September 24th 1805. *Wellington's Private Correspondence*. cit. Longford, 112.
† *Wellington's Private Correspondence*, 7-8. cit. Longford, 115; Nugent, 326-7.

By then he was back in London. At the beginning of November news came that Napoleon, acting with his usual speed and resolution, had cut off the Austrian army at Ulm and forced Mack to capitulate with 70,000 of the best troops in Europe. Two days later, on the night of November 5th, still more momentous tidings reached London: of the annihilation of the Franco-Spanish fleet and of Nelson's death in action. From his victory, redeeming her allies' defeat on land, England took renewed courage. On November 9th, after a popular triumph in which his carriage was drawn by cheering crowds through the streets to the Mansion House, the Prime Minister spoke at the Lord Mayor's Banquet. "On that occasion," recalled Sir Arthur who was present, "he returned thanks in one of the best and neatest speeches I have ever heard in my life. It was in a very few words. The Lord Mayor had proposed his health as one who had been the saviour of England and would be the saviour of the rest of Europe. Mr Pitt then got up, disclaimed the compliment as applied to himself, and added, 'England has saved herself by her exertions, and the rest of Europe will be saved by her example.' That was all – he was scarcely up two minutes – yet nothing could be more perfect."[*]

Later that month, he saw something more of the Prime Minister, spending a few days with him at Lord Camden's seat in Kent where the whole Cabinet was assembled and where the only other guests were the Duke of Montrose and himself. "He was extremely lively and in good spirits," he recalled, "and used to ride 18 or 20 miles every day. . . . On coming home from these rides they all used to put on dry clothes and to hold a Cabinet." He also remembered how the Prime Minister and Lord Grenville became engaged in a keen argument over the dinner table about some point in the *Arabian Nights* of which the former was a great admirer.[†] It must have been on this occasion that Pitt confided in the young general, on whose judgment he had come to rely, that he was in secret communication with the rulers of Spain—then at war with Britain but shattered by their

---

* Stanhope, 118

† "At dinner Mr Pitt drank little wine; but it was at that time the fashion to sup, and he then took a great deal of port wine and water." Stanhope, 117-18, 186. "With Mr Pitt himself I had been on the most intimate social relations from the time I landed in England in September till I went from Deal to join the Army of the Weser in the last days of December. . . . I happen to know that Mr Pitt before he died was in communication with the Spanish Government." *Wellington Mss* cit. Longford, 119.

navy's disaster at Trafalgar—and that the day would come when the conqueror and enslaver of Europe would meet for the first time in that country a national resistance which would enable a British army to intervene on the Continent. To bring Berlin to the sticking-point he was at that moment hurrying every available soldier the country possessed to North Germany. With Napoleon committed to a campaign in central Austria, a Prussian army - though still neutral - threatening his northern flank, and Hanover and Holland almost denuded of French first-line troops, the risk seemed worth taking. The stakes were the liberation of Germany and the Dutch coast and the invasion of Napoleon's overgrown Empire at its weakest point by a British-Russian-Prussian-Swedish force. "We shall see Bonaparte's army either cut off or driven back to France, and Holland recovered before Christmas," Pitt declared.

In that expedition Sir Arthur served, taking command of a brigade from Ireland at Deal where three months before he had landed from India. Asked on a Saturday when he would be ready to start, he had replied, "On Monday," evoking from a member of the Government with whom he had been spending the weekend the comment, "Game, indeed!" "I understood as much of military matters then," he recalled in the days of his fame, "as I have ever done since or do now," and, after his Indian experiences, he found the military system prevailing in England "very faulty." Orders were sent to him from four or five different departments; one general officer who desired him to wait upon him to receive some instructions was actually his junior, which the victor of Assaye observed with his customary tact and good humour: "The order shall be attended to, but I rather believe you will find that I am your senior officer instead of your being mine."*

When the expedition under the command of Lord Cathcart sailed for the mouth of the Weser, it was driven back three times by storms, losing several hundred men on the Goodwin Sands and others on the Heligoland shoals, where eight transports and nearly 2000 troops were lost. Back on the Continent at almost the place from which he had been driven as a young lieutenant-colonel eleven years before, Major-General Wellesley spent that Christmas frostbound among the dismal North German flats, surrounded by French spies and staring, apathetic Teutons and commanding a force no larger than that

* Stanhope, 130-1; Auckland, IV, 256; Dropmore, VIII, 433.

with which he had covered the disastrous retreat across the same ice and mud flats in 1795 before he had governed Mysore and routed the Mahrattas.*

Before that bleak December ended news reached England which broke Pitt's heart. A Russian-Austrian army, instead of awaiting the reinforcements which would have given it overwhelming superiority, had left an impregnable position to attack Napoleon at Austerlitz and suffered disaster. When, returning from Bath, where he had been vainly seeking a cure for the disease that was killing him, the creator of the Third Coalition reached home, he bade his niece roll up the map of Europe on the wall, saying it would not be needed for another ten years. A visitor to Blenheim that Christmas, surrounded by its magnificent historical monuments, pictures and tapestries, found himself longing for a successor to the great Duke of Marlborough, with all his energies and successes, and for the days when England was able to maintain the independence and balance of the Continent.

Four days later, in an interview given to that successor's brother, Lord Wellesley, who had just returned from India after his victorious, but now bitterly attacked Governor-Generalship, the dying Prime Minister spoke with feeling and gratitude of the brilliant young soldier whom he had sent to Germany to serve with the expedition on which he had built such high, but now shattered, hopes. "I have never met a military officer," he said, "with whom it is so satisfactory to converse. He never makes a difficulty or hides his ignorance in vague generalities. If I put a question to him he answered it distinctly; if I wanted an explanation he gave it clearly; if I desired an opinion I got from him one supported by reasons which were always sound. He states every difficulty before he undertakes any service, but never after he has undertaken it. He is a very remarkable man." Just over a week later Pitt was dead.

It may have been the Prime Minister's faith in this, to a politician, phenomenon among military men, which caused the Horse Guards that winter to authorise Sir Arthur's long-delayed promotion to the Staff. To the increase in income so obtained was added in January his appointment to the colonelcy of his old regiment, the 33rd, vacant through the unexpected death of Lord Cornwallis, his

* Stanhope, 130; *Paget Papers*, II, 254; Fortescue, V, 290-4; *Paget Brothers*, 54; Guedalla, 125; *Wellesley Papers*, I, 197.

93

brother's successor in India. "The regiment they have given me and the Staff," he told a friend, "have made me rich." Thus it came about that when, recalled to prevent it from being captured by the French, the expeditionary force ignominiously returned to England at the beginning of February, he found himself in a position to stand for Parliament and provide an establishment in the fashionable west end of London* for the lady who, eleven years before, at her family's insistence, had rejected him on account of his poverty but whom he was now quixotically resolved to make his bride.

It was normal at that time for army officers with means, when not employed on active employment abroad, to combine their military duties with a seat in Parliament. One of Sir Arthur's motives for wishing to leave India had been to defend his brother's administration from the unjust attacks being made on it by his political enemies. With Pitt dead and his friends out of office, there was no hope of political influence offsetting his lack of Army seniority and the prejudice felt by the Horse Guards against him. Any prospect of that Army returning to a conquered continent and of his receiving a command in it commensurate with his eastern achievements and experience seemed negligible. The new Government—a Coalition of the dead Prime Minister's former opponents and critics with the pacific Charles James Fox as Foreign Secretary and its leading member—was dedicated to seeking a stalemate peace. "A revolution (commonly called a change)," Wellesley wrote after his return from Germany to an England which was no longer that of Pitt and Nelson, "has taken place in the government of this country. We are not actually in opposition, but we have no power" - for it was the Whigs and those who sought an accommodation with Napoleon who were in control. "You can have no idea of the disgust created by the harshness of their measures, by the avidity with which they have sought for office and by the indecency with which they have dismissed every man supposed to have been connected with Pitt".†

---

* "Expenses here are very heavy and fortunes very large," he wrote to John Malcolm in India. "Notwithstanding all the taxes, and the rise in price of every article in life, there is more luxury than ever, more appearance of riches in the country, and more persons with large fortunes of moderate extent than there were formerly. You could not exist in the way you would like under a much larger fortune than you possess." To Colonel John Malcolm, February 3rd 1807.

† To Lieut-Colonel John Malcolm, February 25th 1806.

None the less, the returning Major-General had friends and influence enough to secure a seat in Parliament. With the advice of Lord Castlereagh—with whom he had sat on the benches of the Irish Parliament a dozen years before—and through his friendship with his old chief, the Marquis of Buckingham, whose brother, Lord Grenville, was now Prime Minister, he was returned on April 1st for the pocket borough of Rye, which he later exchanged for that of Mitchell in Cornwall. It offered him, at a time when his military prospects seemed hopeless, a tenuous link with the sources of power which might stand him in stead if times were ever to change.*

Immediately after his election he used what remained of a brief spell of leave to travel to Dublin and marry his old flame. It was the first time he had seen her since he parted from her eleven years before. He found her at thirty-four sadly changed, with the prettiness and gaiety of youth gone for ever; a few years earlier—as a result of some emotional crisis—she had suffered from a wasting and "melancholy paleness" or what was then called a "decline" and would today be diagnosed as a nervous breakdown. He was shocked by her appearance and was certainly not in love, but felt bound in honour to proceed. She took his proferred hand with gratitude, but hesitation —for she was in her every instinct a lady—and it was ill for both of them that she did.† For though she adored him with a dumb, passionate adoration, she never understood him, and, Irish, unmethodical and already strongly opinionated and set in her ways, she unwittingly made his newly purchased home in Harley Street disorderly and extravagant, so that he, who loved order and method so much, found little comfort either in it or her. Not that he was cold where women were concerned: but, as he once said, he liked

* "Although I had long been in habits of friendship with the public men of the day and had some professional claims to public notice when I returned to England, I believe I should have been but little known, and should not be what I am if I had not gone into Parliament." To Colonel Sir John Malcolm, June 26th 1813. Brett-James, 267.

† "I should be the most undeserving of beings," she had written to him, "were I capable of feelings less than gratitude in return for the steadiness of your attachment. I do not think it fair to engage you before you are quite positively certain that I am indeed the very woman you would choose for a companion, a *friend* for life." Longford, 117-18. Her husband's view of the matter was given many years later to his friend and confidante, Mrs Arbuthnot. "I married her because they asked me to do it and I did not know myself. I thought I should never care for anybody again, and that I should be with the army, and, in short, I was a fool." Arbuthnot, I, 169.

them "to anticipate one's meaning - that is what a clever woman does - she sees what you mean."

Within a week of his marriage, his leave over, Arthur Wellesley returned to his military duties in England, leaving his wife to follow. They were of a very minor kind. On his return from Germany he had been offered a brigade at Hastings on what had been, before the tide of war receded, the invasion coast, but was now only a backwater. He had not stood on dignity but accepted it, explaining to a friend, "I am nimmukwallah, as we say in the East, that is, I have eaten of the King's salt and, therefore, conceive it to be my duty to serve with unhesitating zeal and cheerfulness where and whenever the King and his Government may think proper to employ me."

For him, as for his country, the interval between the collapse of the Third Coalition in the winter of 1805-6 and the start of the Peninsular War in the summer of 1808 was a time of waiting and frustration. For Britain it saw the deaths, within less than a year, of Nelson, Pitt and Fox; the failure of the latter's ill-starred attempt to make peace with Napoleon on any terms compatible with national honour or even survival, and the successive defeat at the hands of her terrifying adversary of every Continental ally—Austria and Russia at Ulm and Austerlitz, Prussia in the autumn of 1806 at Jena and Auerstadt, Russia again - after a spell of fierce resistance during the Polish winter of 1806-7 - at Friedland in the summer of 1807. "Another year," wrote Wordsworth,

> *" another deadly blow!*
> *Another mighty Empire overthrown!*
> *And we are left, or shall be left, alone,*
> *The last that dare to struggle with the foe!"*

In a war in which the rulers of the sea put an unbreakable ring of salt-water round an invincible land-conqueror and the latter denied the former access to every port and province in his vast territorial dominion, there seemed no place for the man who had commanded more troops in the field and had had more experience of actual fighting and of victory than any other British general then in England. "I am here now," he wrote from Hastings in the summer of

1806 to his Indian friend, Malcolm, "in command of a force stationed in this part of the coast, the old landing-place of William the Conqueror. You will have seen that I am in Parliament, and a most difficult and unpleasant game I have had to play in the present extraordinary state of the parties." Forced to divide his time between Sussex and Westminster, as he sought to defend his brother against Whig threats of impeachment, any active return to the profession of arms to which he was dedicated seemed increasingly remote. For, as he afterwards recalled of this frustrating period in his career, his political activities only added to the prejudice felt against him by his hidebound superiors at the Horse Guards. "They thought very little of anyone who had served in India; an Indian victory was not only no ground of confidence, but it was actually a cause of suspicion. Then because I was in Parliament and connected with people in office, I was a politician, and a politician can never be a soldier. Moreover, they looked upon me with a kind of jealousy, because I was a lord's son, 'a sprig of nobility,' who came into the army more for ornament than use."* And though, because of his membership of the House and his aristocratic connections, he was occasionally consulted by Ministers about their hare-brained projects, as they used the mastery of the oceans won by Nelson and the great admirals to fritter away the country's inadequate military resources in ill-co-ordinated expeditions to every part of the world—one, which was proposed, was a simultaneous attack on New Mexico from the Atlantic and Pacific—their nebulous suggestions of future employment in command of one or other of these never came to anything. Instead, a back-bench Member of Parliament with a Staff commission and an Indian past, he was left high and dry on his station on the erstwhile invasion coast. "Another of my regiments has received orders to march to Deal, where I suppose it is to embark for the Continent," he wrote in the autumn of Jena, when there seemed a momentary chance - quickly dashed by Prussia's collapse - of British intervention in Europe. "If troops are to be sent into Germany, of course, all other views must for the present be abandoned; and I hope that, as four out of five regiments have now been taken from my command to be sent on service, I shall now be sent; I don't care in what situation. I am only afraid that Lord Grenville does not understand that I don't want a chief command if it cannot be given

* *Croker Papers*, I, 342.

to me, and that I should be very sorry to stay at home when others go abroad only because I cannot command in chief."*

In the spring of 1807, there came a welcome change when the Ministry of all the Talents, as it was ironically called, resigned and was succeeded by a Tory Administration - consisting, as someone put it, of "all Mr Pitt's friends without Pitt." Sir Arthur's chief political well-wisher and patron, Lord Castlereagh, once more became Secretary of State for War, while he himself was offered the Irish Secretaryship under the Duke of Richmond as Lord Lieutenant. He accepted on condition that he sould be free to relinquish the office whenever a chance of active military employment presented itself. It brought him a salary of more than £6500 p.a., the Chief Secretary's Lodge in the Dublin Castle world he knew so well, and enough administrative work to satisfy even his tireless capacity for mastering detail as he wrestled with the eternal Irish problems of patronage, religious animosity and injustice, and agrarian poverty and discontent. In the background were the threats of a Catholic rising - it was only nine years since the Rebellion of 1798 - and the possibility of a French landing. As a soldier and a cadet of the Protestant ascendancy, he was well aware how dangerous a combination of these would be. "I lay it down as decided," he wrote, "that Ireland, in a view to military operations, must be considered as an enemy's country."

While, with his habitual force and clarity, he tried to bring system and order to the affairs of a land where disorder was endemic, his attempts to introduce them into his Irish wife's household management failed. All he got for his pains were tears and resentment. For, with her happy-go-lucky Irish disregard for money, Kitty could only see, in his passion for perfection in even the smallest details, a kind of tyranny. Marriage to a man with a genius for mental arithmetic proved as painful to her as divorce from active military command was for him. Early in February, 1807, in her thirty-fifth year, she had given birth to a son; that May, after the move to Dublin, she was pregnant again. The strain on her frail system, undermined as it was by her earlier breakdown, resulted in nervous exhaustion and depression which increased her tendency to worry and hysterical exaggeration - failings with which her husband, with his soldier's distrust of uncontrolled emotion, was

* To the Marquess Wellesley, October 26th 1806; Dropmore, VIII, 353.

constitutionally incapable of sympathising. When she impulsively dismissed a gardener because her maid had drowned herself out of unrequited love, he urged - or, as she chose to believe, insisted - that the man should be taken back, expressing a caustic hope in a letter to her that "the remainder of the maids of the Park will put up with the misfortunes of this world and not destroy themselves." The degree of growing estrangement, and of the frustration which both were experiencing in their ill-matched marriage, is shown by another letter written to her from London that July:

"My dearest Kitty . . . I am much concerned that you should have thought of concealing from me any want of money which you might have experienced. I don't understand how this want occurred or why it was concealed, and the less there is said or written upon the subject the better. For I acknowledge that the conclusion I draw from your conduct upon the occasion is that you must be mad, or you must consider me to be a brute and most particularly fond and avaricious of money. Once for all, you require no permission to talk to me upon any subject you please; all that I request is that a piece of work may not be made about trifles . . . and that you may not go into tears because I don't think them deserving of an uncommon degree of attention."*

Three days later he wrote again: "It is to be hoped that at some time or other I shall be better understood."

Many years later, speaking in confidence to his friend, Mrs Arbuthnot, Wellington poured out his heart about his marriage. He complained bitterly, she wrote in her diary, of "the distress it was to be united to a person with whom he could not possibly live on any terms of confidential intercourse. . . . He had repeatedly tried to live in a friendly manner with her, had determined that he would communicate all his projects to her and endeavoured to make his pursuits and interests the same as hers; but he assured me that it was impossible, that she did not understand him, that she could not enter with him into the consideration of all the important concerns which are continually occupying his mind, and that he found he might as well talk to a child. He added, too, that she had so high an opinion of herself and thinks herself so excessively clever

* Longford, 127.

99

that she never stirs even to accommodate herself to him and never for an instant supposes that, when their opinions differ, she may be in the wrong. He said that her mind was trivial and contracted and, in short, that they never could assimilate in anything. He . . . assured me that he had tried repeatedly to live with her on affectionate terms, for that he had done it for his own sake, that his tastes were domestic, that nothing could make him so happy as to have a home where he could find comfort."*

*　　　*　　　*

When Arthur Wellesley penned these harsh letters to the woman to whom eighteen months before he had so recklessly and blindly given his hand, he was on the point of setting sail on a secret expedition to the Continent. Ever since the early summer the Government of which he was a member had been preparing to send a force of British and Hanoverian troops to the Swedish island of Rügen with the idea of a landing on the Baltic coast to relieve pressure on the Russian army in Poland. At the beginning of June he had written from Dublin Castle to the Secretary of State for War, reminding him of his promise that, if a chance of military employment arose, he should be allowed to resign the Irish Secretaryship. " It may happen," he went on, " that you have it not in your power to employ me as I wish, and it might have happened that I should not have been so employed if I had not been appointed to the office which I fill in this country. But this will not be believed, and it will be understood and said that I had avoided, or had not sought for, an opportunity of serving abroad in order to hold a large civil office. As I am determined not to give up the military profession, and as I know I can be of no service in it unless I have the confidence and esteem of the officers and soldiers of the army, I must shape my course in such a manner as to avoid this imputation." Though refusing his resignation, his colleagues had therefore agreed that, until the expedition sailed, he should be allowed to carry out his duties from London so as not to miss the chance of going with it if he was offered a command.

The projected landing of a British-Swedish force on the flank of the French never took place. For, even before the first British troops under Lieutenant-General Lord Cathcart reached Rügen, the Rus-

* Arbuthnot, I, 168. See also *Gascoygne Heiress*, 223-4; Nugent, 326.

sians suffered a crushing defeat at Friedland on June 14th. Three days later the two emperors, Napoleon and Alexander, met on a raft in the Niemen and agreed to make peace. By the Treaty of Tilsit of July 7th 1807, the Czar, abandoning Britain and Sweden, in return for a promise of Swedish Finland and part of Prussian Poland, recognised Napoleon's unchallenged paramountcy over western and central Europe. France and Russia were to rule the world between them, while Denmark, Austria and Portugal were to be compelled to join in a universal embargo on British trade. And, under a secret clause, the Danish fleet was to be seized by a French army from Hamburg and used as a nucleus of a northern naval confederation in the Baltic to wrest command of the sea from England.

Yet though, like their predecessors, the new Ministers had been too late to save the Russians, they were not too late to save themselves. They were the disciples of Pitt, and, mediocrities and Party hacks though they seemed, they represented all who held that victory was the only salvation for the country. Receiving intelligence that the Danish Fleet was ready for sea and anticipating a French invasion of Holstein, they resolved to send an expedition to occupy the island of Zealand and snatch the coveted ships from the enemy's grasp. They ordered Admiral Lord Gambier to the Sound with seventeen sail-of-the-line, directed transports and troops to Yarmouth and sent instructions to Cathcart to withdraw his army from its exposed position at Rügen and join the fleet off Copenhagen. Demanding from the Crown Prince of Denmark the immediate surrender of his fleet in return for a British alliance and a yearly rent, they scraped together every soldier they could find for the Sound.

During the last week in July, when he was writing in such exasperated terms to his wife in Ireland, Arthur Wellesley received the command he so coveted, sailing from Sheerness on the 31st. It was only of a brigade, and the Horse Guards who, unlike his ministerial colleagues, still distrusted him, appointed another general to act as what he called his "dry nurse."* Yet, though he allowed the latter—Brigadier William Stewart, an excellent officer who had had the misfortune to be taken a prisoner in the ill-fated expedition to Egypt of the previous year—to take charge of the preliminary opera-

---

* "When the Horse Guards are obliged to employ one of those fellows like me in whom they have no confidence, they give him what they call a second-in-command – one in whom they have confidence – a kind of dry nurse." *Croker Papers*, I, 343.

tions when he landed with the advanced-guard in Zealand on August 16th, two weeks later, when his brigade went into action to prevent a relieving force from raising the siege of Copenhagen, he took over from his lieutenant with a brisk, "Come, come, 'tis my turn now." By his brilliant tactical handling of his troops, he showed himself the same expert professional commander that he had been in India.* Even though those he was pitted against were a very different proposition to the dreaded French, it was no longer possible to deny the competence of this soldier-politician and sprig of aristocracy on the battlefield.

As a reward for his handling of the action at Kiöge—the only engagement of the brief campaign and one in which he took 1500 prisoners—he was appointed one of the three parliamentary commissioners to negotiate terms with the Danes when Copenhagen surrendered on September 5th. On his return to England at the end of the month he received, with his fellow commanders, the thanks of Parliament when it reassembled in the New Year. In the meantime, at the wish of his ministerial colleagues and the Lord Lieutenant, he resumed his duties as Irish Secretary. For he was too efficient a man at whatever he did for anyone with whom he worked to wish to part with him.

During that winter while he pursued his administrative and legislative tasks at Dublin and Westminster, he was increasingly consulted by Lord Castlereagh, the Secretary of State for War, on the strategic problems facing the country. While Napoleon, infuriated by his failure to secure the Danish fleet, used his military power to force every country on the Continent to close its ports to British trade, the parliamentary statesmen of Europe's defiant off-shore island—or, as Coleridge put it, "the inisled Ararat on which rested the ark of the hope of Europe and of civilisation"—used their command of the seas to spread their commercial and colonial tentacles throughout the world. But, while they gathered in the fruits of Trafalgar, collecting naval bases in islands and outer Continents where Napoleon's writ could not run and opening up new markets to take the place of those closed to them in Europe, they also tended,

---

* "I immediately made my own dispositions, assigned him the command of one of the wings, gave him his orders, attacked the enemy and beat them. Stewart, like a man of sense, saw in a moment that I understood my business and subsided with . . . good humour in his proper place." *Croker Papers*, I, 342-3.

like their predecessors, to dissipate the country's military resources. Like them, they tried with insufficient forethought and preparation to do too much in too many places. Having sent a fleet through the Dardanelles to coerce Turkey, their predecessors, the Grenville Administration, had had to make a humiliating withdrawal while simultaneously losing an army in Egypt. The brilliant but impulsive Tory Foreign Secretary, Canning, now gambled heavily on wresting the rich South American colonies of Spain from that half-hearted ally of Napoleonic France and, by encouraging a rising of the colonists against their mother country, to secure their trade for Britain. But in the summer which saw the capture of Copenhagen and the Danish fleet, he caught a tartar in Buenos Ayres which, with Montevideo, had been taken by a British force and then recaptured. Rashly committing his force to street-fighting, an incompetent British commander, Lieutenant-General Whitelocke, lost his nerve and capitulated at the very moment when victory seemed within his grasp.

It was to retrieve this disaster and restore British prestige in South America that, in the early summer of 1808, Sir Arthur Wellesley was appointed to command a force of 9000 men assembled at Cork for the purpose of landing in Venezuela to support and foment a rising there. It was not a mission which much appealed to him for, as he remarked, he had a horror of revolutionising a country for a political object.* But he had assured his colleagues after his return from Copenhagen that he would be ready, if called upon, to set out to any part of the world at a moment's notice. That April, just before his thirty-ninth birthday, he had been promoted to the rank of Lieutenant-General - the youngest in the Army List - and, now, four years after he had resigned his command in Mysore, the auspices were beginning to look favourable for his resumption of an active military career.

Yet it was not in the jungles and swamps of central America that Sir Arthur Wellesley was to resume the full-time profession of arms, but in a field chosen for him by the all-powerful European conqueror whose strength he was little by little to erode and whose reputation for invincibility he was ultimately to destroy. In September 1807, a few days after the news of the British seizure of the

---

* "I always said if they rise of themselves, 'Well and good,' but do not stir them up; it is a fearful responsibility." Stanhope, 69.

Danish fleet reached him, Napoleon had given one of his famous displays of temper at a diplomatic reception. "If Portugal does not do as I wish," he shouted at the Portuguese Minister, "the House of Braganza will not be reigning in Europe in two months! I will no longer tolerate an English ambassador in Europe. . . . The English declare they will no longer respect neutrals on the sea; I will no longer recognise them on land!" For with eastern Europe and Russia in his pocket, he felt free to concentrate his entire force against the last corner of the Continent where English merchants had a foothold. The Iberian Peninsula, trackless and remote though it might be, was at his mercy.

Immediately afterwards the French and Spanish ambassadors had quitted Lisbon. Early in October it became known that a French army under General Junot, assembled at Bayonne, was about to cross the Bidassoa and march on Lisbon. On November 8th, terrified by the speed of Junot's advance and shaken by the news of the British defeat and humiliating capitulation at Buenos Ayres, the Portuguese Regent announced that he must "adhere to the cause of the Continent." But he was too late to save his throne. Five days later an intimation appeared in the Paris *Moniteur* that the House of Braganza had ceased to reign. Having signed a secret Convention with Spain by which Portugal was to be partitioned between the two countries, Napoleon sent orders to Junot to press over the mountains at once with every man who could make the pace and so make sure of capturing the Portuguese fleet in the Tagus before it could be removed by the English.

On the last day of November, having marched three hundred miles in a fortnight over rain-deluged mountains, Junot's army straggled into Lisbon with less than 2000 of its original 30,000 men. The Portuguese made no resistance. But the Court and Fleet had gone. On the previous day, taking his treasure and family with him, Prince John had embarked in his flagship and, escorted by British warships, sailed for Rio de Janeiro and Brazil.

Having been thwarted by the British in his attempt to secure, first the Danish, then the Portuguese fleet, Napoleon now resorted to still more drastic measures to break the stranglehold of their naval blockade and destroy the stubborn will of the one nation resisting his bid for universal hegemony. In December 1807, while on a state progress through his Italian dominions, he had issued from Milan a series of Decrees outlawing all neutral vessels which submitted to British search or touched at British ports. His victories in northern Europe that summer had released his immense military resources for operations exclusively against England. Once more, as in the days before Nelson at the Nile and Trafalgar had barred his march to world dominion, he felt free to revert to his dream of a drive across the Mediterranean to the Orient—the source, as he always believed, of Britain's wealth and strength and the goal of his early ambitions. His design was to break the ring of British sea-power by a triple military drive across and round both ends of the Mediterranean. A joint Franco-Russian-Austrian host was to strike at the crumbling Empire of the Turks and the distant approaches to India. In the central Mediterranean Napoleon's brother, Joseph Bonaparte, whom two years earlier he had enthroned at Naples, was to expel the British from Sicily which they had occupied with their troops after Trafalgar. And in the west, a third and greater French army was to march through Spain, and drive them from Gibraltar.

With this intent, in the opening weeks of 1808, Napoleon prepared to seize control of Spain. By a secret Convention signed at Fontaine-bleau in the previous autumn, he had obtained from the Spanish King and his corrupt minister, Godoy, permission for his troops to occupy the principal towns of Biscaya and Navarre under pretence of supporting Junot in Portugal. On February 16th a French Brigade at Pamplona rushed the gates of the citadel after challenging the garrison to a snowball match, seized the magazine and barred out its allies. Similar acts of treachery occurred at San Sebastian, Figueras and Barcelona. Then, having secured the entrances to the Peninsula, Napoleon poured 100,000 troops through the passes and proceeded to take Spain over, lock, stock and barrel.

For a few weeks it looked as if the Spanish adventure had succeeded. Murat, advancing from Burgos, entered Madrid, acclaimed by the populace as a liberator; at Aranjuez the mob rose, prevented the flight of Godoy and the Royal family to South America and forced the King to abdicate in favour of his son, Ferdinand. The latter was then induced by specious promises to cross the French frontier and meet Napoleon at Bayonne. Here he was made prisoner, asked to resign the throne and, when he refused, confronted by his own father and mother who denounced him as a bastard. By May 6th his powers of resistance, never strong, were exhausted and, in return for a French pension, he joined with his father in surrendering his rights to Napoleon. A stroke of the pen, supported by a little force and treachery, had secured France the Iberian Peninsula and - in theory - the Spanish empire of South and Central America. The Pyrenees had been eliminated.

Up to this point everything had gone as Napoleon had planned. The rulers of Spain had been tricked out of their rights like those of a dozen outworn States before them. But the Spanish people now took a hand in the game. They were proud, they were ignorant and they hated and despised all foreigners. Though unanimous in their loathing of Godoy, they had a deep-rooted affection for the Throne which now took the form of a wave of irrational enthusiasm for Ferdinand. When they discovered he had been kidnapped, they became passionately angry. Instead of acquiescing in French rule they rose against it - spontaneously and without warning.

For by deciding to take over what he supposed to be a moribund Spain and place his brother Joseph on its throne in order to enforce his embargo on British trade, Napoleon was fulfilling a prophecy which William Pitt had made before his death in his last conversation with Arthur Wellesley. "Spain," he had predicted, "is the first continental nation which will involve him in a war of partisans. Her nobles are debased and her Government wretched, but the people still retain their sense of honour and their sobriety. Bonaparte will endeavour to tread out these feelings because they are incompatible with his designs, and I look to that attempt for kindling the sort of war which will not cease till he is destroyed." As the French armies marched across the peninsula every mountain valley sprang to arms behind them. For the first time since the outbreak of the Revolution, France was faced by a national movement as popular as her own.

During the last week of May 1808 General Sir Hew Dalrymple, Governor of Gibraltar, received a request from the revolutionary Junta at Seville for money and arms. In their excitement and anger the Spanish people appeared to have forgotten they were at war with the island State which had stopped their trade, sunk their treasure ships, and blockaded their ports; they only thought of England now as a common enemy of the hated oppressor. Moved by the same impulse as their brethren in Seville, the country gentry and clergy of the Asturian valleys, gathered in defiant conclave at Oviedo, decided on May 30th to appeal to London. That night, armed with formal powers by the provincial Council, the historian Toreno and five other emissaries set out and, after an adventurous voyage, arrived at Falmouth on June 6th. The opportunity for which Pitt had sought, and of which his successors had grown to despair, had come at last.

The British people received the Asturian delegates with enthusiasm. They, too, forgot the long war with Spain. They remembered only that Spanish patriots had risen against the French and defied Napoleon. The Government, whose mainspring was Canning, acted quickly. Reluctance to strike was never one of the Foreign Secretary's faults. By the beginning of July peace between the two countries had been proclaimed and preliminaries entered into for a formal alliance.

Castlereagh at the War Office was equally prompt. Waiting at Cork under his favourite soldier, Sir Arthur Wellesley, were 9000 troops destined for Venezuela. Another 5000 under Major-General Spencer were in transports at Gibraltar, 3000 more under Major-General Beresford in Madeira, and 10,000 under Lieutenant-General Sir John Moore in the Baltic, sent there on a hopeless mission to defend Sweden from a combined Franco-Russian invasion. All were put under immediate orders for the Peninsula where, fanned by the arrogance, contempt for religious and national feelings and shameless plundering of the occupying French troops, the flames of popular insurrection had spread to Portugal. At Oporto the Bishop led the peasantry in a successful rising against the pro-French Governor. Junot's hold on his ravished principality shrank in a few days to little more than the vicinity of the capital and principal fortresses.

On June 30th 1808, adding to his command the 5000 men in transports off southern Spain under Major-General Brent Spencer, the Cabinet decided to employ Sir Arthur Wellesley and his 9000 troops at Cork as the advance-guard of a full-scale Portuguese diversion to help the Spanish patriots. A few days before leaving London to join them he entertained the friend who was to take over the work of his Irish department, John Wilson Croker. After dinner the two men sat together over their wine, looking out of the tall windows on Harley Street. As Sir Arthur was silent, Croker asked him what he was thinking about. "Why, to say the truth," Wellesley replied, "I am thinking of the French that I am going to fight. I have not seen them since the campaign in Flanders when they were capital soldiers, and a dozen years of victory under Bonaparte must have made them better still. They have besides, it seems, a new system of strategy which has outmanoeuvred and overwhelmed all the armies of Europe. It's enough to make one thoughtful; but no matter, my die is cast; they may overwhelm me, but I don't think they will outmanoeuvre me. First, because I am not afraid of them, as everybody else seems to be; secondly, because, if what I hear of their system of manoeuvres be true, I think it a false one as against steady troops. I suspect that all the Continental armies were more than half beaten before the battle was begun. I, at least, will not be frightened beforehand."*

*   *   *

Wellesley's confidence in the men he commanded was well placed. Since its tragic experiences in Flanders and the sugar islands at the outset of the Revolutionary War fifteen years before, the British Army had greatly changed. It was still marred by grave faults; too many of its higher officers were martinets with no other qualification for command but age and seniority; too many of its men recruited from the alehouse and the prison. There was far too much drinking, too many brutal and degrading punishments, too much time spent in covering dirty breeches with pipeclay and starching dirty hair with powder, too much mechanical, unthinking, unrealistic drill. But the men, though drawn from the poorest and worst-educated classes in the community, were fine fighting material; tenacious, tough, and full of spunk, they were as inherently hard to beat as they were to rule. "They are a strange set," wrote one who served in their ranks, "and so determined and unconquerable that they will have their way if they can. It requires someone who has authority in his face as well as at his back to make them respect and obey him.†

The unit and living organism of the Army was the Regiment; its Colours the ark of the soldier's covenant. Its legends and rivalries – the sagas of rude, unlettered men - were sometimes, in camp and barracks, a source of administrative embarrassment; on the battle-

* *CrokerPapers*, I, 12-13. For Wellington's later observations on this conversation, see Stanhope, 227.
† Harris, 101-2.

field they became a spur to emulous courage and endurance. It was through such dedicated regimental commanders as Wellesley, who as a young colonel, facing the challenge of the Revolutionary armies, had devoted himself to making his officers and men as keen and efficient in their calling as himself, that the Army had been learning to adapt itself to new methods of tactics and fighting. It had been driven from the Continent by a revolutionary technique of war, and the outdated mechanical models of drill and discipline on which it had formed itself had failed in action. Rather than accept permanent exclusion from Europe it was having to put itself to school.

Through sheer necessity the British Army had begun to climb out of the pit of defeat and neglect into which it had fallen after the great days of Blenheim, Malplaquet and Minden. The officer who bought his promotion like his uniform and commuted by two hours' daily bullying on the parade ground for a life of drinking bumpers on - and under - the Messroom table, was gradually being replaced by the ardent lad who had grown up to hate Bonaparte and viewed his profession as an opportunity for glory. The crimping-house with its sordid tale of mercenary cruelty had yielded to the flashing devil-may-care recruiting-sergeant, parading in his ribbons and finery before the gaping militiamen and extolling the glories of his corps. By the time Trafalgar had cleared the seas for the free movement of British land-forces, a new spirit of martial pride was running again through the half-brutalised ranks. The scarlet and gold regiments of England not only looked smart: they felt smart. "If our commanders are well-chosen and there are some very good ones," wrote Lord Paget, who was himself one of them, "the British Army is in a state that will astonish friend and foe."

Unfortunately, as well as good commanders, it still possessed, in its higher ranks, some remarkably bad ones. And, as it was among the younger rather than the older officers that the new ferment of professional efficiency was working, and as, in promotion to higher command, seniority was what counted with the Horse Guards, the fighting virtues of the British soldier were not always utilised as they deserved to be. The royal Commander-in-Chief, the Duke of York, who presided over that institution and who, because of his genuine care for the welfare of the rank and file, was known as "the soldier's friend,"—and to whom many of the reforms in the Army's training and administration were due,—was, like his brother the King, a great stickler for promotion by seniority rather than by battle experience and intelligence. It had been largely through him that Baird had taken Wellesley's place in command of the Red Sea expedition of 1801, and it was solely owing to the politician Castlereagh that the youngest Lieutenant-General in the Army List had been chosen in his fortieth year to strike the first blow in Portugal.

Chapter Five

THE CHILD OF FORTUNE

" What are these fleets that cross the sea
From British ports and bays
To coasts that glister southwardly
Behind the dog-day haze?

They are the shipped battalions sent
To bar the bold Belligerent
Who stalks the Dancers' Land.
Within these hulls, like sheep a-pen,
Are packed in thousands fighting-men
And colonels in command."

          HARDY, *The Dynasts.*

" Sir Arthur and Sir Harry, Sir Harry and Sir Hew,
Doodle, doodle, doodle, cock a doodle do.
Sir Arthur was a gallant knight, but for the other two,
Doodle, doodle, doodle, cock a doodle do."

          OLD SONG

IT was on July 12th 1808, a day ahead of his command, that Arthur Wellesley sailed from Cork in the *Donegal*, transferring next day to a fast frigate in order to take preliminary counsel with the Junta of Galicia. His orders were to make the utmost Portuguese diversion to assist Spain and, if possible, to expel Junot from Lisbon. True to his unfailing principle of doing everything possible to achieve success, he spent the voyage learning Spanish from a prayer-book given him by his lifelong friends, the Ladies of Llangollen – Lady Eleanor Butler and Sarah Ponsonby – on whom he was in the habit of calling on his journeys from London to Dublin. But when on July 20th he landed at Corunna he found that more than a know-ledge of the language was needed to discover what was happening in Spain. He was welcomed with many stately, old-world ceremonies and by applauding mobs. But no one seemed to have any idea of what was going on in the rest of the Peninsula or even in Galicia itself. All he could gather for certain was that the northern Spanish armies had been defeated a week before by Marshal Bessières at Medina del Rioseco, two hundred miles to the south-east. Even this information was hard to come by: at first the Spaniards said that their general, Blake, had gained a great victory but had failed to follow it up, then that he had gained a victory but had thought it better to withdraw, and finally that he had suffered a slight check. "It is impossible," wrote Wellesley, "to learn the truth."

Though things were plainly not going well for the Spaniards, their chief anxiety seemed to be to keep their allies' troops away from their soil. They particularly wanted Wellesley to employ his army in Portugal, not Spain. Money and arms, they explained, they could not have enough of, but fighting men were needless, for they had plenty of their own.* Remembering the behaviour of their French allies and all they had suffered at British hands at sea, their attitude was natural. Yet it bore no relation to their military position. Dupont, advancing southwards with 15,000 troops, had just taken Cordoba, while Moncey had routed Cuesta at Cabezon and occupied Valladolid. On the very day that Wellesley landed at Corunna, Joseph Bonaparte was entering Madrid to take possession of his new kingdom. Only at Saragossa, where the townsmen had barricaded the streets against a French army, and in the villages behind the advancing columns, where sullen peasants hid their food and abandoned the harvest to cheat the invader, did Spanish deeds match Spanish words.

Yet while Wellesley, after two fruitless days, was taking ship for Portugal, unknown as yet to him the tide in the Peninsula again turned. To all appearance the resistance of Spain was ridiculous: an affair of high-sounding, empty eloquence, of fabulous armies with Don Quixote in the saddle and Sancho Panza in the ranks, of remote provincial Juntas fantastically ignorant of one or other's activities and vainly boasting of imaginary victories, of peasant mobs masquerading as regiments, and monks and romantic professors brandishing the rusty arms of the Middle Ages while Napoleon's legions tramped unopposed along the highways. Yet beneath the unreality

---

* Unknown to Wellesley, his second-in-command Major-General Spencer, who had been operating from Gibraltar, was having the same difficulty with the local Junta at Cadiz. He had been fobbed off with excuses and sent off to a lonely spot on the Portuguese border. "I do not believe," wrote one observer, "there is a point at which they wish an English soldier to land." Plumer Ward, 188.

of the Spanish surface burnt the fires of Spanish pride and patriotism. So long as the hated enemy was far away—in the next province or even, in that land of natural barriers, in the next mountain valley— the average Spaniard persisted in his agelong complacency and his habit of putting off till to-morrow what should be done to-day. But once the tramp of alien feet sounded down his own rocky streets, he went out to kill. As Dupont's blue-coats pressed on beyond pillaged Cordoba, a grimly angry countryside rose in their rear. Unnerved by the stark hostility of the land and people, Dupont fell back towards the Sierra Morena. As he did so the patriots and the ragged army of Andalusia closed in on him. On July 23rd, faced by famine, he lost his head and capitulated at Baylen to General Castaños. Such a thing had not happened to a French army for nearly a decade.

On the following day Wellesley landed at Oporto. Here he found the Bishop in control, an insurgent Junta, a few hundred ragged Portuguese regulars and a crowd of peasants with pitchforks. It appeared that the whole country north of the Tagus, enraged by robbery, sacrilege and oppression, was in insurrection, and that the French were confined to the immediate neighbourhood of Lisbon and a few fortresses east of the river. Ordering his transports to Mondego Bay, where a party of British marines had secured the fort of Figueira, Wellesley went ahead to consult with Sir Charles Cotton, the admiral blockading the Tagus. From him he learnt that all the beaches near the capital were strongly held and that any landing on that exposed coast would be liable to interruption from westerly gales. He therefore decided to put his troops ashore in Mondego Bay - the nearest point at which he could secure an uncontested landing - and march the intervening eighty miles to Lisbon. Summoning General Spencer with his 5000 men from the mouth of the Guadiana, he returned to his transports in Mondego Bay. Here he met with significant news.

For awaiting him were official dispatches from England and a private letter from Castlereagh. It appeared that, as in the days of the expedition to the Red Sea, he had been superseded. Learning that Sir John Moore's army, denied a landing by the mad King of Sweden, was returning home, the Government had decided to send it on to Portugal. But resolved to prevent the command in the Peninsula devolving on Moore, who had made himself unpopular in Downing

Street by his criticisms of Ministerial strategy, it had hastily posted to the expedition two exceedingly senior officers. Then, on his arrival in London, it had allowed Moore to learn in a chance conversation with the War Secretary that he was to be employed only in a subordinate capacity. As was expected, Moore flared up and told Castlereagh what he thought of such treatment. But, contrary to Ministerial hopes, his sense of duty stopped him from resigning. Wellesley, at the outset of his campaign, was thus presented with the prospect of being joined, not only by 16,000 additional troops, but by three superior officers. One of them, Lieutenant-General Sir Hew Dalrymple, the Governor of Gibraltar, had not seen active service since 1794. His second-in-command, Lieutenant-General Sir Harry Burrard, was a Guardsman celebrated for his good nature, excellent table and unassuming intellect who had served in the same capacity under Lord Cathcart in the Danish campaign.[*]

In a private note to Wellesley Castlereagh explained the situation as best he could. Consistent with the employment of the necessary amount of force, he had made every effort to keep in his hands the greatest number of men and for the longest time the circumstances would permit. "I shall rejoice if it shall have befallen to your lot to place the Tagus in our hands; if not, I have no fear that you will find many opportunities of doing yourself honour and your country service."[*] Wellesley kept his temper and replied that he would do nothing rash to secure the credit of success before his seniors arrived, though to his brother, William, he privately wrote, "I don't know what Government proposes to do with me. I shall be the junior of all the Lieutenant-Generals, and of all the awkward situations in the world that which is most so is to serve in subordinate capacity in an army which one has commanded. However, I will do whatever they please."[‡] Then he gave the orders for his troops to disembark.

*   *   *

For the next five days the beaches of Mondego Bay presented an

---

[*] "A very good sort of man, and if he was unfit to command an army, they who gave him the command ought to have known that, for I am sure every one else knew it." Mrs Jackson to George Jackson. Jackson, II, 379.

[†] Castlereagh, VI, 385.

[‡] To the Hon William Wellesley-Pole, August 19th 1808. Wellesley-Pole, 5.

unusual spectacle. It was far from an ideal place to land, but it was the best available. Directed by naval signals from the headlands, relays of flat-bottomed boats put off from the transports, the red-coats sitting tightly wedged on the bucking thwarts with their packs and muskets between their legs. As each boat was rowed towards the rocky, sandy shore, huge breakers, sweeping out of the Atlantic, tossed it high into the air and flung it into a sheet of foam. Here gangs of naked sailors with ropes were waiting to haul it ashore before the next wave should dash it to pieces. When the boats grounded, the sailors seized the soldiers and carried them dry-shod to land. Other boats discharged unsaddled horses who, dazed after their confinement, struggled wildly ashore and then galloped up and down, snorting, neighing and kicking at their pursuers. Every now and then the waves overturned a boat and, despite the efforts of the sailors, later threw up a cluster of stiff, red-coated bodies.

It was not till the morning of August 8th that the last man was ashore and the army ready to advance. During all that week Wellesley worked furiously, trying to create, as in India, a transport and commissariat service sufficiently mobile to enable his force to operate without depending on the countryside for supplies—the basic principle on which all his successes in the East had rested and without which, campaigning in a war-wasted allied country against an enemy who deliberately lived, like the Mahrattas, on plunder, a British army could not hope to surive, let alone prevail. Using as nucleus* two companies of the Irish wagon-train which he had brought with him and engaging drivers, oxen and ox-carts to serve for regular wages and prompt payment under the Commissary General's department—a civilian organisation responsible, under the illogical English system, not to the Horse Guards but to the Treasury —he tried to reduce its commissaries to discipline and efficiency. Most of them, he told Castlereagh, were incapable of managing anything outside a counting-house. Because of this he gave up the idea of using the local Portuguese levies; in any case there seemed little point in overstraining his inadequate commissariat to supply troops whose only military accomplishment appeared to be picking the lice off their breeches. Their discipline was so bad that their rulers were even more afraid of them than the French. Yet, though he could hope for little from his allies, Wellesley was confident that if

* Weller, 32.

he struck quickly enough he could destroy the French before they could unite their forces. The highest estimate of their strength was 30,000, and with this they had to hold down a capital city, meet the threat of further landings and, with a countryside in insurrection, maintain communications with Spain. He guessed from his experience of men and conquest that eight months of occupation had transformed Junot - now styling himself Duke of Abrantes - from a soldier into a prince and his army from a field-force into a garrison.

For his own force he could count on some 13,000 British troops with 2000 regular Portuguese light infantry and horse. His Staff and commissariat were greenhorns, his artillery poorly mounted, his cavalry with only enough horses to mount 240 of his 390 light dragoons.* But, like every great master of war, Wellesley, though he weighed the odds carefully, always thought more of the enemy's difficulties than his own. His chance had come to show what he could do on a European battlefield; it might never come again. Coolly, and with great daring, he resolved to put everything to the test. Having completed his preparations, he marched on August 10th, occupying Leiria, twelve miles to the south, next day.

To maintain contact with the Fleet and his seaborne food-supply, minimise the strain on his transport, and guard against any threat to his left flank from a French army moving across the Tagus from eastern Portugal, he chose the coastal route through Caldas and Torres Vedras instead of the river road by Villa Franca. To save time he sent his advanced guard along the sands to Caldas, thirty miles ahead, following himself with the main body along the Leiria high road. Lacking horses and mules, the troops staggered along the hot sandy track, each man laden with kitbag, greatcoat and camp-kettle, four days' stores of ship's biscuit and salt beef, heavy water-canteen, hatchet, rifle and eighty rounds of ball-cartridge - enough, thought Rifleman Harris, to sink a little fellow of 5 feet 7 inches into the earth.† Around them were the sights and sounds of a mysterious countryside: the white houses in the brilliant glare, the gardens of aloe and cypress, the vineyards and olive groves, the ancient towers and steeples on undulating wooded heights and the barren heaths between, the screeching of the bullock carts with their solid wheels and ungreased axles and the drivers striding beside

* Weller, 32.
† Harris, 18-19; Blakeney, 18-19; *Journal of a Soldier*, 43.

with their goads. At night the air filled with the scents of rosemary, sage and thyme crushed beneath the wagon wheels or burning in bivouac fires, with the noise of frogs and crickets, and the chanting of the carters as they sang their plaintive, interminable hymns to the Virgin.*

As soon as he heard of the landing Junot had dispatched his best general, De Laborde, with 4500 men up the river road to the north to delay the British advance until a force twice as large under General Loison could move down from beyond the Tagus to join him. He himself, as Wellesley had reckoned he would, remained behind with the rest of his army to hold down the capital and watch the British ships off the Tagus. By the 12th Laborde was near Batalha, at the intersection of the two roads to Lisbon. But, finding that the British were moving, not only from the north, but along the beach to the west, to cut him off from Torres Vedras, he left the defence of the eastern road to Loison and retreated southwards towards Roliça. Half-way along the western route from Mondego Bay to Lisbon, he took up a strong position covering the little town of Obidos with its Moorish castle, two days' march south of Leiria.

With less than 300 horses Wellesley could not reconnoitre and cover his advance with cavalry. But he possessed instead a screen of fast-moving, accurate-shooting riflemen with which to probe and soften opposition. For this he was indebted to one of three senior officers now hastening, at the Horse Guards' insistence, to supersede him. Five years before, when Napoleon marched his Grand Army to the Channel shore to invade England, Sir John Moore had been appointed to command and train a *corps d'élite* of riflemen and light infantry at a key point on the Kentish coast. Faced by the natural courage and enthusiasm of the Revolutionary armies, Moore went back to nature to defeat them. He did not discard the traditional discipline of the British Service, but he humanised it. Against the *élan* of the armed *sans-culottes*, so resistless when confronted only by the "stiff solidarity" of the old monarchical armies of the Continent, he opposed an equal enthusiasm based on common-sense, discipline and careful training.

His opportunity to remodel the Army arose out of the need for light infantry. The French had won their battles with a horde of highly individualised skirmishers and sharpshooters going ahead of

* Schaumann, 20; Leslie, 32-5.

their dense half-disciplined columns and firing from every side into the rigid Teuton lines whose only reply were machine-like volleys, imposing on the parade ground but ineffective against such invisible and fast-moving targets. By the time the columns came into range, the defenders were already demoralised, and the rather sketchy discipline of the former - strengthened by successive victories - was seldom tested. An antidote for the *tirailleur* had had to be found. At the outset the British, being almost without light infantry, had relied on hired German Jägers who were little more than armed gamekeepers and foresters. The exigencies of West Indian warfare, like those of American warfare two decades before, caused them to train special companies as protective and reconnaissance screens. The need for more of these being acutely felt during the brief Helder campaign of 1799, the Duke of York had ordered the formation of an Experimental Rifle Corps to which fifteen regiments were ordered to send officers and men for courses of instruction. Trained by two brilliant leaders, Colonel Coote Manningham and Lieutenant-Colonel William Stewart, these were formed in the spring of 1801 into the 95th Regiment of the Line - a Rifle Corps with distinctive green uniform and dark buttons and accoutrements. Disbanded at the end of the Revolutionary War, they were re-formed when the war clouds regathered, armed with the new Baker rifle—a weapon of high precision compared with the smoothbore musket of the heavy infantry—and consigned to Shorncliffe Camp for special training under Sir John Moore. Here, facing across the Channel towards Napoleon's cantonments, they formed with the 14th Light Dragoons and the 52nd and 43rd Regiments - both reconstituted as light infantry - the spearhead of the force designed to repel invasion. For the next three years, until they passed overseas, they were trained by Moore in an amalgam of disciplined team-work and individual initiative, under full war conditions. In an Army notorious for inability to fend for itself in the field, every man of the Light Brigade - taking a leaf from the book of the self-reliant French - was taught to cook and tailor and to take pride in living sparely against the day when he would have to depend solely on himself. The formal brass, feather and pipeclay review so dear to military pedants was abandoned for the field-day - an exercise in which war conditions were reproduced as closely as possible. Everything was made to serve the one great end of reality: the defeat of Napoleon's invincibles.

Armed with a rifle capable of greater accuracy up to 300, or even, in the hands of a master, 500 yards, the rifleman was taught, first in the butts, then in the field, to judge and use cover and varied ground, to fire always to kill and never to waste a shot. He was trained not as a machine but as a craftsman, the consciousness of whose skill - the best guarantee for his survival on the battlefield - gave him courage and self-confidence. Above all, Moore's men were schooled in that art which in all ages is the ultimate arbiter of war; the combination of fire-power and movement. A rifleman in battle was the instrument of an orchestra in which every change of position, whether of individual or unit, was protected by co-ordinated fire, directed at the precise spot from which any interference with that movement might come. His special system of drill was directed to this end. Taught to the recruit by word of mouth in close order on the parade ground, it was subsequently carried out in extended order by bugle-horn and whistle. It aimed at combining the action of highly individualised and rapidly-moving men and units, working together to destroy or outwit the enemy.

At the back of every rifleman's mind Moore instilled the principle that the enemy was always at hand ready to strike. Whether on reconnaissance or protective duty, riflemen and light infantrymen were taught to be wary and on guard: to explore country, gather information, watch and question travellers and inhabitants, investigate and map out roads, paths, fords and bridges. It was their pride never to be caught napping; never to have an outpost or piquet surprised. The British army of the future was to be encompassed at all times and places by an invisible screen of marksmen, watching the enemy from behind every bush and stone, each one an alert and intelligent individual acting in close but invisible concert with his comrades.

*　　*　　*

At the head of Wellesley's army were four companies of the 2nd Battalion of the 95th Rifles, supported by the light companies of the 60th, an earlier regiment of riflemen formed during the American War. On August 15th these, skirmishing ahead of his advanced guard, encountered the French near the windmill of Brilos. Moving as Moore had taught them, an invisible tide of rapid and accurate fire, they quickly gained the village. As the enemy withdrew in good order to the south, one of the green-jackets, stung by the unfamiliar irritation of being fired at by real ball, sprang to his feet and, letting out a yell of "Over! boys, over!" dashed ahead, followed by all four companies, shouting and running over the grass like wildfire towards the distant rise and fixing their bayonet-swords as they ran. Coming up against the main French position at Obidos, they lost two officers and twenty-seven men, and were only saved from serious trouble by the swift advance of Spencer's division in support. Wellesley, though naturally annoyed by this needless loss, could not hide his satisfaction at the dash of his troops. "We are going on as well as possible," he reported to Castlereagh, "the army in high order and great spirits."

There was no time to lose, however, for Loison was nearing Alcoentre, a day's march to the east, and might soon effect a junction with Laborde. After a day of reconnoitring the French position, a general attack was launched early on the 17th. A visitor to the plain of Obidos that morning would have seen the British army drawn up in successive brigades and columns of battalions. He "would not, perhaps," wrote one who was present, "have noticed anything particular. He would have seen the arms piled, and the men occupied as they usually are on all occasions of a morning halt – some sitting on their knapsacks, others stretched on the grass, many with a morsel of cold meat on a ration biscuit for a plate in one hand, with a clasp-knife in the other, all doing justice to the contents of their haversacks, and not a few with their heads thrown back and canteens at their mouths, eagerly gulping down his Majesty's grog or the wine of the country, while others, whiffing their pipes, were jestingly promising their comrades better billets and softer beds for the next night, or repeating the valorous war-cry of the Portuguese.

"But to the person of reflecting mind there was more in this condensed formation than a casual halt required. A close observer would have noticed the silence and anxious looks of the several general officers of brigades, and the repeated departure and arrival of staff-officers and aides-de-camp, and he would have known that the enemy was not far distant, and that an important event was on the eve of taking place."* A British army in a remote province was challenging the imperial legions for a permanent foothold on

* Leslie, 38-9.

Napoleon's Europe. The first battle of the Peninsular War was about to begin.

What had distinguished Wellesley in his Indian wars had been the infinite pains and forethought with which he planned his campaigns and the boldness and dash with which he attacked an enemy when in reach. In this he resembled the great admiral whom he had met in Castlereagh's waiting-room a few weeks before Trafalgar. At Assaye and Argaum, having long perfected every arrangement for supply, he had sprung at the Mahrattas like a tiger. He was now resolved to destroy the inferior force under Laborde barring the Lisbon road before the larger one under Loison to the east could reinforce it, so opening the way to Junot's capital fifty miles on. With this object he meant to use his superior numbers to pin Laborde down by a frontal demonstration in force, while two flanking bodies moved rapidly southwards to encircle him: Trant with his 2000 Portuguese – grotesque-looking ragamuffins in white jackets and immense feathered hats – along the seaboard to the west, and Major-General Ferguson with a much larger force in the hills to the east, ready simultaneously to fend off any intervention by Loison.

Three things prevented him from accomplishing his objective. Ferguson's column descended from the hills too soon instead of continuing along them till it could cut the Lisbon road in the enemy's rear. There was a delay – for there were no maps – in finding the track along which the guns were to move up to pin down the French until it was too late for the latter to disengage without disaster. And one of the battalions demonstrating against the enemy centre mistook its objective, went too far and got itself surrounded, forcing Wellesley to order a premature frontal attack in order to rescue it. As a result Laborde, who was a first-class soldier, aware both of the threat to his flanks and that he was heavily outnumbered, was able to withdraw, with great skill, to a higher ridge two miles in his rear. But the riflemen of the 95th and 60th, driving up the ravines and using every stone and bush for cover, allowed him no time to consolidate. In the end, with the British commander pressing him relentlessly as was his practice when attacking, he was once more forced to abandon his position and fall back, covered by his cavalry, towards Torres Vedras. The French fought magnificently – Wellesley wrote that he had never seen them behave so well, while they returned the compliment by saying they had never been so attacked before. But during the retreat there was a temporary panic and they lost three of their five guns and a number of prisoners. And though the British failed to encircle and annihilate Laborde as they had intended, they had prevented his junction with Loison and opened up the coastal road to the south.

Wellesley's objective now was to secure Lisbon before the French could unite; nowhere else was there a harbour capable of sheltering a fleet against the Atlantic gales and affording a base for future operations in Spain. On the evening of his victory he received news that two brigades from England with a large quantity of stores were off the Peniche peninsula fifteen miles to the south-west, waiting to be put ashore before the next westerly gale dashed them on to the rocks. Next morning, therefore, deviating from the main Torres Vedras road, he pressed on towards Lourinham and Vimiero, a village on the Maceira river, whose sandy estuary, two miles away, offered the only available landing place.

Here, posted on a semi-circle of hills round the estuary, the army took up a covering position on August 19th. Brigadier-General Anstruther's brigade landed that day and Brigadier-General Acland's during the following night, while the piquets and patrols of the light companies, operating with the easy precision of Shorncliffe, kept prowling troops of French cavalry at a distance. This brought the British strength to 17,000 infantry and 18 guns with some 2000 uncertain Portuguese auxiliaries. Moore's transports being already off northern Portugal, Wellesley decided to resume his march on the 21st and, driving towards Mafra between the sea and the defile of Torres Vedras nine miles away, turn the latter before the French could recover from their defeat. The orders for the advance had just been issued when, on the evening of the 20th, a frigate arrived in Maceira Bay carrying Lieutenant-General Sir Harry Burrard. Wellesley immediately went aboard to acquaint his superior with his plans.

They were far too bold for that brave but conventional officer. Burrard's last encounter with the French had been in 1798, when, landing with a brigade to destroy a sluice-gate on the Ostend canal, he had been stranded on the beach by a gale and forced to capitulate. The same fear now haunted his mind. At any moment the French might attack with cavalry and mobile artillery and drive the British who lacked both, into the sea. Instead of landing Moore's 10,000 men at Mondego, as Wellesley had advised, for a dual advance on Lisbon along either side of the Monte Junto *massif*, Burrard was resolved to concentrate his army at Maceira Bay. He therefore wished to keep the troops already landed on the defensive until the remainder could be got ashore. He based his calculations on the belief that Junot would employ his entire force in a counter-attack instead of seeing, as did Wellesley with his clearer insight, that he would try to guard against a rising in Lisbon and a further landing in the Tagus.

Wellesley was naturally bitterly disappointed. He returned to his camp, cancelled his orders and expressed his feelings, so far as he was able, in a note to Castlereagh wishing that Sir Harry had landed and seen things with his own eyes. The resounding *coup* he had planned was not to be. Instead of falling to him after a brilliant victory, Lisbon was to become the subject of a laborious and uncertain siege, which would probably end, like others before it, in a British withdrawal. It was with such reflections that the dapper, alert-looking man with the big nose and close cropped hair, sat on the rough farmhouse table of his headquarters swinging his legs and talking to his Staff, when at midnight a breathless German dragoon announced that Junot was marching to the attack.

He received the report with his habitual calm. He scarcely believed it, for it seemed too good to be true, but sent orders to his piquets and patrols to be doubly watchful. At daybreak, as there was no sign of the French, the army—which, in accordance with his invariable Indian practice, had stood to arms for an hour before dawn—was dismissed with the normal Sunday morning order to parade later for divine service. But shortly after eight, while the men were cleaning their firelocks and washing their linen in the river, the bugles sounded and the drums beat to arms. A column of dust was taking shape on the hills as a strong force of French cavalry. Simultaneously white-coated columns appeared moving along the Torres Vedras-Lourinham road to the east as though to attack the British left.

The army - whose command was to pass in a few hours to Burrard - was drawn up facing south, with five of its eight brigades on a long rugged-topped ridge immediately to the south of the Maceira river where it entered the sea. They had been encamped there since their fifteen-mile march from Roliça on the 19th, to cover the disembarkation of Acland's and Anstruther's brigades on the open beaches at the mouth of the river. A continuation of the ridge to the east—between which and the western ridge the river ran north through a narrow defile before resuming its westward course to the sea—was occupied by only part of a brigade, while two more brigades held a low, round, flat-topped, outlying hill immediately to the south of Vimiero village whose name it bore and which lay a short way to the south of the eastern ridge.

But by nine o'clock it had become abundantly clear that, instead of attacking the British positions from the south, Junot was coming from the east, apparently intending to strike at the islanders' left flank and, rolling them up, drive them, a confused and bewildered mass, into the sea. Any resistance would be broken by the well-worn Napoleonic tactics of clouds of tirailleurs with their accompanying field guns, protected by cavalry, driving swathes of death and terror through the defenders' exposed and strung-out lines before the dense, shouting columns, marching at drum-beat in close support, delivered the coup-de-grâce.

But though the French had still to learn it, there were three unwonted features in the situation before them. The British commander was a highly experienced tactical genius, able to respond to any move of the game which the most veteran French general could devise and with a disconcerting capacity for so placing his forces and reserves that, in any given situation, a unit under attack would be automatically supported by other units. His extended lines of infantry, instead of being helplessly exposed to the bullets and roundshot of the attacking tirailleurs and field artillery, were invariably so placed as to be almost invisible to the attackers until the last moment, being drawn up, not on an exposed skyline, but on the reverse slopes of the positions attacked, using every piece of cover and turn of contour for concealment. And the advancing tirailleurs and field artillerymen, instead of having everything their own way, had first to encounter and fight their way through a strong opposing screen of riflemen, as individually active and self-reliant as themselves and far better co-ordinated and trained as marksmen.

Before either the French could reach his outposts or his sleeping superior land from his ship to take over command, Wellesley recast his dispositions and re-aligned his army to meet the attack. Person-

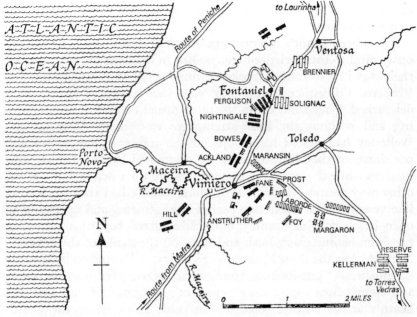

The Battle of Vimiero

ally supervising the operation, he moved four of his brigades from the western to the eastern ridge and placed another to the north and left of it, leaving the two brigades on Vimiero hill to form the right instead of the left of his position. A single brigade remained in reserve on the western ridge above the bay.

For, having left Lisbon on the 15th, Junot had joined forces with Loison on the day after Roliça and occupied Torres Vedras the same evening. Here, reinforced by Laborde's defeated division and his own Reserve, he had assembled 13,000 troops and 24 guns, sufficient, he calculated, to drive the English into the sea. 7000 remained behind to overawe the capital and prevent further landings; others were garrisoning Elvas, Santarem and Almeida in the interior. Having seen so many victories by his master's side, the French Commander-in-Chief felt confident of his ability to destroy an army of amateurs without any pedantic concentration of his forces. His sharpshooters and accompanying field artillery would soon break up their slow, stiff ranks, and then his dense columns and cavalry would do the

125

rest. That the day would end with a scramble on the beaches he never doubted. He did not even take the trouble to reconnoitre the British position.

It had been Junot's intention to attack at dawn – an hour notoriously fatal to inexperienced troops. But in the dark his veterans lost their way in the wooded, broken ground between Torres Vedras and Vimiero. Consequently the day was well advanced before they debouched. They came on in the most casual manner without pausing and without the least attempt to co-ordinate their attacks. Wellesley had placed his troops on the reverse slopes of his hill positions, so that instead of being decimated by the French skirmishers while the attacking columns moved up unscathed, it was the other way round. The riflemen whom Moore had trained, feeling like veterans after their two earlier engagements and operating in open, heathery, pine country, not unlike Surrey, kept up a withering fire from behind every bush and stone on the flanks of the advance. None the less the French, certain of victory, still came on boldly, the skirmishers – "fine-looking young men, wearing red shoulder-knots and tremendous moustaches" – pouring a shower of ball into the heather at the outnumbered but invisible rifles, while the world-famous columns tramped after, shouting and cheering "with more confidence" as Wellesley put it, "and seeming to feel their way less than I always found them to do afterwards."[*]

By this time the British artillery had opened fire at short range. As each shot drove a lane through the oncoming enemy, the green-jackets sniping in the heather began to cheer too. A new shell was being tried out, a hollow affair invented by a Major Shrapnel which burst in the air and scattered grape-shot downwards. The French, though suffering severely, closed their ranks and, like the veterans they were, pressed on. Meanwhile the British waited behind the ridge; Rifleman Harris, who a few years before had been a shepherd on the Dorset hills spending his days watching the sheep crop the turf, thought it the most imposing sight he had ever seen – the motionless lines in the August sunshine, "glittering with bright arms, the stern features of the men as they stood with their eyes fixed unalterably upon the enemy, the proud colours of England floating over the heads of the different battalions and the dark

* Harris, 50; Leslie, 48-9; Ann. Reg., 1808, 222; Napier, I, 211-15, 264; Fortescue, VI, 217-20; Simmons, 102; Croker Papers, II, 122; Weller, 42-58; Sherer, 43.

cannon on the rising ground." Far out at sea Jane Austen's brother, passing down the coast in his man-of-war - embodiment of the remote force which made the battle possible - watched through his spy-glass the smoke on the hills where the French were trying to dislodge the British from the crest.

Every one of Junot's ill-co-ordinated and over-confident attacks broke on the patient discipline and superior, because fully-deployed, fire-power of Wellesley's lines. As every column, already frayed by the British sharpshooters and shrapnel, came into range, it was greeted by a terrible discharge from the extended two-deep line of waiting musketeers or riflemen who, being able to bring every weapon to bear on the leading files of the undeployed French columns, subjected them to a devastating and continuous hail of musketry as each platoon in turn contributed its quota to that rolling barrage of death. Like the Macedonian phalanx when it encountered the open formation of the Roman legion, the French masses dissolved under that converging fire. Then the redcoats, following up with the bayonet, bore down on the confused and faltering column "like a torrent breaking bonds," and the victors of Austerlitz and Jena broke and fled.

Similar disaster befell the French left. Here the 40th and the 71st and 91st Highlanders of Ferguson's brigade, drawn up in three lines, advanced against the attacker's shattered columns with bagpipes playing while the general rode beside waving his hat. An attempt by French cavalry to stem the tide broke on the Highlanders' compact ranks. Everywhere the British were assuming the offensive: even Wellesley's sixty dragoons charged into the mêlée at his quiet, "Now, Twentieth, now is the time!" but, as nearly always with British cavalry, charged so intemperately as to lose formation and suffer needless casualties. By midday, from one end of the field to the other, the French were in precipitate retreat, 15 out of their 23 guns captured, every one of their infantry battalions broken, one of their principal commanders a prisoner and another slain, and the road to Torres Vedras open to the still unused brigades on the British right. Against the victors' 700 casualties, the vanquished had lost nearly 2000 or a sixth of their force.

At that moment, with the demoralised enemy pouring off the field, Wellesley, who had been at every point attacked anticipating every French move, galloped along the ridge his men had so trium-

phantly held, and, raising his hat,* called out to General Burrard
—who, on landing two hours earlier, had chivalrously declined to
take over direction of the battle—"Sir Harry, now is your chance.
The French are completely beaten; we have a large body of troops
that have not yet been in action. Let us move on Torres Vedras. You
take the force here straight forward; I will bring round the left with
the troops already there. We shall be in Lisbon in three days!"

But Sir Harry was not a man to take risks. As he saw it, the
enemy's cavalry was still unbroken, their total force in Portugal
unknown, their fortresses untaken, the whole might of Napoleon's
Empire behind them. His own troops were without cavalry, adequate
transport, gun-carriages or any proper base, and had only twelve
days' provisions. Behind him were open beaches and the uncertain
Atlantic. Nothing that Wellesley could say would induce him to
move till Moore's men had been disembarked. Lacking his brilliant
junior's imagination, he could not picture the confusion and
momentary despair of the French, the excited Portuguese swarming
into the streets of Lisbon for revenge, the confusion that a swift
blow might wreck on an exposed flank and rear. Like most British
generals of his generation Burrard had grown so used to dwelling
on his own difficulties that he had ceased to be able to think of the
enemy's. He could not see that the boldest measures might now be
the safest. Nor could the Adjutant-General and the Quartermaster
General, both nominees of the rule-of-thumb Horse Guards and
both of whom supported him against Wellesley's entreaties.†

So, summing up the events of an astonishing twenty-four hours
and hardly knowing whether to lament or rejoice more at his
alternating fortunes, the superseded victor wrote to his brother next
morning.

"We gave the French an unmerciful beating yesterday. Sir Harry
Burrard arrived on the evening of the 20th, and I did everything
in my power to induce him to march on; which he resisted till he

---

* Rifleman Harris of the 95th saw the incident and recalled it in his memoirs: "It is
something to have seen that wonderful man even do so commonplace a thing as lift his
hat to another officer on the battlefield." Harris, 130. See Fortescue, VI, 231.

† But Moore, landing on the spot a few days after the battle, took Wellesley's view.
"Several of our brigades," he wrote in his journal, "had not been in action; our troops were
in high spirits and the French so crestfallen that probably they would have dispersed. They
could never have reached Lisbon." Moore, II, 258-9.

should be reinforced by Moore - a decision with which I was not pleased any more than I was with the manner in which it was made. Sir Harry did not come on shore that night; and, as I am the 'Child of Fortune' and Sir Harry did not choose to march towards the enemy, the enemy came to us with his whole force and attacked us in our position, and we gained a most complete victory.'*

In the course of that day, August 22nd, the counsels of prudence and timidity were reinforced by still higher authority. Sir Hew Dalrymple landed from Gibraltar and assumed command. He was in no mood to listen to Wellesley's arguments. He belonged to a school of warfare which had perished on the battlefields of the Revolution fifteen years before but which still lingered on in his mind: of an exquisite and leisurely eighteenth-century art only to be mastered by rigid and lifelong adherence to exact and formal rules. It was bad enough for a Corsican brigand like Bonaparte to run amok and break all the rules without a jumped-up young Irish general copying him on the strength of a few irregular campaigns in India. What had enraged Sir Hew still more was a letter from Castlereagh urging him, nearly twenty years Wellesley's senior, to take that officer's advice. He was damned if he would.

But though Sir Hew and Sir Harry had no conception of the magnitude of their junior's achievement and victory, Junot and the French were in no doubt about it. Early on the afternoon of August 22nd, General Kellermann arrived in the British lines under a flag of truce and proposed an immediate armistice and a formal convention for a French evacuation of Portugal. It seemed to the two senior British commanders by far the best thing that could happen. They had been ordered to expel the enemy from Portugal as a prelude to the liberation of Spain - a more improbable mission than any even normally given to a British general - and here were the French offering to go of themselves. Even Wellesley, though he privately complained of "Dowager Dalrymple and Betty Burrard haggling with Kellermann over inadmissible terms,"† saw that there was now nothing else for it. The chance of exploiting his victory had been

---

* To the Hon William Wellesley-Pole, August 22nd 1808. Wellesley-Pole, 6-7.

† See a reference in Lady Bessborough's correspondence to letters from Wellesley to the Duke of Richmond "that makes one's blood boil." Granville, II, 33.

lost; Junot, reinforced, was back at Torres Vedras, and the only hope of taking Lisbon, let alone of reducing the interior fortresses, was by a series of prolonged sieges in a country notoriously lacking in natural resources, with the rains approaching and the equinoctial gales threatening to cut communications with the Fleet. And with Dalrymple as Commander-in-Chief the only sane course seemed to be to bring hostilities to an end as quickly as possible. For, after his prolonged spell as Governor, the old gentleman was manifestly incapable either of managing an army in the field or of taking the advice of those who could.

Wellesley, therefore, did as he was ordered and signed the armistice with his two seniors. Though he disapproved profoundly of their stupid and craven failure to exploit the victory he had won, he did not wish, as he said, to raise "a faction" - something he abhorred in a soldier - against them. In the making of the Convention that followed he had no part. Neither Sir Hew nor Sir Harry knew anything of diplomacy. Like all their race, the French generals were able bargainers, and their wits, sharpened in the turmoil of Revolutionary society, enabled them to take their opponents' measure. Their army was to evacuate Portugal but on the most advantageous terms, in British transports with all its arms and equipment and taking with it whatever "property" it had legitimately acquired in Portugal. In other words - though this was not officially admitted - it was to take its plunder. Landed at a western French port, it was then to be free to re-enter the struggle.

*   *   *

For Wellesley all this was bitterly disappointing. After being denied a chance for five years to show what he could do in command of an army and what he had indeed already done in India, he had twice in four days defeated a veteran French commander and veteran French troops, on the second occasion so signally that Junot's routed and flying force was at his mercy and the road to Lisbon wide open. Instead he had been forced by his incompetent superiors to halt his victorious troops where they had fought, leaving them to be poisoned by the stench of the dead and half-starved for lack of rations in a neighbourhood where everything had been eaten up. "I wish that I was away from this army," he wrote to his brother, William, three days after the battle. "Things will not flourish as we are situated and organised, and I am much afraid that my friends in England will consider me responsible for many things over which I have no power. There is no more confidence in me on the part of the Chiefs than if I had been unsuccessful, and I am the only person in whom the army have any. The Chiefs ask my opinions about everything and never act according to it." "The General has no plan, or even an idea of a plan," he added in a postscript two days later, "nor do I believe he knows the meaning of the word *Plan*. I entered fully into a discussion upon the situation of the army the day before yesterday, in which I pointed out the inutility of augmenting his army here and the danger of the measure if he should not - and he could not - augment his means of supply, and I gave him papers to read upon the subject of his future operations. He has not uttered one word to me upon that subject from that time to this. And Moore" —who had arrived off the coast with his 10,000 men from Sweden, only to be placed under the same stultifying command—"told me last night that he had said to him, 'You may either land your corps or not as you think proper,' as if it was a matter of perfect indifference whether this army should have 10,000 men in addition or whether 15,000 additional mouths should be fed by means calculated for half the number. The people are really more stupid and incapable than any I have yet met with, and, if things go on in this disgraceful manner, I must quit them."*

They did. Three weeks later, on September 16th, he wrote to his brother again,

"What do you think of my having now four battalions under my command, there being two major-generals with six and a brigadier-general with four? What do you think of their having deprived my general officers of their brigades, broken them up, separated the regiments which they had led to victory, some of which they had had under their command for years, separated their staff officers from them, and deprived two of them of their brigades entirely? They have annoyed the soldiers, too, as much as they could, and they have put themselves to an inconvenience to detach the regiments which were under my command to distant

* To the Hon William Wellesley-Pole, August 24th and 26th 1808. Wellesley-Pole, 6-8.

garrisons, the soldiers from the marches they had already made having no shoes to their feet and feeling a very natural desire to see the place for which they had fought.

"Then my orders and regulations in respect to the discipline and supply of the army are treated as so much waste paper; contradicting orders are issued without even a reference to them; and there never was such a state of confusion as we now are in this respect. To this add that they have illegally broken the contract which was made under my authority for the supply of meat to the troops; and the consequence is that a great proportion of the army is now upon salt provisions. . . .

"I am aware that there is a party that will run me down for coming away, but I have never cared much for what people say of me without cause, and I shall care less for it than ever, I believe, now. In short, I have determined to quit the army if these Gentlemen continue in the command of it, and I was never more convinced of anything than that I judge right in making this determination. In respect to the situation in which I shall be when I shall have quitted the army I am entirely indifferent. I'll return to Ireland if the Ministers wish it; if they don't, I don't desire it. If I should not return to Ireland I'll remain upon the Staff in England; or, if that is impossible, I'll do nothing and amuse myself with hunting and shooting."*

A fortnight before he had told John Malcolm that, if he could be of any use to the men who had served him so well, he would stay with them forever, but that, as things were, he could do nothing for them, and he had therefore informed Castlereagh of his desire to resume his political duties as Chief Secretary for Ireland if convenient for the Government. "I am sick of all that is going on here," he told the Lord Lieutenant, the Duke of Richmond, "and I heartily wish I had never come away from Ireland and that I was back again with you."

Before he returned to England, however, he did a service of some importance to the country and to the future of the war in the Peninsula. On September 17th he addressed a letter to his fellow Lieutenant-General, Sir John Moore, who, though with infinitely

---

* To the Hon William Wellesley-Pole, September 16th 1808.

greater experience of war than either, had also been placed under the orders of the incompetent Sir Hew and Sir Harry. Moore, though a man of rare nobility, had made himself unpopular with the Tory Ministers by his forthright criticisms of their strategy, and, though out of a high sense of duty, he had accepted the humiliating subordinate appointment they had given him, he had left them in no doubt as to his indignation and resentment. Wellesley, who was a member of the Government, knew this and offered his good offices to heal the breach.

"I write to you on the subject to which this letter relates with the same freedom with which I hope you would write to me on any point in which you might think the public interests concerned. It appears to me to be quite impossible that we can go on as we are now constituted; the Commander-in-Chief must be changed, and the country and the army naturally turn their eyes to you as their commander. I understand, however, that you have lately had some unpleasant discussions with the King's Ministers. . . . I wish you would allow me to talk to you in order that I may endeavour to remove any trace which they may have left on the minds of the King's Ministers. . . . Although I hold a high office under the Government, I am no party man, but I have long been connected in friendship with many of those persons who are now at the head of affairs in England; and I think I have sufficient influence over them that they may listen to me upon a point of this description, more particularly as I am convinced that they must be as desirous as I can be to adopt the arrangement for the command of this Army which all agreed is the best.

"In these times, my dear General, a man like you should not preclude himself from rendering the services of which he is capable by any point of form. Circumstances may have occurred, and might have justified the discussions to which I have referred; but none can justify the continuance of the temper in which they are carried on; and yet, till there is evidence that it is changed, it appears to be impossible for the King's Ministers to employ you in the high situation for which you are the most fit, because during the continuance of this temper of mind there can be no cordial or confidential intercourse.

"In writing this much I have perhaps gone too far and have

taken the permission for which it was the intention of this letter to ask. . . ."*

Moore accepted the letter in the spirit in which it was written, and the two men who alone had the capacity to lead the army in its hazardous mission, and in whom alone the army had confidence, met in the palace of Queluz outside Lisbon. One or other of them, Wellesley said, must liberate Spain. "You," he added, "are the man, and I shall with great willingness act under you."†

On the day after this interview Wellesley left Lisbon to resume his office as Irish Secretary. Unbeknown to him, on the same day that he wrote his letter to Moore, the Government, alarmed by the outcry aroused by the Convention, decided to recall Sir Hew and Sir Harry to attend a Public Inquiry in England.

* * *

It was not till the end of August that people in Britain had heard of the victories in Portugal. At the beginning of that month hopes had dropped sharply. "Nothing," wrote that well-informed diplomat, Francis Jackson, after the Spanish defeat at Medina del Rioseco and Joseph's entry into Madrid, "is to be expected from Spain. If Sir Arthur Wellesley lands he will find himself between the fire of two corps, each of which is equal to his own." But soon afterwards news came of the capitulation of Dupont's army and the landing in Mondego Bay. By the third week in August, with Joseph's evacuation of his capital eleven days after he had entered it and the repulse of the French by the people of Saragossa, British faith in the Spanish rising touched a higher point than any yet reached. The Government's popularity rocketed: a Radical mass meeting at the Mermaid tavern, Hackney, voted the King and his Ministers thanks for helping Spain to show how Europe could be delivered from despotism. "Now for some good news from Wellesley," wrote Lord Grey, the ex-Whig Foreign Secretary, "and we will give a *feu de joie* and drink bumpers!"‡

And in the evening of the 31st it came - brought to London by two

* To Lieut-General Sir John Moore, September 17th 1808.
† Stanhope, 244.
‡ Granville, II, 321; Cartwright, 368-9. See also Jackson, II, 256-8; Crabb Robinson, I, 272; Wellesley, I, 231.

travel-stained officers. "I can hardly believe," wrote an entranced lady, "that it is the same scattered scarecrow, Arthur Wellesley, I used to play at romps with that has done this!"* The country went mad with joy: the long years of military defeat were over and the charm of Napoleon's ascendancy broken. Never again, wrote that staunch champion of her country, Lady Bessborough, would one be told that British troops were inferior to those of other nations and that it was ridiculous to attempt to cope with the French. There could be no more croaking now; "huzza," shouted Captain Paget of the *Cambrian*; "for the old British bayonet!" It was said that Junot had capitulated and that the British had already entered Lisbon. "I hear," wrote Lady Errol, "that hero Kellermann, who last November was dictating strict humiliating terms to Emperors and Kings, was obliged to go down upon his knees to Sir Arthur Wellesley. . . . I like it *loads* and quantities."†

The terms of the Convention proved, therefore, a terrible shock. The first hint of it came on September 3rd when a half-hysterical Portuguese Minister lodged a complaint at the Foreign Office against the disregard shown by the contracting British generals for his country's rights and property. As Ministers had not so much as heard of any truce, they were at a loss what to make of this: supposing the French army to be at their mercy, they set the whole thing down as a forgery. It was not till the middle of the month that confirmation from Dalrymple reached them.

Yet, appalled as Ministers were by the Convention, they were far more appalled by its effect on the country. Announced in an Extraordinary Gazette on September 16th, it struck the public mind, excited beyond measure by Wellesley's dispatches and Spanish victories, with the force of a tornado. It was worse than Whitelocke's capitulation at Buenos Ayres; "twice in a twelvemonth," wrote Francis Jackson, "have we had the game completely in our own hands and twice has it been wantonly thrown away." The generals, including Wellesley himself, became the most unpopular men in England; they were cartooned on gallows and hooted in the streets as cravens. After fifteen years of defeat and frustration the heroism of British fighting men had snatched victory from the French, and their commanders had thrown it away! Some went so far as to

* Festing, 149.
† Jackson, II, 261-2; *Berry Papers*, 292; *Paget Brothers*, 87; Wilberforce, II, 147.

denounce the Convention - popularly, though wrongly, identified with the name of Cintra - as downright treachery; a wag declared that he would henceforth spell humiliation with a "hew." The Opposition naturally made the most of it, and all the simple souls who had seen in the Spanish rising the noblest expression of human virtue and freedom since the birth of mankind cried out that the Spaniards had been betrayed. "Britannia sickens, Cintra, at thy name!" wrote Wordsworth, who was so angry that he not only composed a denunciatory pamphlet and a sonnet but tramped through the dales to address a public meeting.

It was to an England in this frenzy of popular indignation - with himself as the centre of it - that Wellesley returned in the first week of October 1808. "I arrived here this day," he wrote to his brother the Marquess, "and I don't know whether I am to be hanged, drawn and quartered, or roasted alive. However I shall not allow the mob of London to deprive me of my temper or my spirits; or the satisfaction which I feel in the consciousness that I acted right."* For in its fury against the three generals who had signed the Armistice and, as they supposed, the Convention - though in this last he had no part - the public had forgotten, even if it had ever realised, that it was Wellesley who alone had won the unique and seemingly miraculous British victory whose scandalously wasted fruits were the cause of all this uproar. And as he was the only politician of the offending trio, and as his had been a political appointment, all those opposed to the Government united in abusing him. The great Whig parliamentary demagogue, Sam Whitbread, the brewer, while he regretted "the lost opportunities for national glories" thrown away by the armistice and Convention, expressed himself delighted to see the pride of the Wellesleys lowered; "how the devil," wrote the radical journalist, Cobbett, "will they get over this? Now we have the rascals on the hip. It is evident that *he*" (Sir Arthur Wellesley) "was the prime cause - the only cause - of all the mischief, and that from the motif of thwarting everything *after he was superseded*. Thus do we pay for the arrogance of that damned infernal family." He even went so far, when Wellesley returned to his post in Ireland, as to accuse him of cowardice.†

* To the Marquess Wellesley, October 5th 1808. See *Croker Papers*, I, 344.

† Gore, *Creevey*, 54 "He had the discretion not to make any noise upon his landing. He snugged it in, in the *Plover* sloop, and off he went as fast as post-horses would take him to

To all this the grossly maligned victor of Roliça and Vimiero made no public reply. "I am accused of being the adviser of persons over whom I had no control and who refused to follow my advice, and I am made responsible for the acts of others," he wrote to Lord Buckingham. "The real share which I have had in the transactions - which in my opinion have deservedly incurred the displeasure of the public - cannot be known till they will be inquired into. . . . I know of no immediate remedy for these difficulties of my situation excepting patience and temper. And I thank God that the undeserved abuse which has been heaped upon me has not altered the latter. In respect to the conduct of my case I have determined I will publish nothing nor authorise the publication of anything by others. This forbearance is particularly incumbent upon me, as the whole subject must be inquired into. I have also determined that I will not involve others in scrapes because they differed in opinion with me previously to the 22nd August, notwithstanding that difference of opinion and alteration of system were the cause for the military expediency of allowing the French to withdraw from Portugal. I am afraid that I shall experience some difficulty in carrying this intention into execution because the truth must come out; but I will endeavour not to bring others (viz. Sir Harry Burrard) into a scrape, not only out of regard to him, but because I think it fatal to the public service to expose officers to the treatment which I have received and to punishment for acting upon their own military opinions."*

When the Court of Inquiry met on November 14th at Chelsea in the Great Hall of Wren's Royal Hospital under the chairmanship of General Sir David Dundas - popularly known as "Old Pivot" from his addiction to the drill-book - Wellesley was completely exonerated. So—for that was what the Horse Guards who had appointed them desired—were Sir Hew and Sir Harry. On December 22nd by six votes to one the Court approved the armistice; by four to three, a little reluctantly, the Convention. As, if Sir Arthur's advice after Vimiero had been taken, there would have been no need for an armistice, which he had only signed because the Commander-in-Chief requested him to do so, and because, his advice to follow up his

that place where one man is not known to another, and where a man may walk about and be hidden at the same time. This must, however, have been a little mortifying to the high Wellesley." *Political Register.* cit Longford 163

* To the Marquess of Buckingham, October 11th 1808.

victory having been rejected, it was the only practicable course in the circumstances; and, as he had never signed the Convention and had had no part in negotiating its terms, it was impossible to fault him.

While the Court of Inquiry was sitting in London, dramatic events were happening in Spain. Here Sir John Moore, who, on Sir Arthur's advice, had been confirmed as Commander-in-Chief of the British forces in the Peninsula, had marched with 20,000 men from Lisbon across the Portuguese mountains into Leon and Old Castile to co-operate with the Spanish armies in freeing their country, while another 17,000 troops had been sent from England to Corunna to reinforce him under Wellesley's old rival and comrade, Sir David Baird. Having been earlier passed over by the Government he had offended, Moore thus found himself in command of the largest army Britain had sent to Europe since the time of Marlborough. He had used it with startling effect. For all their boasting, enthusiasm and self-confidence, the Spaniards, thanks to their utter unpreparedness and indiscipline, had failed miserably in the field and been routed in a series of disastrous battles by Napoleon, who had entered Spain to destroy them with 120,000 veteran troops, bringing his forces in the Peninsula to more than 300,000. On December 4th, despite a popular rising in the capital to keep him out, he had entered Madrid. It looked as though the resistance of Spain was at an end and that the whole country, including Portugal, must fall to the all-triumphant Emperor of the French.

Yet during the first week of December, while the resistance of the Madrid populace was still in the balance, Moore reached a heroic decision. Despite the collapse of the Spanish armies and the consequent abandonment of his own isolated and now hopelessly outnumbered force, he had decided to strike at Napoleon's communications and, by doing so, halt him in his otherwise irresistible advance on Portugal and southern Spain. "I mean," he wrote to his second-in-command, Baird, "to proceed bridle in hand, for if the bubble bursts and Madrid falls we shall have to run for it."

Three days before the Court of Inquiry finished its proceedings at Chelsea, Napoleon in Madrid learnt that the despised British, instead of scurrying back to their ships as he had supposed, were, with inconceivable impudence and hardihood, striking at his communications and attempting, into the bargain, to surprise and overwhelm one of his marshals, Soult, who with an inferior force to theirs was unsuspectingly mopping up what Spanish resistance remained in Old Castile. Like a tiger whose tail had been twisted, he reacted with characteristic speed and fury and, driving across the Guadarrama mountains in deep snow, descended into the northern plains in overwhelming force, determined to encircle and destroy the British. Warned in the nick of time, Moore turned in his tracks and just escaped the jaws closing around him. There followed a terrible three weeks' midwinter retreat across the Galicia mountains. But the British, having drawn the main French forces into a remote corner of Spain, reached their transports in safety. Moore himself fell in a victorious rearguard action at Corunna fought to cover the embarkation. Foiled of his prey, Napoleon had already returned to France as a result of news that Austria—driven beyond endurance by the imperious demands of his trade embargo against British goods and roused by the past summer's events in Portugal and Spain—was arming once more for war.

Chapter Six

DOURO AND TALAVERA

It may be questioned whether any general, even Napoleon
himself, ever brought about so many startling surprises.
COLONEL G. F. R. HENDERSON, *The Science of War*

I shall do the best I can with the force given to me, and if the
people of England are not satisfied they must find someone else
who will do better.
ARTHUR WELLESLEY

WHEN the British army, ragged, lousy and emaciated, returned to
England at the end of January, 1809, there was little enthusiasm left
for Spain to whose support it had so chivalrously gone. The romantic
dreams of Spanish valour and patriotism had vanished in a night.
The returned soldiers presented the Spaniards as heartless cur-
mudgeons who had barred their doors and hidden their food and
wine; as cravens who had fled from the battlefield leaving their
would-be liberators surrounded. Nobody had a good word to say
for them or their beggarly country: a land, it seemed, of rain-
soaked, frozen uplands and stinking hovels swarming with lice and
fleas, where a clean bed and a coal fire were as little known as kindli-
ness and honesty.

News of further Spanish disasters followed the return of Moore's
troops. Venegas was routed by Victor at Ucles, Corunna and Ferrol
were yielded by their governors a few days after the British evacuation, and Joseph Bonaparte was crowned at the end of January in
Madrid. In the next month St Cyr, overwhelming the Spaniards at
Vallas, made himself master of all Catalonia, while, after 50,000 of
the defenders of Saragossa had perished and a third of the city had
been reduced to rubble, 16,000 pestilence-stricken survivors staggered out to surrender.

Yet though the north and centre of Spain was lost, the British
colours flew over Lisbon. Command of the sea enabled Britain to

140

dominate the wide perimeter of the Peninsula: her troops withdrawn from one point on the coast could be moved more swiftly than Napoleon's road-bound legions to another. Seville and Cadiz were still unconquered. The Spaniards had suffered disasters but their resistance was unbroken. The extension of French conquests only hardened it. No sooner had Soult's army, followed by Ney's, over-run Galicia than that province - hitherto indifferent to the war - rose in passionate revolt. The moral forces which had made the Revolution and which had ever since operated against its excesses came into play. The exuberant lawlessness which prompted Napoleon to filch the Spanish crown, and the private of his Guard to rob the peasant's household peace, aroused instincts deep in the human conscience. Spain might still be medieval, but nowhere were indi-viduals more ready to respond to elemental moral promptings. The doctrine that a Revolutionary army was entitled to live on a con-quered country was met by the equally Revolutionary doctrine that a country so treated was morally obliged to destroy the invader. Scarcely a day passed that February without ten or twenty of the French being killed; the banks of the Tagus were lined with peasants armed with fowling pieces, whose victims fell before they knew they were being attacked. The Spanish temperament, with its fierce individualism, heroic obstinacy and passion for revenge, lent itself to such warfare. So did the landscape with its wild, inaccessible hills and immense distances.

It had been Sir John Moore's view that Portugal could not be held if the Spanish armies collapsed. Since Corunna the 10,000 troops left in that country had been expecting a French advance on Lisbon and an early recall to London. But events were taking place on the Continent which suggested the wisdom of still keeping a British force in the peninsula, if militarily possible. For in central Europe, as in Spain, the exercise of the new Charlemagne's will was so vehement and unscrupulous that sooner or later he drove all opposed to it to desperation. The enslaved peoples of the Continent watching, in the aftermath of Baylen and Vimiero, Napoleon's veterans receding into Spain had realised that there was only one Grand Army. And, though Prussia, like Russia, was in the con-queror's camp, the nascent forces of nationalism found a focus in what was still the greatest of the Germanic States. The Court of Vienna might be frivolous, hidebound and incapably inefficient, yet, despite three defeats at the hands of France in the past thirteen years, Austria was still a great Power. For centuries the rampart of Christendom against the Turk, compounded of half a dozen fighting races – Teutons, Magyars, Tyrolese, Croats, Czechs, Poles – she could put an army of more than 300,000 well-trained men into the field. After Austerlitz she had played a waiting part, watching the Russian campaign in Poland with what seemed to Englishmen a craven neutrality and participating in the outward forms of Napoleon's New Order. She had accepted his Continental System, closed her ports to Britain's trade and even declared war on her. Yet all the while she was secretly preparing for a renewal of a struggle which she knew to be inevitable. In the summer of 1808, encouraged by the news from Spain, she had established a national Landwehr, embodying the French conception of a nation in arms. Under the direction of the Archduke Charles – the ablest soldier in Germany – her arsenals were being replenished, her artillery re-horsed and her army reorganised in *corps d'armée* on the Napoleonic model. And while they continued to return soft answers to Napoleon's remonstrances, the young Emperor Francis and his Minister, Count Stadion, steadily prepared for war. After the fall of the Spanish Bourbons it seemed their only hope. In the autumn of 1808 they had opened secret negotiations with England.

This had been one of the reasons which had brought Napoleon hurrying back from Spain to Paris before Corunna. Once more the old protagonists, Teuton and Gaul, were moving into the lists, and it was in Britain's interest to do everything possible to encourage the clash. For British constancy in the Peninsula might again re-animate Europe. During March 1809, at the instance of Lord Castlereagh, the Secretary of State for War, the Government gave its approval to a memorandum prepared by Sir Arthur Wellesley in which he gave it as his considered belief that, with a Portuguese army disciplined by British officers and drill sergeants, from 20,000 to 30,000 British troops, including 4000 cavalry, could hold Lisbon against anything up to 100,000 French. "I have always been of the opinion," he wrote, "that Portugal might be defended whatever might be the result of the contest in Spain."

What commended this plan to the Government was its modest demand on man-power; indeed, its author stated that any larger force would at present be out of the question since everything it needed would have to come from England - arms, ammunition, ordnance, clothing, accoutrements, even flour and oats. It was, therefore, decided that, despite the prejudice of the Horse Guards and the political animosity felt against him by the Whig Opposition, Wellesley should himself put into execution the plan he had recommended. On April 6th he was formally appointed Commander-in-Chief of the British forces in the Peninsula with instructions that the defence of Portugal was to be considered his first and immediate object. At the same time troops were dispatched to join those already at Lisbon.

During the early months of 1809, fresh from his ordeal by popular clamour and the Cintra Court of Inquiry, Sir Arthur had been suffering a good deal of domestic disquiet. His wife had caused him distress by borrowing - or, as he put it, "misappropriating" - the housekeeping money to pay the gambling debts of her younger brother, and had then, out of fear, tried to conceal the fact from him, causing him - the most meticulous of men in such matters - to be dunned by tradesmen. Early in March the wife of his youngest brother, Henry, had caused a major scandal by eloping in a hackney coach with Lord Paget, the commander of Moore's cavalry in the Corunna retreat. If Harriette Wilson can be believed - which is doubtful - he himself sought relief at this time in the arms of that celebrated courtesan who, in her memoirs published sixteen years later, alleged that he visited her on several occasions before "he betook himself again to the wars." He certainly seems, then or earlier, to have helped her with money, for he told Mrs Arbuthnot in 1825, after Harriette's publisher had tried to blackmail him, that he had frequently given her some when she wrote to beg for it. But, as he also said that he had never seen her since his marriage and, as he was an exceptionally truthful man, his association with her may have been confined to the months immediately after his return from India, and her allusion to his drying her tears before he returned to Spain may well have been pure fabrication.*

It must at least have been with feelings of deep relief that he

---

* Hariette Wilson, 74-5, 78; Arbuthnot, I, 378. Arthur Wellesley is said to have helped another lady, a Mrs Stuart, from the same establishment - Mrs Porter's fashionable and notorious house in Berkeley Street - when she was stranded on her way to join her husband in India. Elers, 57; Longford, 168. He was, at heart, a very kind man who always helped old acquaintances in trouble, even disreputable ones.

returned that April to his chosen profession. He resigned his political office and gave up his seat in Parliament. For the next five years he was to be a soldier and nothing else and was never to leave the field of war. He sailed from Portsmouth on April 15th 1809, narrowly escaping shipwreck in a night storm off the Isle of Wight. Warned by a message from the captain that the vessel was about to founder and that he should put on his boots and come up on deck, he replied, with his habitual calm, that he preferred to stay in his cabin and that he could swim better without boots.

On April 22nd he landed at Lisbon, having made the voyage in a week. He was greeted with immense enthusiasm by the people of Portugal whom he had liberated by his campaign of the previous summer, and by the army which he had commanded in the greatest British victory fought on the Continent since Minden and Malplaquet. He might not be appreciated yet by the people of England, but here he was a hero.

The situation facing him would have daunted any other commander. With 20,000 British, 3000 Hanoverians of the King's German Legion and 16,000 uncertain Portuguese regulars, his chances looked anything but rosy. A hundred and sixty miles to the north Marshal Soult with 23,000 veterans was menacing Lisbon from Oporto, while Marshal Victor, with 25,000 more, having routed the Spaniards at Medellin, threatened the Portuguese capital from the east. Between them lay General Lapisse with another 6000 near Ciudad Rodrigo. A further 200,000 French troops were scattered about the Peninsula, mostly in garrisons.

Yet, as Wellesley saw, the situation had its possibilities. On April 8th, two weeks before he landed at Lisbon, the Archduke Charles had issued a proclamation to the German peoples announcing that his army was marching to secure their liberties and inviting them to repudiate their puppet rulers. At the same time the Tyrolese mountaineers, emulating the Spanish guerrillas, rose against the pro-French monarchy of Bavaria and reaffirmed their ancient allegiance to the Hapsburgs. As a result considerable forces had been recalled from Spain to France and, as the war in Germany intensified, more were likely to follow. The Marshals whom Napoleon had left behind had been curiously slow to exploit their advantages and, absorbed in supply difficulties and personal rivalries, had fallen far behind the time-table set them. And neither of the two widely-separated armies facing Lisbon were concentrated for immediate battle. Instead, both were spread out over the countryside. For Revolutionary licence in billets and the Revolutionary principle of making war support war were having their usual result. The storming of Oporto had been accompanied by an orgy of drunken rape and murder, and British patrols reconnoitring to the north found houses and churches wrecked, householders murdered and their furniture lying smashed in the streets, altars and sanctuaries rifled and tombs polluted. Outside Oliveira the dangling bodies of the priest, the chief magistrate and the town clerk testified to the thoroughness of the Napoleonic doctrine of hostage.* Everywhere the Portuguese peasantry, who would otherwise have regarded the coming of the French with indifference, were roaming the hills in angry, restless groups.

It was Wellesley's way, like Napoleon's, never to let his own difficulties obscure his enemy's. He divined that the very weakness of his forces and their previous inaction had put the French off their guard. If he was quick enough, he might be able to overwhelm and expel one of the two armies threatening Portugal before its commander realised its peril. Selecting Soult's army as the smaller, he ordered an immediate concentration at Coimbra on the Mondego river, ninety miles to the north of Lisbon. From here it was little more than four days' march up the coast to Oporto.

Within two days of landing he had made his plans. On May 1st - his fortieth birthday - he rode out of the pine woods into Coimbra amidst cheering crowds and showers of rose petals and flowers.† By the 4th he had assembled in the town 16,000 British and 2400 Portuguese. Only a few fine regiments like the 29th remained of the force which had beaten Junot; the rest of the old Peninsular army had returned to England after Corunna. Most of the men were young soldiers and militiamen hastily drafted into second battalions. Wellesley had resolved, therefore, to keep them under his immediate eye and strike with a compact force at the main body of the French - then estimated at some 13,000 - in Oporto. A subsidiary corps of 6000, mostly Portuguese, under Beresford, was to strike northeastwards to Lamego to guard the army's right flank and if possible,

---

* Leslie, 108-9. See also Fortescue, VII, 134; Schaumann, 155-6; Burgoyne, 42; Tomkinson, 7; Boothby, 259-60.

† Burgoyne, 39.

prevent the enemy's retreat into Spain along the northern bank of the Douro. 4500 British and 7000 Portuguese were left in central Portugal to guard the Tagus against Victor.

As in the old days of India, Wellesley showed his belief that ninety per cent of war was an affair of commissariat and transport. His correspondence at this time was of clothes and horseshoes, guns and nails, ammunition and hammers, above all oxen and ox-wagons and—since his aim involved a coastal advance—barges and fishing-boats. To increase the fighting strength of his army for its dash to the north, he added to five of his eight infantry brigades one of the Portuguese battalions which Major-General Beresford and a handful of British officers and NCOs had been training during the winter. And, remembering the invaluable services of the skirmishing line at Roliça and Vimiero, he attached to every brigade a company of the 60th armed with the new Baker rifle—for the 95th and the two Light Infantry regiments from Shorncliffe were still waiting to sail from England to join him. Most original departure of all, he divided his main striking-force into three what became known as divisions—autonomous both for command and logistics—the strongest consisting of three brigades and the others of two each. This was henceforward to become a permanent feature of British military organisation.

The advance began on May 7th as soon as the transport arrangements were complete. During the next three days the army covered nearly fifty miles. At dawn on the 10th, in the course of a turning movement along the coast, its advanced guard nearly succeeded in surprising and surrounding an enemy force on the heaths near the mouth of the Vouga. On the 11th after a brisk encounter, it drove back 4500 French from the heights above Grijon. By nightfall it had reached the little town of Villa Nova on the wooded banks of the Douro opposite Oporto.

Wellesley had moved with such speed that it was not till that night that Soult realised his danger. Even then he merely contented himself with destroying his pontoon bridge over the Douro. He had escaped the British once in December, when Napoleon's sudden march prevented Moore from surprising him at Saldana. Now, like the Mahrattas behind the Kaitna before Assaye, he felt himself secure. The river, as broad as the Thames at Westminster, was in full flood, and, having removed all vessels to its northern bank, the Duke of Dalmatia could see no reason for hurry. His chief care was for the five miles of open country between Oporto and the sea where he feared that the British, using the fishing-boats gathered for their out-flanking movement over the Vouga, might try to rush the estuary. He took little care of the steep banks above the city; only a madman, he felt, would dream of throwing part of his army over that angry spring flood with an undefeated enemy on the other shore.

But the Marshal had overlooked his adversary's experience of crossing Indian rivers. He had forgotten, too, his Napoleonic bold-ness. At dawn on May 12th, reconnoitring the Douro from the Sierra height east of Villa Nova, Wellesley found that the rocky banks opposite were deserted at a point where the lie of the cliffs and a sudden bend in the river broke the vision of the French sentries in Oporto. Meanwhile his scouts, seeking for boats, had discovered a barber who had not only concealed a small skiff in a thicket but knew where there were four unguarded wine-barges on the northern bank. With the help of a local prior these were ferried over without raising an alarm. At the same time it became known that a scuttled ferry-boat at the village of Barca d'Avintas, four miles above the town, had been only superficially damaged.

Wellesley immediately decided to throw every man he could across the river, relying on the unorthodoxy of his tactics for surprise. He was taking an immense risk, but with the future dependent on a swift victory before Soult could fall back on his re-serves, he meant to put everything to the test. While Major-General Murray with two battalions of the King's German Legion and two squadrons of the 14th Light Dragoons was sent to cross at Barca d'Avintas, thirty men of the Buffs were piled into each of the four barges and hurried over to seize a large, empty seminary on the cliffs near the eastern outskirts of Oporto. The ground in front was care-fully covered by three batteries concealed in the gardens of a con-vent on the Sierra height. It was not till the barges had crossed for the third time, when half the Buffs were established on the northern bank, that the enemy awoke to what was happening.

During the ensuing counter-attack Wellesley's eighteen guns from across the river mowed down every frontal assault on the seminary, while more and more troops, including the 48th and 66th, were ferried over to support the Buffs. When Lieutenant-General Edward Paget, the hero of the Corunna rearguard, was dangerously wounded his place was taken by a thirty-six-year-old Salopian, Major-General Rowland Hill, who continued to hold the position against every attack. Soon after midday Soult, realising the situation was taking an ugly turn, threw in a brigade which had been guarding the southern quayside of the city. Immediately hundreds of Portuguese emerged from the houses and began to paddle boats across to the southern bank. In these Wellesley rushed over the 29th Foot and the Brigade of Guards whom he had concealed in the streets and gardens of Villa Nova. The Guards were to have embarked first, but the Worcesters - resolved that none should go before them - passed back word that they were so packed in the narrow streets that it was impossible to open their ranks.* Crowding into the boats, they landed in any order and stormed into the town. The whole city was by now in the wildest confusion, the inhabitants cheering from the windows, the streets filled with cannon and musket smoke and many of the houses on fire. At this point Soult, seeing the game was up, ordered a general retreat along the eastern road before it became too late. In the town jail Private Hennessy of the 50th - taken at Corunna - cried out to his fellow Portuguese captives at the sound of the firing that it must be the English, for their own bloody countrymen would never make such a fight! A moment later he was beating out the brains of the French sentry as the first detachment of the Buffs battered on the door.†

By that time the battle was over and Wellesley was sitting down to eat the dinner cooked for Soult. The latter, leaving behind him 300 dead, 1500 prisoners and six French and seventy captured Portuguese guns, was in full retreat. His losses would have been still heavier had Murray done his duty, but that officer, encountering the entire French army as he advanced westwards from Avintas, drew aside and let them pass unchallenged. A superb charge by a squadron of the 14th Dragoons redeemed the occasion, but the bulk of the enemy escaped. With only a weak force of cavalry and with his artillery and supply baggage still on the far side of an unbridged river, Wellesley, who had to husband every man of his little army, could not sustain a close pursuit.

At a total cost of twenty-three killed, two missing and ninety-eight wounded, he had defeated the more urgent of the two threats

* Leslie, 111-12.
† Charles Napier, I, 113. See *Peninsular Sketches* 85-95; Ellesmere, 144.

to Lisbon, driven a French Marshal from an almost impregnable position and freed the second city of Portugal. Nor was his triumph yet at an end. For on the following day Soult, still retreating eastwards, learnt that Beresford, advancing across the Douro from Lamego with his Portuguese-British corps, had unexpectedly thrown back Loison's division and occupied the town of Amarante on the only highway left into Spain.

With Wellesley behind him there was only one thing to be done. Soult, who did not bear an Imperial baton for nothing, acted promptly. He left the high road and struck northwards into the wild, tangled Sierra de Santa Catalina. To do so he had to abandon all his remaining transport and guns and expose his men to an ordeal as severe as the retreat to Corunna. For nine days they struggled over perilous mountains and flooded rivers until, after losing everything they possessed, they reached Galicia. By May 19th a quarter of their number had perished or fallen by the way, many suffering a terrible fate at the hands of the revengeful hill-folk. A British commissary saw French soldiers nailed alive to the doors of barns and others trussed and emasculated with their amputated members stuffed into their mouths.*

Having outrun their supplies in a countryside that offered nothing but wine, the British were unable to prevent their escape. For a week in torrential rain they struggled after them, bivouacking on soaking hills and marching fifteen or sixteen miles a day over rocks till their shoes were cut to ribbons. A commissary, entering Ruivaens on May 18th, found the village street full of exhausted troops with pale and famished faces, standing up to their knees in mud. As Wellesley wrote that day to Castlereagh: "If an army throws away all its cannon, equipment and baggage and everything which can strengthen it and enable it to act together as a body, and abandons all those who are entitled to its protection but add to its weight and impede its progress, it must be able to march by roads through which it cannot be followed by any army that has not made the same sacrifices." Hearing that Victor had advanced into eastern Portugal almost to Castelo Branco, he therefore withdrew his

---

* Wellesley, who had been equally horrified by the sight of Portuguese civilians hanging from trees by the roadside, wrote to Soult on May 12th assuring him that he would take the greatest care of the French sick and wounded prisoners in Oporto and that, so far as he was able to prevent it, no one should injure them. *Dispatches.* IV, 304.

victorious troops and reunited his army at Abrantes. In three weeks he had secured his northern flank and done all, or almost all, that he had set out to do, avenging Moore and inflicting on Soult 4000 casualties and the loss of all his guns, stores and transport.*

*   *   *

On May 22nd the Tower guns announced the news of Wellesley's crossing of the Douro. On the day before, having apparently shattered the Austrians in a series of lightning victories and entered their capital in triumph, Napoleon had thrown discretion to the winds and, contemptuously underestimating his enemy, had started to cross the Danube in the presence of 80,000 Austrians. The Archduke Charles had counter-attacked when half the Grand Army was on the far bank and, in two days of desperate fighting round the villages of Aspern and Essling, had inflicted on it more than 20,000 casualties. The battle, which made those of the Peninsula seem almost skirmishes, showed that Napoleon was mortal. With his army in peril, hopes everywhere rose. In Britain, where a formal alliance with Austria had been signed on April 24th, preparations were hurried forward for a great amphibious operation against Antwerp and a landing at the mouth of the Scheldt.

It was in the light of these hopes that Wellesley, having twice in nine months driven the French out of Portugal, prepared in June, 1809, to march into Spain. With the withdrawal of French troops to German battlefields and the temporary elimination of Soult, the war in the Peninsula had taken a turn which even the most optimistic could not have foreseen two months before. The entire French forces in the north-west were out of action or tied down in operations against the patriots of Galicia and Asturias, who in their mountain fortresses were now more than holding their own against the corps of Ney and Mortier. Elsewhere Spaniards were fighting bravely in Catalonia and Aragon, while the defeated armies of Estremadura and La Mancha, with the astonishing resilience of their country, were reforming south of the Tagus and in the Sierra Morena. But the greatest sign of Spain's recovery was the mastery which her rustic guerillas were establishing on every foot of her

---

* Schaumann, 156-7. See also Burgoyne, 41-4; Oman, II, 346-63; Gurwood, 258; Fortescue. VII, 165-7; Weller, 71-85; Munster, 177-8; *Peninsular Sketches*, 85-95; Maxwell, I, 140-4.

soil not actually occupied by the invader. So intense was this spontaneous explosion that the French found themselves unable to obtain the most elementary intelligence of British and Spanish movements and were hard put even to maintain communication between their own armies.

In these circumstances the British Government, wishing to denude northern France and the Dutch coast of defenders, had given Wellesley authority to extend his campaign beyond the Portuguese frontier. In its anxiety to release transports for the coming invasion of Europe it even agreed to make him temporarily independent of England by sending him 8000 additional troops. These included the veteran first battalions of the Light Brigade for which he had expressly asked and the Chestnut Troop of the Royal Horse Artillery. By June, though the bulk of his reinforcements had still to arrive, he had some 25,000 British and German effectives—the Portuguese were still unfit for service beyond their own borders—with another 4500 in hospital. Facing them in Spanish Estremadura between the Tagus and Guadiana were Victor's 23,000, watched - from the south bank of the Guadiana - by a ragged horde of more than 30,000 Spaniards, partly survivors of Medellin and partly new recruits, commanded by General Cuesta. The latter's proposal was that the British and Spanish armies should combine in one of those elaborate encircling movements which since Baylen had been the lodestar and bane of Spanish strategy. Its weakness lay in the assumption that Victor would remain motionless while his destroyers surrounded him.

"The ball is at my foot," Wellesley wrote to the British Minister at Lisbon on June 11th, "I hope I shall have strength enough to give it a good kick." But before he could join in this project he had to overcome immense difficulties. After five weeks' continuous marching and campaigning his troops were in need of shoes and clothing, as well as drastic reorganisation. Above all they needed transport and pack animals to enable them to advance through regions notoriously deficient in fodder and forage. This, in a land in which everything had to be paid for in cash, was not made easier by a serious shortage of specie; owing to the Treasury's currency troubles at home the British Commander for several weeks lacked money to defray even the most essential expenses. This in turn complicated the question of discipline. For the troops—many of them recently recruited from the poorest and most disorderly elements in the community—being unpaid, took to straggling and plundering the countryside. "They are a rabble," Wellesley reported to Castlereagh, "who cannot bear success any more than Sir John Moore's army could bear failure; there is not an outrage of any description which they have not committed. . . . We are an excellent army on parade, an excellent one to fight, but we are worse than an enemy in a country. Take my word for it, either defeat or success would dissolve us."* With so large a proportion of Irish militiamen in the ranks discipline was almost as much a problem on shore as it had been a decade earlier at sea. Its solution was not simplified by recent well-meaning political interference with the powers of provost-marshals or the application of the laws of civil evidence to the procedure of courts-martial - a piece of parliamentary folly against which Wellesley protested bitterly.

Not till June 27th was the army ready to move forward from Abrantes. By that time any chance - if it ever existed - of getting between Victor and Madrid had passed, for, having eaten up Estremadura, the Marshal had crossed to the north bank of the Tagus and withdrawn towards Talavera. Following him with 21,000 British and German troops—4000 more and the Portuguese remained under Beresford to defend Portugal—Wellesley reached Plasencia, the capital of High Estremadura, on July 8th. Here he was only 125 miles from Madrid and within sixty of the Spanish army which was encamped near the Bridge of Almaraz on the Tagus.

Two evenings later, having ridden over from Plasencia, the British general inspected the latter's force by the light of torches and amid strains of medieval music. It was his first glimpse of a Spanish army. It was a strange spectacle: the swarthy faces of the sturdy young peasants in their soiled motley uniforms, the fiery, undisciplined way they handled their arms, the fantastic hats and long Toledo swords of the officers, the shaggy Barbary steeds of the cavalry and the wild movements of their riders. But the most remarkable sight of all was the aged Captain-General of Estremadura precariously held on his horse by two pages. In spite of countless medals, gold lace and traditional trunk hose, he looked in his bobtailed wig more like an elderly German shopkeeper than a soldier.

* To Lord Castlereagh, June 17th 1809.

Nearly seventy years of age, Don Gregoria de la Cuesta had been ridden over three months before by his own cavalry at Medellin and was now forced to travel in a vast, lumbering coach drawn by nine mules. As, however, he never inspected the ground or reconnoitred the enemy, but, like a true countryman of Don Quixote, based his actions on strong imaginative hypotheses that had little or no relation to reality, this constituted no handicap in his eyes. He regarded Wellesley with contempt as a pretender to the art of war.*

On this occasion he scarcely spoke to him, being consumed with a jealous suspicion that he was intriguing with his rivals at Seville to deprive him of his command. The plan of campaign was therefore drawn up in consultation with his Chief of Staff, a very voluble officer of Irish descent named O'Donoju. Crossing to the north bank of the Tagus the Spaniards - 33,000 strong - were to advance eastwards to Oropesa where they were to join forces with the British moving from Plasencia. The two armies were then to advance on Talavera and overwhelm Victor. Their northern flank was to be protected by a small contingent of Portuguese irregulars - the Lusitanian Legion - skirmishing eastwards along the southern slopes of the Sierra de Gredos under an adventurous young Englishman, Colonel Robert Wilson. Other Spanish forces were to remain behind to hold the mountain passes of Baños and Perales to the north-west against any attempt of Soult to move down the Portuguese frontier against Wellesley's base at Plasencia. Meanwhile General Venegas with 23,000 troops of the Army of La Mancha was to emerge from his lair in the Sierra Morena and, driving through Mazanares and Aranjuez towards Madrid, was to prevent the French troops in the neighbourhood of the capital from reinforcing Victor.

But, as Wellesley soon found, strategic plans in Spain were one thing, their execution another. Even for the British army to perform its part in this elaborate converging movement, food and supplies were necessary. And none, despite grandiloquent promises, were forthcoming. Even in the fertile Vera of Plasencia the troops went hungry. Though the march into Spain, with its clean houses, pretty women, clear air and crisp, brisk language, at first delighted

* "A perverse, stupid old blockhead," John Colborne called him. Seaton, 30. See also Schaumann, 174-5, 182; Shand, 37; Castlereagh, VII, 85; Stanhope, 46-7; H. M. C. Bathurst, 99; Leith Hay, I, 168; Stewart, 382-3; Leslie, 471.

them, like Moore's men before them they found it meant short commons. The Supreme Junta was far too busy disputing with its subordinate authorities, the Provincial Juntas of Andalusia and Valencia, to spare any time for provisioning a heretic army. Nor, when it was prevailed upon by an importunate Ambassador to issue requisitions for its wants, would the Estremaduran peasantry honour them. The truth was that for all practical purposes Spain – distracted and poverty-stricken – was without a government. British generals and soldiers found it hard to understand this and in default attributed their sufferings to sloth and treachery.

Part of the trouble arose from the incurable optimism and boast-fulness of the Spanish authorities: part from the inexperience of British commissaries who had still to learn the art of extracting sustenance from a wasted countryside. One irascible divisional commander, driven frantic by the wants of his men and horses, threatened to hang a commissary who, flying for redress to the Commander-in-Chief, was curtly informed: "If General Sherbrooke said he would hang you, he certainly will, so you'd better comply!" Sir Arthur himself complained bitterly of his difficulties. "We really should not be worse off in an enemy's country," he wrote to the British ambassador to the Supreme Junta, "or indeed so ill, as we should there take by force what was required. . . . It is ridiculous to pretend that the country cannot supply our wants. The French army is well fed and the soldiers who are taken in good health and well supplied with bread, of which indeed they left a small magazine behind them. This is a rich country in corn in comparison with Portugal, and yet, during the whole of my operations in that country, we never wanted bread but on one day on the frontiers of Galicia. . . . The Spanish army has plenty of everything, and we alone, upon whom everything depends, are actually starving. I am aware of the important consequences which must attend the step which I shall take in withdrawing from Spain. It is certain that the people of England will never hear of another army entering Spain after they have received the accounts of the treatment we have met with; and it is equally certain that without the assistance, the example and the countenance of a British army, the Spanish armies, however brave, will never effect their object. But no man can see his army perish by want without feeling for them when he knows they have been brought into the country in which this want is felt by his own act and on his own responsibility and not by orders of any superior authority."*

None the less the British commander persisted in his bold course. He knew that a successful march on Madrid while Napoleon was hamstrung on the Danube might have incalculable consequences for Europe. He therefore disregarded the preparations which Soult was reported to be making for a dash over the mountains to Plasencia. With Beresford watching the Portuguese frontier, and the high passes of Baños and Perales securely held by the Spaniards, little harm seemed likely to come of them. Even if the worst came to the worst, the British could always withdraw to the south bank of the Tagus and trust to that broad river to delay the French. Behind him Wellesley knew that the Light Brigade - 3000 of the finest troops in Europe - were hurrying after him from Lisbon by river and road. His victories had given his youthful army faith in him, and he believed in himself. Unlike his fellow generals, he felt no fear of the politicians at home, for he was almost one of them himself.

On July 16th 1809, the British moved forward from Plasencia. The heat was intense and clouds of dust marked the line of columns moving eastwards over the rolling, barren plains. During the next few days the most popular figures in the army were the lemonade vendors - large, muscular men from Valencia of swarthy complexion, bushy eyebrows and gigantic sombreros, who followed the march with barrels slung on their backs, promenading the thirsty lines at every halt with shouts of " *Limonada! Limonada fresca!*"†
By the evening of the 20th the troops had covered the sixty miles to Oropesa. Here on the following day the Spanish general and his staff reviewed them, staring in astonishment at their rigid, silent lines. The British were much less favourably impressed: the sight of the aged Captain-General—"that deformed-looking lump of pride, ignorance and treachery," as Rifleman Costello called him—glaring at them from the cushions of his mule-drawn coach inspired no confidence. Nor did the sprawling march and easy discipline of his followers: the lolling, chattering groups in the uniforms of half a dozen different reigns smoking their cigarillas by the roadside, the

* To John Hookham Frere, July 24th 1809.
† Leslie, 126, 134, 136; Costello, 23; Schaumann, 168, 174-5.

interminable siestas, the air of chaotic antiquity that overhung the Spanish army like a cloud of garlic.

On July 22nd the allies, advancing together, reached Talavera. Here the immense, snow-capped wall of the Sierra de Gredos, with its forest slopes shimmering in the heat, inclined southwards to within a few miles of the Tagus. The Spanish cavalry - blue dragoons followed by green - went clattering through the streets after the French outposts, sending up showers of sparks, while the inhabitants yelled, " *Viva España! Viva España!*" and made cutthroat signs, the priests particularly distinguishing themselves by their fanatically truculent attitudes.* Beyond the town, however, the advance guard came up against strong artillery posted on the banks of the Alberche, and there was a check. But in the July drought the river was only knee-deep,† and a great opportunity opened out before the allies. For so well had the guerrillas done their work of blanketing French communications that Victor's army, outnumbered by two to one, had been taken completely by surprise.

Yet the chance of an overwhelming triumph was lost by Cuesta's obstinacy. All next day, while the hungry British waited impatiently for the word to attack, he resisted Wellesley's entreaties with excuse after excuse. "He contrived," wrote the latter, who had risen at 2 a.m., "to lose the whole of yesterday in which, although his troops were under arms and mine in march, we did nothing owing to the whimsical perverseness of his disposition." Only after the enemy, recovering their senses, had vanished eastwards along the Madrid highroad, did he announce his readiness to advance. Then, though Wellesley pointed out that there were at least 50,000 French in the neighbourhood of the capital who, now that the alarm had been raised, would immediately concentrate, and reminded him that no news had been received of Venegas's advance from the south, he became as reckless as he had formerly been prudent. Nothing would content the old gentleman but to launch his army in headlong pursuit on the capital. All that day the astonished British watched it pour past - a bewildering kaleidoscope of turbulent, half-armed brigands emerging from clouds of dust, regular regiments in blue and scarlet marching in perfect order, of cavalry staff-officers, priests, musicians, women, carts, guns and artillery wagons, and

* Schaumann, 169.
† Anderson, 33

herds of sheep, pigs and cattle.* It looked like the last army of the Middle Ages pouring out to do battle with the French Revolution.

Wellesley, who was still awaiting the carts, supplies and mules promised by the Junta and whose men had been on half rations for the past two days, refused to accompany Cuesta. To advance farther

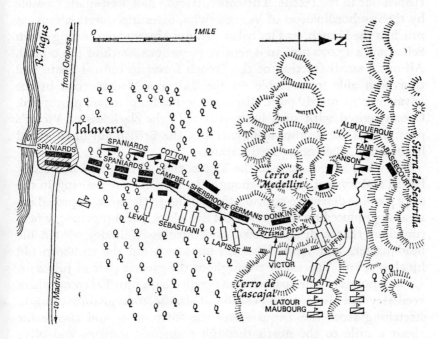

The Battle of Talavera

into so inhospitable a hinterland in the face of a superior enemy without any certainty of being able to feed his troops would have been insanity. The most he would consent to do was to send two infantry brigades and a small force of cavalry beyond the Alberche to maintain contact with his uncontrollable allies. With the rest of his army he took up the best defensive position he could find between the Tagus and the mountains, and there awaited, with such patience as he could, the inevitable return of the Spaniards.

They were not long. On the afternoon of the 26th they came

* In other words, "a Spanish army – ill-commanded, ill-appointed, moderately disciplined and in most respects inefficient." Leith Hay, I, 145-6.

streaming back down the great highway in a confused mob, shouting that the French were after them. Having reached Torrijos, thirty miles to the east, they had come up against a force of 46,000 men formed by the junction of Victor's First and Sebastiani's Fourth Corps with the bulk of the Madrid garrison which King Joseph had rushed out to the rescue. The concentration had been made possible by the insubordination of Venegas who, detesting Cuesta almost as much as the French, had halted at Aranjuez instead of pinning down Sebastiani's 17,000 men in defensive operations south of the capital. All but a small fraction of the French forces in central Spain had thus been able to assemble on the Talavera-Madrid road in the advancing Spaniards' path. Discovering that his plan had miscarried, Cuesta retired with such haste that only the slackness of Victor's pursuit and the prompt deployment of the British advanced guard beyond the Alberche averted a rout.

But when he got back to the Tagus, the old Spaniard perversely halted and refused to cross, though the British were waiting in the only possible defensive position three miles to the west. Repeated entreaties produced no result. Not till five o'clock next morning when, conscious that a disaster faced both armies, Wellesley visited his headquarters and went down on his knees, did the stubborn old hidalgo relent. Thereafter throughout the greater part of July 27th - a very hot day - the Spanish army trailed back into Talavera, where Wellesley had allotted it a position of almost impregnable strength, stretching from the Tagus along the town walls and thence for about a mile to the north through embanked gardens and olive groves. Here its 32,000 men were able to dispose themselves in triple lines with powerful reserves of cavalry in support.

It was otherwise with the British, whose lines extended for a farther two miles to the north where the plain ended in a stony ravine at the foot of the Sierra de Segurilla. Their right and centre were in open country without shade or cover, their left on a steep conical hill called the Cerro de Medellin which, climbing gradually up a scrubby, rolling ridge from the Talavera plain, fell precipitously into the narrow mountain valley to the north. To hold this against 46,000 veteran troops—for the Spaniards, being incapable of manoeuvre, could be easily contained—Wellesley had little more than 17,000 British and 3000 Germans. Even when drawn up only two deep, they barely covered the ground. With the exception of the

29th and 48th - the Worcesters and Northamptons - few were seasoned troops, and the artillery - thirty field pieces mostly of light calibre - were hopelessly overweighted by the enemy's eighty guns.

Even before the Spaniards reached the security of their lines at Talavera trouble began. The brigades which had been sent forward to cover their retreat, falling back through the olive groves to the west of the Alberche, were almost overwhelmed by the speed of Victor's advance. Wellesley himself, making a survey from the top of a tower as he supervised the withdrawal of his young troops, only escaped capture by a last-minute dash down the stairs to his waiting horse in the courtyard below. The situation was restored by a counter-attack by the 45th and some German companies of the 60th, who both displayed admirable steadiness. But this preliminary rescue operation cost the British nearly 500 men whom they could ill afford.

The situation for the British commander could hardly have been more uncomfortable. His men were half starving, and behind them lay a wasted and barren countryside. Retreat in the presence of the enemy's immense strength in cavalry was out of the question for, once the Spaniards abandoned the shelter of the walls and ditches of Talavera, pandemonium would break out on the single highway to the west. The only hope was to fight it out. If the French chose to attack—and there was every sign that they meant to—only the courage and coolness of the fighting man could avert disaster. Scarcely since the morning of Agincourt had a British army been in a more perilous position.

So certain was Victor of his prey that he did not even wait till next day. As soon as it was dark, without troubling to consult Joseph and his Chief of Staff, Marshal Jourdan, he launched exploratory attacks against the British. After a preliminary cavalry demonstration in front of Talavera - which provoked a tremendous discharge of musketry along the entire Spanish line and the instantaneous flight of four Spanish regiments, terrified by the noise they had made - he attempted to seize Wellesley's two main strong-points. That nearest the allied centre, a formidable redoubt on a knoll just clear of the olive groves, was too stoutly held by Colonel Donkin's brigade for the French to be able to make any impression. But farther north, where, owing to inadequate staff work and the confused retirement of the afternoon, the defenders' lines were still undefined, a division under General Ruffin penetrated through the piquets of the King's German Legion to the top of the Cerro de Medellin. Major-General Rowland Hill, the commander of the division appointed to hold the height on the morrow, was returning from Talavera, where he had been dining, when he was attracted by the sound of firing. Remarking to his brigade-major that he supposed it was the old Buffs making some blunder as usual, he was half-way to the summit when he found a Frenchman's hand on his bridle. Setting spurs to his horse—his companion was shot dead at his side—he collected the 29th and led it in line up the hill to drive the enemy out before they could consolidate. Losing all cohesion in the darkness, the latter, though greatly outnumbering the Worcesters, were unable to withstand their well-directed volleys and, after half an hour's fighting, were driven back into their own lines.

No further attempt was made against the British that night. In the stillness, nervous sentries could hear the French officers going their rounds on the opposite hillside, while the sound of wheels and cracking whips and the light of torches showed where cannon were being placed in preparation for the morrow. Wellesley, who scarcely dared to delegate anything to his inexperienced Staff, spent most of the night supervising the movement of artillery which he had now ordered to the top of the Cerro de Medellin. That another attempt would be made on the hill he could not doubt, for its capture would spell his army's doom. The question in his own and every other mind was would his men hold.

Few who witnessed it ever forgot the dawn of July 28th 1809, as it rose over the French lines. It was like the morning of St Crispin four hundred years before. As it grew light more than 40,000 troops could be seen in serried columns beyond the Portina brook, which flowed from north to south between the rival armies. The greatest concentration was on the sloping hillside to the east of the Cerro de Medellin. In front hundreds of *tirailleurs* were awaiting the signal to advance. Farther back on the skyline regiment after regiment of cavalry was drawn up in gleaming casque and multi-coloured uniform. Only opposite the thirty thousand Spaniards around Talavera was the ground comparatively deserted. Every man in the British army could see where the attack would fall. As the officers rode along the lines—stretching two-deep like a scarlet snake over the rolling hills and plain—they noticed how unwontedly pale and silent their men were.*

Shortly after daybreak the smoke of a gun curling in the air and the report of a single cannon gave the signal for the attack. Immediately a tremendous cannonade broke from twenty-four pieces of artillery opposite the British left. When the shot tore gaps in the ranks, Wellesley made the six battalions holding the Cerro de Medellin withdraw beyond the brow of the hill and lie down with their arms in their hands. At the same time the bugles sounded to call in the skirmishers before they became submerged by the advancing French; true to their training, however, they fell back slowly with the regularity of a field-day so that General Hill—startled for once out of his habitual sobriety of speech—called out, "Damn their filing, let them come in anyhow!" As the earth shook with the thunder of guns and the shot whizzed and whistled overhead, the Commander-in-Chief stood on the hill wondering if his men could take it.†

He need have had no fears. As the French neared the summit with loud shouts Hill's battalions rose as one man, doubled forward in perfect formation and taking the time from their officers, poured - in succession of platoons - volley after volley of rolling musketry into the surprised columns. Then Sir Arthur called to them to charge, and, as the 29th and 48th rushed forward, "a wall of stout hearts and bristling steel," the triumphant cries of " *Vive l'Empereur!*" changed to "*Sauve qui peut!*" The victors of Austerlitz had again underestimated the discipline and fire-power of the British line. For half an hour the struggle swayed down the steep eastern slope, the British firing, running, and cheering till the last Frenchman had been driven across the Portina brook, leaving the hillside covered with dead and dying. By eight o'clock in the morning it was all over.

By now the sun was high in the sky and the day was growing hot. The gunfire died away, and burial parties from both sides and men filling their canteens mingled, fraternising, in the stagnant pools of the Portina brook. Having proved their manhood, the young British soldiers felt a curious elation, and their hearts warmed towards the famous warriors they had repelled. Many shook hands and conversed by signs: a lieutenant of the 29th handed a French officer two

* Schaumann, 184; Munster, 505; Leslie, 147; Oman, II, 521.
† Leith Hay, I, 151-2; Leslie, 147-8; Schaumann, 185; Oman, II, 523.

crosses of the Legion of Honour which he had taken from bodies on the hillside. Among the rocks of the Sierra de Segurilla half a mile to the north desultory sharpshooting broke out between French *triailleurs* and some Spaniards of Basscourt's reserve division which Wellesley, fearful of an infiltration round his left, had hastily borrowed from Cuesta. But elsewhere almost complete peace had fallen on the battlefield.

Meanwhile the French generals were in acrimonious consultation on the summit of the Cerro de Cascajal facing the scene of the late encounter. Jourdan, who had opposed the attack from the start, could see no point in further fighting. A few weeks before, orders had come from Napoleon to withdraw Ney's and Mortier's corps from the Galician and Asturian mountains and concentrate them under Soult for a grand new offensive against Portugal with the aim of "beating, hunting down and casting the British army into the sea." The Emperor, writing from the Danube, had been unable to foresee that when his orders arrived the British would themselves be marching on Madrid, but his concentration of 50,000 men in Salamanca province offered a splendid opportunity for striking at Wellesley's rear. Accordingly on July 22nd instructions had been sent to Soult to march with all speed through the pass of Baños on Plasencia. There seemed no point in wasting good troops in fruitless frontal attacks when Wellesley's ultimate encirclement and destruction was certain. But Victor – like all the Revolutionary leaders a passionate egotist – wanted all the triumph for himself and was in no mood to wait for his fellow Marshals. The British, he insisted, were still outnumbered by two to one, and the hour for annihilating the Emperor's principal enemy had arrived. With threats to report any cowardice to Napoleon, he insisted that the attack should be renewed.

Early in the afternoon a general resumption of the bombardment showed that he had carried his point. In the town of Talavera a few faint-hearted Spaniards, who did not know the courage and endurance of the English, dashed headlong through the streets and out to the west along the Oropesa road.* There, twenty miles away in insufferable heat, the three finest regiments in the British Line – the 95th, 52nd and 43rd, whom Moore had trained at Shorncliffe – were marching under "Black Bob" Craufurd as even they had never

* Schaumann, 189.

marched before, pressing forward at their light infantryman's quick pace through the stifling dust. Every man carried, besides rifle and ramrod, eighty rounds of ball and a pack weighing at least forty pounds. Yet though few had eaten anything that day but a crust of mouldy bread, and the heat was so great that more than one rifleman fell dead as he marched, not a man voluntarily left the column. For far ahead the men could hear the rumble of the guns, and, from the lips of cowards flowing past them into the west, the tale of a British army fighting against overwhelming odds.*

* * *

This time the attack was general and directed against almost the entire British line. It was preceded by a short but intensive bombardment by the eighty guns of the French 1st and 4th corps which overwhelmed, though they did not silence, the thirty British and six Spanish guns opposed to them. On the British right, close to the junction of the allied armies, Major-General Campbell's 4th Division - stoutly supported by some neighbouring Spanish cavalry - not only repelled by their superior musketry the assaults of General Laval's Dutch and German troops but in the course of a counterattack captured seventeen guns. The feature of the fighting was the steadiness with which Campbell controlled his men and prevented them from going too far in their success.

In the open ground farther north Lieutenant-General Sherbrooke's 1st Division of Guards and Hanoverians was less skilfully handled. Here, following a more prolonged bombardment, two strong divisions led by Generals Sebastiani and Lapisse moved forward in column at about three o'clock against the British centre. Waiting in the usual extended two-deep line, deployed in crescents so as to enfilade each of the advancing French columns, Sherbrooke's men held their fire till the leading files of the enemy columns were within fifty yards and then followed up their devastating volleys with bayonet charges. The French were flung back in confusion, but the Guards and Germans, losing cohesion in their advance, pursued them beyond the Portina brook and were shattered in their turn by the advancing waves of the enemy's second columns which their

* Leith Hay, I, 137; Simmons, 15-16, 32; Costello, 19-20; Smith, I, 18-19; Leach, 81; Leslie, 155-6; George Napier, 108-9.

commanding officers had forgotten. In the ensuing rout the Hanoverians lost their general and half their strength and the Guards 611
out of 2000 men. Within twenty minutes a great breach had been
made in the weakest part of the line, with 15,000 French infantry and
7000 waiting cavalry about to drive through it in triumph.

At this moment the battle was saved by Wellesley's quickness of
thought and action. Anticipating the disaster about to befall the advancing Guards and Hanoverians, as they approached in strung-out
disorder the dense French supporting columns, he filled the fatal
gap in the British line behind them by ordering Major-General
MacKenzie's reserve brigade to advance obliquely northwards so as
to form, in the nick of time, a stop-gap. Three regiments – the 24th,
31st and 45th – numbering little more than 2000, plugged the hole
and held up forces seven times as numerous while the Guards and
Germans re-formed behind them. Warwicks, Huntingdons and
Nottinghamshires—many of them wearing the accoutrements of
the militia regiments from which they had been hastily drafted a
few months before—fought with the steadiness of veterans. Mac-
Kenzie and a third of his men fell, but the line held. An unexpected
charge by the 14th Light Dragoons, led by Major-General Stapleton
Cotton, who had last ridden over the French as a boy of sixteen at
Le Cateau fifteen years before, halted one column at a decisive
moment. Meanwhile, keeping a firm grip on the battle, Wellesley
brought down from the Cerro de Medellin the 48th Foot and
launched it against the advancing enemy's right flank. As the steady
volleys of the Northamptons raked the crowded columns, the *élan*
of the French began to ebb. Lapisse fell at the head of his men, and
the Guards and Germans returned cheering to the fight. The British
centre was saved.*

Scarcely had the great shout of triumph from the tired, smoke-
grimed victors died away when a new scene opened to the north of
the Cerro de Medellin. Here, though Victor inexplicably failed to
renew his frontal attack on the hill—so enabling Wellesley to reinforce his centre with the 45th at the crucial moment—the divisions
of Ruffin and Villatte, following the winding course of the Portina
brook, had pressed up the ravine between battle-scarred slopes and
the rocky Sierra de Segurilla. Since the new movement threatened to
envelop the British left, the Commander-in-Chief, who, having

* Oman, II, 537-43; Fortescue, VII, 244-51; Munster, 231; Leith Hay, I, 156-8.

restored his broken centre, had resumed his commanding station on the Cerro de Medellin, gave orders to Brigadier Anson's cavalry brigade, waiting below, to mount and clear the valley.

As the trumpeters sounded the charge and the horsemen, comprising the British 23rd Light Dragoons and the 1st Hussars of the King's German Legion, broke into a gallop, a second cheer went up from the troops watching the arena from the heights above the valley. Then, as that cloud of valiant, shouting dust moved forward towards the French, there was a fatal check. A deep cleft concealed by long grass ran right across the path of the charging squadrons. The Dragoons, who were leading at the gallop, had no time to draw up; many, riding knee to knee, vanished into the gully or were carried to the rear by their frightened horses. But the survivors re-formed on the far side of the ravine and resumed the charge. Galloping out of hand, as so often with British cavalry, right up to the French who had hastily formed squares, they swept past them and, though one out of every two troopers fell, routed a regiment of Chasseurs beyond. Meanwhile Spanish horse artillery, unlimbering just out of shot of the now unsupported French squares, began to fire into their ranks. Other British and Spanish cavalry advancing down the valley under Brigadier-General Fane and the Duke of Albuquerque prevented the French infantry from extending, while the guns on the Cerro de Medellin joined in the massacre from above.

By this time all but 5000 of the French had been engaged. The afternoon was growing late, and, ignoring Victor's protests, King Joseph determined to call off the battle. News had reached him that Venegas was advancing from the south on the capital, and he dared not throw in his last reserves with Cuesta's army still unused on his flank. Had the latter been capable of manœuvre and Wellesley had dared to move it from its entrenched position to cut the road to Toledo and Madrid, the French could have faced complete disaster. Soon afterwards they began to fall back along the entire front, though their guns continued firing till nightfall. As it grew dark the parched grass on the slopes of the Cerro de Medellin caught fire, and hundreds of helpless wounded were engulfed in the flames. All night their cries continued while the moon rose dimly over the battlefield and exhausted comrades slept where they had stood.

To the inexpressible relief of the British the attack was not renewed on the 29th. Shortly after dawn drums and bugles were heard from the west, and the Light Brigade, after covering forty-three miles in twenty-two hours, marched on to the charred battlefield, with the Chestnut Troop trotting in its midst. Around its path lay thousands of dead and dying, piled in stiff or still faintly stirring hillocks of soiled scarlet and blue amidst dismounted guns and shattered ammunition wagons, broken horse-trappings and blood-stained shakos. But, as the bugle-horns rang out, the survivors broke into cheers. For, though more than 5000 of their comrades - or a quarter of their strength - had fallen, they knew at last that the battle was theirs. The French, leaving behind seventeen guns and 7000 dead and wounded, were in full retreat to the east. Then, as there was no longer any need to stand to arms, the regiments marched down from the Cerro de Medellin to encamp in the olive grove at its base, bearing their tattered, shot-ridden colours with them.*

*   *   *

"Never was there such a murderous battle," Wellesley told his brother. He himself, though miraculously unhurt, was hit by a spent bullet and his coat was shot through, while every member of his staff was either wounded or unhorsed. "Our loss has been very great, that of the enemy larger," he wrote on the morrow of the victory. "We had about two to one against us; fearful odds; but we maintained our positions, and gave the enemy a terrible beating."† Three times in eleven months - at Vimiero, the passage of the Douro, and now at Talavera - he had given the lie to the popular belief, deeply founded after fifteen years of Revolutionary and Napoleonic victories, that the French were invincible and that British generals were designed by Providence for losing battles. "Now my dear Augustus," an English lady wrote to her son in Stockholm on August 16th, when the tidings of Talavera reached London, "walk about the streets with looks of pride and exultation, bear high your head and glory in being a Briton!"

Yet within a few weeks all was again in the dust. Austria - her army shattered at Wagram - had made peace, the British expedition to the mouth of the Scheldt on which such high hopes had been

---

* For detailed accounts of Talavera see Oman, II, 500-61; Fortescue, VII, 223-61; Weller, 91-107; Longford, 190-7; Maxwell, I, 159-66.

† To John Charles Villiers, July 29th 1819.

built, had failed disastrously, and the Kentish ports were filled with pale-faced ghosts from fever-haunted Walcheren. At Hythe, Sir John Moore's camp became a hospital, and the cemetery was piled high with the graves of the riflemen he had trained.*

Twice that year had a British army come home in such a plight. "Everything goes so ill," wrote the lady who had bidden her son rejoice over news of Talavera, "that I have no courage to write: I don't know what we are to look or hope for." For even the battle which, in their exultation at their soldiers' courage, the people of England had hailed as the successor of Agincourt and Crecy, had proved Pyrrhic and fruitless. The British army in Spain was starving and in retreat, its wounded – deserted by the Spaniards – had fallen into the hands of the enemy, and the dashing Wellesley, instead of marching into Madrid, was in danger of encirclement. Far from proving the second Marlborough that some had predicted, he had ruined everything, it was said, by his recklessness. Hitherto one of the luckiest men in military history, Captain Gomm – the future Field-Marshal – assured his aunt, he seemed likely to set the whole country in mourning. "We have defeat and miscarriage everywhere," wrote Pitt's one-time colleague, William Windham.†

For the aftermath of Talavera had proved a tragically unhappy one. A sickening stench hung over the battlefield, and, though the exhausted troops tried to bury the swollen corpses, the task was beyond their powers and they were reduced to burning them in piles. Thousands of wounded, driven almost frantic by the flies and heat, had to be rescued from Spanish plunderers, who swarmed everywhere stripping their allies and murdering their foes. In Talavera all the churches and convents were turned into hospitals, but the authorities were unable to cope with the demand. Cries for help, and above all for water, sounded from every side; one passer-by saw hundreds of amputated legs and arms being flung out of the windows of the town.‡

Pursuit for the moment was out of the question. Of the four British divisions which had taken part in the battle, only the smallest – Campbell's – was in a state to fight again without rest and regroup-

---

* The second battalions of the 43rd, 52nd and 95th went to Walcheren while the first battalions had gone to Spain.
† Windham, II, 354-5; Gomm, 137; Granville, II, 345; *Marlay Letters*, 126.
‡ Schaumann, 193-4; Leith Hay, I, 166-7; Smith, I, 19; Simmons, 32.

ing. Hill's had lost a quarter of its strength, MacKenzie's a third and Sherbrooke's nearly two-fifths. Rations, cut down by half on the army's arrival at Talavera, were now reduced to a third. To crown all, the Spanish Commander-in-Chief's jealousy of Wellesley had become ungovernable. "I should get the better of everything," the latter wrote to Castlereagh, "if I could manage General Cuesta, but his temper and disposition are so bad that this is impossible."

Fortunately the French, after their unwonted mauling, assumed the British to be stronger than they were and continued to withdraw eastwards. A curious game of shadows ensued, both sides misconceiving the other's position. Joseph was principally concerned for his capital: troops of Venegas's army had at last appeared before Toledo, occupied Aranjuez and pushed northwards along the main Andalusian road to within twenty miles of Madrid. He naturally assumed that they were acting in conjunction with Wellesley and Cuesta and that a joint advance on the city was imminent. Sending his brother, the Emperor (of whom, like all his Marshals, he was terrified) a cock-and-bull report about having overwhelmed the English before breaking off the fight to repel Venegas, he left Victor with 18,000 men behind the Alberche to watch the Allies and hurried eastwards to Illescas to save his capital. No sooner had he gone than Victor became equally alarmed at a threat from the north-west, where Sir Robert Wilson, pushing on with his ragged Lusitanian Legion beyond the head waters of the Tietar, had reached Escalona on the upper Alberche. Fearful of being cut off from Madrid, the Marshal hastily withdrew to Santa Cruz, where his retreat on the capital was only stopped by Joseph's imperative orders.

Meanwhile Wellesley and Cuesta were equally in the dark, though their misapprehension took the form not so much of mistaking shadows for dangers as of assuming dangers to be shadows. In the hope that the elusive Venegas had at last drawn off part of Joseph's army, they proposed to move forward at the beginning of August. The British commander, however, made two reservations: that the carts and wagons promised him should arrive first, and that no serious attack should develop from the north against his communications with Portugal. Up to the middle of July he had had little fear of Soult, whom he supposed to have been too badly mauled at Oporto for further fighting. At Talavera, however, he learnt that the French 5th and 6th Corps under Mortier and Ney had been withdrawn from the northern coastal provinces and had appeared in the valley of the upper Douro. Yet as late as July 30th he refused to believe that the three French Marshals could together muster more than 20,000 men for a drive on Plasencia.

But on the evening of August 1st, while still waiting for transport and supplies, Wellesley received alarming tidings. A strong French force had entered Bejar, fifty miles north-east of Plasencia, and had driven back the Spaniards from the Pass of Baños. It then transpired that, despite Cuesta's assurances, the force detailed to hold the pass was less than three thousand. With Plasencia on the main road to Portugal thus open to the enemy and several hundred British lying wounded in the town, Wellesley had no choice but to turn back and deal with the intruder before more serious damage was done. After a stormy conference with Cuesta in which he refused to divide his army, he set off at dawn on August 3rd, leaving the Spaniards to guard his 4000 wounded at Talavera. His effectives, including the Light Brigade, now numbered only 18,000.

When that afternoon he reached Oropesa he learnt from a captured dispatch, hastily forwarded by Cuesta, that Soult was advancing across his rear, not with 15,000 troops as he had supposed, but with nearly 50,000. Driving south from Salamanca with three *corps d'armée*, the Marshal had entered Plasencia on August 2nd and was now hastening eastwards to seize the vital Tagus crossings at Almaraz and Arzobispo on which the British army depended for its alternative communications with Lisbon through the Guadiana valley and Badajoz. Already he was too near the Almaraz crossing for Wellesley to have any hope of reaching its northern end without fighting on the way. Indeed, that very evening British and French cavalry patrols were in action at Naval Moral, twenty miles west of Oropesa.

There was only one thing to do: to cross to the south bank of the Tagus by the bridge of Arzobispo and march with all speed over the mountains to secure the south side of the broken bridge and ford at Almaraz while there was still time, leaving Cuesta to follow as best he could. Already on receipt of the news the old gentleman had started for Oropesa, a crossing at Talavera being out of the question since the roads south of it were impassable for artillery. Early next day the Spaniards poured into the little town to the fury of the British, who, ignorant of the reason for their retreat, imagined that they had abandoned their wounded comrades at Talavera out of cowardice. Many of these came limping after the flying Spanish army in every state of misery: the rest were left to the mercy of the French or died by the wayside for want of transport.

At this moment of crisis, possibly the gravest in Wellesley's career, Cuesta announced his intention of remaining where he was and fighting. The British commander immediately had it out with the old man. If with a broad river and a single bridge in his rear he chose to expose the last principal army of Spain to the attack of nearly 100,000 Frenchmen—for a junction of Soult's and Joseph's forces now appeared imminent—he could not be prevented. But, whatever happened, the British were going to cross by the bridge at Arzobispo at once. Having announced his resolution, Wellesley put it into execution without losing a moment. That afternoon - August 4th - as in the insufferable heat a motley, cursing crowd of soldiers, muleteers, artillery, baggage, carts piled with wounded, mules, donkeys and screeching bullock carts poured over the bridge, a little group of field officers stood on a hill near Oropesa scanning the plain through their telescopes. Presently their leader pointed to a distant cloud of dust beginning to rise over the western hills. It was Soult's advance guard. "Mount," ordered Sir Arthur Wellesley, and the cortège cantered off southwards towards the bridge to rejoin the retreating army.*

For the next two days the British hurried westwards across the wilderness of rugged and waterless hills that lay to the south of the Tagus. The dust was suffocating and the heat beyond conception. At points the track, such as it was, ran along the side of precipices and the guns had to be dragged up by hand. Yet none was lost; the men, who were without bread, grumbled furiously, but their officers found that they had only to put on a soothing and encouraging expression to turn their miseries to jest. Food was the main difficulty: but for plundering the few living things found on the way, the whole army would have perished.

By nightfall on August 7th the main British body had reached the mountains around Deleytosa, twenty miles south of Almaraz. Here on the previous day the Marquis del Reino's troops guarding the crossing had been joined by the Light Brigade and the 87th and 88th Foot after a fifteen hours' march over waterless hills. They arrived

*Schaumann, 198-9; Oman, II, 583.

just in time to prevent Ney from forcing the river. For the next fortnight they remained guarding the solitary ford, camping by day on a wooded hill and marching down each night to bivouac by the water's edge. They lived on wild honey, which caused dysentery, and dough cakes made by pounding coarse corn from the fields between stones. Dough Boy or Doby Hill, as they called it, long lived in the memory of the Light Brigade as a kind of nightmare. A few remembered its picturesque beauty, but to the majority the only impression was one of aching hunger, heat, mosquitoes and noisome exhalations from the rotting vegetation in the river flats.

The rest of the army, camping beside the cork and oak forests at Jaraicejo a day's march away, fared little better. The drought was so intense that the men's eyelids smarted perpetually, their lips split and the skin peeled off their faces. Every few days the grass would break into flames, making enormous fires which spread for miles over the rolling terrain like gigantic serpents. The bivouacs swarmed with scorpions, snakes, mosquitoes and enormous flies, and the pools were full of leeches which clung to the nostrils of the horses and the mouths of the men. The countryside, already plundered by Victor earlier in the year, was destitute of almost every necessity; the British stores at Plasencia had fallen into the hands of the enemy, and those at Abrantes were too far away. The men, famished and discouraged, grumbled bitterly at their officers, and the officers at their commander. Many spoke gloomily of Verdun and a French prison; Sir Arthur, it was said, could fight but could not manœuvre.[*] He himself wrote to his brother, Lord Wellesley, who had just relieved Frere as Ambassador at Seville, that the army would have to leave Spain if its present treatment continued. "No troops can serve to any good purpose unless they are regularly fed, and it is an error to suppose that a Spaniard or a man or animal of any country can make an exertion without food." "With the army which a fortnight ago beat double their numbers," he added in a third letter written to his brother that day, "I should now hesitate to meet a French corps of half their strength."

Yet, so long as he could, Wellesley clung to his position. For not only did it bar the southward road across the Tagus to Seville and Cadiz, but it lay on the flank of any westward advance against

---

[*] "We were then young soldiers in the art of war!" Tomkinson, 214. See also Leith Hay, I, 174, 177-8; Schaumann, 204-5; Oman, II, 600-5; Fortescue, VII, 276-7, 279.

Beresford and Portugal. Cuesta, after losing half his rearguard at Arzobispo and thirty guns—including most of those captured by the British at Talavera—had retired into the hills on the south bank and was now holding an almost impregnable position at Mesa de Ibor, a few miles to the west of Jaraicejo. Meanwhile Joseph had withdrawn eastwards in search of Venegas, while Ney's corps had had to hurry back to the north to deal with an eruption of the Asturian and Galician patriots into the plain of Leon. As for Soult, in the barren lands between the Tagus and the Vera de Plasencia his men were growing as hungry as Wellesley's. Sooner or later, they, too, would have to retreat.

But there was a limit to what flesh and blood could bear, and by the middle of August the British army had reached it. Hunger, dysentery and fever had reduced men and horses to bundles of bones, and, according to Commissary Schaumann, the soldiers' wives – usually decently clad and faithful to their husbands - went round on starved donkeys offering themselves to anyone for half a loaf.* After it became known that Venegas, as dilatory when threatened by disaster as when proffered victory, had been routed on August 11th at Almonacid, there ceased to be any object in the British remaining in the Spanish hinterland. There was no means of doing so either. "I must either move into Portugal where I know I shall be supplied," Wellesley informed General Eguia, Cuesta's deputy—for the old man had had a paralytic stroke—"or I must make up my mind to lose my army."

On August 21st, to their inexpressible relief, the troops set off to march by Trujillo and Merida to the fortress of Badajoz in the Guadiana valley, a hundred and thirty miles to the south-west. Half-starved and fever-stricken, they arrived on September 3rd and entered cantonments along the Portuguese frontier. Here they could be supplied from Elvas and Lisbon. To Spanish complaints that they were betraying Spain and laying Andalusia open to invasion, Wellesley replied that the responsibility lay with those who had been acquainted with their wants and made no attempt to relieve them. In any case, with the winter approaching, Seville was almost as well secured by his new position on the French flank as it had been by his presence on the direct road south of the Tagus. With this object he agreed to remain for the time being in the Guadiana valley - at

* Schaumann, 205.

that season notoriously unhealthy - thus exposing his men to new ravages of typhus and malaria. But beyond that, protest though the Junta might, he would not go. Nothing would induce him to co-operate again with Spanish generals or rely any longer on Spanish promises for food. He had lost a third of his army by doing so, and it was enough.*

* Of the Spaniards he wrote at the time to his brother, William. "The Spanish troops will not fight; they are indisciplined, they have no officers, no provisions, no magazines, no means of any description. If we enter into a co-operation with them the burthen of the war must fall upon us, and with us will rest the disgrace of its certain and unavoidable failure. This is not an exaggerated picture. I was slow as every man is to believe all the bad I had heard of the Spaniards, but I assure you there is nothing so bad in the shape of troops, and nothing so inefficient as the enthusiasm of which such a boast is made and which such pains are taken to excite and keep up. At the same time the Spaniards really detest the French, and I believe it will be scarcely possible for Bonaparte to establish a Government in Spain." To the Hon William Wellesley-Pole, August 29th 1809, Wellesley-Pole, 22.

Chapter Seven

THE MAKING OF AN ARMY

"They may do as they please. I shall not give up the game here
as long as it can be played."

WELLINGTON

AFTER Wagram the whole Continent, from the Urals to the Atlantic, and from the North Cape to the Pyrenees, was at peace under the shadow of the Eagles. But beyond that shadow were still the sea and the sierras. Nearly a hundred and fifty British ships of the line, two hundred frigates and five hundred sloops and brigs, manned by 130,000 seamen and marines, kept watch round the long European coastline. In the Mediterranean one of the largest fleets England had ever maintained in those waters exerted an invisible influence on every State round its shores. Driven from the Continent, the cautious, tenuous, ubiquitous diplomacy of England still sent out its disturbing waves from a three-decker's tilting quarter-deck.

The most awful quality of that blockade was its persistence. In his attempts to defeat it Napoleon imposed intense suffering on the peoples of Europe. Legitimate trade became paralysed. The principal comforts of life were unobtainable by all but the richest; pathetic attempts were made to manufacture coffee out of dried carrots and sunflower seeds, and tobacco out of gooseberry leaves and cabbages. Evasion was met by ruthless repression. "Have the crew and gear of the fishing boat which communicates with the English seized at once," Napoleon ordered, "make the skipper speak! If he should seem to hesitate squeeze his thumbs in the hammer of a musket." When his brother, Louis, struggling to avert the ruin of the little mercantile nation he had been sent to rule, petitioned for some relaxation of the regulations, he was made to abdicate and Holland was incorporated in France. The whole of Europe, a Papal nuncio reported, had become a prison house.[*]

* Jerningham, I, 310.

Little by little in his resolve to smash the English and slake his insatiable will, Napoleon was alienating those very forces of natural instinct and inclination which had swept him on the surge of revolution to power. Outside the favoured ranks of the Grand Army *la volonté générale* was ceasing to sustain him. Those whom he sought to unite in a single uniform European State, free of racial feeling and prejudice, he drove through poverty and repression back on ancient loyalties and separatist feelings. His ultimate legacy to the Continent he dominated was not unity but a romantic and intensely dangerous nationalism.

*   *   *

Nowhere was the reaction of that disconcerting, centrifugal force so swift and sure as in Spain. Even the most crushing French victories were unable to stem it. After the disaster of Almonacid in the autumn of 1809 and the retreat of the British army to the borders of Portugal, the Supreme Junta, desperate to retrieve its credit, had refused to remain on the defensive in the passes of the Sierra Morena. Instead, contrary to every canon of strategy and common sense, it had launched a new offensive from the mountains of the south, west and north-west. Advancing against a more numerous and infinitely more efficient enemy with the advantage of interior lines, the ragged Spanish armies, after a brief, initial success at Tamames near Salamanca, suffered the inevitable consequence of such folly. On November 19th, Areizaga, the rash and inexperienced general whom the Junta in a desperate gamble had appointed to command the joint armies of Andalusia and Estremadura in place of Cuesta, was routed by Soult at Ocaña. Fifty of his sixty guns were taken and half his 50,000 men killed or taken prisoner.

Yet the very magnitude of the victory only increased Joseph's difficulties. It tempted him to play for stakes beyond his means. Unable in the barren uplands of Castile to raise revenue to support his Court and denied aid by a brother who believed in making war pay for itself, the titular King of Spain coveted above all things the rich valleys of Andalusia. So long as the Spaniards held the Sierra Morena in force he dared not, with the British undefeated on his flank, risk a second Baylen by advancing through the passes. But now, with the last army of Spain scattered and the British withdrawing in disgust into Portugal, the road to the south was open.

The only obstacle remaining was Napoleon who had ordered that, until the British army had been expelled from the Peninsula, other objectives must take second place. But his brother's plight for money was so excruciating and his clamour so pitiful that the Emperor for once followed the military line of least political resistance and let him have his way. He did not actually grant him permission to invade Andalusia but, absorbed in the preparations for his own divorce and approaching wedding to the defeated Emperor of Austria's daughter, he refrained from answering his letters. Interpreting his silence as consent, Joseph at the beginning of January, 1810, left Madrid at the head of his army for the south.

In this he was abetted by Soult, who had succeeded Jourdan as Chief of Staff. The Marshal knew as well as his master that no new commitments ought to be undertaken in the Peninsula until the hard core of British resistance had been broken. But the art treasures of the Andalusian monasteries made an irresistible appeal to his princely tastes. He also had secret hopes of a Spanish throne. He therefore collected all the troops who could be spared from the north and interior and poured them through the passes of the Sierra Morena, brushing aside the remnants of Areizaga's army. Jaen fell on January 23rd, Cordoba on the 24th and Seville on February 1st. Five days later Sebastiani, driving far to the south, reached the Mediterranean at Malaga.

Yet the final prize eluded the French. Immediately the Andalusian capital had fallen Victor set out for Cadiz. It looked as though nothing could save the port and the Spanish fleet. But the Duke of Albuquerque, hurrying south from Medellin, threw his ragged army into the town just in time. Meanwhile the local Junta appealed to the British. Their commander immediately sent every man he could spare. By the end of March 9000 British and Portuguese under Sir Thomas Graham and 18,000 Spanish regulars were holding the narrow, fortified isthmus which separated Cadiz and the Isle of Leon from the mainland. All Victor could do, after a few vain attempts to force the outer forts and a still vainer appeal to Napoleon for naval help, was to sit down and blockade the town. Besiege it he could not, for it was open to the sea.

Thus, by the time spring returned to Spain, the principal French field army was irretrievably committed to siege and garrison operations in Andalusia. Three corps, totalling 70,000 troops - twice as many as the British effectives in Portugal - were tied down in the south. For, despite Joseph's sanguine hopes, his new dominion proved no more susceptible of government than his old. Like the north and centre, it could only be held by bayonets. Kindly proclamations and promises were utterly unavailing. Though here and there a few, chiefly among the possessing classes in the towns, accepted a French king as the price of a quiet life, the average Spaniard contemptuously refused to acknowledge the usurper. Sooner than do so he preferred to see his lands ravaged, his house and chattels burnt, his wife raped and his children butchered before his eyes. It was a choice that, as Goya's fearful cartoons reveal, thousands were to make during the next three years.

For, as both French and British learnt to their amazement, the Spaniards were as formidable behind their native rocks as they were ineffective on the battlefield. The French horsemen, in their serried ranks and gleaming casques, might cry " *Retirez-vous, coquins!*" to the ragged levies on the open plain,* but it was another matter when they entered the sierras or tried to force their way through the portals of the grim little towns in the hills. There the unconquerable spirit of the people burnt only the brighter for disaster. In every province of the conquered land it was the same: no suffering could daunt this stark, uncompromising race. No sooner had the half-starved, tattered Spanish armies fled from the plain than they reformed in the hills, descending again the moment the victors had moved on. Wherever to feed themselves the conquerors seized the peasant's corn and livestock, armed guerrilla bands sprang up as though by magic. Villainous faces, livid with hatred, peered from behind every boulder; revengeful fingers in waiting cellar and glade stole along fowling-piece and knife. The very priests took to the hills to stalk and kill: one Franciscan friar boasted he had slain six hundred invaders with his own hands.

No Frenchman was safe. For nearly four years Napoleon's daily losses in Spain averaged a hundred.† In the remoter fastnesses—and there was no highway that did not run through or near one—the guerrilla forces at times assumed the dimensions of small armies.

---

* Stanhope, 22.
† Fortescue, VI, 178. See Sherer, 249-50.

Their leaders - many of them men of the humblest origin - were as elusive as they were daring. They would sally out from some impregnable eyrie, attack couriers, foraging parties, convoys and even field detachments. But, once they had learnt their limitations, they carefully refrained from meddling with any force stronger than their own. They merely waited for it to pass on or straggle. Some of these chieftains acquired an almost European reputation: Martin Diez - El Empecinado or Inky Face - a labourer's son from Aranda who haunted the mountains on the borders of Old and New Castile and once seized and held the town of Guadalajara for a day; Mina, the student, who stormed Tafalla in Navarre; Camilo who made thousands pay with their blood for the violation of his wife and daughter; the savage Don Julian Sanchez who provided Wellington with a tribute of decapitated couriers and the contents of their dispatch cases and who vowed that, if he caught Soult, he would slice him into strips beginning at his feet. One of his colleagues boiled a general alive and sawed another in half.*

The effect on French *morale* was grave and cumulative. The war in the Peninsula became detested even by the toughest *moustache*. This was a very different proposition from campaigning in a land populated by timid Italians or docile, home-keeping Germans. Plunder ceased to be a pleasure: the mildest foraging expedition assumed the character of a nightmare. Every convoy needed a powerful escort; every village and town, if it was to be of the slightest value to Joseph's tax-gatherers, had to be garrisoned. Denied all but a pittance for military essentials by Napoleon, King Pepe, as he was called by his scornful subjects, was unable to pay even the salaries of his Court. Confiscation brought in little, for no one - even a traitor - was willing to buy in a land where the military were so powerless to protect property. And as the French generals never knew where their invisible foes would attack next, they were driven to disperse their forces ever wider to maintain order and preserve their communica-

* On December 17th 1809, in a letter to a friend in England, Wellington wrote: "The Spanish people are like gunpowder - the least spark inflames them; and, when inflamed, there is no violence or outrage they do not commit and nothing can stop their violence . . . The Spaniard is an undisciplined savage who obeys no law, despises all authority . . . and is ready with his knife or his firelock to commit murder. At the same time, bad as they are, their vices and defects and the lamentable state of their country afford some hopes of the issue of the contest, and we cannot with honour withdraw from it till we shall be obliged to do so." To Lord Burghersh, December 17th 1809.

tions. The more they did so, the weaker they became at any given point.

* * *

It was Wellesley's supreme merit as a commander that, despite his strong prejudice against the Spaniards, he grasped the importance of this. "If we can maintain ourselves in Portugal," he wrote, "the war will not cease in the Peninsula, and, if the war lasts in the Peninsula, Europe will be saved." With his insight into realities he saw that, so long as the guerrillas fought on and his army remained in the field, the French would be in a quandary. If they dispersed enough strength to smother the growing conflagration, they would sooner or later expose some part of their forces to a blow from the British. If they concentrated against the latter, they would be unable to keep the flame of rebellion under control.

In the dark hour after the retreat from Talavera, therefore, when almost every other Englishman despaired of Spain, the British Commander-in-Chief urged the Government to persist. He was still doing so three months later when the Spaniards by their incredible folly had lost the battles of Ocaña and Alba de Tormes and exposed Andalusia to invasion. "If they had preserved their two armies or even one of them, the cause was safe," he commented bitterly. "But no! nothing will answer but to fight great battles in plains, in which their defeat is as certain as the commencement of the battle."* Yet he continued to contend that, with 30,000 British and 40,000 disciplined Portuguese troops, he could hold Lisbon. Ministers, he told Lord Liverpool, would betray the honour and interests of the country if they abandoned the campaign. "If you are beaten," he declared, "you cannot help it, but do not give up unnecessarily."†

For, so long as the guerrillas tied down the bulk of the French armies in garrison, police and convoy duty, only limited forces could be assembled for an advance across the barren Portuguese mountains. And by delaying actions, driving the countryside and utilising its defensive features, Wellesley felt that he could deal with any force of less than seventy or eighty thousand. He told the Secretary of State that the French were desperately anxious for the British to

* To Bartle Frere, December 6th 1809.
† To Liverpool, November 14th 1809.

withdraw but that they could only bring sufficient strength against Portugal by abandoning other objects and jeopardising their whole fabric in Spain. If they invaded and failed to force his army to evacuate, they would be in a very dangerous situation, and, the longer they could be delayed, the more they were likely to suffer.

In this, Wellesley took account of the peculiarities of Portuguese geography. Ostensibly the long, narrow land was defenceless: the mountains ran, not along the frontier from north to south, but from east to west, and the main river valleys flowed from the Spanish hinterland to the coast, so splitting the defenders into isolated groups. With the Tagus and the mountains cutting the country into isolated lateral strips and with almost every road leading to Lisbon, an army acting on the frontier ran a grave risk of being cut off from the capital.

Yet the map was deceptive. The river valleys – Douro, Mondego, Tagus and Guadiana – were not so much thoroughfares as deep gorges, almost as hard to penetrate as the mountains through which they seeped their way. The only easy approach from Spain to Lisbon was the Merida highway to the south of the Tagus. But this was dominated by the great fortresses of Badajoz and Elvas – still held by the Spaniards and Portuguese. And it led an invading army not into the capital but merely to the opposite shore of the broad Tagus estuary, which could not be forced in the face of British naval power. Only at Santarem, nearly forty miles to the north or, at best, at Villa Franca a little lower down, was there a bridge or ford.*

This gave the British Commander an opportunity to offset his inferiority in numbers. While he held the southern approach with a comparatively small force, he could concentrate his best troops to the north of the Tagus. Fighting a delaying action with light infantry and road demolitions, he could force the invaders to advance over the northern mountains where their supply difficulties would increase with every mile, and only give battle when they were on the verge of the coastal plain. Here, where there were several strong positions barring every track out of the mountains, his own communications, based on the sea, would be as short as theirs were long.

Even if the French, with their almost inexhaustible reserves of conscripted man-power, could not be held at the edge of the coastal plain, Wellesley had a further resource. His great object was to

* See Stanhope, 70.

hold Lisbon and the Tagus estuary, for, so long as he did so, his army would remain in being and the enemy's dilemma only increase with every advance. The danger was lest, in holding on too long, his army should be unable to escape. Situated several miles up the estuary and with its water approaches vulnerable to shore artillery, Lisbon had none of the obvious defensive advantages of Cadiz.*

Yet it had others which did not escape the British commander's experienced eye. Though it could not be defended from its own ramparts without allowing the enemy's artillery to reach the river below it, the peninsula on which it stood was long and narrow and, nearly thirty miles to the north of the city, was still little more than twenty-five miles wide. Here it was intersected by a deep chain of rugged hills stretching from the Atlantic to the Tagus and rising in places to 2000 feet. Three years earlier Junot, preparing to defend Lisbon against a British advance from Mondego Bay, had noted "the excellent position of Alenquer and Torres Vedras, the right of which could be extended to the Tagus, the left to the sea."† On his subsequent visits Wellesley had carefully noted them too.

In September 1809, after his withdrawal of his army to the borders of Spain and Portugal, he learnt that he had been made a viscount for his victory at Talavera. In his absence abroad his brother, William, had chosen his title, taking it from the little Somerset town of Wellington in whose vicinity his remote Wellesley ancestors had once held land. On September 16th, Sir Arthur no more, he first signed himself by the name by which he was henceforward to be called. It was thus as Viscount Wellington of Talavera and Baron Douro that he visited the Portuguese capital on secret and exploratory business in October 1809. There, after spending two weeks on horseback with his chief engineer, Colonel Fletcher, exploring the hilly country between the Atlantic and the Tagus through which any invader approaching Lisbon by land would have to pass, he issued to that officer on October 20th confidential instructions for making what were to be known as the Lines of Torres Vedras. Three lines of defence were to be constructed, crowned by earthworks and protected by artificial inundations - an inner one at

---

* "It is difficult, if not impossible, to bring the contest for the capital to extremities and afterwards to embark the British army. . . . Lisbon is too high up the Tagus." To Castlereagh, August 25th 1809.
† Castlereagh, VI, 379.

the extreme southern tip of the peninsula to cover a possible embarkation, a principal line twenty miles to the north based on the central massif of the Cabeça de Montechique, and an outer line six miles farther north extending east and west from the Monte Agraça above Sobral. In all more than fifty miles of earthworks, redoubts and abatis were to be made under British supervision by gangs of Portuguese labourers and militiamen: precipices were to be scarped, forests cleared and stone walls piled on mountains. But fearful lest the over-confident French should hear of these elaborate preparations and, anticipating a prolonged siege, improve their haphazard supply services, the British general confided his intentions to no one but those directly concerned. So secretly were the works set in hand that months elapsed before even senior officers of the Army suspected their existence.

All this was characteristic of the man - foresight, patience, reticence. If genius is an infinite capacity for anticipating and taking pains, Wellington possessed it in supreme measure. He left little to chance. He foresaw every contingency and took the necessary steps to meet it. While he was instructing his engineers, he was also consulting with the Government and the naval Commander-in-Chief about embarkation arrangements and transports. This officer, Vice-Admiral Berkeley, he found somewhat of a trial, though, with his usual capacity for accommodating honest differences with any man who meant well, he ultimately established a reasonable working relationship with him. "His activity," he told his brother, William, "is unbounded, the whole range of the business of the country in which he is stationed, civil, military, political, commercial, even ecclesiastical, I believe, as well as naval, are objects of his attention: and he interferes actively in everything. In my life I never saw a man who . . . has such a passion for new invented modes of doing ordinary things and such a contempt for everything that is practicable. I tremble when I think that I shall have to embark the Leopards"—Napoleon's name for Wellington's troops and a source of much amusement to them—"in front of Bonaparte, aided by such a man, who has already twenty new invented modes of putting Leopards into boats, and of getting boats off a coast to a ship, besides new plans and inventions for the execution of all the ordinary services that can occur."*

* "I am already . . . teazed to death by this man with propositions for new modes of

To prevent an eleventh hour panic in the Portuguese capital, Wellington asked the Government that transports should be stationed permanently in the Tagus; both to give confidence to his troops and to accustom the civilian population to the sight. In the event of failure in the field - which he did not anticipate - he was resolved to embark and bring away his army safely. He, therefore, made sure that he could do so. "Everything is prepared for us," he told the Secretary of State for War, "either to go or stay." If the former, it should be, he said, "like gentlemen out of the hall door, and not out of the back-door or by the area."

*   *   *

The distinguishing feature of this great soldier's mind was that it dwelt as much on the future as on the present. He was a strategist not merely in space but in time. He husbanded it not only for to-day's battle but for to-morrow's. In this he embodied the genius of his country - patience. He could bide his time and, unlike his passionate adversary, knew when to refrain from action. "It will give Spain the chance of accidents," he wrote of his Fabian plan in December, 1809, "and of a change in the affairs of Europe."*

In his calculating, undemonstrative way he was at heart an optimist. He saw the inherent flimsiness of Napoleon's dominion; its foundations were not sound in time. "The Austrian marriage is a terrible event," he wrote in the spring of 1810, "and must prevent any great movement on the Continent for the present. Still I do not despair of seeing at some time or other a check to the Bonaparte system. Recent transactions in Holland show that it is all hollow within, and that it is so inconsistent with the wishes, the interests and even the existence of civilised society, that he cannot trust even his brothers to carry it into execution."† Ephemeral disaster, how-

---

doing everything in the Commissariat, the Artillery, etc. etc. which coming from such an authority I cannot treat with the contempt they deserve. I am obliged to give answers, to reason, to temporise, to delay and to get rid of this impracticable nonsense in the best and least offensive mode in my power." To the Hon William Wellesley-Pole, January 26th 1810. Wellesley-Pole, 30-1. "Your Admiral who has nothing to do in his own department of the Service is a terrible bore in all countries." *Idem.* 31.

* To Bartle Frere, December 9th 1809.
† To Brig-General Craufurd, April 4th 1810.

ever shattering, never blinded the vision of this cool, dispassionate observer. "The affairs of the Peninsula," he noted in March 1810, "have invariably had the same appearance since I have known them; they have always appeared to be lost. . . . The contest however still continues."

Yet this temperate optimism was never based on wishful thinking. An eight years' apprenticeship in the cynical school of Indian warfare, followed by the campaigns of Vimiero and Talavera, had purged him of all illusions. He looked facts unflinchingly in the face, and men too. Of the latter his views were seldom sanguine: he kept even his generals at arm's length and viewed his junior officers, till they had proved themselves otherwise, as slapdash amateurs who would always bungle things unless he took care to prevent them. His opinion of the rank and file was still lower: he told his brother, William - his chief confidant - that it was the worst British army that had ever been sent out of England. "The conduct of the soldiers," he wrote to the Secretary of State in January, 1810, "is infamous. They behave well generally when with their regiments and under the inspection of their officers; but when detached and coming up from hospitals, although invariably under the command of an officer and always well fed and taken care of, they commit every description of outrage. They have never brought up a convoy of money that they have not robbed the chest, nor of shoes or of any other article that could be of use to them . . . that they do not steal. . . . At this moment there are three general courts-martial sitting in Portugal for the trial of soldiers guilty of wanton murders, robberies, thefts. I assure you that the military law is not sufficiently strong to keep them in order."* He admitted, however, that, though these terrible outrages continued, the army was greatly improved since he had taken its discipline in hand.

A cadet of the ruling Protestant ascendancy of Ireland, his vision of the world was that of an aristocrat struggling to preserve order, peace and civilisation in an untidy welter of violence, confusion and unreason. Nor was it unsuited to the realities of the Iberian peninsula in a Revolutionary age. Not expecting too much of men, Wellington seldom tried them too high and, knowing where they were likely to fail, was always ready with the necessary corrective at the right place and moment. No one was ever a greater master of cold, scathing

* To the Earl of Liverpool, January 24th 1810. See also Brett-James, 199-200.

rebuke that, without exaggeration or provocative heat, left the victim without answer or escape. "It is not very agreeable to anybody," he told a refractory Portuguese magnate, "to have strangers quartered in his house, nor is it very agreeable to us strangers who have good houses in our own country to be obliged to seek for quarters here. We are not here for our pleasure."

During the quiet winter months of recuperation which followed the collapse of his hopes after Talavera, the British Commander-in-Chief—using the respite offered by Napoleon and Joseph—was transforming his still half-amateur army into a professional fighting force. Under his easy, high-bred manner he reshaped it with a hand of steel. In this he was helped by the fact that he was a man of the world and of the highest fashion. Though of frugal and even Spartan tastes, he was accustomed to the best society, was said, though on dubious authority, to have kept a mistress - in her due place* - and understood the lure of pleasure. He was well able to deal both with senior officers who claimed a gentleman's right to go home for the winter to hunt and manage their estates, and with subalterns who neglected their regimental duties for the charms of the Lisbon opera house. "My Lord," one of his brigadiers began, "I have of late been suffering much from rheumatism . . ." "And you wish to go to England to get cured of it," snapped the Commander-in-Chief, turning his back: "By all means. Go there immediately."†

The rule of such a chief was as unpalatable to gentlemen who thought themselves above discipline as to marauders who deserted for drink or left the line to plunder. Just as the malingerers and column-dodgers of the base hospital at Belem - the notorious *Belem Rangers*, "noted for every species of skunk" - were driven back to their regiments that winter by an icy wind, so gay sparks who tried

* According to Lady Sarah Napier - a prejudiced witness - in the field, Lennox, II, 229. See also Burgoyne, I, 70-1. But he certainly regarded such frailties as weaknesses never to be publicly paraded. He privately expressed a wish that his brother, the Marquess, should be castrated "or that he would, like other people, attend to his business and perform too - it is lamentable to see talents and character and advantages such as he possesses thrown away upon whoring" - and wrote scathingly of a court martial which had "honourably acquitted" an officer of broiling in a brothel, as though any activity in a brothel, however otherwise blameless, could be regarded as honourable, "since there is no man who unfortunately commits the act (of going to a brothel) who does not endeavour to conceal it from the world and his friends." To the Hon. William Wellesley-Pole, April 6th 1810; to Brig-General John Slade, October 12th 1809.

† McGrigor, 304-5.

to find in Lisbon a second Drury Lane were recalled in chilling terms to their duties. "The officers of the army," they were reminded, "can have nothing to do behind the scenes. . . . Indeed, officers who are absent from their duty on account of sickness might as well not go to the playhouse, or at all events upon the stage and behind the scenes."*

Nor would this unsympathetic commander permit his officers the liberty of politics. He stigmatised the croaking which prevailed in the army as a disgrace to the nation. "As soon as an accident happens," he complained to one of his divisional generals, "every man who can write, and who has a friend who can read, sits down to write his account of what he does not know and his comments on what he does not understand."† Such letters, diligently circulated by the idle and malicious, not only found their way into English newspapers, encouraging the anti-war Opposition and conveying valuable information to the French, but aroused partisan feelings in the field. These he would have none of; his wish, he stated, was to be the head of an army not a party, and to employ indiscriminately those who could best serve the public, be they who they might.

Yet his discipline was never negative. He made it his business to teach his officers the same meticulous care and attention to duty in which he had schooled himself. Success, he told them, could only be attained by attention to minute detail and by tracing every part of an operation from its origin to its conclusion, point by point and ascertaining that the whole is understood by those who are to execute it. An indefatigable worker, he expected everyone about him to be so too. He made it a rule, he said, always to do the work of the day in the day. Regular habits, a superb constitution and a well-regulated mind had been the foundations of all his triumphs. "When I throw off my clothes," he once remarked, "I throw off my cares, and, when I turn in my bed, it is time to turn out."‡ He taught his army to do the same.

At the root of this punctilious, fastidious, clear-sighted man's nature was a deep and abiding sense of duty. It was not an inspired and burning passion like Moore's or Nelson's; he made no pretence of being at home in such altitudes. But, though his feet were firmly

* To Colonel Peacocke, October 26th 1809.
† To Brig-General Craufurd, July 23rd 1810.
‡ *Leaves from the Diary of an Officer*, 37. He always got up directly he was called.

planted on his mother earth - one on the battlefield and the other in Bond Street - he was inherently a man of his salt. He spoke the truth, honoured his bond and kept faith. He regarded a lie as an act of cowardice and a breach of promise as a vulgar betrayal. He had learnt to eradicate these easy frailties from his own character, just as he had taught himself to be frugal and reticent in his youth, when he had had to master his Irish ebullience and artist's sensitivity in order to survive in a *milieu* of thrustful elder brothers and inadequate family resources. Adherence to bond and duty was not so much a natural bent of his rather mysterious nature—in which ran suppressed rivers of deep emotion—as a close-fitting mask which he had early donned in self-protection and to which in due course his own features had come to conform. Yet it was one which, like his talent for economy, perfectly served his country's need. He spared himself no care or labour which could further her ends and made every man and every penny go as far as man or penny could go.

In November 1809, at the close of his second Peninsular campaign, he was a slight, upright, wiry-looking man of forty with keen grey eyes and an aquiline nose. "I was much struck with his countenance," recalled Lieutenant Sherer who saw him for the first time at a divisional inspection after the retreat from Talavera, "and his quick glancing eye, prominent nose and pressed lip, and saw, very distinctly marked, the steady presence of mind and imperturbable decision of character, so essential in a leader." His habitual dress, though neat to the point of dandyism, was almost consciously unostentatious: a plain blue frock coat, a small, glazed, cocked hat without feathers, a short cape and strapped grey trousers. He eschewed plumes and gold lace, went about without a Staff, and was usually followed at a discreet distance by a single orderly. He liked seeing things for himself without fuss. "I will get upon my horse and take a look," he used to say when any problem requiring visual investigation was put to him. "Our post," wrote one of his junior officers, "was next the enemy. I found, when anything was to be done, that it was his also."*

At this time the Commander-in-Chief was far from universally popular. In England the glamour of his early victories had faded. He

---

* Kincaid, 14. "He was just such a man as I had figured in my mind's eye and I thought that the stranger could betray a grievous want of penetration who could not select" (him) "from amid five hundred in the same uniform."

was blamed for the rashness of his summer campaign, the loss of his wounded and the hardships of the retreat from Talavera. His family was assailed by Opposition pamphleteers as a tribe of proud, rapacious Irish Tories with greedy fingers in every public pie; his brilliant elder brother, Lord Wellesley—a Spanish grandee grafted on an Irish potato, as the Prince Regent called him—was almost the best-hated man in England with his intolerable viceregal airs, his notorious debts, his "common whore," Sally Douglas, who, rumour said, he had taken in state on his mission to Spain. Arthur Wellesley's own elevation to the peerage was regarded as a Tory job, and the £2000 a year pension voted him in Parliament was publicly attacked by the Common Council of the City of London. Even his army, unable to understand the broader issues underlying the campaign of 1809, thought of him as a rash Irishman, a brilliant tactician but no strategist, who had gambled away the lives of his men at Talavera and callously allowed them to rot in the Guadiana marshes to please his Spanish allies. A surgeon at the military hospital at Lisbon told Charles Napier that Lord Wellington deserved hanging for his reckless waste of life.

Yet those who were brought into contact with him seldom retained such impressions for long. He was so industrious, clear-headed, sensible and efficient. For everything he did he had a reason and, when he chose to explain it in his clear, lucid way, it always proved unanswerable. As he himself wrote of Marlborough, he was remarkable for his cool, steady understanding.* If any of his senior officers quarrelled—as in those days of hot tempers, hard drinking and prickly honour they were very apt to do—he was always ready with his moderation, balance and good sense to compose the difference. "A part of my business and perhaps not the most easy part," he told the fiery Craufurd, who had conceived a grievance against a brother officer, "is to prevent discussions and disputes between the officers who may happen to serve under my command. . . . I hope that this letter may reach you in time to induce you to refrain from sending me the paper which you inform me you have written."†

For here was a Commander-in-Chief who did not stand upon ceremony or take personal offence. It was hard to quarrel with him: he saw your point of view while clarifying and enforcing his own

* Stanhope, 31.
† To Brig-General Craufurd, May 29th 1810.

"You and I necessarily take a different view of these questions," he told Craufurd, "I must view them in all their relations; your view of them is naturally confined to their relation with your own immediate command." Much of this time was spent in trying to adapt impossible War Office and Treasury regulations to the exigencies of a Continental campaign for which they had never been designed. Yet he refused to inveigh against them needlessly or to allow his subordinates to do so; all that could be done, he told the latter, was that they should assist each other as much and clash as little as possible. Adhering steadfastly to his chosen path, he was always ready to compromise on inessentials: to go down metaphorically on his knees, as he had done before Cuesta at Talavera. "Half the business of the world," he wrote, "particularly that of our country, is done by accommodation and by the parties understanding each other."*

This genius for being reasonable, coupled with his clarity and common sense, enabled Wellington - unlike most men habituated to discipline and command - to deal with politicians. Being free from Moore's troublesome sense of moral indignation, he never made them uncomfortable with tedious reiterations of principle. So long as they ultimately came along with him, he always allowed them a way to wriggle round their difficulties. And though he left them in no doubt as to what he wanted and meant to do—there is nothing in life, he once remarked, like a clear definition—he never expected or asked them to do the impossible. "In my situation," he told a colleague, "I am bound to consider not only what is expedient but what is practicable."† He remembered that Ministers had to do so too. He realised that they were harried and abused in Parliament and the country, that there was a shortage of money and troops. He made no more claims on them than were absolutely essential, told them the exact truth, and explained, in language which the busiest fool could understand, the common-sense reasons for his requests. He only pressed them when he had to: "would it be fair or indeed honest in me," he wrote to the British Ambassador at Lisbon, "to ask for a man more than I thought absolutely necessary."

For, frigid and bleak though he sometimes seemed, Wellington had a curiously detached sense of justice. He could be just even in his

* To Rt Hon J. Villiers, September 20th 1809.
† To Rt Hon J. Villiers, December 6th 1809.

own cause. Having explained to Lord Liverpool, who had succeeded Castlereagh as Secretary of State for War, exactly why he needed transports in the Tagus, he added that none of his reasons were worth anything if the ships were needed elsewhere. Such moderation, despite the sacrifices it involved, had its reward. It established a sense of confidence between Cabinet and general: made them conscious of their mutual dependence. When Wellington really needed support from England he could ultimately rely on receiving everything that was available.

Thus it came about, while the ordinary Englishman despaired of Portugal and expected nothing better than an evacuation,* a Government with a precarious majority accepted Wellington's contention that it should be held. This was the more praiseworthy in that any fighting there was bound to be defensive and could offer few prospects of political glory. But after seventeen years of almost unbroken war British statesmen were at last learning how to wage it. "We must make our option," the Secretary of State for War wrote, "between a steady and continued exertion upon a moderate scale and a great and extraordinary effort for a limited time which neither our military nor financial means will enable us to maintain permanently. If it could be hoped that the latter would bring the contest to a speedy and successful conclusion, it would certainly be the wisest course; but unfortunately the experience of the last fifteen years is not encouraging in this respect."† Instead of seeking in every corner of the globe like their predecessors for opportunities "to give a good impression of the war in England," Ministers, therefore, concentrated on building up expanding strength in Portugal. In this they were helped by the fact that in the fifth year after Trafalgar and Austerlitz there was not much left outside Europe for them to conquer and nowhere inside it save Portugal where they could hope even to retain a footing. The capture of the last French Caribbean islands in the summer of 1809 released the garrisons of no less than seventeen British stations for service elsewhere. By the following summer a small but steady flow of reinforcements was heading for Portugal from every corner of the world.

Yet the growth of this confidence and support was a gradual thing

* Wellesley, I, 258; Lennox, II, 228, 233.
† Fortescue, VII, 562.

and largely of Wellington's own creation. The failure of the Wal-cheren expedition, the defeat of Austria and the resignation and death of the Prime Minister, the Duke of Portland, had brought about in the autumn of 1809 a political crisis so grave that, without either Castlereagh or Canning, the new Perceval Administration—forced to trim its sails to every parliamentary wind—seemed unlikely to survive.* "The Government are terribly afraid that I shall get them and myself into a scrape," Wellington wrote in April 1810, "but what can be expected from men who are beaten in the House of Commons three times a week?"† Yet, though he did not expect them to last he calmly took the responsibility of urging them to cling to Portugal, knowing that, if he failed, the full weight of the disaster would fall on his own head. At best the defensive campaign he was planning could win him little credit - one, as he said, in which there could be few brilliant events and in which he was almost bound to lose the little reputation he had. "I am perfectly aware," he wrote, "of the risks which I incur personally, whatever may be the result of the operations in Portugal. All I beg is that, if I am to be responsible, I may be left to the exercise of my own judgment."‡

For he was under no illusions as to the weight of the impending attack. As soon as he learnt of the Austrian armistice he had warned the Government to dispatch transports to the Tagus on the first intimation that Napoleon was reinforcing Spain. "You may depend upon it," he wrote, "that he and his Marshals must be desirous of revenging upon us the different blows we have given them and that, when they come into the Peninsula, their first and great object will be to get the English out."§ For this he knew they would face heavy risks and losses.

He therefore scrupulously sought to spare his army. Contrary to the expectation of Ministers, who feared that he would try to snatch another desperate victory like Talavera,¶ he refrained from every move that could expose his troops. To Spanish pleas for new adventures he opposed a bleak and undeviating *non-possumus*. "Till the evils of which I think I have reason to complain are remedied," he

---

* In fact, it survived for more than twenty years under three different Prime Ministers – the last of whom was Wellington himself.
† To Vice-Admiral Berkeley, April 7th 1810.
‡ To Lord Liverpool, April 2nd 1810.   § To Lord Castlereagh, August 25th 1809.
¶ "Depend upon it, whatever people may tell you, I am not so desirous as they imagine of fighting desperate battles." To Liverpool, April 2nd 1810.

informed his brother, the Ambassador, "till I see magazines established for the supply of the armies and a regular system adopted for keeping them filled, and an army upon whose exertions I can depend commanded by officers capable and willing to carry into execution the operations which may have been planned by mutual agreement, I cannot enter upon any system of co-operation with the Spanish armies."* Save for Cadiz, he left that country alone; he had fished, he remarked, in many troubled waters, but Spanish troubled waters he would never fish in again.

*　　*　　*

For more than six months after Talavera the British army did not fire a shot. As soon as the collapse of the Spanish offensive in November made its continued presence in the sickly Guadiana valley unnecessary, Wellington marched the bulk of it over the mountains into northern Portugal. Here he cantoned it along the Mondego and in the upland valleys of Beira, while Craufurd with his riflemen watched the Spanish frontier and Hill with two Anglo-Portuguese divisions kept guard south of the Tagus. The main activities of the winter were training and sport, while the men recovered their strength and spirits and the hospitals emptied. The officers engaged in coursing, shooting and horse-racing, the rank and file in poaching and fishing. It was surprising how quickly under such a regimen everyone's confidence returned.

For, as Wellington had the good sense to see, from the drunken Irish spalpeen to the lordling from the hunting shires, it was a young army and a sporting one. Its readiness to lark was an index of its readiness to fight. Its allies, the Portuguese, suffered a good deal from its high spirits but learnt to take them in good part; the young gentlemen of the Rifle Corps invariably gave chase to any officer of the Caçadores who passed them on the march, galloping after him - to the delight of the troops - with horns and hunting cries up to the head of the column.† At Villa Viçosa the officers of the 23rd Light Dragoons - survivors of the charge at Talavera - dressed up one of

---

* To Marquess Wellesley, October 30th 1809.

† "We never carried the joke too far, but made it a point of etiquette to stop short of our commanding officer, who was not supposed to see what was going on." Kincaid, *Random Shots*, 159-60.

their members as an English bishop in red velvet breeches, white gaiters trimmed with lace, an old dressing-gown and clerical band and collar, and, arming him with a huge lemon stuck on a stick, processed behind him bearing their helmets in their hands while a devout populace cheered itself frantic.* The innumerable Portuguese ecclesiastics and their strange superstitions proved an irresistible butt for such high-spirited boys; young Charles Napier, recovering from a wound in the face, gravely offered a splinter from his jaw-bone to a monk as a relic, explaining that it was a piece of St Paul's wisdom tooth given him in a dream by the Virgin Mary. The larking spirit broke out even at headquarters. Taking tea one day in the parlour of Vizeu Convent, Wellington was surprised to see one of the nuns turn on her head and, throwing her heels in the air, reveal not only a wealth of conventual petticoat but the boots and trousers of a British officer. It proved to be Captain Dan Mackinnon of the Coldstream Guards, who was always "running, chasing and climbing" and whose practical jokes became a legend throughout the Peninsula.†

Under the skylarking surface the army was busy preparing for the grim tasks which lay ahead. The great men whom Moore and Wellington successively taught and inspired, like Donellan of the 48th and Wallace of the Connaught Rangers, were reducing their regiments to a perfection of discipline which was to astonish friend and foe. Yet it was not in the bleak hill cantonments above the Mondego but forty miles to the east along the Spanish frontier that the flower of the Army was to be seen. Here the Light troops Moore had trained were watching the French at the edge of the plain beyond the Agueda under the brilliant soldier who had led them through the horrors of the retreat to Corunna and Vigo. Robert Craufurd was now just on forty-six, five years older than his chief and nine than the youngest divisional commander, and a little soured by adversity and long-delayed promotion. He was still only a junior brigadier, but on March 1st 1810, his brigade, consisting of the first battalions of the 43rd, 52nd and 95th, a troop of horse artillery, a regiment of

* "I only wished that Lord Wellington might by chance have encountered this cavalcade; how quickly it would have dispersed." Schaumann, 210.

† Stanhope, 14-15. On another occasion he impersonated the Duke of York at a Spanish port until, wearying of the gravity of Iberian hospitality, he suddenly plunged headfirst into a bowl of punch, thereby creating a minor international incident. Wellington, however, always forgave him. Gronow, I, 61-2.

G.D.   193   N

Hanoverian hussars and two battalions of Portuguese Caçadores – about 4000 men in all – was reconstituted in Wellington's reorganisation of his army, as the Light Division. Its instructions were to screen the army, maintain communications with the Spanish frontier fortress of Ciudad Rodrigo and keep the Commander-in-Chief punctually supplied with intelligence of every enemy movement.

Never was reconnaissance more brilliantly carried out. Since the retreat from Corunna and his return to Spain Craufurd had been improving on Moore's rules in the light of experience. To the original handiwork of his master he had added a wonderful polish. Impulsive and hot-tempered in action, "Black Bob", like Wellington, was a man of immense method. He once insisted on a commissary keeping a journal like a log-book so that he might see how and where he spent every moment of his time. Wherever he went himself he carried a pocket-book and whenever he encountered anything worthy of remark, down it went. From this he elaborated his divisional Code of Standing Orders which governed all movements on the march, in camp and on outpost duty. It was designed, like his Chief's earlier field-orders to his troops in India, to ensure an automatic response to every order and to give his entire force the precision of a single section on the parade-ground. "All sounds preparatory to turning out and marching," it began, "will commence at the quarters of the Assistant Adjutant-General and be immediately repeated by the orderly bugles attending on the officers commanding regiments. As soon as possible after the first sound all the bugles are to assemble at the quarters of the commanding officers of regiments from whence all the other sounds will be repeated."

From this start everything went with a steady, unhalting, unhurrying swing which only an earthquake could have interrupted. Officers and camp-colourmen went ahead to the night's quarters, the baggage was packed and loaded, and, an hour after the first, a second bugle call sounded for the companies to fall in. Thereafter buglehorns in carefully-timed succession brought the companies together and set the regiments marching to the accompaniment of music. Step and perfect dressing were observed until the word was given to march at ease. During the march guides, who had already gone over the ground, directed the head of the column, and every officer and NCO kept his appointed place. Straggling was forbidden: no man was to leave the ranks save with his company commander's permission and only after a signed ticket had been issued. Anyone straying or stopped by the camp-guard without a ticket was to be arrested, tried by drumhead court-martial and flogged.* In crossing streams and other obstacles, no regiment, company or section was to defile or break rank unless the preceding unit had done so: any man who disobeyed was to be given a dozen lashes on the spot.† Where defiling was necessary, it was to be carried out with precision by the proper words of command. Hurrying or exceeding the regulation step were forbidden; half an hour after the start and at hourly intervals - to be governed by the proximity of water - the division was to halt for five minutes, during which time, and at no other, the men were to fill their water-canteens.

The reason for all this—mercilessly enforced and, at first, much disliked—was made clear to all. Every battalion defiling on the march caused a delay of ten minutes or, in a brigade of three battalions, of half an hour. In a country like Portugal, with innumerable water-courses, many hours could be lost in this way. The tail of the division might arrive at its destination hours late, perhaps drenched to the skin, and be confronted at the day's end with all the confusion and discomfort of bivouacking in a strange place in the dark. Experience demonstrated the wisdom of Craufurd's rules: punishment, at first frequent, became almost negligible. "The system once established," wrote an officer, "went on like clockwork, and the soldiers became devotedly attached to him; for while he extracted from all the most rigid obedience, he was, on his part, keenly alive to everything they had a right to expect from him in return."‡ The beauty of such discipline, as the editors of the Standing Orders pointed out, consisted of doing everything that was necessary and nothing that was not.

Craufurd, by sterner methods engendered by the realities of war, systematised Moore's training of common sense and humanism. His rules made it second nature for men to do the right thing. By obeying them all grew accustomed to looking after themselves in all circumstances. The troops of the Light Division did not give way to

* *Standing Orders*, 24. On the march to Talavera, before he had evolved his system, Craufurd took away the ramrod of every man found straggling, later punishing every one who paraded without one. Harris.

† Kincaid, *Random Shots*, 46. "Sit down in it, Sir, sit down in it," Craufurd himself would cry if he saw a soldier avoiding a puddle. Seaton, 173.

‡ Kincaid, *Random Shots*, 17, 50; Sherer, 59-60.

fatigue after a long march and drop asleep when they halted, later to awake in the dark, cold, supperless and miserable. Instead, the moment the bugle sounded for them to dismiss, they bustled about securing whatever the neighbourhood could contribute to their night's comfort. Swords, hatchets and bill-hooks were soon busy hacking at every tree and bush: huts were reared with roofs and walls of broom, pine branches or straw, fires were lit and camp-kettles set boiling; and presently, when the regulation pound of beef had been fried, tired but happy souls, their feet toasting round the cheerful blaze, would fall on their meal with a will, taking care, however, like good soldiers, not to consume anything which belonged to the morrow's ration. And, before they slept, wrapped in sedge mat or cloak and leather cap and with sod or stone for pillow, every man carefully arranged his accoutrements ready for nocturnal emergencies.*

The value of all this became plain in the presence of the enemy. Seven minutes sufficed to get the whole division under arms in the middle of the night and fifteen to bring it in order of battle to its alarm posts, with the baggage loaded and assembled under escort in the rear. And this, as Johnny Kincaid wrote, not upon a concerted signal or at a trial, but at all times and certain. The moment the division or any of its units halted, guards and piquets were posted automatically, while every road was examined, cleared, and reported upon so that the troops could move off again at once in any direction. Unless otherwise ordered, one company of every battalion served as outlying piquet, placed sentinels at all approaches and stood to arms from an hour before sunrise until a grey horse could be seen a mile away.† Officers on outpost duty were expected personally to examine all inhabitants for information, reconnoitre all fords, morasses, bridges and lanes in the neighbourhood and post sentries in pairs, who were relieved every two hours, in all commanding hedges and woodlands, and at night on the reverse slopes of hills. If attacked, sentries were instructed to give the alarm and fall back obliquely so as not to reveal the position of the main guard. In addition patrols were sent out every hour to visit posts and bring back information.

With less than 3000 British infantry so trained and their Portu-

* Kincaid, *Random Shots*, 88-90. See also Leslie, 83-5. Sherer, 59, 60.
† *Standing Orders*, 47-8; Smith, I, 185; Kincaid, 33-5.

guese and Hanoverian auxiliaries, Craufurd for six months guarded a river line of more than forty miles between the Sierra da Estrella and the Douro, broken by at least fifteen fords and with an open plain in front. His men were never less than within an hour's march of 6000 French cavalry with 60,000 infantry in support. Yet they never suffered their lines to be penetrated or allowed the slightest intelligence of Wellington's strength and movements to reach the enemy. "The whole web of communication," as Sir Charles Oman has written, "quivered at the slightest touch."*

On one occasion, on the night of March 19th 1810, a greatly superior force of *voltigeurs* attempted to surprise a detachment of the 95th Rifles at the bridge of Barba del Puerco. A French general had been informed by a Spanish traitor that the British officers were in the habit of getting drunk every night, and accordingly assembled six hundred picked troops at midnight under the rocks at the east end of the bridge. Creeping across in the shadows cast by the rising moon, with every sound drowned by the roar of the mountain torrent below, they succeeded in surprising and bayoneting the two sentries at the other end before they could open fire. But a sergeant's party higher up the rocks saw them and gave the alarm to the piquet company. Within a few minutes the rest of the regiment, with hastily donned belts and cartridge boxes slung over flapping shirts, led by Colonel Beckwith in dressing-gown, night-cap and slippers, was tumbling them down the rocks and across the bridge whence they had come. The French casualties in the affair were forty-seven, the British thirteen. It was the first and last attempt to surprise a Light Infantry piquet at night.†

It was through this screen and its patrols of riflemen and hussars, ranging far beyond the enemy's lines into Spain, that Wellington obtained his knowledge of French movements. It was work which required, as Kincaid said, a clear head, a bold heart and a quick pair of heels, all three being liable to be needed at any hour of the day or night. Founded on the training, habits and virtues of a few hundred humble British soldiers, its effect on the course of the European war was incalculable. For, in conjunction with the work of the Spanish guerrillas, it deprived the enemy of all knowledge of

---

* Oman, III, 238.

† Kincaid, *Random Shots*, 52-6, 59; George Napier, I, 113; Simmons, 56; Costello, 28-9; Oman, III, 236-8; Burgoyne, I, 69; Fortescue, VII, 465.

Wellington's strength and dispositions. While the British commander knew from day to day what was happening on the other side of the lines and saw his enemy silhouetted, as it were, against the eastern sky, the French faced only darkness. This outweighed all their superiority in numbers. For it meant that, when the time came to strike, Goliath with his mighty sword lunged blindly. David with his pebble and sling had no such handicap.

Chapter Eight

A FABIAN RETREAT

Napoleon's plan was always to try to give a great battle, gain
a great victory, patch up a peace, such a peace as might leave an
opening for a future war, and then hurry back to Paris. We
starved him out. We showed him that we wouldn't let him
fight a battle at first except under disadvantages. If you do fight,
we shall destroy you; if you do not fight, we shall in time
destroy you still.

WELLINGTON

WITH the summer of 1810 the hour of decision, long delayed by
Joseph's Andalusian adventure, was drawing near. The quarter of a
million French troops originally in Spain had been joined by another
sixty thousand: forty thousand more were waiting on the frontier at
Bayonne. But, contrary to expectation and his own repeated declara-
tions, the Emperor did not appear in person to lead them. Instead, he
stayed behind to enjoy his new wife and parade her before his subjects in France and the Rhineland. This was in part the result of
inclination: like his soldiers, Napoleon had come in the past two
years to detest the very name of Spain. He affected to treat the war
there as a mere colonial campaign, waged beyond the pale of civilisation against barbarians and the handful of British mercenaries who
so wickedly assisted them.

Yet there was more in Napoleon's decision than reluctance to
sacrifice time and reputation to a tedious campaign. He knew the
importance of the Peninsula too well to miss any chance of com-
pleting its conquest. He did not maintain 300,000 soldiers there
merely to provide a throne for his brother Joseph. For all his victories on the Danube, his Imperial marriage and the defeat of the
Walcheren invasion, he was uneasy. For, though he tried to conceal
the fact even from himself, the English, inch by inch, were forcing
him on to the defensive. Two and a half years before, he had entered
Spain to secure a bridge into North Africa and make the Mediterranean a French lake. But instead of breaking the ring of sea-power

199

his venture had ended in his opponents themselves securing a bridge-head in Europe and, what was worse, retaining it in the teeth of his personal intervention. With their sea-ring still unbroken, they were perpetually stirring up trouble round the European circumference. In the previous year they had made Austria their cat's-paw. Now, though he had dealt with that Power, Russia - hampered in her trade by the Continental blockade - was in turn growing restless. For so long as England's cruisers could carry her corrupting wares and gold to every back-door in Europe, there was always a court of appeal for Napoleon's dissatisfied friends and clients.

Because of this, Napoleon refused to commit either himself or the flower of his army to Spain. He knew too well that it might soon be needed elsewhere. He sent the Young Guard but not the Old, and transferred only a limited number of troops from central and eastern Europe. Instead he made up new drafts by anticipating the next two years' conscription and calling up 40,000 lads between the ages of sixteen and nineteen. This, together with growing taxation, did not enhance his popularity. After two years of war in the Peninsula a balanced budget had degenerated into a deficit of fifty-seven million francs. The Emperor did his best to reduce the drain of the campaign by cutting payments to the Peninsular armies and by imperative orders to Joseph to raise more money from his Spanish subjects. When that unhappy monarch, still anxious to win their hearts, raised objections, his kingdom was summarily divided into military districts under Governors directly responsible to Paris. Their corrupt and exorbitant demands destroyed his last chance of establishing an honest and therefore tolerable administration.

In place of himself Napoleon sent against the British the most experienced and cunning of all his Marshals, André Masséna, Prince of Essling and Duke of Rivoli. But, jealous as always of any power that might rival his own, he refrained from giving him any general authority and left Soult in Andalusia, Suchet in Aragon and Augereau in Catalonia in independent command. This system of *divide et impera* enabled him to play off one Marshal against another and intervene personally in distant operations without leaving Paris. But it scarcely made for vigorous prosecution of the war. Masséna's Army of Portugal was confined to Ney's 6th Corps on the frontiers of Leon, Reynier's 2nd Corps in the Tagus valley and Junot's 8th

Corps in Old Castile, numbering, together with Montbrun's Cavalry Reserve and the garrison and administrative troops, some 138,000 men or perhaps 70,000 field effectives. Large though this force was compared with the British army, which it outnumbered by two to one, it was not big enough for its purpose.

In fact, as the test approached and the impression gained ground in England and Portugal that an evacuation was inevitable, the British Commander-in-Chief remained grimly confident. "I am prepared for all events," he wrote to the Military Secretary, "and if I am in a scrape, as appears to be the general belief in England, although certainly not my own, I'll get out of it!"* He saw, as always, the inherent weakness in the imposing French structure – the rival Marshals, the lack of financial and administrative confidence, the slapdash arrangements for feeding and transporting so great a host through the wilderness. "This is not the way in which they have conquered Europe," he wrote to his brother, as June followed May and still Masséna made no move. "There is something discordant in all the French arrangements for Spain. Joseph divides his kingdom into *préfetures*, while Napoleon parcels it out into governments; Joseph makes a great military expedition into the south of Spain and undertakes the siege of Cadiz, while Napoleon places all the troops and half the kingdom under the command of Masséna and calls it the Army of Portugal. . . . I suspect that the impatience of Napoleon's temper will not bear the delay of the completion of the conquest of Spain."†

Wellington judged rightly. Masséna's difficulties were immense. The Marshal did not minimise them when he addressed his officers on taking up his appointment on May 15th. He had not wanted to come to Spain at all. He was fifty-two and, after nearly twenty years of continuous war in an age when men aged rapidly, was losing his vigour. The spoils of victory and plunder had begun to soften his native toughness; he had learnt to love ease and luxury, including a most expensive and exacting mistress. The prospects of carrying an army of 70,000 men and their innumerable followers through two hundred miles of desolate mountain inhabited by vindictive savages appalled him. The very sight of that gaunt land filled

* To Colonel Torrens, March 31st 1810. See Simmons, 51, 64; *Two Duchesses*, 345; Charles Napier, I, 129.
† To Rt Hon H. Wellesley, June 11th 1810.

him, as it did all Napoleon's Marshals, with an intense longing for Paris.

None the less Masséna was a great soldier – an old fox up to every trick of the game and worthy of Wellington's mettle. He was not a man in whose presence it was safe to take risks or to blunder. His chief lieutenant, the forty-year-old Ney, was one of the most daring captains of his age – the Sarlouis cooper's son who had routed Mack at Elchingen and, by his assault on the Russian lines at Friedland, won from Napoleon the title of the "bravest of the brave." During the years when most of the British general and regimental officers had been drilling on provincial parade-grounds or garrisoning remote naval stations and sugar islands, the leaders of the Army of Portugal had been fighting and conquering in every corner of Europe. Continental warfare had been their trade since boyhood. They regarded the English as clumsy novices and the Portuguese as cowardly *canaille*. They never doubted, in the words of Masséna's proclamation, that they would drive the Leopards into the sea. It was only a question of gathering the necessary bullocks, mules and wagons to drag their guns and munitions over the mountains.

A cautious and methodical man, Masséna took his time. He had a European reputation to preserve, and neither he nor his master meant there to be any mistake this time. Thrice in three years had a French army set out for Lisbon. The first under Junot, now a corps commander in the Army of Portugal, had reached it only to be ignominiously expelled by the British after Vimiero; the second under Napoleon himself had had to turn back to crush Moore's threat to its communications; the third under Soult had met with disaster on the banks of the Douro at the hands of the same young general who had defeated Junot and was now once more in command of the British-Portuguese forces. The new advance was, therefore, to be no impetuous dash like Junot's costly march over the Estrella in November, 1807, but a slow, methodical avalanche which, gathering irresistible weight, should roll the British into the sea.

The first step was to clear the northern road to Lisbon by capturing the Spanish and Portuguese frontier fortresses of Ciudad Rodrigo and Almeida at the eastern edge of the mountains. Ney moved forward with 30,000 men against the former in the last week of May. Ciudad Rodrigo was not a very formidable place – an old-fashioned, third-rate fortress and much neglected like everything else in Spain which belonged to the State. But the septuagenarian who commanded it and its garrison of 5000 Spaniards put up an unexpectedly stubborn defence, so much so that Wellington found himself in an embarrassing position. For, as week followed week and the fortress still held out, both the Spanish authorities and his own soldiers began to clamour for its relief. It seemed shameful for a British army to stand by almost within gunshot and watch a brave ally being pounded and starved into surrender.

Yet nothing could move Wellington from his purpose. He had formed a clear conception of the campaign he wished to wage—one scrupulously adapted to his military and geographical resources—and he was not going to be deflected from it by any momentary advantage. Nor was he going to harass and tire his men by conforming to the enemy's movements. Permanent defence of Ciudad Rodrigo and the Portuguese frontier was out of the question against the forces threatening him; the sole services General Herrasti and its defenders could do was to hold out as long as possible and so gain additional time before the inevitable advance on Lisbon. Though only a day's march from the British advanced-posts in the mountains, the besieged fortress was situated on an open plain within easy reach of Masséna's massive cavalry. It could not be relieved without a pitched fight. And to give battle in such a position with 33,000 men, half of them untried Portuguese, against an almost equal French force would be to court heavy losses, even if by some miracle Ney could be defeated before the enemy's main body came to his aid. And Wellington knew that he was going to need every man he possessed, whereas the French could replace their losses many times over. Against such considerations neither sentiment nor hope of glory counted for anything with him. His officers grumbled at the humiliation, but a few were more far-seeing. "He is blamed for this," wrote Charles Napier, hitherto one of his severest critics, "but he is right and it gives me confidence in him. He is a much better general than I suspected him to be.*

Ciudad Rodrigo held out in the burning midsummer heat till July 10th when, after the walls had been breached and a quarter of the garrison had fallen, Herrasti surrendered. Wellington had reason to be satisfied, for his allies had gained him six valuable weeks. Having expended 11,000 shells and 18,000 round-shot on

* Charles Napier, I, 129-33.

reducing the place, the French were forced to make a further wait till they could bring up fresh supplies. Meanwhile Craufurd with the Rifle and Light Infantry screen continued by brilliant skirmishing to impede their progress, making them deploy in front of every obstacle. So superbly trained and handled were his troops that the enemy never knew whether they were opposed by a few hundred men or the whole British Army.

Yet in his confidence in his own and his men's skill Craufurd tempted fate too far. In spite of Wellington's warnings not to linger in the open plain, he was still retaining his position on the exposed bank of the Coa when, in the third week of July, the enemy moved forward against the Portuguese fortress of Almeida. He thus needlessly exposed his four thousand men – the very eyes of the army – to attack by a force six times as large, with a raging stream and a single bridge in his rear. For, as one of his officers remarked, Craufurd was as enamoured of his separate command as any youth of his mistress.

The result was that on the morning of July 24th—in the half-light between night and day which Wellington had foretold as the danger period—Ney, probing his adversary's strength, suddenly realised the weakness of the British rearguard and immediately launched his entire corps, including two cavalry brigades, against the thin, over-extended line of skirmishers. A company of the Rifles on the left were overwhelmed by a cavalry charge, and within a few minutes Craufurd, who had failed to get his guns over the bridge in time, was faced with disaster.

The situation was saved by the steadiness of the infantry of the Light Division. While the hussars and artillery galloped under heavy fire down a steep hairpin-bend road for the bridge, the men of the 43rd, 52nd and 95th, covering their retreat and that of the Portuguese, fell back from wall to wall firing as coolly and steadily as on a Kentish field-day. Cut by the weight and speed of the French advance into isolated groups, they continued to fight as they had been taught in small sections, every officer and man knowing exactly what to do. "Moore's matchless discipline was their protection," wrote Charles Napier, "a phantom hero from Corunna saved them!" A final stand by the 43rd, the Rifles and a company of the 52nd on a small knoll of pine trees immediately in front of the bridge enabled the remainder of the division to take up a strong position beyond the Coa where it should have been stationed from the first. Five companies of the 52nd still fighting on the eastern slopes above the knoll were almost cut off and were only saved by a brilliant counter-attack led by Colonel Beckwith in person. By the time the last man had crossed the stream more than three hundred of the light infantry, including twenty-eight of their fine officers, had been lost.

Yet the disaster so rashly courted had been averted. Ney's subsequent attempt to rush the bridge in a deluge of rain proved as expensive to his troops as Craufurd's over-confidence had been to his, more than five hundred falling under the fire of the British guns and marksmen, now posted among the rocks of the western bank. And though Masséna in his dispatches, which were published with fanfares in the Paris papers, claimed to have inflicted immense losses on the defenders whose strength he estimated at ten thousand – more than three times the real number – the general impression left on the attackers was one of deep respect for the fighting qualities of the British. Indeed, one of Ney's brigadiers, General Foy, gloomily recorded in his diary that the despised islanders were better soldiers than the French, at any rate than the young conscripts with whom Napoleon was beginning to flood his veteran regiments.

Not unnaturally Wellington was extremely angry. Through Craufurd's folly he had come within an ace of losing the Light Division. Yet in his dispatches he refrained from any censure of his hot-headed lieutenant, transmitting his report without comment and taking the responsibility for the needless loss of life on his own shoulders. It was one of the idiosyncrasies of this stern, lonely man, who never forgave the least disobedience to his orders in any other subordinate, that he always treated Craufurd with exceptional tenderness. If he was to be hanged for it, he told his brother, he could not accuse a man whom he believed had meant well and whose error was one of judgment, not of intention. "That is not the way in which any, much less a British, army can be commanded."

During the week which followed the engagement on the Coa the French formally invested Almeida. Contrary to Wellington's expectation they made no attempt to mask the town and press over the mountains towards the Coimbra plain. Nor did they move south of the Tagus, where Hill with his two divisions were still watching for an enemy attempt to break through Alemtejo – the southern province of Portugal south of the Tagus - and, by a passage of the river near Abrantes, cut off the main allied army from Lisbon. The truth was that, owing to Soult's preoccupation in Andalusia, Masséna had not sufficient force for the dual advance against the capital which Wellington had always feared. And, having lost nearly two thousand draught animals and used up his forward ammunition during the siege of Ciudad Rodrigo, the Marshal was in no position to hurry. Not till August 15th did his troops commence active siege operations.

With the fortifications of Almeida in far better repair than those of Ciudad Rodrigo and garrisoned by 5000 Portuguese regulars under a British brigadier, Wellington began to hope that the advance over the mountains might be held up until the October rains. But on August 26th an unexpected disaster occurred. A chance bomb, falling in the courtyard of the castle of Almeida, just as a convoy of powder for the ramparts was being loaded opposite the open door of the main magazine, exploded a trail of powder from a leaky barrel and in a moment sent castle, cathedral and half the town into the air. Two days later the garrison surrendered. There was no ammunition left and, though the British commander tried to brazen it out, his Portuguese lieutenants, seeing no point in further resistance, betrayed the fact to the enemy.

It was a heavy blow. Yet it did not find Wellington unprepared. "The object of the allies," he had written when he first planned the campaign in the previous autumn, "should be to oblige the enemy as much as possible to make his attack with concentrated corps. They should stand in every position which the country could afford such a length of time as would enable the people of the country to evacuate towns and villages, carrying with them or destroying all articles of provisions and carriages."* Before the siege of Almeida began he had ordered his engineers to prepare charges on all the principal roads into the interior.† He now gave instructions for the systematic evacuation of the entire countryside between the frontier and the coastal plain at Coimbra. Everything was in train for a retreat to Lisbon and the mountain lines his engineers had been secretly preparing. For, though outnumbered and on the defensive, Wellington had no intention of letting Masséna call the tune. He

* Memorandum for Lieut-Colonel Fletcher, October 20th 1809.
† Burgoyne, I, 97.

was resolved to retain the initiative and make that wily Marshal and his Army of Portugal dance to his own piping.

Yet the success of his Fabian strategy turned on two uncertain factors: the attitude of the British Government and the behaviour of the Portuguese nation and army. For the ruthless plan he was about to put into execution was certain to try both high. From the Cabinet he was asking loyal and sustained support for a costly and apparently inglorious retreat at a time when they were facing bitter opposition in country and Parliament. From the Portuguese he demanded even more: the depopulation and ruin of their country-side and its abandonment to a cruel and hated enemy.

Nor was this his only demand on Portugal. Having only 30,000 British effectives with which to hold the mountain lines before Lisbon, he was dependent on the Portuguese regular army to make good his deficiency in numbers. It could only do so by fighting. "If the Portuguese do their duty," he had written at the beginning of the year, "I shall have enough to maintain it; if they do not, nothing that Great Britain can afford can save the country."* The difficulty was to make them fight. On its record the Portuguese Army was no more to be depended on than the Spanish. When Wellington had landed in the country two years before, it was undisciplined, unarmed and demoralised. The very idea of its resisting the French seemed unthinkable. It had allowed Junot to seize Lisbon with less than 2000 men. Its habit of flying at the first shot amid excited cries of "Vamos!" had caused the British soldier to coin a new and uncomplimentary word – to vamose.†

But Wellington was a realist. He knew from his Indian experiences that cowardice in the field was not caused by racial degeneracy but by failure to cultivate the military virtues. "We are mistaken," he wrote, "if we believe that what these Portuguese and Spanish armies want is discipline, properly so called. They want the habits and spirits of soldiers—the habits of command on one side and of obedience on the other—mutual confidence between officers and men."‡ The Portuguese army was a mob, without training, order, drill, *esprit de corps* or mutual confidence. Its officers were self-indulgent loafers in peacock feathers who gamed, drank, smoked and stank and, never

* To Rt Hon J. Villiers, January 14th 1810.
† Costello, 31; Fortescue, VII, 125, 135, 137; Leslie, 40, 47, 73.
‡ To Marshal Beresford, September 8th 1809.

having trained themselves for anything else, thought of nothing in the hour of danger but saving their skins.* Their men, ignorant and uncared-for peasants or unwilling artisans impressed by a periodic round-up of the public gardens, naturally followed their example. They were not brave, because no one had ever given a moment's thought to making them so.

Wellington, who had not been a Sepoy general for nothing, treated the reorganisation of the Portuguese Army under British discipline as a matter as important as the defence lines before Lisbon. In March, 1809, as a result of a treaty with the Regency, William Carr Beresford, a forty-year-old British Major-General, had taken over its command with the rank of a native Marshal. A big, commanding-looking man with a regal air and a blinded eye - the bastard of an Irish Marquis - he had a way with him that took the fancy of the Portuguese, much as they disliked his strenuous severity. With a few hundred young British officers and drill-sergeants to help him, he became under Wellington's supervision, organiser, schoolmaster and dictator of the Portuguese Service. He made it in everything but name and race an integral part of the British Army. Not only did it adopt the latter's drill-books, evolutions and bugle calls, but its ranks were completely re-clad and re-armed from British depots and magazines. After a few months of hard work and unrelenting discipline, the ragged Portuguese had been transformed into small, dark replicas of their powerful allies.

By the summer of 1810 more than 25,000 of them had been trained and drilled on the new method and brigaded with British formations. Their uniforms were clean, their arms smartly and efficiently handled and their conduct regular and obedient. With their bronzed faces, broad sturdy shoulders, steady ranks and fine equipment, they really looked like soldiers. Nobody could predict what they would do under fire, but their British officers believed that, if initiated with discretion and not exposed to too grave a risk of failure at the start, they would acquit themselves creditably. "The great object," wrote Captain Gomm, "is to give them confidence in themselves."†

*   *   *

---

* See Boothby, 149.

† Gomm, 155, 173. See also Schaumann, 229; Gomm, 153-5; Burgoyne, I, 65; Tomkinson, 42; Leslie, 40; Leith Hay, I, 190; *Peninsular Sketches*, 74-7; Sherer, 114-15, 143, 157; Fortescue, VIII, 428-31.

With such imponderables still unresolved, Wellington withdrew his rearguard westwards before the French advance in September, 1810. The Portuguese peasantry behaved with stoic grandeur. Such was their hatred of the enemy and their instinctive patriotism that tens of thousands left their homes at a few days' notice, destroying their crops and driving their flocks before them. The wealthier classes, including the burghers in the towns, having more to lose, fell short of this high standard. A few even went so far in their desperation as to enter into secret communication with the enemy: at Figueira there was talk of a wild plot sponsored by French spies to massacre the British wounded and seize the town.* More serious was the resentment of educated and patriotic Portuguese at a retreat which they could not understand and which threatened to reduce them to penury. Protesting bitterly at what they regarded as a British betrayal and the prelude to another evacuation, they demanded an early stand. Even the Lisbon Regency, which had approved Wellington's plans, joined in the clamour against him.

In England, too, the public was growing restive. What, gentlemen abed argued, was the use of paying ever-rising taxes to maintain an army abroad, if that army did nothing but retire without fighting? To the taxpayer, harassed by Continental blockade and commercial crisis, Portugal, like Spain before it, seemed a bottomless pit. Ministers—forced to budget for an unprecedented expenditure of £85,000,000 and faced on every side by shortage of money—did not disguise their anxiety from their general in Portugal. Perceval, the new Prime Minister, warned him that, had he been able to foresee the immense drain of the campaign, he would never have dared to authorise its continuance.

Wellington was not a dictator like Napoleon, but a British general subject to public and parliamentary opinion. In view of Masséna's strength he had planned after the fall of Almeida to retire slowly to his lines without a fight, leaving hunger and disease to do the work of guns and muskets. But faced by riots in Lisbon and pessimism at home, he modified his dispositions. Having a profound sense of political responsibility, he decided that it was his duty to restore confidence by a successful action before withdrawing behind his winter defences. In its present attitude towards land operations Parliament could not be trusted to tolerate a long and apparently

* Smith, I, 32-3; Simmons, 100.

hopeless siege, and the clamour for evacuation – now universally expected – might well become more than a weak Government could withstand. The only remedy was to give the latter a new lease of life by a timely victory.

Yet on one thing Wellington was determined: that it should be a victory, so far as was humanly possible, without risk. He would pay no more for it than he could afford. He had already, anticipating such a situation, prepared a defensive position on the last mountain barrier dominating the road along the southern bank of the Mondego which he supposed the French would take to Coimbra. Here at the Ponte Murcella he ordered the immediate concentration of his army. Hitherto it had been operating in two widely separated sections, the larger, including the bulk of the British troops, under his personal command in Beira, the remainder under Hill in the Alemtejo to guard against any advance south of the Tagus either by the French 2nd Corps or Soult's Army of Andalusia. But Reynier's sudden northward march in mid-September to join Masséna had temporarily relieved Hill of the fear of a subsidiary drive to cut the British communications with Lisbon. Carrying out his instructions without a moment's delay, the latter set off to reinforce Wellington with seven thousand British and thirteen thousand Portuguese. His leading division reached the Mondego on September 20th; the remainder on the following day. By his promptitude he brought the allied strength before Coimbra to more than 50,000 and made a successful action against Masséna possible. "The best of Hill," his chief observed, "is that I always know where to find him."

Wellington did not fight the French in the position he had selected on the south bank of the Mondego, because they did not come that way. Relying on inadequate Portuguese maps and ignorant Portuguese traitors, Masséna chose an abominable track running through Trancosa and Vizeu far to the north of the river. Advancing over a wilderness of barren and incredibly tumbled hills, the invaders found that it had been denuded of every living thing except partisans. The militiamen of the national Ordenanza – called out by Wellington to resist invasion – waited in their mountain fastnesses until the main French army had passed and then descended in sudden, savage cascades on the baggage-train and supply columns. Laboriously negotiating a stony, narrow and precipitous track which had to be constantly cleared with picks and crowbars, guns, carts and horses fell far behind the infantry and became an easy prey. Five days after the main body left Almeida a party of two thousand militiamen under their Irish commander, Colonel Trant, nearly succeeded in capturing the Grand Park of the Army with all its heavy guns, and took a hundred of its guards prisoner. Only their indiscipline when confronted by regular fire saved it.

All this was as Wellington had planned. By drawing the French into a depopulated desert he was making it impossible for them to follow their usual practice of living on the countryside. And by raising the Ordenanza against them he was compelling them to dissipate strength in small detachments to maintain even a semblance of communication with Spain. The savagery with which the invaders responded to the guerrilla warfare he had launched only increased their difficulties. When Masséna avenged the capture of his Provost-Marshal by burning a village and shooting two militiamen as brigands, the Portuguese grew still fiercer and took to torturing their prisoners.

By taking the longer northern route, Masséna gave the British ample time to complete their concentration in front of Coimbra. His advance guard under Ney entered a deserted Vizeu, twenty miles short of the coastal plain, on September 18th when Hill's men, unknown to him, were already descending into the Mondego valley after their rapid march from the south. The position chosen by Wellington to bar the new French advance was the ridge of Busaco, some eight miles to the north-east of Coimbra. Stretching for nine miles from the Mondego in the south to the Sierra de Alcoba in the north, it towered above the wooded hills west of Mortagoa like a wall of bleak, heathery rock. Rising at one point to 1800 feet and falling away almost precipitously in rugged dells and dykes to the east, it was, apart from its length, an ideal position in which to fight a defensive battle. Of the 51,000 troops available to hold it, only 26,000 were British, for the promised reinforcements from England and the West Indies were still delayed by adverse winds and Walcheren fever. But no place could have been better chosen for giving the 25,000 Portuguese regulars brigaded with the British army a chance to win their spurs and acquire confidence.

Throughout September 21st, 22nd and 23rd the Allied troops toiled through gorse and heather to their allotted positions: so steep was the slope that one elderly colonel had to be carried up in a blanket by four sergeants.* Hill's and Leith's 2nd and 5th Divisions from the south took their places on the right of the ridge on the morning of the 26th, Leith nearest the centre and Hill on the flank commanding the Mondego gorge. Wellington's headquarters were at the Convent of Busaco in the left centre where the *chaussée* from Vizeu and Mortagoa climbed over the highest point of the ridge before dropping down into the Coimbra plain. From here a wonderful view extended far over the Atlantic to the west, and eastwards to the mountains across the tumbled, wooded foothills through which Masséna's army was labouring, its advance troops skirmishing with the retiring outposts of the Light Division and its muskets shining in the evening sunlight like distant lightning.†

The 26th, though pinched by a cold wind from the Estrella, was a beautiful day with bright September sunshine. From their lofty station the British looked down, as far as the eye could see, over dark, glittering columns winding under clouds of dust along every valley and forest clearing and coming steadily out of the east. It was not an armed force alone but a great multitude - horse, guns and foot, ambulances and commissariat, interminable trains of wagons, tribes of mules with their attendants, sutlers, camp followers and women. "So this," wrote an onlooker, "was the famous French army, the terror of the world, the conqueror of Italy, Spain, Egypt and Germany! It had been victorious at Jena, Austerlitz, Marengo, Ulm and Vienna, and on the morrow we were going to try conclusions with it."‡ But the British were not at all perturbed. Though for weeks every one had been expecting an evacuation, exhilarated by the clear air of that lonely spot and its Olympian prospect they were full of confidence. So was their leader. "If Masséna attacks me here," he said, "I shall beat him." The Portuguese had only to stand their ground and there could be no question of the result.

Masséna, watching Craufurd's rearguard withdrawing up the steep, heathery hillside, was equally confident. He snapped back at a brigade commander, who dwelt on the strength of the position, that he had seen many stronger. He did not believe that the Portuguese could fight, and he still thought that Hill and Leith, out-

---

* Anderson, 42.   † Schaumann, 244.
‡ See also Schaumann, 246-7; Leith Hay, I, 230; Tomkinson, 42; Fortescue, VII, 506; Grattan, 28; Gomm, 181.

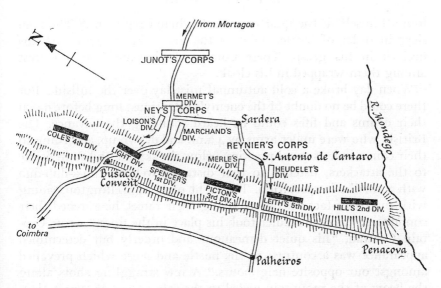

The Battle of Busaco

manœuvred by Reynier's rapid march to the north, were far away in the Alemtejo. The sharp edge of the ridge concealed the British regiments from his eyes and its great height placed them beyond the range of his field guns. But he knew the power and *élan* of his soldiers in attack and he had enjoyed too many victories over the veteran armies of the Continent to doubt the ability of his 62,000 to overwhelm 20,000 British. Four weak divisions, which were all he supposed before him, could not withstand three army corps. "I cannot persuade myself," he remarked, "that Lord Wellington will risk the loss of a reputation by giving battle, but if he does, I have him! To-morrow we shall effect the conquest of Portugal, and in a few days I shall drown the Leopard."

That night the French bivouac fires twinkled from a thousand points in the foothills in front of the ridge; it seemed as if Masséna was trying to frighten his foe off the hilltop by the size of his host. The British, concealed among the cedars and pine-woods of the western slopes, encamped in darkness. Here a young Scottish gentleman, travelling all day from Oporto to Lisbon through a wild and deserted countryside, heard at the entrance of a glen the strains of "The Garb of Old Gaul" played by a bagpipe and a moment later

213

found himself in the quarters of a Highland regiment.* The men slept in order of battle, quiet as the grave, every man with his firelock in his grasp. Their Commander-in-Chief took his rest among them wrapped in his cloak.

When day broke a cold autumnal mist lay over the hillside. But there could be no doubt of the enemy's intentions: long before dawn their drums and fifes could be heard sounding the advance. The British, who were under arms by 4 a.m. and drawn up, according to their commander's usual practice, below the skyline and so invisible to the attackers, listened to that distant, swelling rub-a-dub-dub with a thrill of expectation. The sight of Lord Wellington, riding with matter-of-fact unconcern along their ranks, heightened their confidence: "as each soldier took his place in the lines," wrote Captain Grattan, "his quiet demeanour and orderly but determined appearance was a contrast to the bustle and noise which prevailed amongst our opposite neighbours." A few straggling shots along the brow of the mountain added to the sober sense of expectation.

Disregarding the lessons of Vimiero, Corunna and Talavera, Masséna launched his attack against the long British line in dense columns. He disposed his assault-troops in two massive fists timed to strike successively. The 14,000 infantry of Reynier's two divisions on his left or southern flank were drawn up in serried battalions on a single company front astride a low outlying spur opposite the centre of the ridge. Here, where a rough country track climbed over a low saddle between the villages of San Antonio de Cantaro and Palheiros, they were to drive in two columns over the pass and, descending the far slope to the Coimbra highroad, wheel northwards round the rear of Wellington's main position. As soon as they had reached the summit, two divisions of Ney's 6th Corps to the north were to swarm up either side of the *chaussée* from Mortagoa and break what Masséna took to be the centre of Wellington's line at the Busaco Convent. The third division of Ney's Corps and the whole of the 8th Corps were held in reserve on the Mortagoa road to complete the rout when the British centre had been surrounded.

The flaw in this plan, apart from its underestimate of Allied numbers and fighting capacity, was its assumption that, by striking at the centre of the ridge, Reynier could roll up Wellington's flank. Over-confidence in the rapidity of his own dispositions and a com-

* Scott, II, 403. He fought by their side next day as a volunteer.

plete absence of reconnaissance had blinded Masséna to the fact that Hill's two divisions from the Alemtejo were in position beyond what he supposed to be the extreme right of the British line. Thinking of the British in terms of the Flanders campaign of 1793, he had failed to realise their new efficiency and, least of all, that of their commander.

Starting shortly before dawn in a thick mist and preceded by a cloud of *tirailleurs*, Reynier's two divisions started up the hillside at speed. But the precipitous gradient and indented, rocky ground quickly broke them up into small breathless crowds climbing diagonally and straggling. Merle's division on the right took the lead, driving in the British skirmishers by sheer numbers and infiltrating in the mist nearer and nearer to the crest. Then suddenly the swirling vapour lifted and the *voltigeurs*, " with all the characteristic activity, alacrity, firmness and incessant progress of a French attack," could be seen in the bright sunshine swarming up the rocks and loading and firing their muskets as they advanced.* The British field guns, quickly opening up, drove lanes of shot through the struggling masses of Heudelet's division and, supported by the fire of a mixed British and Portuguese brigade, brought it quickly to a halt. But farther to the north Merle's division, 6500 strong, reached the top, more by accident than design at a point in the long drawn-out British line where there was a gap between two battalions of Major-General Picton's 3rd Division.

The one weakness in Wellington's position was its extent; with the limited fire-power of the time, a front of nine miles was too much for 51,000 men to hold easily. But the gaps were more apparent than real, for from their commanding height the defenders had ample time to foresee where an attack was impending, while behind their lines a lateral track, carefully prepared by their prescient commander and running just below the skyline out of sight of the enemy, made it easy to transfer troops quickly to any threatened point. Mobility and flexibility were the keynote of Wellington's dispositions; as always, he had so placed his forces that any part of the line under pressure could be at once reinforced from some other. Only the morning mist had enabled Merle to reach the summit before the British could arrive to repel him. Already the 45th and 88th Foot and two Portuguese battalions were hurrying from different

* Leith Hay, I, 236.

directions to the spot. As the French were reforming on the little plateau and recovering their breath, the 88th suddenly appeared on their right advancing towards them, supported by four companies of the 45th.

The 88th were a tough crowd from the bogs of western Ireland with a bad reputation for filching Portuguese chickens and goats. But they were born fighters and their Scottish colonel - Alexander Wallace - had made them one of the crack regiments of the army. Looking them full in the face with his steady, cheerful countenance, he addressed them as they stood to their arms before forming column: "Now, Connaught Rangers, mind what you are going to do; pay attention to what I have so often told you, and, when I bring you face to face with those French rascals, drive them down the hill - don't give the false touch but push home to the muzzle! I have nothing more to say, and if I had it would be of no use, for in a minute or two there'll be such an infernal noise about your ears that you won't be able to hear yourselves." As the Rangers bore down with the bayonet, and Wallace, dismounting, placed himself at their head, the enemy hastily opened fire. "All," wrote an officer, "was confusion and uproar, smoke, fire and bullets, officers and soldiers, French drummers and French drums knocked down in every direction, British, French and Portuguese mixed together, while in the midst of all was to be seen Wallace fighting - like his ancestor of old - at the head of his devoted followers and calling out to his soldiers to press forward."* "Upon my honour," Wellington called out to him, reining in his horse, "I never witnessed a more gallant charge than that just now made by your regiment."

Had the French been allowed longer to recover their ranks, they might have established themselves on the summit in the centre of the British line. But the Commander-in-Chief's foresight, Wallace's promptitude and the fiery valour of his men saved the situation. Within a few minutes, aided by the fire of a Portuguese battalion and two guns which Wellington had galloped up from the left, eleven French battalions, including one of Napoleon's favourite regiments, were being bundled down the hillside. They left behind them nearly 2000 dead and wounded.

Half an hour later, though the bulk of Heudelet's division remained halted among the heather by the fire of the British and

* Grattan, 33.

Portuguese above, a single brigade under General Foy, serpentining through the rocks, reached the summit at the same spot. The scene was thereupon repeated. This time it was not Picton's division that cleared the ridge but Leith's, moving along the lateral track from the right to strengthen the threatened centre and left at the orders of the Commander-in-Chief who, as at the crucial moment of Talavera, had anticipated the danger and taken timely steps to meet it. Scrambling up the crest, the 9th or East Norfolks, supported by the 38th and the Royals, unexpectedly appeared on the ridge in front of the French, and, deploying, opened a terrible fire from a hundred yards. Then, with General Leith riding beside waving his plumed hat, the regiment bore down with fixed bayonets. Sooner than await that avalanche of steel, the enemy turned about and raced for the slope and, tumbling headlong down the hill, left it strewn with blue-clad bodies.

The sun was now climbing high in the heavens, and, though a further attack was developing on the left, a feeling of exaltation prevailed in the allied lines.* On either side of the steep *chaussée* which wound up the hillside to the convent Ney's two divisions were struggling through the gorse and heather. The going was even harder than in the centre, and the riflemen of the Light Division and the shrapnel of Captain Ross's troop of Horse Artillery did much execution in the toiling ranks. But the French continued to press on with great gallantry. At the sound of firing to the north, Wellington had galloped for a mile along the ridge to the point where Craufurd's men were holding the ravine up which the highroad ran; here he calmly reconnoitred the advancing foe through his field-glass regardless of the bullets spattering around him. Throughout the fighting he had appeared at the crucial moment at every threatened point, giving his orders, as Captain Moyle Sherer had heard him earlier in the day, in a loud, firm, decisive but reassuringly calm voice, "If they attempt this point again, Hill, you will give them a volley and charge with the bayonet, but don't let your people follow them too far down the hill." "He had nothing of the truncheon about him," Sherer noted: "nothing important, foul-mouthed or fussy: his orders on the field are all short, quick, clear and to the purpose."†

A few hundred yards to the left of his Commander-in-Chief's

* Leith Hay, I, 237.   † Sherer, 148-50.

vantage point, Craufurd was standing at the edge of the hill watching the Rifles and the Portuguese contesting every foot of ground with Loison's column. Yet it was not on the skirmishers of the 95th and the 1st Caçadores among the heathery boulders below that he was relying. Drawn up in the sunken roadway behind him, out of sight of the enemy, were the eighteen hundred bayonets of the 43rd and 52nd. Just as the French drums were beating for the final charge and their officers, capering up and down like madmen, were waving their hats on their swords and urging their men to rush the last twenty yards and seize Ross's guns on the skyline, Craufurd turned to the two famous Light Infantry regiments lying behind him and shouted, "Now 52nd, revenge the death of Sir John Moore!" With a great cheer the men rushed forward and poured such a fire from the crest into the astonished enemy, following their ordered volleys up with the bayonet, that the whole six thousand were dashed in a few minutes to the bottom.

By eleven o'clock the battle was over. Though firing continued for the rest of the day Masséna made no further attempt on that high, defiant ridge. Of the 40,000 infantry he had thrown into the attack more than a tenth had fallen or been wounded or taken prisoner, including five generals. The British and Portuguese, who, with 33,000 fresh troops still unengaged, had suffered only a quarter of the French casualties, remained complete masters of the field. Twenty-four battalions had repelled and put to flight forty-five. And of the allied units engaged nearly half had been Portuguese. The latter were naturally immensely elated; they had proved themselves men on the open field and taken heavy toll of the hated invaders. "It has given them," wrote the Commander-in-Chief, "a taste for an amusement to which they were little accustomed."*

The objects for which he had given battle had been achieved. His allies had learnt their strength and his countrymen had been heartened. But neither he nor Masséna were men to be deceived for a moment as to the true situation by a single inconclusive engagement, however exhilarating or depressing. Both were cool, experienced hands in the bloody business of war. Almost before the battle was over the French commander had begun to seek a way round the left of the British position; he realised that he had underestimated his enemy and must be more patient. Moving into the mountains of the

* For Busaco see Weller, 124-40; Fortescue, VII, 500-32; Longford, 224-30.

Sierra de Caramula early on the 28th, his cavalry patrols found a rough track leading to the coastal plain some thirteen miles to the north of Coimbra. Wellington, who knew of the road's existence, had ordered Trant to hold it with his Portuguese militiamen, but the latter, handicapped by their lack of discipline, were unable to reach it in time. Sooner than run any risk of being cut off from the crossing of the Mondego at Coimbra or of being hustled in his retreat to his chosen position before Lisbon, Wellington gave the order to retire.

So it came about that on the night of September 28th 1810, the British marched down from the cold, misty mountain and vanished into the south. The troops, in high spirits after their victory, were naturally surprised at the withdrawal. To the Portuguese, rejoicing at their unexpected reprieve, it seemed utterly unaccountable. They now became sure that Wellington meant to abandon them. The earlier scenes of mass evacuation were now repeated; at a few hours' notice the inhabitants of Coimbra were hustled out on to the highroad with their goods piled on the few carts the army had left unrequisitioned and bearing pitiful bundles on their heads and in their hands. Within a day the pleasant old university town became a solitude. The road was thronged with thousands of helpless creatures, many of them bare-footed and in rags, trudging between the retreating columns or trailing disconsolately across the adjoining fields.*

Yet neither the wailing of old women calling on the saints in wayside oratories nor the frantic expostulations of the Portuguese Government could make any impression on Wellington. "I should forget my duty to my Sovereign, to the Prince Regent and to the cause in general," he informed the War Minister at Lisbon, "if I should permit public clamour or panic to induce me to change in the smallest degree the system and plan of operations which I have adopted after mature consideration."† As there was no position south of the Mondego on which he could stand until he reached his prepared lines, a further seventy miles of country had to be wasted. Meanwhile the Light Division and the cavalry of Anson's brigade, retiring at their own pace, kept the French at a safe distance. Not till

* Gomm, 185; Seaton, 146; Anderson, 41, 44-5; Tomkinson, 50; Burgoyne, I, 121; Leslie, 211; Schaumann, 261; Sherer, 162-4; Leith Hay, I, 242-3.
† To Dom Miguel Forjaz, September 6th 1810.

October 1st did the last British troops march out of Coimbra. As they passed through the deserted city, now blazing in many places, the Rifles were stopped by the agonised cries of the criminals and lunatics left behind in the town gaol. Within a few minutes the poor creatures, hastily set at liberty, were leaping and howling in a delirium of joy along the bridge over the Mondego, with the wide world before them and the French dragoons at their heels.*

As the retreat continued along the road up which Wellington had advanced on Lisbon two years before, British discipline, admirable at first, began to grow a little ragged. In Condeixa, where the commissariat was destroying stores, the streets were ankle-deep in rum into which passing soldiers dipped their caps as they marched; others helped themselves to shoes and shirts which the harassed commissaries handed out to all and sundry.† At Leiria an olive tree beside the road was hung by orders of the Commander-in-Chief with the corpses of two soldiers caught in the act of plundering a church. Uninhabited but furnished buildings with open doors were too tempting for men who had enlisted to escape the constable and who reflected that what they did not help themselves to to-day the enemy would take to-morrow. Others plundered out of high spirits: at the deserted convent of Batalha, where the hallowed body of John of Portugal was preserved, a finger of the warrior king mysteriously found its way into the regimental baggage of the 95th.

On the last night of the retreat - October 7th - the equinoctial rains, which had hitherto held off, set in with full fury. Next day the line of march presented a terrible spectacle. Along roads littered with smashed cases and broken wagons, dead horses and exhausted men, moved a dense mass of misery - mothers carrying children on their backs, fine ladies wading in torn silk and bedraggled lace knee-deep in mud, nuns beside themselves with fear at their expulsion from familiar convents or, grown bold from necessity, with arms linked with those of friendly British soldiers.‡ Mingled with them were herds of starving bullocks, sheep, donkeys and mules. Behind, led by the Provost Marshal's guard with the Busaco prisoners, tramped the British regiments. Here, too, depression had set in after the high hopes of the battle. With grim faces and tattered uniforms dripping from torrential rain, the men marched the last

* Kincaid, 17; George Napier, 149.   † Kincaid, 18.
‡ Schaumann, 261, 263; George Napier, 149; Leslie, 210-11; Gomm, 184, 187.

stage of the three hundred-mile retreat from Almeida imagining that the best before them was a shameful evacuation. During the rapid marches of the past week rations had started to run short; a draft of red-cheeked, chubby youths from England, who had just joined the 95th, recalled with ravenous longing, as they trudged their twenty miles a day, the ship's dumplings they had left behind.* Alternately deploying and marching, the weary rearguard still kept the French at bay, though the latter, sensing victory, were growing bolder every hour. Already their cavalry were pressing ahead, as Masséna, snatching at the glittering prize of Lisbon, began to close in for the kill.

Then, as pursued and pursuers approached Torres Vedras, the lines rose out of the mountains to greet them. Scarcely any one even in the British army had any idea of their existence. Scores of guns disposed in elaborate redoubts and earthworks looked down from every height. Trenches had been dug, parapets raised, palisades, abatis, *chevaux de frise* and *trous-de-loup* made, forests, orchards, mounds and houses levelled to the ground, every hollow and ditch that could give cover against the cross-fire of the guns filled in, and every hillside turned into a vast, exposed, featureless glacis. In other places streams had been damned to form impassable marshes and defiles blasted into precipices. Wellington's engineers had used the respite Napoleon had given them to good advantage. For nearly a year thousands of Portuguese labourers had been working to turn a broken range of hills into an impregnable barrier. Every pass had been barred, every roadway transformed into a death-trap. Behind, echeloned in immense depth, were other forts and redoubts whose guns covered every way to Lisbon. And on either flank of the twenty-nine miles of mountain wall the British Navy was on guard. Already, as the enemy's left moved along the Tagus highway, the gunboats of the river flotilla went into action.

The French were dumbfounded. Masséna had had no idea that any serious obstacle lay in his path. The Portuguese traitors at his headquarters had told him that the approach to Lisbon from the Mondego was through open, uneventful country. "*Quel diable!*" he exclaimed when they laid the blame on those who had failed to discover what Wellington had been doing to their familiar hills, "*il n'a pas construit ces montagnes!*" In his haste to destroy the British

* Kincaid, 11-12.

before they could reach their boats, the Marshal had concentrated his entire force in a single great surge and left his communications to look after themselves. He had even exposed his hospitals at Coimbra to Trant's wild militiamen with the result that the latter, overwhelming the inadequate guard, had seized the town on October 6th and borne off 4500 French wounded to Oporto. And now he found his way barred by what he saw at once was an impregnable barrier.

The more he looked at it, the less he liked it. After a half-hearted attack in the rain on October 14th against an outlying mound near Sobral—from which the British withdrew to their main lines after inflicting heavy losses on his men—Masséna decided that any attempt to storm the heights would end in a massacre. So strong were the British works that they could be held by artillerymen and second-line troops alone, while, in accordance with Wellington's plan, the main army remained in the field ready to strike down any attackers who succeeded in scaling their slopes and penetrating through the cross-fire of their guns. And behind them, as Masséna soon learnt, lay other and still stronger lines.

For the British had fallen back to their ultimate base - the sea. The French with their strung-out land communications had advanced far from theirs and were at their very weakest. Around them was a wasted wilderness. Behind them the Portuguese guerrillas were closing in on every road. Within a fortnight Masséna, wishing to send a letter to Napoleon, was forced to detach half a brigade under General Foy to carry it back to Spain. Only the fact that Wellington's orders to destroy all crops and food had here and there been disobeyed, and the ability of the hardy French to live on next to nothing, enabled the Army of Portugal to retain its position at all.

Yet though Masséna could not go forward, he would not go back. Neither he nor his master had given up hope of driving the British army from Lisbon. Though it could be provisioned from the sea, its impregnable stronghold could only be held permanently if the British Government and people were prepared to go on maintaining it. And the tone of the Opposition in Parliament and the country and the almost pitiful weakness of the Perceval Administration gave Napoleon cause for hope. It was worth letting Masséna's army die of starvation in front of Wellington's lines if by doing so it could wear down the patience of Britain.

For, in his moments of frankness with himself, Napoleon was beginning to see that everything depended ultimately on this. If the tide of French conquest which had flowed to the ramparts of Lisbon could be held there till the British tired of their purpose and came away, the liquidation of Spanish resistance would follow and, with the west of Europe finally subdued, he would be able to turn his full forces against the still unconquered east. But, if the British remained, the war in Spain would continue to consume his armies until, once more, he was forced to fight on two fronts. For, owing to the blockade and the Continental System by which he sought to break it, the Emperor's relations with the Czar were steadily deteriorating. "I shall have war with Russia," he told Metternich in September, "on grounds that lie beyond human possibilities, because they are rooted in the cause itself." In October, at a moment when he still believed that his troops were marching into Lisbon, he had requested Alexander to seize six hundred ships trading in his ports under American and other neutral flags but carrying goods of suspected British origin. And the Czar, yielding to the pressure of his merchants and relying on Napoleon's preoccupation in the Peninsula, had refused.

Therefore, though Wellington complained of Opposition journals which kept "the people of England in a state of constant alarm and agitation" and urged the Government to take counter-measures to prevent every newswriter from running away with the public mind, their effect on policy was negligible. Ministers continued to support their general in Portugal, and the solider part of the public, preferring anything to the half-pacifist Whigs, stood by them and prayed for a victory before Lisbon and a continuance of the campaign.

So the tide of French conquest remained held and then, unable to advance farther, began, as is the way with tides, to recede. Though no one knew it except perhaps Wellington, its flood days were over for ever. Henceforward it was to ebb, at first slowly, yet with ever-growing momentum.

For a month Masséna clung to the waterlogged, wind-swept fields in front of Wellington's lines while his men grew daily more ravenous and his pack and draught animals died in thousands. The British, fed from their ships and snug in their entrenchments, were so sorry for the starving French sentries that they tossed them biscuits from the points of their bayonets and secretly traded them surplus rations and tobacco in return for brandy.* But, though the spirits of his men were high, Wellington refused to attack. He knew the skill of Masséna and the tenacity of the French, and he was not going to waste lives needlessly. " I could lick those fellows any day," he remarked, " but it would cost me 10,000 men, and, as this is the last army England has got, we must take care of it."†

On the morning of November 15th the British outposts noticed that the haggard sentinels in front of their lines had grown strangely stiff: closer examination showed that they were dummies made of straw. The French had withdrawn during the night under cover of a fog. For the next four days the allies followed them northwards along the Tagus. " This retreat," wrote a soldier of the 71st High-landers, " brought to my mind the Corunna race. We could not advance a hundred yards without seeing dead soldiers of the enemy.... The retreat resembled more that of famished wolves than men. Murder and devastation marked their way; every house was a sepulchre, a cabin of horrors!"‡ Those who had evaded Wellington's orders to evacuate their homes had paid dear for their disobedience.

On November 18th the French halted in front of the riverside town of Santarem, thirty miles north of the lines of Torres Vedras. Here Masséna, in the hope that Wellington would throw aside his caution and attack him, had prepared a strong position and concentrated the bulk of his army. But the British Commander, restraining Craufurd from a frontal attack with the Light Division, persisted in his " safe game." He was at the head, he explained, of the only army remaining in being in the Peninsula or in Europe able to contend with the French, and he was not going to lose a man of it without the clearest necessity. Four months of winter had still to go, and during that time Masséna should have only two alternatives: to stay where he was and starve, or to face the horrors of a mid-winter retreat over the mountains.

Of the two evils for the French, Wellington regarded the latter as the lesser. " I am convinced," he wrote to the Secretary of State, " that there is no man in his senses who has ever passed a winter in Portugal who would not recommend them to go now." Yet Masséna

* Costello, 56; *Journal of a Soldier.*
† Fortescue, VII, 555.
‡ *Journal of a Soldier,* 100. See also Smith, I, 37; Simmons, 121; Leach, 179.

did not go. Something might yet turn up to cause the stubborn British Commander-in-Chief to weaken or disperse his forces. Concentrated in a strongly defended triangle between Santarem, Thomar and Punchete, the equally stubborn French marshal waited with his savage, hungry men for a false move on the part of his opponent and a chance to get between him and Lisbon.

But Wellington merely kept his restraining guard round the French position and watched his enemy growing daily weaker. He made no attempt to snatch a victory, for he knew that hunger and disease would do his work as quickly and far more cheaply than guns and bayonets. Nor did he seek by any showy triumph to draw Masséna's selfish, sluggish colleagues from Andalusia and northern Spain to his aid. It was only necessary to wait patiently for everything to be added. "If we can only hold out," he wrote, "we shall yet see the world relieved."

Chapter Nine

THE TURN OF THE TIDE

In the War in which we are engaged, no man can pretend to say
how long it will last.

WELLINGTON

THE fourth French offensive against Portugal had failed. By an inflexible exercise of will and sound judgment Wellington had done precisely what he had said he would do, though a few months before scarcely a man in England or even in his own army had thought it possible. " Being embarked," he had written, " in a course of military operations of which I hope to see the successful termination, I shall continue to carry them on to their end."*

Yet, though he had defeated the enemy's offensive, he had made no attempt to take it himself. His plan did not admit of risks, and he would not deviate from it by a hair's breadth. So long as his adversary chose to remain entrenched among the hills and marshes around Santarem - one of the strongest positions in Portugal - time and hunger were on Wellington's side. He did not intend to give the wily victor of Zurich the slightest opportunity. He preferred, he told Ministers, the sure game and the one in which he was likely to lose the fewest men.

Masséna clung on manfully. In a starving match in which the dice were loaded against him, he persisted where almost any other commander would have despaired. He wrung sustenance - of a sort - out of the very rocks and fed his men on roots and garbage; it could scarcely, wrote the British commander, be called subsisting. Where the latter had given his foe a month in which to starve, the old Marshal held out for three. It was an astonishing example of what a French army could do.

At the back of Masséna's mind lay the hope that sooner or later one of his fellow Marshals would relieve him and enable him to resume the offensive. He knew that Soult, with his 70,000 troops

* To Charles Stuart, October 6th 1810.

226

and his viceroyalty at Seville, had little love for him, but he believed that Napoleon would force him to act. Though the guerrillas in the mountains had cut off all normal communication between Santarem and Spain, Foy, dispatched from Torres Vedras in October, had reached Paris at the end of November. And by Christmas, as Masséna had guessed, the Emperor ordered Soult to the Tagus.

Yet it was one thing to tell the Duke of Dalmatia to take an army across Estremadura and the Alemtejo in midwinter to release the Prince of Essling: another for him to do so. Not only had Wellington transferred 10,000 troops under Hill to the south bank of the Tagus to barricade Masséna in from that side, but the principal crossing at Abrantes was guarded by a powerful Portuguese fortress. Between the great river and Seville, two hundred miles distant, lay six other fortresses - Badajoz, Olivenza, Elvas, Campo Mayor, Albuquerque and Jerumenha - as well as two Spanish field armies operating from almost inaccessible hills under La Romana's lieutenants, Mendizabal and Ballasteros. Without abandoning the siege of Cadiz and the whole of Andalusia—and this Napoleon had expressly omitted to order—Soult could not assemble a force sufficient to overcome such obstacles, even if he could master the equally insuperable difficulties of supplying it.

Instead, therefore, he gathered 20,000 troops - the most he could collect without relaxing his hold on the rich, turbulent cities of Cordoba, Malaga, Jaen and Seville - and set out on December 30th for Estremadura. His aim was to reduce as many of the Spanish and Portuguese frontier fortresses as possible and so create a diversion which would draw part of Wellington's forces away from Masséna. Napoleon was having to pay the inevitable price for his refusal to appoint a supreme commander in the Peninsula and his attempt to direct operations from Paris. Indeed, had the Spanish generals played their cards as Wellington advised, Soult in pursuit of his master's orders could soon have been in as grave a plight as Masséna.

Luckily for him the Spanish leaders as usual threw away their advantages. Like most of his fellow Marshals, Soult, indolent and neglectful on the crest of the wave, reverted in adversity to the stark, Revolutionary dynamism which had made him. Marching in two columns to feed his troops, he reached Olivenza in under a fortnight. Whereupon General Mendizabal, regardless of the hopeless inadequacy of its long-neglected fortifications, threw in part of his field army to enlarge the garrison. When a week later its incompetent commander surrendered, 4000 Spanish troops were needlessly lost.

Worse followed. On January 26th 1811, Soult laid siege to the great fortress of Badajoz, commanding the Guadiana valley and the main highway into southern Portugal. He had little hope of taking it, but he calculated rightly that the threat would force Wellington to detach troops for its relief. So long as Masséna clung to his positions round Santarem, the British commander dared not employ more than a division of his own beyond the Tagus. But he at once released La Romana's entire Spanish force to reinforce Mendizabal. Unfortunately at that precise moment La Romana fell ill and died, and before his successor, Castaños, could arrive on the scene, the incompetent Mendizabal had blundered into a major disaster. On February 19th 1811, though outnumbering Soult by two to one, he allowed himself to be surprised and routed on the Gebora river under the walls of Badajoz. The Spaniards had done exactly what Wellington had urged them not to do. They had destroyed their own army.

Though with its formidable walls and position Badajoz was capable of withstanding a long siege, Wellington could do nothing more to relieve it so long as Masséna stood his ground. Yet not only did his plans for a future offensive turn on its relief, but its fall while the enemy threatened Lisbon would open the floodgates to a new French invasion of Portugal and undo all that he had accomplished.

Aid, however, was forthcoming from another quarter. For all operations against the common foe in the Peninsula were, as Wellington had seen from the first, one and indivisible. By pinning down Masséna and so drawing Soult to his aid, he had caused the latter to withdraw troops who were holding down liberating forces elsewhere. A third of Soult's 20,000 had been taken from Victor's army before Cadiz. And this left Victor only 19,000 with which to contain 25,000 Spaniards, British and Portuguese.

Major-General Thomas Graham, the commander of the British contingent in Cadiz, grasped his opportunity. This sixty-two-year-old Scottish laird, who had begun his military career as a volunteer at the siege of Toulon only eighteen years before, was by now a master of war. To march to the sound of the guns had become part of his nature. As soon as the French began to withdraw troops from their lines, he and the British Admiral, Sir Richard Keats, started to urge their Spanish colleagues to break the siege by transporting part of the garrison, including the British contingent, to Tarifa to attack Victor's lines in the rear. To recommend it to the Spanish Commander-in-Chief, General Manuel La Peña, he offered to serve under his command. In this he exceeded his instructions, but in view of the urgent need to take pressure off Wellington, it seemed a lesser evil than to do nothing. Unhappily La Peña was a byword for incompetence even among Spanish generals. He was the kind of officer who opposed everything except the enemy.

The expedition sailed from Cadiz on February 21st, 1811. Consisting of 9500 Spaniards, 4900 British and 300 Portuguese, it landed at Algeciras two days later, where it encountered the usual tale of broken Spanish promises and unprovided rations and transport. But with fierce Scottish insistence and threats to withdraw to Gibraltar, Graham broke the spell of the eternal *mañana*, and on February 28th the Allied army set out to march the sixty miles up the coast to Cadiz. On March 5th on the plain of Chiclana it encountered Victor, who, like all his kind in a tight place, had reverted to the speed and spirit of the Revolution and, raising the siege, marched to the attack. The battle which ensued turned on the possession of the Barrosa ridge which through incredible folly La Peña allowed to fall into the enemy's hands but which Graham's men, with wonderful valour, against odds, recaptured. Six guns, an imperial eagle, and a wounded general of division remained with the victors.

Throughout the engagement the Spaniards on the beach never moved; La Peña had reduced himself and his men to a state of complete prostration. It was the inevitable consequence of the habit into which the military system of Spain had fallen; Don Quixote at his most fantastic now sat in the saddle of the Conquistadores. "They march the troops night and day without provisions or rest," Wellington wrote to Graham after the battle, "abusing everybody who proposes a moment's delay to afford either to the famished and fatigued soldiers. They reach the enemy in such a state as to be unable to make any exertion or to execute any plan, even if any plan had been formed; and, when the moment of action arrives, they are totally incapable of movement, and they stand by to see their allies destroyed, and afterwards abuse them because they do not continue, unsupported, exertions to which human nature is not equal." Graham was so angry that next day he withdrew to Cadiz without even acquainting La Peña, and the French, who were on the point of retiring to Seville, resumed their blockade.

Four days after Barrosa, in despair at the news of Graham's landing behind Victor's lines and of an advance by a Spanish patriot army from the Rio Tinto against Seville, Soult summoned the Governor of Badajoz to surrender. It was his only hope of averting disaster. To his utter astonishment the infirm and desponding Spaniard, who had succeeded to the command of the fortress on the death of its gallant commander, General Menacho, surrendered next day without having sustained a single assault. A breach had been made in the walls, but he had 8000 troops, 150 guns and ample ammunition, and had just learnt that a British army was hastening to his relief. Luckily Soult could not exploit his triumph further, for his concern now was not Masséna's starving army but his own rear. Leaving Mortier with 11,000 troops to hold the captured fortress, he hurried back to save his Andalusian capital and the blockade of Cadiz.

Even had Soult been free to advance towards the Tagus, it would now have availed Masséna nothing. For on the evening of March 5th - the day of Barrosa - his army reduced almost to its last biscuit, the Marshal had begun his retreat to the north. A month earlier, with an escort of 2000 men, Foy had fought his way through the mountains and the encircling guerrillas to bring him his first news of the outer world. The orders he bore from Napoleon promised early relief, but they were already six weeks out of date when they arrived, and by the end of February it was plain that any help would come too late. Of the 73,000 first-line troops who had originally invaded Portugal or joined Masséna since, only 44,000 survived. Every foot of the country they occupied had been scoured for food and more than five thousand horses had been eaten. To have delayed another week would have seen the end of the Army of Portugal's capacity to move at all.

Already judging the long-maturing plum ripe and in daily expectation of reinforcements in the Tagus, the patient Wellington was preparing to close for the kill. When on the morning of March 6th his men moved cautiously into Santarem, the full nature of the French disaster became apparent. The road was covered with dead soldiers and abandoned carriages; the houses filled with sick and dying in the last loathsome stages of disease. Many lay on the floor in full uniform, their arms still grasped in their hands as if asleep, or sat in chairs, stiff and upright, with shakos on and pinched features frozen in death. The route their comrades had taken was marked by straggling wretches with pallid, swollen faces which they turned with inexpressible pathos on their pursuers. The Rifles in the British van threw them their biscuits in pity as they passed.

But their pity turned to anger as they saw what they had done. For everywhere were burning and ravaged houses, mutilated peasants with slit throats and gouged-out eyes, polluted churches and rifled graves. The whole countryside had been transformed into a waste fit only for wolves and vultures. The few surviving inhabitants looked like skeletons risen from the tomb. Gaunt and ghastly figures fed off the grass in the fields or scoured the woods for acorns and rotten olives. Violated women lay bleeding in charred and unroofed houses, the streets were strewn with putrid carcasses, children with bones sticking through their skin clung to the bodies of dead parents. Searching for a stream on the first night of the British advance, Rifleman Costello stumbled on a fountain into whose waters the brains of three peasants were oozing, while all that had possessed life in the village "lay quivering in the last agony of slaughter and awful vengeance." Here a Caçadore found the mangled bodies of his father and mother lying across the threshold of his home, while within his only sister was stretched dying on the floor. Staring wildly around him, the unhappy man rushed out and flung himself on a passing batch of prisoners, killing one and wounding another before he was pulled off by the guards. Another spectre stole towards a group of cadaverous Frenchmen and then suddenly, spitting on his hands, pulled out a club from under his cloak and beat out their brains.*

*　　　*　　　*

Under the shock of defeat Masséna's army had reverted to type. From the shambles of the Terror a whole generation had gone out to wage war and carry the Revolution into the lands of their neigh-

* Costello, 58-60, 69; Anderson, 62-4; Schaumann, 274-6; Kincaid, 40-1; Simmons, 138-9, 151-2; Donaldson, 165-6, *Peninsular Sketches* II, 293.

bours. Since 1792 the French had been a nation in arms.* Welded by enthusiasm and fear into a single instrument of force, these active, handy little fellows with their broad shoulders and spreading shakos, their short-waisted, roomy, swallow-tailed coats and large, baggy trousers, had terrorised the world. Nothing seemed able to tire or deter them; they would swarm up the steepest hill under the deadliest fire with such fury that their foes were paralysed before they arrived. Matchless in *élan* on the field, they were equally brilliant on the march or in the bivouac; there was scarcely a man of them who could not cook his savoury *potage* and make himself comfortable in the most inhospitable conditions. They had elevated plunder into a military science and could support themselves in a wilderness: they would nose out the last sack of peasant's corn or potatoes from the bottom of a well or the back of a bricked-up chimney and return next day with a shrewdly pointed bayonet for more. And like their Emperor and his Marshals, they generally contrived to take something home to France with them. "A French soldier, ever with something valuable about him," wrote Grattan, "was quite a prize to one of our fellows."

Cocksure and arrogant even in adversity—Wellington complained that after Vimiero Junot had insisted on walking into dinner in front of him†—the conquerors of Europe possessed a certain charm. They were so gay, so ready to forget their hardships and make the best of the world which was their prey. They could be cheerful in the most unlikely places. George Napier described how after Sahagun he found a pocket of famished prisoners in a cellar and ordered them bread and wine. "This being done," he wrote, "the poor fellows were as merry as possible and began dancing and singing; and one of them took a little fiddle from his pocket and commenced playing quadrilles with as much energy and life as though he were playing to a parcel of ladies."‡ At their happiest there was something infectiously good-natured about them. Little, swarthy Frenchmen in front of the British lines would stick pieces

---

* When Haydon visited Paris in 1814 he found scarcely a driver of a fiacre, a waiter at a café, or a man in middle life who had not served in a campaign or been wounded.

† "Although I was the stranger and although of the two I was certainly the victorious general." Stanhope, 247. See also Simmons, 132; Haydon, I, 259.

‡ George Napier, I, 51; Leslie, 52. See also the delightful description of French gaiety by that unrelenting gallophobe, Haydon. Haydon, I, 247-8.

of bacon on their bayonets or hoist up their canteens with cheerful shouts of "I say come here - here is ver good rosbif! - here is ver good brandy!"* Wellington was perpetually having to take measures to stop fraternisation between the outposts; French officers were always inviting their British counterparts to plays and concerts and attending in turn their horse-races, football-matches and dog-hunts.

In triumph, towards an adversary they respected like the British, the French could be astonishingly chivalrous. "Gentlemen," cried General Laborde to his captives after Roliça, "now that you are my prisoners, we are no longer enemies."† Ney, told that Charles Napier, captured at Corunna, had an aged and widowed mother, sent him home by the first ship without waiting for an exchange. After Talavera a wounded captain of the 87th was sent into the British lines under a flag of truce so that he might breathe his last among his countrymen. "Ours, indeed, was a noble enemy," wrote Rifleman Costello, "they never permitted us to flag for want of stimuli, but kept us for ever on the *qui vive*. We anticipated little terror from capture." For the French soldiers' attitude towards the British was purely professional: they regarded them as fellow craftsmen worthy of their steel: as pupils who had made good. "*Eh bien, c'est égal*," cried the captured *moustache* to the Rifles standing around him, "*les écoliers sont dignes de leurs maîtres*. The French have taught you some terrible lessons, and you understand, at length, the art of making war as it should be."‡

In this lay the moral weakness of the French; they had learnt to glorify war for its own sake. Strength they valued above all other virtues. They literally believed in violence. They took brutality, death and destruction as matters of course; they were still the children of the guillotine. The packed theatres during the Terror; the crowd laughing at the bear, Martin, who ate the *moustache* in the Jardin des Plantes; the soldiers gambling on the bodies of their dead comrades in the hospital at Minsk while propped-up corpses with painted faces and masquerade dress were ranged along the blood-stained walls,§ were all symptoms of an acceptance of brute force and horror as part of the nature of things. Behind the gaiety of desperation and the conqueror's resplendent mask peeped the crazed eyes of the savage. The Grand Nation was still in the grip of a terrible fever.

* Buckham, 332-3.   † Leslie, 59.   ‡ Costello, 125.   § Festing, 198-9.

To such a people there was nothing fundamentally wrong in murder, plunder, and rape for these in their view were the inescapable lot of the conquered. The French atrocities at Santarem were not only the result of individual misery and desperation: they were the corporate Revolutionary reaction to opposition. They were like the September massacres. For months organised parties of soldiers had gone from village to village and farm to farm using torture as a military art in their efforts to extract the last crumb from the starving peasant.* During the retreat mass murder and arson were pursued as part of a deliberate policy, just as in Spain a few months before Suchet had ordered the entire population of Lerida to be driven into the castle yard and sprayed with grape-shot until the Governor surrendered. Because the Portuguese had chosen to waste their countryside at Wellington's orders, they had now to learn what it was to thwart the will of the French. Towns were systematically fired, and historic monasteries like Alcobaça - the pride of Portugal - were burnt to the ground on Masséna's orders. An orderly-book found near the Convent of Batalha gave the number of soldiers daily employed in the destruction of villages and houses;† peasants pressed as guides were automatically shot at the day's end to prevent their providing information to the British. In some places unexploded bombs and shells were even hidden in chimneys so that returning inhabitants should be blown to pieces when they attempted to light a fire. The line of retreat resembled the trail of a horde of barbarians rather than a European army.

The British soldiers - rough and brutalised though many of them were - were horrified at what they saw. They refused to accept such ruin and misery as a natural outcome of war. They distributed their own rations - already grown meagre with the pace of the advance - among the pallid children by the wayside, and compared the scenes before them with the gentle, ordered land they had left behind. "These were sights," wrote the dashing, gay-hearted Johnny Kincaid, "which no Briton could behold without raising his voice in thanksgiving to the author of all good that the home of his child-

* George Napier, 170-2.
† Wellington to Liverpool, March 14th 1811; Tomkinson, 80. See also Gomm, 204, 206, 209; Picton, I, 385; Charles Napier, I, 160; Grattan, 56; Anderson, 61-2; Schaumann, 284-5; Burgoyne, I, 124; Donaldson, 164; George Napier, 188.

hood had been preserved from such visitations."* The same thought passed through the mind of his Commander-in-Chief when he replied - a little petulantly - to a letter from Lord Liverpool complaining of the rising expense of the campaign. "I have no doubt that if the British army were for any reason to withdraw from the Peninsula," he wrote, "and the French Government were relieved from the pressure of military operations on the Continent, they would incur all risks to land an army in His Majesty's dominions. Then indeed would commence an expensive contest; then would His Majesty's subjects discover what are the miseries of war, of which, by the blessing of God, they have hitherto had no knowledge; and the cultivation, the beauty and prosperity of the country and the virtue and happiness of its inhabitants would be destroyed, whatever might be the result of the military operations. God forbid that I should be a witness, much less an actor, in the scene."†

The enemy's retreat increased Wellington's difficulties. Hitherto close to his base in the Tagus, it had been comparatively easy to feed his army; now, with forward magazines to be established in a wasted wilderness, his problems grew with every mile. At any moment his adversary - a master of defensive warfare - might turn and overwhelm his vanguard before the main body could come up. Even with its full strength deployed, his army was still no bigger than Masséna's, for a considerable part of it was beyond the Tagus where it had been sent to relieve Badajoz. And while the French could ultimately replace their losses by new conscriptions, with Wellington the loss of every man told; he had in his keeping England's only army and was responsible for its safety to a jealous and critical public assembly.‡ Unless he reached the Spanish frontier with it intact, all he had achieved in Portugal would be in vain.

Yet Wellington could not afford to allow his foes a moment to recover so long as they stood on Portuguese soil. Unless he could prevent them from crossing the Mondego, they would be free to

---

* Kincaid, *Random Shots*, 131. See also Gomm, 206; Charles Napier, I, 165; George Napier, 174-5; Donaldson, 166. "Soup kitchens were established by subscription among the officers. ... The soldiers evinced the same spirit of humanity, and in many instances, when reduced themselves to short allowance from having outmarched their supplies, they shared their pittance with the starving inhabitants." Walter Scott, *The Vision of Don Roderick*. Note XV.

† To Lord Liverpool, March 23rd 1811.

‡ "I knew that if I lost 500 men without the clearest necessity, I should be brought upon my knees to the bar of the House of Commons."

consolidate behind it and turn the still unwasted provinces of northern Portugal into a base for new operations against Lisbon. The river ahead was held by a few thousand Portuguese irregulars under Colonels Trant and Wilson; no resistance they could make could be prolonged. The only hope of saving northern Beira and Oporto from the same fate as Santarem was to press Masséna so hard that, not daring to force the river with the British army at his back, he would turn eastwards into the mountains. For this reason Wellington clung to his rear like a terrier behind a bull. Whenever his quarry halted he attacked or threatened his flanks.

He was careful to do so – and this was the beauty of his tactics – with the minimum of risk. The hilly and wooded terrain through which he had to advance was perfectly adapted for the defensive; a strong country like Portugal, he observed, afforded equally good positions to both sides. His method was to use the Light Division, with its superbly trained skirmishers and marksmen, to distract the enemy with sham frontal attacks, while Lowry Cole's 4th Division, Thomas Picton's 3rd and Brigadier Pack's Portuguese edged at high speed round their flanks. This happened when the French rearguard under Marshal Ney tried to stand on March 11th at Pombal, twenty miles south of the Mondego, and again next day at Redinha, half a dozen miles on. On each occasion Ney, sooner than risk encirclement, withdrew from a strong position after a few hours' skirmishing. British casualties in the two engagements were small – 14 officers and 228 men killed and wounded. They would have been smaller still but for the stupidity of Major-General Erskine, the cavalry officer who was commanding the Light Division in Craufurd's absence on leave in England. For this gallant but bull-headed soldier was apt to become so heated in battle as to forget his orders and attack everything he saw. By doing so he threw away valuable lives.

At dawn on March 13th Masséna, still closely pursued and finding the passage of the Mondego at Coimbra barred by Trant's militia, turned eastwards and made for the mountains. He thus gave up his last chance of revictualling his army inside Portugal. Before him lay only the barren hill track to Celorico and Almeida. In his decision he was partly influenced by the fear – a groundless one – that the British were about to land troops from the sea on his flank. The wraith of Nelson still pursued his eternal vendetta against his country's foes. "We have saved Coimbra and Upper Beira from the enemy's ravages," Wellington announced, "we have opened communications with the northern provinces and have obliged the enemy to take for their retreat the road by Ponte Murcella on which they may be annoyed by the militia acting in security upon their flank, while the allied army will press upon their rear.*

As they turned across the line of their pursuers' advance, the French had to quicken their pace to avoid disaster. So sudden was the change of plan that at one moment, owing to the failure of a trooper to get through from Ney, Masséna was nearly captured by a vedette of the King's German Legion - an accident which fanned the smouldering enmity between the two Marshals into open flame. During the 14th the British vanguard, driving from one hilltop to another, was continuously attacking, and by nightfall Masséna, having retreated fourteen miles, was forced to sacrifice the bulk of his remaining baggage and wheeled transport. Five hundred horses and mules were hamstrung and left to die in torment on the outskirts of Miranda de Corvo, where the sight of their bleeding flanks and pleading eyes further increased British resentment against the French.

Next day, after marching all night, Masséna reached the valley of the Ceira. Here at Foz do Arouce the 3rd and Light Divisions found Ney's rearguard at four o'clock in the afternoon on the wrong side of the flooded stream. Though his main force was still far behind, Wellington at once gave orders to attack. It was the Coa in reverse, with Ney in Craufurd's shoes. A rush for the bridge by the Light Division resulted in a panic which, but for Ney's brilliant leadership, might easily have become a rout. As it was, four hundred Frenchmen were drowned or taken prisoner.

During that day new signs of demoralisation had appeared in Masséna's ranks. From precipitate his retreat was becoming disorderly. The road was strewn with gold and silver crucifixes and rich ecclesiastical vestments, trampled in the slush amidst derelict wagons and limbers and dying soldiers. The deserted bivouacs, with the bulkier articles of wasteful spoil heaped in piles outside huts made out of demolished houses, looked like the camps of predatory Tartars. The atrocities committed on the civilian population became still more pathological; mutilated corpses were propped

* To Lord Liverpool, March 14th 1811.

up as though alive in chairs at cottage doors and in holes in garden
walls, and entire families were found murdered in their beds as if
for sport.*

But the pace of the retreat was also becoming too rapid for the
pursuers. In ten days they had advanced more than a hundred miles,
constantly fighting their way over steep wooded country, intersected
by gorges and swollen mountain streams, and sleeping by night on
the ground in drenched clothes. Even the British had far outmarched their supplies, while the Portuguese commissariat - never
strong - had broken down altogether. Several Caçadores actually
died of starvation on the march. On the 16th, therefore, Wellington
called a halt to reorganise his transport and magazines. He had
never subscribed to the Revolutionary belief in the possibility of
the impossible. Men could not, he wrote indignantly to the Regency
at Lisbon, perform the labour of soldiers without food.

At the moment when Wellington halted to preserve the tempered
steel of the weapon he wielded, he learnt of the surrender of Badajoz.
It was a terrible and unlooked-for blow. To eject the French before
they could consolidate, he at once dispatched Lowry Cole's 4th
Division to reinforce the 2nd under Beresford in Estremadura. This
reduced the strength of his main army to 38,000. When on the 17th
- in torrential rain - it resumed its advance, it was numerically
weaker than the enemy it was pursuing.

But Wellington knew by now that Masséna was in no state to
fight. On the night of March 18th 1811, after a rearguard action at
Ponte Murcella, the French abandoned all attempts at any further
stand and made a forced march of twenty miles over the mountains.
During the following day the allied cavalry gathered in 800 stragglers, while the Portuguese militiamen, descending from their hiding places, slew many more. By the 22nd Masséna's main body had
reached Celorico, thirty miles from the Spanish frontier and a few
days' march from its bases at Ciudad Rodrigo and Salamanca. The
invasion of Portugal was virtually over.

Masséna's pride would not let him admit it. His army's morale
had been undermined by starvation, but he still retained a French
Marshal's belief in the capacity of the human will to achieve the
impossible. He refused to trail ignominiously back over the Spanish
frontier at the point where he had crossed it so triumphantly

* Gomm, 204, 207; Schaumann, 290-2; Simmons, 143-4; Grattan, 57-9.

eight months before. Having temporarily shaken off his pursuers, he conceived the idea of marching his sullen, shoeless, mutinous army across the four-thousand-foot mountains of central Portugal into the Tagus valley and there renewing the threat to Lisbon. When Ney defied his orders and tried to take his corps back to Salamanca, Masséna had him arrested. The Army of Portugal, almost beside itself with rage, turned its back on its bases and set off under its grim chief towards the south-east.

But after two days the remaining corps commanders, Reynier and Junot, faced by stark starvation, announced that their men could go no farther. Masséna at last recognised the inevitable and countermanded his orders. He was almost too late. On April 29th, while his main body was falling back on Ciudad Rodrigo, Wellington's advance guard surprised two of his divisions in the mountain town of Guarda, taking three hundred prisoners and hustling the remainder out in such haste that they again left their dinners untasted. Had the British had their guns and cavalry up, they might have taken far bigger game. But their supply difficulties were overwhelming. Fleaed, bugged, centipeded, beetled, lizarded and earwigged, as an officer of the Light Division wrote, the men had been marching for days from four in the morning till seven at night, living on maggoty biscuits and even at times, according to Charles Napier, on shoe-leather.*

On the afternoon of April 1st they came up with the French army, standing on the line of the Coa at Sabugal. Next day, as Masséna seemed disposed to linger, Wellington resolved to drive him out. Long-awaited reinforcements from England and Lisbon had now joined him, increasing his strength by 6000, while that of the enemy had sunk to under 40,000. A loop in the river, inside which Reynier's 2nd Corps was somewhat dangerously extended, gave him his chance, and at dawn on the 3rd, the 3rd, 5th and Light Divisions and two brigades of cavalry moved forward towards the river. Unfortunately a fog, so thick that the cavalry were unable to see the ears of their own horses, delayed the start of the two flanking divisions. Then, as part of a chapter of accidents, Erskine refused to wait and sent the leading brigades of the Light Division under Colonel Beckwith across a deep ford - the wrong one - straight into

* "Though not a bad soldier, hang me if I can relish maggots!" Charles Napier, I, 164. See also *Journal of a Soldier*, 104-5; Donaldson, 169-70; Simmons, 156-7.

the middle of the 2nd French Corps. Thus a battalion of the 43rd, four companies of the Rifles and three of Portuguese Caçadores – 1500 men in all – found themselves committed without support to an attack on a strong position held by at least three times their own number.

Their training and Beckwith's magnificent leadership, aided by the fog and rain, saved them. Three times they attacked up the slope, only to be driven back by growing force. Yet each time as they withdrew they kept up a steady fire from behind the stone walls, re-formed and returned with the bayonet. Beckwith, a thirty-nine-year-old giant who had commanded the 95th under Moore at Corunna, proved himself worthy that day of his master. His calm, resounding voice could be heard wherever the danger was greatest. "Now, my lads," he would cry, "we'll just go back a little if you please. No, no," he continued as some of the men began to run, "I don't mean that – we are in no hurry – we'll just walk quietly back, and you can give them a shot as you go along." All the while he continued riding in their midst, the blood streaming down his face from a head wound, until he judged the moment was ripe and faced about, crying, "Now, my men, this will do – let us show our teeth again!"*

Yet two battalions could not oppose an army corps indefinitely. The odds against them hardened with every minute. They were rescued, just as the French were launching a fourth attack to hurl them into the river, by their companion brigade under Colonel Drummond. Disregarding an order from Erskine, that officer, true to the traditions of the Light Division, had marched to the sound of the guns with both battalions of the 52nd, the 1st Caçadores and four more companies of the 95th. The 3500 light infantrymen supported by two guns of Captain Bull's troop of horse artillery thereupon resumed the offensive and, though still outnumbered, carried the French position. "I consider," wrote Wellington, "that the action fought by the Light Division with the whole of the 2nd Corps, to be one of the most glorious that British troops were ever engaged in."

* Kincaid, *Random Shots*, 164-9; Kincaid, 68-71. See also Oman, IV, 188-94; Smith, I, 45-6; Fortescue, VIII, 100-11. Throughout the battle a little spaniel, belonging to one of the officers of the 95th, kept running about barking at the balls. "I once saw him," wrote Kincaid, "smelling at a live shell, which exploded in his face without hurting him." Kincaid, 71.

The battle of Sabugal ended when the mist suddenly lifted, revealing to the French commander not only the true situation of the Light Division but the sight of the 3rd and 5th divisions preparing to fall on his flank. He did not wait but, as Picton's men forded the river and opened their attack, withdrew rapidly under cover of a storm towards the Spanish frontier. Next morning the British resumed their advance, pressing on eastwards without catching a glimpse of the enemy all day. But the road was strewn with torn clothing and discarded arms, and there were signs that Masséna was no longer in control of his men, whose atrocities had become those of a rabble rather than of an army. At one place all the villagers were trussed in rows with their heads in a stream; at another the chief magistrate's wife, with her lower garments torn off and blood pouring from her ears and mouth, was found lifeless under a granite rock in the middle of the street.*

Under Wellington's patient hand the Army of Portugal was disintegrating. Deep down, though it took a great adversary to reveal it, there was a fatal flaw in the French military system. The colossus had feet of clay. The *moustache*'s god was the victorious engine of war under whose banners he marched: his religion his Emperor's will. Break that engine, thwart that will, and one robbed him of his faith and martial cohesion. The belief in Napoleon and his star was a mighty force; it could at times be most moving, as in the captured veteran who under the surgeon's knife flung his amputated arm into the air crying, " *Vive l'Empereur! Vive Napoleon!*"† But it was not a faith founded on the verities of existence. At its heart lay a pathetic and childlike lack of realism. The French were the slaves of an illusion.

In one corner of Europe at any rate that illusion had for the first time begun to crumble. There had seldom been a more striking exercise of military will-power than Masséna's attempt to defy the forces of winter and hunger and drive Wellington out of Lisbon. It had failed, with every circumstance of horror and humiliation. For a moment the link which bound the French soldiers to their leaders seemed to snap; their invincible unity shrivelled at Wellington's cool, common-sense touch. The war in Spain, they cried

---

* Two officers of the 95th testified separately to this revolting atrocity. Simmons and Kincaid. See also Smith, I, 46-7; Donaldson, 180; Schaumann, 292.

† Bell, I, 149.

bitterly, is the fortune of generals, the ruin of officers and the grave of soldiers!*

Yet Masséna's army was only one of many. Behind it lay the entire martial machine created by the Terror, and a great nation with a military tradition far older than that of the Revolution. Though it had lost more than a third of its strength and nearly all its horses and baggage, it still had immense powers of recuperation. Masséna, a great captain, was well aware of this. He refused to despair. His magazines and reinforcements were near, and he could give his hungry, shoeless, sullen men a rest. A few weeks' quiet, he knew, would work wonders.

On April 5th 1811, the defeated army recrossed the Spanish frontier; on the 11th it reached its base at Salamanca. The British, still far ahead of their supplies, could not pursue farther. As it was, the pace of their advance over the mountains had been a miracle of improvisation. Blockading the small French garrison left in Almeida, they followed the enemy across the frontier and went into cantonments along the line of the Agueda and Axava. Entering Spain after the vulture-haunted horror behind them was like, in the words of one of them, stepping from the coal-hole into the parlour. Around them for the first time since they left the lines of Torres Vedras were cultivated fields and inhabited villages. They even slept in beds, ate off tables and met girls with rosy faces.†

In twenty-eight days the British had advanced more than three hundred miles. Since the autumn they had inflicted on the principal French army then in the field nearly 40,000 casualties. Of these 8000 remained in their hands as prisoners, 2000 had fallen in battle and the remainder had perished – as Wellington had planned – of hunger and disease.‡ The British Commander-in-Chief – three years before an unknown Sepoy general – had become a major European figure. His name was now as familiar as that of Suvoroff or the Archduke Charles. The whole world read the proclamation which he issued in April to the people of Portugal, telling them that their country had been cleared of the enemy.

* Leslie, 216.
† Kincaid, 72; *Random Shots*, 177. See also Tomkinson, 95; Charles Napier, I, 193; Gomm, 210.
‡ Oman, IV, 203; Fortescue, VIII, 112.

Chapter Ten

AT THE GATES OF SPAIN

People in England must not be in too great a hurry. They must
give us time to do things by degrees, and I hope I shall be able
to perform them without great loss; which after all our boasting we cannot well bear. If there is a war in the North I think
we shall make Boney's situation in Spain this year not a bed of
roses; if there is not a war in the North this year it is impossible that his fraudulent and disgusting tyranny can be
endured much longer; and, if Great Britain can only hold out,
I think we shall yet bring the affairs of the Peninsula to a satisfactory termination.

WELLINGTON TO CHARLES ARBUTHNOT
May 28th 1811

FOUR days after the British re-entered Spain from the west, three
young Catalans gained admission to the fortress of Figueras, five
hundred miles away, and let in the guerrillas to destroy the garrison.
Though more than 300,000 of Napoleon's troops occupied the Peninsula, patriot forces, nourished from the sea by British cruisers,
fought on in the Asturian, Biscay and Galician mountains, in
Navarre and Estremadura, in the Sierra Nevada and in Murcia. On
the east coast, where Suchet had captured Tortosa that January and
laid siege to Tarragona, a Spanish army still held Valencia, and even
in the conquered districts, hundreds of small French detachments –
together amounting to whole divisions – were needed to prevent
open rebellion and guard the roads and towns from the fierce, predatory partisans who infested the hills. The ruin the war had brought
daily swelled the latter's numbers; every man who lost his livelihood
or could not pay his debts took to the wild and indulged the delicious
passion of revenge. Civil government and the collection of taxes were
alike impossible. King Joseph – *el Rey Intruso* – was in Paris, pleading
in despair with his inexorable brother for leave to abdicate. His
troops had not been clothed nor fed for months, unpaid contractors
had stripped his palace of its valuables, and his ambassadors abroad

were in the direst poverty. "I live here," he had written from his capital, "in the ruins of a great monarchy."

Napoleon paid little heed to his brother's lamentations. To avert the scandal of an abdication he bullied the unhappy man into returning to Madrid with a promise of a small monthly allowance. He also ordered three new divisions to Spain which, together with conscript drafts, made good Masséna's losses and brought the French potential in the country to nearly 370,000. But though he had no other campaign on hand and all Europe remained in a stunned peace, he stayed away from the Peninsula himself. With his over-centralised State dependent on him for its smallest decision, he dared not bury himself again in that trackless, medieval labyrinth of desert and sierra. He feared that, as in 1808, absence there might cause him to lose his grip on the Continent. And, with England's tentacles feeling inwards out of every sea, he was beginning to realise that he might lose it once too often.

For Napoleon's Empire was not so strong as it looked. It rested solely on the sword. Not only the European peoples, ground down by taxes, trade prohibitions, conscriptions and forced billetings, but their rulers, were living for the day when they would be free again. All eyes were turned on Spain and the unexpected triumph of the British army. And far away at the other end of Europe, among steppes and impenetrable swamps, the great outer barbaric Power of Russia, still scarcely aware of her terrible strength, was turning from the policy of collaboration begun at Tilsit to a state of suspicious watchfulness. On the last day of the old year, as Masséna's retreat from Torres Vedras became known, her Czar retaliated against Napoleon's lawless annexation of the Baltic port of Lübeck by a ukase admitting colonial goods into his dominions.

*   *   *

The successive collapse of the Third Coalition, of Russia and Prussia at Tilsit and of Austria in 1809, had temporarily deprived most Britons of faith in the Continent's power to shake off Napoleon. The failure of the Spanish armies, on which such exaggerated hopes had at first been built, had deepened this conviction. Only a small handful of Tory statesmen had persisted in believing that, so long as England maintained her undeviating opposition to French aggression, Europe was certain to rise again and in the end to triumph. As late as June 1811, a patriot could express the hope that Russia would not break with France too soon, since a Continental war would only result in further subjection. But the belief, born of Ulm, Jena, Friedland and Wagram, that Napoleon could not be defeated on land, was now being banished by successive British triumphs in Portugal. During the early months of 1811 the bells of London were set repeatedly ringing. In February a jubilant City learnt of the final elimination of French power from the Indian Ocean. In March and April came the tale of Graham's triumph at Barrosa, of the French retreat from Santarem, of Redhina, Foz do Arouce and Sabugal, of Masséna's shattering losses,* and of the re-crossing of the Spanish frontier.

The greatest factor in Britain's reviving belief that France could be overthrown on the battlefields of the Continent was its new-found faith in Wellington. His Fabian warfare had produced results which scarcely anybody - even the most sanguine - had expected. Here, in "our Nelson on land" as Scott called him, was a man of genius not deterred by obstacles or fettered by prejudices.† Even the French admitted him to be the first captain in Europe after Napoleon. Instead of being chased out of Lisbon and off the Continent as almost every one had predicted, his troops were herding the victors of Austerlitz across the stony hills of Portugal like sheep.

All this increased the Tory Government's prestige and lowered the sinking stock of those pessimists who wished to make peace and let Napoleon have his will of Europe. With their expectations that Wellington was about to be flung into the sea and their explanations that Masséna's withdrawal was only a ruse, the Opposition leaders had been made to look uncommonly foolish. The Whig argument that, because Bonaparte had conquered Europe, he must conquer the Peninsula had been given the lie: "a child," wrote a triumphant Tory, "must see the cowardice and error." They had not been so easy to see a few months before.

One sign of the Government's growing strength was the return to the Horse Guards of the Duke of York, who had been forced to

---

* "Saturday. – Dispatches from Lord Wellington. Park and Tower guns firing – a complete fight . . . a great number of the enemy taken and destroyed, very many guns spiked and left behind, ammunition blown up, villages burnt, roads covered with dead men and horses, hot pursuit." *Paget Brothers*, 148, 159.

† *Croker Papers*, I, 32; Scott, II, 480; Gomm, 224; Granville, II, 362; Simmons, 183.

resign in the spring of 1809 by a major scandal caused by the sale of commissions by his former mistress. On May 25th 1811 he resumed his old office as Commander-in-Chief, an Opposition motion against his reinstatement being defeated by 296 votes to 47. The Army was delighted to be freed from what Charles Napier dubbed the offensive oppression of Sir David Dundas; during the next few weeks "Old Pivot's going to pot!" was the toast of many a Mess both in England and the Peninsula. The change was welcome, too, to Wellington, whose attempts to adapt the time-honoured administration of his army to the necessities of warfare had been consistently thwarted by the rigid old Scots martinet. On the eve of Masséna's advance he had been driven to complain that, though directing almost the largest British army that had taken the field for a hundred years, he had not the power of making even a corporal. He was constantly distracted by the tyrannical stupidity and lack of elasticity of the bureaucratic mind at home. No man was ever a greater practical administrator than Wellington; none ever more conscious of the necessity of meticulous attention to every minute detail: to what he described as tracing a biscuit from Lisbon into the man's mouth on the frontier, and to remembering that "a soldier with a musket cannot fight without ammunition and that in two hours he can expend all he can carry." But he was therefore all the more critical of the kind of administration - so dear to little minds - which obscured clear and simple organisation by a mass of needless paper. "My Lord," he wrote to the Secretary of State, "if I attempted to answer the mass of futile correspondence that surrounds me, I should be debarred from all serious business of campaigning. . . . So long as I retain an independent position, I shall see no officer under my command is debarred by attending to the futile drivelling of mere quill-driving from attending to his first duty, which is and always has been, so to train the private men under his command that they may without question beat any force opposed to them in the field."

* * *

The victorious spring of 1811 brought Wellington strategic as well as administrative problems. He had liberated Portugal, but, in doing so, had immensely increased his own difficulties of supply. His army was now operating two hundred miles from the sea, and

everything it needed - food, ammunition, equipment and replace-
ments - had to be brought up by mule and bullock-cart over the
mountains. Since its dual devastation, first by his own orders and
then by the French, there was nothing to be got from the country -
a wilderness in which vultures and foxes now lived their lives almost
undisturbed. Though six French armies of comparable size were
operating in the Peninsula, the total allied force numbered only
40,000 British and 32,000 Portuguese, of whom fifteen per cent were
normally on the sick list. Nothing could be looked for in the open
field from the Spaniards - "that extraordinary and perverse people,"
as Wellington called them. His was the only army in the Peninsula
capable of withstanding the French in pitched battle.

Yet though the strategic initiative theoretically remained Napoleon's, Wellington intended to keep the tactical initiative he had
won. It still lay in his mighty adversary's power to return to Spain
in person or to reinforce his troops on the Portuguese frontier
with one or more of the armies operating against the guerrillas of
the north, east, south and interior. But the British Commander-
in-Chief knew that, if he did so, two things must happen. First, that
those armies, by concentrating in a desert, would be faced with
starvation, while his own force, supplied from the sea, would be
able to exploit the defensive strength of the country until they were
compelled to disperse. Second, that the foes they had left behind,
both in Europe and Spain, would take advantage of their absence to
raise the standard of liberation, harry their communications and
attack their rear. From the enigmatic Czar in his palace on the
Neva, to the dispossessed peasant in his hiding-hole in the Asturian
rocks, Wellington's lonely and outnumbered army had secret
sympathisers and allies in every corner of Europe. "I am glad to
hear such good accounts of affairs in the North," he wrote that
spring of a rumoured quarrel between Napoleon and Alexander;
"God send that they may prove true, and that we may overthrow
this disgusting tyranny. Of this I am very certain that, whether true
or not at present, something of the kind must occur before long."*

For by continuing to resist, the Anglo-Portuguese army and the
Spanish guerrillas between them had made the French fight in a
land where they could not maintain themselves. Inch by inch, they
were draining Napoleon's man-power and money. Sooner or later

* To Liverpool, May 23rd 1811.

they would force him to draw on the resources of France itself; when that happened, Wellington wrote, the war could not last long. England must therefore be patient and persist, for her own sake and that of the world. The price, however great, was well worth paying.

In the meantime his policy remained what it had always been: to avoid needless risks and husband every man and weapon until they could be used offensively. "If we adhere strictly to our objects," he wrote, "and carry on our operations in conformity to directions and plans laid down, we shall preserve our superiority over the French, particularly if they should be involved in disputes in the north of Europe."* Portugal was still to be the coping stone of his strategy; nothing was to be based on Spain and her unpredictable leaders. The army must rely on the Tagus, the Mondego and the Douro for everything it needed. Only thus could it maintain itself in a barren and chaotic Peninsula or be able to strike, when the hour was ripe, across the plains of Leon at the French life-line from Madrid to Bayonne.

Yet so long as Almeida and the Spanish frontier-fortresses of Ciudad Rodrigo and Badajoz were in the enemy's hands, Wellington's base for the future was insecure. Without them he could not advance into Spain, as he had done in 1809 and his predecessor had done in 1808. With the French in Badajoz dominating the Guadiana and the southern road into Alemtejo, he could not strike at their northern communications without exposing his own in the south. The temporary loss of Ciudad Rodrigo and Almeida had been allowed for in his original plan. He had sacrificed them to draw the French into his trap. He had also planned their early recapture - a feat which, in Masséna's exhausted state at the end of his big retreat, would have been well within the power of a British-Portuguese army of nearly 60,000 men.

But the unexpected surrender by the Spaniards of the great southern fortress at the moment when his projects were coming to fruition had thrown out his calculations. "It is useless now," he wrote sadly, "to speculate upon the consequences which would have resulted from a more determined and protracted resistance at Badajoz." Because of its loss he had had to divide his army and send 22,000 troops, including two British divisions and a brigade of cavalry, south to Estremadura. This left him, even after reinforcements had

* To Charles Stuart, April 21st 1811.

come up from Lisbon, with only 38,000 in the north - a force insufficient to reduce Ciudad Rodrigo before Masséna could reinforce
and re-equip his army.

The only remedy was to recapture Badajoz before its fortifications
could be repaired. Yet so long as Masséna held Almeida - the key to
northern Portugal - Wellington could neither reinforce his southern
army for this purpose nor lead it in person. A hundred and forty
miles of villainous, winding mountain-track separated Badajoz from
his headquarters on the Coa, and none of his present lieutenants in
Portugal were fit to direct major operations. Rowland Hill, Cotton,
Leith and Craufurd were all on sick leave in England, Graham was
at Cadiz. Sir Brent Spencer, the senior divisional commander in the
north, lacked nerve in any independent situation and could not be
left on his own for more than a few days. Beresford, who in Hill's
absence had been appointed to the southern army, was a fine administrator and trainer of men but had had comparatively little experience in the field and was only a mediocre tactician. And the
situation before Badajoz, if it were to be retrieved in time, called for
genius.

It did not get it. Beresford succeeded in recapturing the little
fortress of Campo Mayor, taken four days earlier after a gallant
stand by its Portuguese garrison, and forced the 11,000 troops left
behind by Soult to retreat hastily into Spanish Estremadura. In a
skirmish with their rearguard outside the town on March 25th
two hundred men of the 13th Light Dragoons routed three squadrons
of French horse and chased them for seven miles right up to the walls
of Badajoz, riding over the enemy's siege-train on the way. Had
they been supported by the rest of Beresford's cavalry, sixteen invaluable heavy guns would have fallen into their hands with incalculable consequences to the rest of the campaign. But, as Wellington complained, there was hardly an officer in the Army who knew
how to handle two cavalry regiments together. The Dragoons'
charge, he pointed out in a stinging order of the day, was merely
the indisciplined stampede of a rabble galloping as fast as their
mounts could carry them; he even threatened, if they ever behaved
in such a manner again, to take away their horses.*

* To Sir W. C. Beresford, March 30th 1811. "The formation and discipline of a body of
cavalry," Wellington had written in India in January 1804, "are very difficult and tedious,
and require great experience and patience in the persons who attempt it. . . . Nothing can

Meanwhile the fortifications of Badajoz were being rapidly restored under the energetic direction of its French Governor, General Phillipon. All hope of a speedy *coup* vanished when it was found that the Spaniards, in spite of repeated warnings, had allowed the only regular bridge of boats in the allies' possession to fall into enemy hands. As a result Beresford was unable until April 6th to cross to the south bank of the Guadiana – the essential preliminary to a siege. By that time the fortress, provisioned for several months, was sufficiently strong to withstand anything short of a full-scale attack by experienced sappers and heavy battering-guns. And Beresford had neither.

Nor had Wellington. The British Army, being designed for colonial and amphibious operations, had never been equipped or trained for the elaborate business of reducing Continental fortresses. It relied for this on its allies. No siege-train had been sent to Portugal, which the Government had looked on as a purely defensive theatre of war. The only heavy guns in the country, apart from a few which had been landed from the fleet to hold the lines of Torres Vedras, were the antiquated cannon in the Portuguese fortresses. A number of the latter were laboriously brought up during April from Elvas, the great frontier fortress of Alemtejo, fifteen miles away. Meanwhile Beresford followed Mortier's rearguard into southern Estremadura, recapturing Olivenza and advancing along the Andalusian highway as far as Zafra. His cavalry even penetrated to Llerena, seventy miles north of Seville.

At this point Wellington arrived from the north to study the situation. Calculating that Masséna was in no state to resume the offensive for some weeks, he left his headquarters at Villa Fermosa on April 16th and reached Elvas on the 20th, wearing out two horses on the way and losing two dragoons of his escort in a swollen stream. On the 22nd, while reconnoitring Badajoz, he was all but captured himself by a sudden sortie. During the next two days he drew up detailed instructions for the siege, and arranged for the

---

be more useful in the day of battle than a body of disciplined cavalry, nothing can be more expensive and nothing more useless than a body of regular cavalry half and insufficiently disciplined" (Gurwood, 140). During the Peninsular War he wrote in indignation of "a trick our officers of cavalry have acquired of galloping at everything, and then galloping back as fast as they gallop on the enemy. ... All cavalry should charge in two lines, of which one should be in reserve." Longford, 275.

support of 15,000 Spanish troops in the neighbourhood. Then, on April 25th, after giving Beresford discretion to fight or retire should Soult - as he expected - advance from Seville to relieve the fortress, he set off again for the north on receipt of disquieting news from his deputy, Spencer.

For Wellington had underestimated both the obstinacy of Masséna's injured pride and his army's capacity for recovery. Re-equipped from bases in Leon and reinforced by drafts from Bessières's Army of the North, the French were ready to take the field again within three weeks of their arrival at Salamanca. It was an achievement which could have been accomplished by no other army. Behind it was the certain knowledge of the grim old Marshal - born of twenty years of Revolutionary politics - that, unless he redeemed his misfortunes quickly, it would be too late. His only chance of deflecting Napoleon's wrath was to take the offensive at once.

His capacity to do so turned chiefly on the retention of Almeida. If the 1300 troops left there under General Brennier could be re-provisioned, the northern door into Portugal would remain open, and, with Badajoz also in French hands, Wellington would be in a cleft stick. To guard both entrances into Portugal he would then be forced to divide his inadequate forces permanently. Masséna's problem was to relieve Almeida in time. Lacking the means to breach its walls, the British could not storm it. But in the chaos of the French retreat little provision had been made for victualling the place, and it could only hold out for a few weeks. Already the British sharpshooters had driven its few cattle from their only pasture on the glacis,* and the garrison had been reduced to half rations. Every effort, therefore, was made at Masséna's headquarters to prepare a convoy for its relief at the earliest possible moment.

It was this which brought Wellington hurrying back from the south. Knowing Spencer's limitations, he had given him orders not to contest the passage of the river but to retire, if pressed, westwards. Yet, with Badajoz still to be regained, Wellington now knew that the early reduction of Almeida was vital. If Masséna moved to its relief, he would be compelled, at whatever risk, to fight. For unless he could cover it until famine had done the work of his missing siege-train, Napoleon would still be free to renew the invasion of Portugal.

* Kincaid, 72-3.

By an immense exertion Masséna had assembled 42,000 infantry and 4500 cavalry beyond the Agueda to escort the convoy. Wellington, with two of his eight divisions absent in Estremadura, had only 34,000 foot and 1800 horse. Of these not more than 26,000 were British. His troops, cantoned over an area of twenty square miles, hailed his return on April 29th with considerable relief. It was not that they feared the odds, but, having tasted victory, they had little wish to revert to the dreary, familiar tale of blunders, retreats and evacuations. With "Old Douro," as they called him, they felt safe. The sight of his long nose in a fight, Johnny Kincaid said, was worth a reinforcement of ten thousand men any day.*

His first act on rejoining was to order an immediate concentration. It increased the difficulties of feeding his troops, but there was no alternative. Had Almeida been covered by a dominating hill position like Busaco, his numerical inferiority would have given him little anxiety, especially as he had forty-eight guns to the thirty-eight which was all his adversary had been able to horse. But the beleaguered fortress stood just outside the mountains, on the high rolling plateau to the east of the Coa where Masséna's cavalry – borrowed mostly from Bessières's Army of the North – were bound to prove dangerous. Having to fight in the open, Wellington chose the best position he could find. He withdrew his troops from the more exposed Agueda to within five or six miles of Almeida. Here, with his left entrenched among the woods and rocks in front of the town, he disposed the army along a line of low hills behind the narrow gorge of the Dos Casas. With a clear field of fire before them he felt complete confidence in the ability of his well-trained infantry and artillery to hold up any frontal attack.

The weak point was on the right, five miles to the south, where the main road from Ciudad Rodrigo into the Portuguese hinterland crossed the Dos Casas at the village of Fuentes de Oñoro - the Fountain of Honour. Behind it on rising ground Wellington posted the best part of four divisions - Spencer's 1st, Picton's 3rd and the newly-formed 7th, and, when it came in after covering the withdrawal, the Light Division as a reserve. The village itself he picketed with 28 companies of light troops - British, Portuguese and German. The stronger ground on the left was held by the 5th and 6th Divisions

* Kincaid, 73-4. See also *Random Shots*, 168; Gomm, 215.

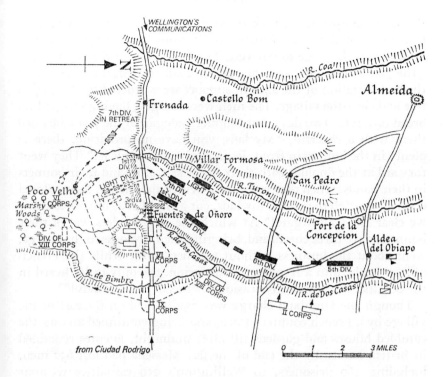

The Battle of Fuentes de Oñoro

alone. With his usual skill Wellington concealed his men in such a way that it was difficult for Masséna before attacking to discover their stations or strength.

The French crossed the Agueda on May 2nd 1811, by the bridge of Ciudad Rodrigo, the British rearguard retiring before them all day in skirmishing order across the Espeja plain. Early on the 3rd they came up against Wellington's position. After examining it Masséna decided to throw his whole weight against Fuentes de Oñoro in the hope of breaking his adversary's line and driving him into the Coa. To this end he concentrated five of his eight infantry divisions opposite the British right, and at about two o'clock in the afternoon launched them against the village - that is, at the precise point where Wellington, watching from a hill above Fuentes, was expecting them. They came forward in the usual way, in three dense columns, and, after a hard fight in which they lost heavily, gradually forced

253

the allied sharpshooters back through the narrow streets. Then, before they could recover breath, Wellington launched his counter-attack from the ridge to the west. Two battalions of the 1st Division - the 71st or Glasgow and the 79th or Cameron Highlanders - with the 2nd battalion of the 24th in support were ordered to advance in line and clear the village. The men were hungry, having received no bread ration for two days. But Colonel Cadogan of the 71st addressed them with a cheerful, "My lads, you have no provision, there is plenty in the hollow in front, let us down and divide it!" They went forward at the double, with their firelocks trailed and their bonnets in their hands; when they came into view of the enemy, their colonel cried again, "Here is food, my lads, cut away! Let's show them how we clear the Gallowgate!" At which the Highlanders waved their bonnets, gave three cheers and, bringing their firelocks to the charge, went about the business without another word. While the French officers broke into a frenzy of exhortation, the only order heard in the Scottish ranks was an occasional, "Steady, lads, steady!"*

Though the Highland charge was finally held on the east of the village by a French counter-attack, and firing continued among the tumbled houses and gardens till after midnight, Fuentes remained in British hands. By the end of the day Masséna had lost 652 men, including 160 prisoners, to Wellington's 259 casualties without having achieved anything. Next morning, in beautiful weather, the two armies faced one another across the river, but the attack was not resumed. After a little mild cannonading, both sides occupied themselves in collecting their wounded, with the usual spontaneous outbreak of fraternising. The French then fell to parading, marching and band-playing in order to impress the British, and the British, characteristically, to playing football.

Meanwhile both generals were engaged in more serious business. Masséna, as after Busaco, was probing to his left with his cavalry to discover whether there was a way round the British flank. Wellington, knowing there was and anticipating the move, was extending his right to meet it. The newly arrived 7th Division, consisting of 900 untried British infantry, 2200 Portuguese and 1500 foreign auxiliaries,† was moved towards Poco Velho, a village in the plain

* *Journal of a Soldier*, 107.
† Oman, IV, 620. Half of them French emigrés and half Brunswicker mercenaries recently despatched from England. Of the latter Wellington wrote: "I am not very fastidious about

two and a half miles south of Fuentes. There was danger in this, for it offered scope to the French cavalry, but there was no other way in which Wellington could both cover Almeida and prevent Masséna from cutting his communications across the Coa. The troops who in happier circumstances would have extended his right beyond his adversary's reach – as at Busaco – were far away in the Guadiana valley, trying to recover Badajoz.

As soon as darkness fell Masséna began to move his men southwards towards Poco Velho and the woods beyond. His plan was to turn the right of the allied line with three infantry divisions and four brigades of cavalry – some 17,000 bayonets and 4000 sabres in all. Then, at the critical moment, when the British were rushing reserves to their threatened flank, three more divisions under General Drouet of the 9th Corps were to renew the frontal attack on Fuentes, and, in conjunction with the sweep from the south, break the back of Wellington's line. Meanwhile Reynier's 2nd Corps, by a demonstration across the Dos Casas, was to prevent the British 5th and 6th Divisions from moving to the aid of their engulfed right and centre.

The test began at dawn when, in morning fog, the French cavalry emerged from the woods beyond Poco Velho and fell on the small force of British and Hanoverian horse guarding the extreme right of the army. The latter, displaying great coolness and gallantry, fell slowly back on the village, where the French infantry joined in the attack about an hour after daylight. Here two isolated battalions of Major-General Houston's 7th Division were severely mauled and forced to retreat on their main body to the north-west. They were only saved by the self-sacrifice of a regiment of German hussars which repeatedly showed front and charged. By this time Masséna's intention was clear. His horsemen were ranging over the open plain south of Fuentes with the obvious intention of cutting off the raw 7th Division, while dense columns of infantry were emerging from the woods beyond the captured village of Poco Velho.

Wellington, who always seemed to see clearest in a crisis, at once altered his dispositions. "Oh! they are all there, are they," he remarked as the weight of the attack became clear, "well, we must

---

troops; I have them of all sorts, sizes and nations; but Germans in the Peninsula pass for Englishmen, and it is really not creditable to be a soldier of the same nation as these people." *Supplementary Despatches*, VII, 38.

mind a little what we are about." Realising from the numbers deploying against his right that nothing formidable was to be feared on his original front, he moved the 3rd and 1st Divisions southwards to form a new line at right angles to the old, pivoting it on the rocky hillside about Fuentes de Oñoro. By doing so he temporarily sacrificed his communications with Portugal, but their retention was no longer compatible with the blockade of Almeida. Seeing war as an option of difficulties, he yielded the lesser object for the greater. For so long as he held the heights between Fuentes and the Coa, the French would still be unable to relieve Almeida without storming his lines. Nor could they remain astride his communications for long without exposing their own to his counter-attack. And not even a French army could exist in those wasted mountains without supplies.

At the same time Wellington ordered the 7th Division to fall back to the right of his new position. To prevent the French from cutting it off he moved the Light Division from the high ground above Fuentes down on to the plain. By a happy chance Craufurd had arrived from England on the previous evening, and the light infantry, delighted to be rid of Erskine's galling rule, were in the highest spirits.* They set out on their mission with complete confidence in their ability to cope with Montbrun's cavalry. By brilliant manœuvring and steady, deadly fire, they closed the gap between the army and their imperilled comrades, enabling the latter to continue their withdrawal without molestation. They then started, with the help of Cotton's cavalry, to fall back to the British lines.

The full weight of the French attack now turned on them. Robbed of their expected prey, four brigades of cavalry, supported by three infantry divisions, closed in on the Light Division and its four attendant regiments of British dragoons and German hussars.† With two miles to cover, Craufurd's 2900 British and 900 Portuguese seemed doomed. But though Montbrun's splendid horsemen, "trampling, bounding, shouting for the word to charge," worked themselves into a frenzy of excitement, riding at times almost up to

* No one was more pleased than the Portuguese Caçadores. The moment Craufurd appeared, they began shouting, to the hilarious joy of the Rifles, "Long live General Craufurd who takes care of our bellies!" Costello, 79. See also Smith, I, 49.

† The 1st Dragoons (The Royals), the 14th and 16th Light Dragoons, and the 1st Hussars of the King's German Legion.

the British bayonets, they made no impression on those cool custo-mers, the riflemen. Instead of breaking, as so many Spanish and European armies had done when charged on the open plain, the Light Division moved with the precision of a field-day slowly and steadily back in a line of bristling battalion squares, while Cotton's cavalry, retiring by alternate squadrons, repeatedly charged and so immobilised the French guns. Between the marching squares Major Bull's troop of horse artillery kept unlimbering and opening up at the French cavalry. It was a magnificent professional spectacle, en-acted before the admiring gaze of both armies. William Napier, who was present, drew it many years later for posterity. "There was not during the war," he wrote, "a more dangerous hour for England."

Yet the Light Division reached the rocky ground between Fuentes and Frenada with the loss of only sixty-seven men. Very few were killed and none taken prisoner. The cavalry suffered most, 157 falling out of 1400. At one moment two guns under Captain Norman Ramsay, lingering too long to keep the French at bay, were cut off by a horde of cuirassiers. "A thick dust arose," wrote Napier, "and loud cries and the sparkling of blades and flashing of pistols indicated some extraordinary occurrence. Suddenly the multitude became violently agitated, an English shout pealed high and clear, the mass was rent asunder and Norman Ramsay burst forth, sword in hand, at the head of his battery, his horses breathing fire, stretched like greyhounds along the plain, the guns bounded behind them like things of no weight, and the mounted gunners followed close, with heads bent low and pointed weapons, in desperate career." Simul-taneously a squadron of the 14th Light Dragoons and another of the Royals bore down to the rescue. A few minutes later, as the last of the light infantry were nearing the shelter of the rocks, an incident revealed the extent of the peril through which they had passed. Some skirmishers of the 3rd Foot Guards, extended on the slope in front of the army, failed to form square at the approach of the French cavalry and were crumpled up in a minute.

The three-mile withdrawal from Poco Velho was over, and the French wheeling from the south were now faced – like their com-rades in the east – with a solid box of guns and muskets strongly entrenched on rocky ground. Attention now veered to Fuentes de Oñoro where a fierce battle was raging immediately in front of the angle in the new British line. Breaking into the village two hours after daybreak, 5000 infantry of the French 6th Corps and three battalions of picked Grenadiers from the 9th gradually forced back the 71st and 79th Highlanders through the barricaded streets and stone-walled gardens. But, though losing more than a third of their number, including their leader, Colonel Cameron, the Highlanders contested every inch of the way. Reinforced by the 24th and the light companies of the 1st and 3rd Divisions, they still clung to the church and graveyard and the upper part of the village.

About midday, with the flanking movement held up in front of Wellington's new line, Masséna threw the greater part of Drouet's* 9th Corps into the village. Charging across the Dos Casas and up the narrow, corpse-heaped streets, two divisions reached the church and the highest houses in an irresistible torrent of shouting, cheering manhood. The survivors of the Highlanders were forced on to the open hillside, where they continued firing sullenly at the dense columns forming between them and the village. Behind them at the top of the hill stood Mackinnon's Reserve Brigade of the 3rd Division, composed of the 45th, 74th and 88th Foot. At that moment Edward Pakenham, the Deputy Adjutant-General, galloped up to Colonel Wallace of the 88th, who was intently watching the combat. "Do you see that, Wallace?" he said. "I do," replied the Colonel grimly, "and I would sooner drive the French out than cover a retreat across the Coa." On Pakenham's observing that he supposed the Commander-in-Chief could not think the village tenable, Wallace passionately protested his regiment's ability to take it and keep it too. Whereupon Pakenham rode off to consult Wellington.†

A few minutes later he returned. "He says you may go - come along!" On this the whole of Mackinnon's brigade moved down the hill to the attack, led by the Connaught Rangers in column of sections with fixed bayonets. As they drew level with the torn and blackened Highlanders, the latter gave them a cheer, but the Rangers passed on in grim silence. When they came in sight of the French 9th Regiment drawn up outside the church, Captain Grattan, at the head of the leading company, turned to look at his men. At which, he recorded, "they gave me a cheer that a lapse of many years has not made me forget." Then the whole martial concourse - Irish, Scottish and English - went forward after the 88th in a surge that swept the huddled columns away with it. Crowded together in the

*Or Count D'Erlon as he was later called. † Grattan, 67

narrow streets the French were powerless to resist. By two o'clock the whole village down to the riverside was clear of the enemy.

Masséna made no further attempt to recapture Fuentes or to assault Wellington's flank. He had had enough. Two thousand two hundred of his men had fallen, or nearly three casualties to every two of the allies. For the next two days he paraded his army in front of the British trenches with much beating of drums and flaunting of colours. But it made no impression on the stolid islanders who, digging themselves in, merely congratulated themselves on having withstood the attack of such fine-looking fellows. On May 10th the French, growing hungry, began to withdraw eastwards and, recrossing the Agueda, retired to Salamanca. On the strength of their having driven in Wellington's flank for three miles, the Paris newspapers claimed a victory. But as Wellington's sole object in fighting had been to prevent their relieving Almeida, which remained unrelieved, the victory was clearly his.*

Yet he made no vaunt of his success. It had been far too uncomfortable and near-run an affair to linger over with satisfaction. " If Boney had been there," he told his brother, " we should have been beaten." He might have added, however, that, had Boney been there, he would not have fought at such odds. In his letters home he dwelt more on the price which had been paid for victory than on victory itself. "I hope you will derive some consolation," he wrote to Major-General Cameron on the death of his son, "from the reflection that he fell in the performance of his duty at the head of your brave regiment, loved and respected by all that knew him." To the Government, appealing for subscriptions for the homeless villagers, he observed in his usual laconic style that the village of Fuentes de Oñoro, having been the field of battle, had not been much improved by the circumstances. His chief concern seemed to be to impress on the country the strength of his adversary and the magnitude of the task ahead. If he was to swing the tide of war from the defensive to the offensive, he knew he would need every man and pound that could be spared.

For though the band of the 52nd marched off the burning and vulture-ridden plain playing the "British Grenadiers"—"a little like

* Oman IV, 288-346; Longford, 251-4; Weller, 156-70; Glover, 148-59; Maxwell, I, 226-9; *Peninsular Sketches*, 187-98; Ellesmere, 129; Grattan, 68; *Journal of a Soldier*, 110-12; Oman, IV, 330-5; Fortescue, VIII, 168-75; Schaumann, 303-4.

dunghill cock crowing," noted Charles Napier, "but the men like it"
—and though the count of British dead was less than two hundred
and fifty, no one knew better than Wellington the toll the summer's
campaign was likely to take of his little army. Already scores of
wounded were dying in the crowded, gangrenous hospitals; Captain
Grattan of the 88th saw two hundred soldiers lying in an open
farmyard waiting for the surgeons to amputate. And because, under
his cold, undemonstrative exterior, he was aware that the cost of a
Peninsular battle only began on the battlefield, Wellington grudged
anything which diminished, by however little, the gains which had
to be purchased at so dear a price. Of all the great captains, none ever
husbanded his men so frugally or counted their triumphs more
carefully.

The aftermath of Fuentes de Oñoro tried his parsimonious temper
high. Five days after the battle, when General Brennier's starving
men in Almeida were at their last gasp, the negligence of two senior
British officers allowed them to escape in the night. 900 out of 1300
got through to the defile of Barba del Puerco and ultimately to
Masséna's lines, after destroying the fortifications. Such carelessness
caused Wellington to write bitterly that there was nothing on earth
so stupid as a gallant officer.*

With the north secured, he now turned his attention again to
Badajoz. Aware that Soult would make every effort to relieve the
fortress, he gave orders for the 3rd and 7th Divisions to march for
the Guadiana and reinforce Beresford. They set out on May 14th,
leaving 29,000 men to guard the Coa. Wellington followed next day,
passing them on the way. But before he could reach Elvas, he learnt
that he was too late. Beresford, hearing that Soult was hastening
northwards, had raised the siege and placed himself in his way at
Albuera. A great and bloody battle had been fought there on the
16th.

*　　　*　　　*

Beresford's efforts to reduce Badajoz had not been happy. His tools
for doing so had been inadequate, and they had been concentrated
against the wrong objects. The investment had begun on May 5th -
the day of battle at Fuentes de Oñoro - and the trenches were opened

* Supplementary Despatches, VII, 566.

on the 8th. But nothing went right; the antiquated cannon from Elvas did more damage to themselves than to the ramparts, and the inexperienced sappers and working-parties in the trenches suffered severely both from foe and weather. Instead of concentrating, as Soult had done, on the weaker and easier objectives, they endeavoured to throw their siege-works round the Castle and the great fort of San Cristobal on the north bank of the river. These were wholly beyond their means. They had made little impression when on May 12th it became known that Soult was marching north across the Sierra Morena and was already at Santa Ollala, scarcely eighty miles away. Next day reports of his progress became so alarming that Beresford decided to call off the siege and ordered the immediate return of the battering guns to Elvas. By the night of the 13th he was on his way to meet the French Marshal at Albuera.

Beresford's decision to fight south of the Guadiana was based partly on reports of Soult's numbers, partly on the strength of the Spanish forces on which he could call. Three Spanish armies, amounting in all to 15,000 men, were operating in southern Estremadura. They included two divisions under Blake from the garrison of Cadiz – freed from danger by Graham's victory at Barrosa – which had recently landed at the mouth of the Guadiana and joined Ballesteros at Xeres de los Caballeros, twenty miles south of Albuera. As at Wellington's instance Castaños, the Spanish Commander-in-Chief, had placed himself in the most commendable way under Beresford's command, the latter was able to order the immediate concentration of 37,000 men, including 10,000 British and 12,000 Portuguese.

In a letter of May 15th to his brother, William—to whom, though seldom to others, he revealed his heart and concealed anxieties— Wellington had written, "I am obliged to be everywhere and, if absent from any operation, something goes wrong." What happened next day at Albuera, 150 miles away across the mountains over which he had so recently ridden to rejoin his main army, showed how right he was. For on that day there took place, under Beresford's command – or lack of command – an engagement of which Wellington wrote afterwards, "Another such battle would ruin us." Soult's army, though comparatively small, was formidable. It was homogeneous, capable of the highest speed and composed of some 24,000 of the best soldiers on the Continent. The 15,000 Spaniards on whom Beresford relied for numerical superiority were, however brave individually, incapable of manœuvre. Such a force, as had been repeatedly proved in the Peninsula, was liable to become a terrible handicap on the battlefield. And both in cavalry and artillery the French were far stronger - an important consideration in an open corn-country. The position Beresford had chosen to bar the French advance was a low, undulating ridge fourteen miles to the south-east of Badajoz and just west of the Albuera river. But Soult did not oblige him with the frontal assault he was expecting. Instead he concentrated five-sixths of his force on the allies' right flank, with the object of cutting their communications and, after rolling up their line, destroying them with his cavalry on the open plain.

Beresford was taken completely by surprise. The Spanish army, plunged into irretrievable confusion, save for a few isolated and fragmentary units never got into action at all. It merely got in the way of the British, one of whose brigades was almost totally destroyed, thirteen hundred out of sixteen hundred men being killed, wounded or taken prisoner by a charge of Polish lancers. At one moment the triumphant horsemen all but captured Beresford and his staff, who had to draw their swords to defend themselves. The day was saved by the stubbornness of the British infantry; and, the Spaniards being virtually out of it, the battle assumed the form of a duel between two French divisions and two British brigades - 8000 bayonets against 3000 - firing at each other through heavy rain across a shallow depression. One regiment - the 29th, the heroes of Talavera - lost 336 out of 476 men, the 48th, 280 out of 646, the 31st, 155 out of 398, while the 57th—who that day gained their title of Diehards from the laconic command of their dying colonel—lost 428 out of 616. When Wellington visited the battlefield five days later, he found the fallen, as he put it, "literally lying dead in their ranks." Pride in their regiments and a dogged refusal to admit themselves beaten in the presence of old rivals and comrades, and some invincible spark in the English heart, had kept these stubborn soldiers to the sticking-point.

By this time, with English and French dying alike in shoals, the battle reached an impasse which both commanders seemed incapable of ending. Beresford was like a man in a dream; nobody seemed to know what to do or how to bring the interminable and murderous contest to a decision. Soult was equally shaken and appalled. He neither threw in his reserves nor called off the fight, but remained, like his bewildered adversary, a pained spectator of the meaningless massacre.

The battle was resolved by the action of the 4th Division under a thirty-nine-year-old Irishman – Major-General Lowry Cole, who had once been a suitor of Kitty Pakenham, Wellington's wife. He took it upon himself, without orders, to deploy and throw into the fight a brigade of 2000 men of the Royal Fusiliers and Royal Welch Fusiliers, supported by the rest of his Anglo-Portuguese division. "Then," wrote William Napier describing the sequel, "was seen with what a strength and majesty the British soldier fights . . . Nothing could stop that astonishing infantry. No sudden burst of indisciplined valour, no nervous enthusiasm, weakened the stability of their order; their flashing eyes were bent on the dark columns in their front, their measured tread shook the ground, their dreadful volleys swept away the head of every formation, their deafening shouts overpowered the dissonant cries that broke from all parts of the tumultuous crowd as, slowly and with a horrid carnage, it was pushed by the incessant vigour of the attack to the farthest edge of the height. There the French reserve endeavoured to sustain the fight, but the effort only increased the irremediable confusion, the mighty mass gave way and, like a loosened cliff, went headlong down the steep. The rain flowed after in streams discoloured with blood, and fifteen hundred unwounded men, the remnant of six thousand unconquerable British soldiers, stood triumphant on the field."*

The battle lasted seven hours. The total allied loss was 5916 out of 35,284; that of the 6500 British infantry 4407, or more than two-thirds. The French lost nearly 7000 out of 24,260. These casualties were so staggering that both commanders felt they had been defeated. While Beresford sadly regrouped his shattered units to resist a fresh assault, Soult withdrew slowly towards Seville under cover of his cavalry. "They could not be persuaded they were beaten," he wrote of those who had so unexpectedly foiled him. "They were completely beaten, the day was mine, and they did not know it and would not run."

When Wellington read the melancholy account of the battle which Beresford had sent him, he said directly, "This won't do; it will

* Napier. See also Sherer, 210-25.

drive the people in England mad. Write me down a victory."* The dispatch was altered accordingly, and Albuera was enrolled among the most glorious battle honours in the British Army's history. Its losses had been largely needless, and could be ill spared, but it had achieved its purpose and, though Phillipon took advantage of Beresford's absence to level the allies' siege-works, the investment of Badajoz was resumed. Nor was the battle without consequences of a moral kind. The French, gallant and experienced soldiers though they were, never wholly recovered from the effects of that terrible day. Thereafter the memory of it haunted them in the presence of the British infantry like a blow across the eyes.

* * *

In the brief if rather breathless pause gained by Fuentes de Oñoro and Albuera, Wellington attempted once more to reduce Badajoz with the means at his disposal. He relied on the greater speed with which he could concentrate and the ignorance in which the guerrillas kept the French generals of one another's movements. Marching fifteen miles a day, the 3rd and 7th divisions reached Elvas on May 24th, once more bringing the half-crippled Anglo-Portuguese force in the south to 24,000 effectives. Fourteen thousand of them reinvested Badajoz, while the remainder under Rowland Hill, who had providentially arrived from England, pushed Soult's outposts as far down the Andalusian highway as was compatible with safety. Here on the 25th, at Usagre, forty-five miles south of Albuera, Lumley's cavalry scored a brilliant and unexpected success, ambushing and destroying three hundred of Latour-Maubourg's greatly superior force of horse for a loss of less than twenty troopers.

The second British siege of Badajoz, however, proved no more successful than the first. Like Beresford, Wellington lacked both the

---

* Stanhope, 90. "The battle of Albuera was a strange concern," Wellington wrote of Beresford and his fellow commanders to his brother William. "They were never determined to fight it; they did not occupy the ground as they ought; and they were ready to run away at every moment from the time it commenced till the French retired; and, if it had not been for me, who am now suffering from the loss and disorganisation occasioned by that battle, they would have written a whining report upon it which would have driven the people of England mad." To Hon William Wellesley-Pole, July 2nd 1811. Yet he also wrote to Beresford to comfort him: "You could not be successful in such an action without a large loss, and we must make up our minds to affairs of this kind sometimes, or give up the game."

heavy guns and the trained sappers to prepare a way for his infantry. There were only twenty-five Royal Military Artificers, as the engineers were called, in the whole Peninsula.* Most of the big guns assembled by Colonel Dickson, the young British commander of the Portuguese artillery, dated from the seventeenth century. When on June 6th, a week after opening the trenches, a storming party essayed an inadequate breach in the ramparts of San Cristobal, ninety-two men out of a hundred and eighty were lost. A second equally vain attempt three days later resulted in another hundred and forty casualties, half of them fatal. Two hundred more were killed or wounded by enemy shells and mortars in the wet, exposed trenches. By June 10th the ammunition of the siege-guns was almost exhausted. Realising that he was attempting something beyond his means, Wellington thereupon raised the siege. Immediately afterwards, though the garrison was almost down to its last ration, he withdrew his blockading screen. Important as the re-capture of Badajoz was to him, there was something even more essential - his Anglo-Portuguese army. He would not risk its ultimate safety for any secondary object, however great.

For the expected had happened. Not only had Soult, rallying after Albuera, called up his reinforcements, but the Army of Portugal was coming down from the north to his assistance. On May 10th 1811, five days after the battle of Fuentes de Oñoro, Masséna had been superseded by Marshal Marmont, the thirty-six-year-old Duke of Ragusa. This brilliant soldier, who had fought by Napoleon's side in almost every major campaign since Toulon, had not yet inherited his predecessor's feud with Soult. He not only acceded to the latter's request for help but, reorganising his depleted formations at astonishing speed, set off for the south with his entire force on June 1st. Revictualling Ciudad Rodrigo on the way, he crossed the Tagus by a flying bridge at Almaraz and reached Merida by the middle of the month with 32,000 men. Here he was joined by Soult and reinforced by Drouet's 9th Corps. With more than 60,000 troops between them the two Marshals were in an immediate position to advance on Badajoz at once.

Wellington had also concentrated his forces, and more quickly than they. Admirably served by his assistant adjutant-general, Colonel John Waters, and the host of Spanish spies whom that genial,

* Oman, IV, 417. See Blakiston, II, 273-5.

chameleon-like Welshman controlled,* he knew every change in the enemy's dispostions almost before it happened. At the end of the first week in June, Spencer, acting on his orders, set off to join him with his four divisions from the North. Marching twenty miles a day in heat so intense that more than one of the proud infantry of the Light Division dropped dead sooner than fall out like the weaker brethren of other corps, they crossed the Tagus by pontoon at Villa Velha and reached Elvas before their adversaries got to Merida.†

Even with this reinforcement Wellington had still only 54,000 troops, of whom less than two-thirds were British. He had no intention of being forced to fight against odds in an open plain or of being hustled into a hasty and costly retreat. He therefore with-drew to the north of the Guadiana on June 17th, before the enemy's junction was still complete, and took up a carefully chosen position on the Portuguese frontier. When two days later the French moved forward from Merida in the direction of Albuera, they found that the shadow they were seeking had vanished.

On June 20th the two Marshals entered Badajoz, to the joy of Phillipon's hungry garrison. The next week was critical. Less than ten miles to the west Wellington with an outnumbered Anglo-Portuguese army was holding a twelve-mile line of hills stretching from Elvas through the Caya valley and Campo Mayor to the little walled town of Ougella near the Gebora. He could only retreat at the cost of exposing the key fortress of Elvas and laying Portugal open to a fourth invasion. But he had chosen his ground and placed his troops with such skill that they could neither be overlooked nor outflanked; nothing could expel them but a frontal attack on a position which was almost as strong as that of Busaco.

This, with the memory of other attacks against hill positions chosen by Wellington fresh in their minds, the two Marshals refused to attempt. Although Latour-Maubourg's cavalry, keenly scrutin-ised by British outposts in the Moorish watchtowers along the wooded heights, made a great show of strength, a homogeneous

---

* For a delightful account of his activities, see Gronow, I, 15-16.

† Tomkinson, 106; Smith, I, 50; Simmons, 188. "I do not believe that ten of a company marched into the town together," wrote a private of the 71st Highlanders. "My sight grew dim, my mouth was dry as dust, my lips one continued blister." *Journal of a Soldier*, 114.

army of 63,000 French for five days declined the chance of battle with an Anglo-Portuguese force of 54,000.

By June 27th the danger was over. Impelled by invisible forces, the great French concentration had already begun to disperse. On that day the most southerly of the divisions facing the Portuguese frontier marched in haste southwards. For, finding that Soult had pared his Andalusian garrisons to the bone to relieve Badajoz, the forces of resistance in southern Spain had seized their opportunity. They were assisted by Blake and 11,000 Spanish regulars whom Wellington had detached to threaten Seville as soon as Soult moved north. At the same time another 14,000 Spaniards from Murcia poured into Andalusia from the east.

From that moment Soult's glance, as Wellington had foreseen, turned from Portugal back to his endangered viceroyalty. He thought no more of taking Elvas and Lisbon but of saving Seville and Granada. Five days after the relief of Badajoz he informed Marmont that he must return to his capital. His fellow Marshal was naturally furious; he had not come to his assistance, he declared, merely to take over his frontier duties and free the Army of Andalusia for police work. He only consented to remain on the Guadiana at all on condition that Soult left him the 5th Corps and the whole of Latour-Maubourg's cavalry.

Even with this Marmont's strength was reduced to less than 50,000. Yet, since it was still sufficient to stop Wellington from either resuming the siege of Badajoz or uncovering Elvas, the deadlock on the Caya and Guadiana continued until the middle of July. It was an extremely uncomfortable fortnight for the British. The whole neighbourhood was a shadeless, dusty inferno of tropical heat, swarming with snakes, scorpions and mosquitoes and notorious for fevers. The only consolation was the knowledge that the enemy was suffering just as severely.

Wellington knew, moreover, that Marmont could not retain his position. The twin laws of Peninsular warfare were operating against him. Being dependent like all French generals on the resources of the country, he could not maintain himself in a desert. Nor, having provinces of his own to police, could he leave them for long without fatal consequences. He had entrusted his beat in Leon to the reluctant Marshal Bessières and his Army of the North. Like

Soult, Bessières now found himself beset with troubles of his own. Instigated by Wellington, the ragged Spanish Army of Galicia seized the opportunity of the southward drift of the campaign to take the offensive and threaten the plain of Leon. Though it was driven back as soon as the French were able to concentrate, the partisan bands of the two great guerrilla chiefs, Porlier and Longa, descending from the Asturian mountains, played such havoc along the enemy's lines of communication that for several weeks the whole north was paralysed. So good did the hunting become that another famous chieftain, Mina, forsook his preserves in Navarre to join them. Many French garrisons were completely isolated and even Bessières's headquarters at Valladolid was beleaguered. Meanwhile the celebrated throat-cutter, Don Julian Sanchez, and his villainous ragamuffins* succeeded in once more isolating Ciudad Rodrigo from the outer world.

On July 15th 1811, having provisioned Badajoz for six months and eaten up the entire countryside, Marmont withdrew north-eastwards towards the Vera of Plasencia and the road over the mountain passes to Leon. With several thousands of his men down with Guadiana fever, Wellington gratefully followed his example and marched his army northwards through Portugal to the Tagus, leaving Rowland Hill with the 2nd Division and Hamilton's Portuguese to guard Elvas. For the next few weeks the army was cantoned in the hill villages around Portalegre and Castello Branco, while it recovered its health and made up its depleted ranks with fresh drafts from England. Here it was in a position to watch the Army of Portugal and move northwards to Ciudad Rodrigo or southwards again to Badajoz as events dictated.

Without great difficulty Wellington had regained his freedom of action. For after three years' fighting, his foes, though numerically superior, had lost their offensive spirit. They had re-provisioned Ciudad Rodrigo and Badajoz. But the armies with which they had done so had been forced to withdraw and disperse, and before long they would have to reassemble and re-provision them again. Sooner or later the chance for which Wellington was waiting would come. It would have come already if only the Spaniards had learnt from their bitter experience the necessity for discipline and military

---

* "I could never divest myself of the idea of Forty Thieves when I looked at him and his gang." Gomm, 244. See also Kincaid, *Random Shots*, 187-8; Schaumann, 325.

training, or had pocketed their pride and, like the Portuguese, let the British teach them. But their movements remained as chaotic and ill-co-ordinated as ever, and the wider opportunities offered by the French concentration on the Guadiana were missed. The Army of Murcia was routed by Soult and thrown out of Andalusia, the Army of Galicia was forced to retreat to the hills, while on the east coast Marshal Suchet stormed Tarragona and prepared to invade Valencia. Wellington's was still the only dependable force fighting the French in the Peninsula or in Europe. " One would have thought," he wrote after his exacting experience, " that there would have been a general rising. This is the third time in less than two years that the entire disposable force of the enemy has been united against me. But no one takes advantage of it except the guerrillas."*

Yet the help given to Wellington by the Spaniards, bankrupt though they were in official policy, was far greater than met the eye. Porlier, the guerrilla chief, surprised Santander in August; Martinez with 4000 starving indomitables immobilised the French 7th Corps for the entire summer in front of Figueras; Ballasteros, making deft use of British sea-power, kept descending and re-embarking at various points along the Andalusian coastline, sending Soult's harassed columns scurrying on wild-goose chases through the mountains. Hardly a day passed without some foray against Napoleon's three hundred mile life-line from Bayonne to Madrid. One Catalonian band, to the Emperor's apoplectic fury, even crossed the Pyrenees and ravaged an outlying canton of France. And the reinforcements which he had ordered to Spain in the spring were delayed on the road for weeks by the countless diversions caused by such warfare. It was not till the autumn that they began to reach their destinations.

By that time Ciudad Rodrigo was again threatened. Not only was its garrison blockaded by British light troops and Spanish guerrillas, but rumours had begun to reach the French that a siege-train had been landed in the Douro and that serious preparations were in progress for an assault. Early in August 1811, Wellington's army, reinforced from England, had marched once more over the skyborne Sierra de Gata to its old haunts between the Coa and Agueda - stretching, in Johnny Kincaid's words, off to the north in

* Fortescue, VIII, 250.

pursuit of fresh game. For its chief meant either to take the fortress or to force the French into a new concentration to save it.

Marmont could not afford to let the gateway to Leon go by default. Nor could his colleague, Dorsenne, who had just succeeded to the command of Bessières's Army of the North; an Allied march across the Douro plain would cut at the very roots of his troublesome dominion. Early in September the two French commanders took counsel and agreed to unite their forces to revictual Rodrigo. On the 23rd they met, with nearly 60,000 men, at Tamames, twenty miles to the east of the fortress. With them came a hundred and thirty field guns and a convoy of more than a thousand supply-wagons, gathered with immense difficulty from a denuded countryside.

Wellington could not maintain the siege against so great a force. His army, despite reinforcements, still numbered less than 46,000, 17,000 of them Portuguese. 14,000 more – mostly newcomers from England – were suffering from malaria or a recurrence of Walcheren fever. With only 3000 cavalry to Marmont's 4500, the British commander had no choice but to leave the plains for the safety of the mountains. Here, on the rocky fringe at Fuente Guinaldo, fifteen miles south-west of Ciudad Rodrigo, and a farther twenty miles back near Sabugal, he had prepared with his usual foresight two formidable positions. The second, in particular, was of immense strength.

Yet he was much slower in going back than usual. For, sensing the nearness of his own offensive, he grudged yielding a foot more ground than was necessary. Behind his lines he had been building in the utmost secrecy an elaborate system of forward bases, packed with munitions and stores for a winter assault on Ciudad Rodrigo. The reports which had reached the French were true; a battering-train from England had been landed in July in the Douro, whence a thousand country carts and an army of Portuguese labourers were painfully moving it over the mountains to Almeida. Here other Portuguese were at work restoring the ruined fortifications to house and guard it till it was needed. Elsewhere Colonel Fletcher and his engineer officers, in default of rank-and-file sappers, were training tradesmen and artificers from the infantry for sapping and siege-duties and setting others to work making fascines and gabions.

Wellington did not wish the enemy to stumble on these preparations. Though he made no attempt to prevent Marmont's entry into

Rodrigo on the 24th, he left the 3rd and Light Divisions within a few miles of the fortress to keep watch while the rest of the Army remained a little farther back, strung out along a sixteen-mile front to cover his accumulations of artillery and stores from raiding cavalry. After Marmont's failure to attack on the Caya, he did not expect him to do more than provision the fortress and retire. He had been profoundly impressed by a captured letter to Napoleon's Chief-of-Staff, in which the Marshal complained that, whereas the British had a vast number of supply-carts and twelve thousand pack animals, Masséna had scarcely left him a dozen wagons.* For once, too, the guerrillas had failed to provide exact information. Wellington knew that Napoleon had been sending reinforcements into Spain, but he failed to realise how many. He estimated their number at around ten thousand. In fact there were thirty thousand, of whom more than half had been assigned to the Armies of Portugal and the North.

Yet Wellington was right about Marmont's intentions. The Marshal only meant to relieve Ciudad Rodrigo; he was not equipped to do more. Unlike Masséna, he had grasped the impossibility of campaigning in the Peninsula without organised transport and supplies. And, as his opponent knew, he had none save what he had brought to provision the fortress. But he was young and confident, and, like a true Frenchman, could not resist the opportunity of glory. On September 25th 1811, it suddenly seemed as if a good deal might be coming his way.

* * *

On the morning of that day Major-General Picton's 3rd Division, still standing at its observation post on the plateau of El Bodon, six miles south of Rodrigo and as many more in front of the army's concentration point at Fuente Guinaldo, saw moving towards it along the road out of the relieved fortress squadron after squadron of cavalry, followed by thirteen or fourteen battalions of infantry. Some of the latter were reported to be wearing high plumes and bearskins and were believed, though wrongly, to belong to the

---

* Fortescue, VIII, 254-5. "We have certainly altered the nature of the war in Spain," wrote Wellington. "Marmont says he can do nothing without magazines, which is a quite new era in the French military system."

Imperial Guard. It was part of a reconnaissance in force which Marmont had sent out for the purpose of discovering what Wellington wished to hide - his preparations for reducing Ciudad Rodrigo. Four brigades of cavalry under General Montbrun, supported by a division of infantry, were moving through El Bodon on Fuente Guinaldo, while two other cavalry brigades under General Wathier were starting on a sweep to the north through Espeja.

It was the larger of these two forces, comprising nearly 3000 horse and 8000 foot, which came up against the 3rd Division, 5000 strong, on the El Bodon plateau. Driving through the British outpost screen Montbrun suddenly became aware that the troops in front of him, instead of being concentrated for battle, were spread over a front of nearly six miles with huge gaps between them. On this he decided to probe more closely and, without waiting for the infantry, sent the whole of his cavalry in to attack two British battalions which, with some Portuguese guns and three squadrons of horse, were posted across the main road.

The French cavalry were on their chosen ground, an open plain. They saw before them the kind of situation which had proved the prelude to so many triumphs on the battlefields of the Continent. They went forward in a glorious sweep of flashing helmets and sabres to scatter the outnumbered infantry and massacre them as they ran. The Portuguese gunners, though keeping up a heavy fire at point-blank range, were overpowered and forced to take shelter; many were cut down. But the 5th Foot behind them - the Northumberland Fusiliers - instead of flying, advanced in square on the amazed dragoons before they could recover breath and, pouring in three deadly volleys, scattered them and recaptured the guns. This unorthodox performance temporarily restored the situation, and for the next hour, ordered by Wellington to hold on at all costs until the isolated units on their flanks could be withdrawn, the 5th and its companion regiment, the 77th - a unit still fresh from England - resisted every attack. All the while the 1st Hussars of the King's German Legion and the 11th Light Dragoons* kept charging the enemy's cavalry to gain time.

By the time that the French gave up their frontal attacks for the

* Later the 11th Hussars. The Hanoverian Hussars were many years later absorbed into the Prussian Army, where they continued to bear the battle honour, El Bodon, on their helmets.

less costly and more profitable tactics of infiltration, the remainder of the division had been disengaged and was in retreat towards the south. The 5th and 77th then formed a single square and, preceded by a supporting Portuguese battalion, brought up the rear. For the next two hours the 3rd Division withdrew in column of regiments across a perfectly flat plain with Montbrun's cavalry riding furiously round it. Once the rearguard square was assailed from three sides simultaneously; for some minutes nothing could be seen but a cloud of dust and smoke checkered by the glint of helmets and sabres. Then the 5th and 77th emerged, still marching. Other regiments – in particular the 74th, 88th and 94th – distinguished themselves in that perilous six miles' retreat, repeatedly bringing the French horsemen to a halt almost on the point of their bayonets while the hussars and dragoons kept charging and re-forming in turn to prevent the enemy getting into battle order. By the end of the day every officer of the 11th Light Dragoons bore the marks of the foeman's weapons either on his person or his horse.*

As the French began to weary, the division, to quicken its pace, formed column of march along the high road. Only the rearguard remained in square. The enemy's artillery now took a hand in the game, galloping up and unlimbering on the flank. Those who fell under the hail of round-shot and grape had to be abandoned, but the stolid infantry remained unshaken, continuing at a normal marching pace and keeping exact stations in readiness to form square should Montbrun's dragoons charge. If they dared to, the lads of the 88th cried out, every one of their officers should have a *nate* horse to ride upon.† By their side, with his familiar cane cocked over his shoulder, rode their big, bony, foul-mouthed divisional commander, Thomas Picton, exuding the genial confidence which always marked him in time of danger. "Never mind the French," he told an officer who seemed too intent on the enemy's cavalry, "mind your regiment. If the fellows come here, we'll give them a warm reception!"‡ All the while he kept moving from battalion to battalion, warning the men to keep proper distance and dressing and telling them that the credit and honour of the army as well as their own safety depended on it. When, as they drew near the

* Burgoyne, I, 142-3. See also Grattan, 112-14; Schaumann, 329; Donaldson, 223; Oman, IV, 568-70.
† Grattan, 116.   ‡ Donaldson, 223.

lines of Guinaldo, Montbrun's squadrons began to swing inwards as though for a final charge, he took off his hat and, using it to shade his eyes from the fierce noonday glare, gazed long and sternly at them. Then, as with an immense clatter of hoofs and clanking of sabres they rode up to within half a pistol shot, he called out, "No, it is but a *ruse* to frighten us, but it won't do."* At that moment the 3rd Dragoon Guards hove in sight, coming up at a swinging trot, and the French horse drew off. The division was saved.

Wellington's anxiety did not quite end there – deservedly for once – for he had a little under-estimated his adversary. The Light Division under Craufurd had also got delayed, though more because of its chief's habitual reluctance to relinquish independent command than through any interference by the enemy. By the morning of September 26th, with the French on three sides of it and an almost impassable mountain on the fourth, its position had become decidedly ticklish. However, with its usual dexterity it extricated itself and joined the army at Guinaldo during the same afternoon, to Wellington's undisguised relief. "I am glad to see you safe," he snapped at his erring lieutenant.

"I was in no danger, I assure you."

"No, but I was through your conduct."

"He's damned crusty to-day," was Craufurd's comment.†

Even before the remainder of the army came in, the crisis had passed. In a sense it had never existed, for the French commanders, mesmerised by Wellington's reputation for the defensive, declined – as he had always foreseen – to attack. Instead they spent an entire day waiting for their reserves and picking out through their telescopes insuperable, but mostly imaginary, obstacles on the heights before them.‡ Nor was there ever the slightest apprehension of danger in the British lines. In the view of his men Wellington was now invincible; "every one," wrote Simmons of the 95th, "felt the greatest security in his out-manœuvring Johnny and bringing out the division in safety." It was during the reaction of that slightly tense afternoon that a drunken private of the Light Division, stumbling in his unholy state into the Commander-in-Chief's proximity,

---

* Grattan, 167.

† Fraser, 180; Maxwell, I, 241-3; Fortescue, VII, 265; Weller, 191; Oman, IV, 559-82.

‡ Thiebault, IV, 66.

loudly hailed him as "the long-nosed b— that beats the French."[*]
It was precisely the same conviction which caused Marmont and
Dorsenne to decide to retreat.

Before they could do so Wellington himself had gone. During
the night he suddenly retired on his main defence-line in front of
Sabugal, leaving his camp-fires burning to deceive the enemy. He
had taken enough risks for the moment and was going to run no
more. Throughout the 27th the enemy followed cautiously, a brisk
rearguard action taking place between a French division and the
Fusilier brigade of the British 4th Division at Aldea da Ponte. By
nightfall Wellington had his entire 45,000 men in the position he
had chosen. The French had a good look at it and withdrew towards
Salamanca on the following evening. By the time they regained
their base they had consumed the greater part of the food they had
brought for the garrison of Ciudad Rodrigo.

*　　*　　*

That was the end of the campaign in the north. Yet before finis was
written to the Anglo-French account for 1811 there was a reper-
cussion far away in the south. Marmont's short-lived concentration
had drawn away the troops who should have been supporting
Drouet's 9th Corps—left in Estremadura at midsummer to watch
Hill and prevent a third attack on Badajoz. Other units belonging to
Soult's Army of Andalusia had been drawn southwards by Ballasteros's amphibious activities around Algeciras. Drouet was thus
left in a kind of vacuum, with Hill's 2nd Division and Hamilton's
Portuguese more or less equally matched against him on the other
side of the frontier. But, being without regular supplies, he was
forced to disperse his troops to plunder. This placed him at a disadvantage.

Rowland Hill was quick to realise it. Under the placid and good-
humoured exterior which caused his men to christen him Daddy
Hill, this shrewd, brilliant officer - still only in his fortieth year -
had as fine an eye for war as any of Napoleon's Marshals. Seeing in
October that one of Drouet's divisions had got dangerously far from
its companions while levying contributions on the wild country to
the north of Merida, he sought Wellington's leave to attack. It was

* Tomkinson, 117.

immediately given. Taking 3000 British and 4000 Portuguese infantry and 900 cavalry, Hill left Portalegre in the utmost secrecy on October 22nd. General Girard with 4000 foot and 1000 horse was at that moment at Caceres, sixty miles away and nearly as far from his base at Merida. Everything depended on catching him before he suspected the presence of a superior allied force. On the first day Hill marched thirty miles. The winter rains and gales had begun, and his men, soaked to the skin and half-frozen, herded at night on the open hills. For three days they pushed on in almost continuous rain, the old soldiers convinced that they could smell the *crappos* ahead by the stink of their tobacco and onions. On the 26th, when they were only eight miles from Caceres, they learnt that the French had taken alarm and begun to retreat on Merida. Next day the British and Portuguese marched parallel to their foes, covering twenty-eight miles to their twelve and crossing two mountain ranges. By nightfall they were within five miles of Girard's halting place at Arroyo dos Molinos, a little town among the clouds of the Sierra de Montanches.

For the fifth night running the pursuers bivouacked in their wet clothes in a gale, six thousand feet above sea level. Orders were given to preserve absolute silence; no fires were to be lit or bugles sounded, and the men, dismissed to cheerless ditches and fields, were warned to parade at two in the morning. Long before dawn on the 28th they were off, moving through mountain fog and icy, driving rain to surround Arroyo dos Molinos. When day broke they were already closing in on it from three sides. The surprise was complete. One column, consisting of the 1st battalion of the 50th and the 71st and 92nd Highlanders, broke into the town just as the French main body was about to move off, charging down the street with their pipes playing, "Hey Johnny Cope, are ye waukin yet?" As they went through, upsetting baggage and baggage-carts and pushing the astonished French before them, General Girard, beside himself with rage, ran out of the house where he had been at his breakfast, gnashing his teeth and stamping on his cocked hat to think he had been so tricked. One of his brigades had already marched and was beyond pursuit, but the remainder were caught and engaged on the plain outside the gates by the other allied columns. Within half an hour all was over. Four or five hundred of the enemy led by Girard got away over the mountains, eight hundred were killed and nearly fifteen hundred taken prisoner, including the second-in-command, General Bron. Three guns, several hundred horses and much booty were also captured. The British losses were seven killed and seven officers and fifty-seven men wounded. The *parlez-vous*, as a subaltern of the 34th put it, had been handsomely trounced.*

* Bell, I, 13-17; Blakeney, 215-31; *Journal of a Soldier*, 117-20; Burgoyne, I, 149; Oman, IV, 599-606; Fortescue, VIII, 270-6; Long, 137-45, 169.

Chapter Eleven

OVER THE HILLS AND FAR AWAY

Or may I give adventurous fancy scope
And stretch a bold hand to the awful veil
That hides futurity from anxious hope,
Bidding beyond it scenes of glory hail,
And painting Europe rising at the tale
Of Spain's invaders from her confines hurl'd,
While kindling nations buckle on their mail,
And Fame, with clarion-blast and wings unfurl'd,
To freedom and revenge awakes an injured world?
WALTER SCOTT
The Vision of Don Roderick, 1811

ENGLAND was becoming too strong for Napoleon. Despite persistent difficulties—unemployment in her hungry, chaotic industrial towns, bankruptcies and strikes, riots and machine-breakings—her power still increased. Her Government of alleged Tory nonentities survived parliamentary crisis after crisis and continued, quietly and persistently, to send troops to Portugal, to throttle the Continent's trade and raise troubles for France in every corner of the world. And all the while British manufacturers seeped into Napoleon's forbidden fortress, and the stranglehold on the world's colonial products tightened. A month before El Bodon 3500 troops from India conquered Java - the last and richest of the overseas possessions of France's satellites.

With minute forces, to which sea-power lent a magic cloak of invisibility and mobility, she could concentrate against any spot, leaving vast Continents and archipelagos almost unguarded and destroying her isolated foes piecemeal. But in Portugal and Spain, under Wellington's guiding hand, she used sea-power as the basis of a more ambitious strategy, building up an army in the trackless mountains of that inaccessible peninsula and threatening Napoleon's southern ramparts. The utterly unaccountable victories of the thin red line over one after another of his best generals had given hope to all Europe; in the flashes of its musketry it seemed that the *Grande Armée* was not invincible after all.

278

Napoleon's empire stretched from the Ems to the Adriatic and from the Baltic to the Ebro. Rome, Barcelona, Hamburg, Cologne, Geneva, Lübeck, Osnabrück, Trieste, Genoa and Ragusa were all French cities. Round this immense territory stood an outer ring of subservient States, controlled by the Emperor's kinsfolk and Marshals: the Napoleonic kingdoms of Italy, Spain, Naples, Westphalia and Sweden, the Swiss Confederation, the Confederation of the Rhine and the Grand Duchy of Warsaw. Austria was his ally, Denmark, Bavaria and Saxony his vassals, the Turks were at war with Russia - the only State in the world still able to put a great continental army into the field against him. Except for Portugal, whose reigning House had had to fly to Brazil, there was not an established Government in Europe which openly adhered to England's cause.

Yet they nearly all sympathised with her and tried in every way open to them short of actual revolt to give expression to their feelings. Napoleon's unifying New Order seemed to ungrateful Europeans only an intolerable and tyrannic interference with their commerce and revenues: a heartless denial of spices, dyes and cottons, tea and tobacco. Confiscated sugar and coffee were burnt by French soldiers while hungry crowds silently watched in the streets; the whole of Europe seemed sunk, in Fichte's phrase, in the bottomless abyss of one arbitrary will. Everybody was needy: everyone lived in fear. Trade was at a complete standstill, and England represented the sole hope of its revival. A Dutch merchant, questioned about his allegiance, remarked that the Emperor was all but omnipotent, but there was one thing he could not do - make a Dutchman hate an Englishman.

The year that followed Torres Vedras had been one of terrible scarcity in France. While Masséna's starving scarecrows trudged eastwards over the Portuguese mountains, their wives and mothers stood in the snow outside empty bakeries.* The peasant's fear of the return of priest and émigré to filch his fields was being slowly banished by the reality of an eternal war which, though still far from the borders of his homeland, threatened to rob him of all he possessed. Despite constantly rising taxes the deficit in the national revenues by the end of 1811 was nearly fifty millions. So acute was the shortage of money that Napoleon was forced to cheat the very dead, cancelling by Imperial Decree the arrears of pay owed to his fallen soldiers.

* Majolier, 13-15.

279

And the cause of all this trouble was England's refusal to loosen her sea grip or to withdraw from the Peninsula. In his darker hours Napoleon was coming to despair of Spain. If only, he was heard to say, he could get the English out and throw that country back to Ferdinand or the Cortez! It was like an open wound that was slowly draining his strength; if the obdurate islanders persisted, he did not know what he should do. In the face of their obstinacy he resorted to a passionate unrealism. He sent repeated orders to his Marshals for some grand sweeping advance that should clear the Peninsula, based always on information months out of date or on facts and figures which only existed in his own imagination. When they failed to carry these out, he turned on them furiously as he had turned in happier days on his admirals. At other times he issued grandiloquent proclamations assuring the world that England's end was near: that he had drained her of men and money and that her inglorious campaign in the Peninsula had bared her for the final blow which should free Europe and Asia. Having long been accustomed to astonish and deceive mankind, Napoleon, as Wellington said, had come at last to deceive himself.

As he contended with the advancing tide, the Emperor fell once more into the old fault which had vitiated his grandest achievements – overweening impatience. He would not withdraw before the flood, biding his time, but would go out at once and overwhelm it. To every sign of rebellion among his European underlings he responded with uncontrollable rage. On August 11th 1811, he broke out in one of his famous tirades against the Russian Ambassador. War, he shouted, was bound to follow the Czar's repeated defiance; he would march to Moscow with half a million men and two thousand cannon; he would enforce the independence of the Occident.

A conqueror, like a cannon-ball, Wellington observed, must go on; if he rebounds his career is over.* Before the end of 1811 Napoleon had issued his orders for the mobilisation of the Grand Army against Russia. He called up another 120,000 conscripts and recalled forty of his best battalions from Spain, filling their places with raw drafts from France. Refusing to draw in his horns – a thing he now seemed incapable of doing – he left the Peninsula to look after itself while he directed his forces elsewhere. He did not abandon it: he merely ignored it.

* Rogers, *Recollections*, 195

So obstinate was Napoleon's refusal to consider the Anglo-Portuguese army as a serious menace that he ordered a concentration on the far coast of Spain. The capture of Tarragona in the summer of 1811, and of Sagunto in October, opened - or seemed to open - a way not only to Valencia, where Blake, supported by British cruisers, was holding out with 30,000 troops, but to the complete elimination of organised Spanish resistance in the east of the Peninsula. Accordingly, while the infatuated Emperor prepared himself to march into the heart of Russia with the greatest army the world had ever seen, he made Marmont detach a third of his force to strengthen Suchet in front of Valencia.

By this incredible act of folly he temporarily reduced the Army of Portugal to 30,000 men. Relying on British inability to move during the winter, and on an utterly groundless belief that Wellington had 20,000 sick and - in the teeth of all evidence - that his Portuguese troops were worthless, the Emperor unbolted the door into northern Spain at the very moment when his greater plans depended on keeping it barred. It was the chance for which his adversary had waited so long.

Ever since the summer Wellington had been secretly preparing for an assault on Ciudad Rodrigo. Two reasons had caused him to concentrate against the northern fortress in preference to the southern. The hill country round it, being healthier than the Guadiana valley, was more suitable for a spell of indefinite waiting, while, by leaving Badajoz alone, he avoided the risk of drawing Soult from his unprofitable ventures in the south - the sham siege of Cadiz, the pursuit of Ballasteros's phantom army over the Ronda hills, and the occupation of Andalusia. When Rodrigo had fallen and the entire Anglo-Portuguese army could be moved against Badajoz, it would be time enough to distract the Duke of Dalmatia from the honey-pot into which he had crammed his head.

So after El Bodon Wellington had cantoned his men in the hill villages between Guarda and the Agueda which they regarded as their natural element; "Garnerin's balloon," wrote one of them, "was never more seated in the clouds than we are at this moment." Here, watching every movement of the French like a cat its prey, he completed his preparations during the final months of 1811. Sanchez's guerillas and Wallace's Connaught Rangers closed in unostentatiously on Rodrigo, filching more than two hundred cattle as they grazed on the glacis, and, when General Renaud, the Governor, tried to recover them, capturing him too. The roads were put in order, Dickson's siege-guns were dragged from the Lower Douro over the mountains to Almeida, a new kind of bullock-cart, with iron axle-trees and brass boxes, was manufactured in hundreds, and mules were assembled in the unprecedented proportion of one for every six infantrymen and two for every four cavalrymen.* Meanwhile in their scattered cantonments among the clouds the regiments were busy making fascines and gabions. All this was done with such elaborate devices to deceive that scarcely anyone, even his own army, was aware of Wellington's intentions. The storming apparatus was spoken of as a sham preparation for keeping the enemy on the qui vive. To those learned in such matters it scarcely seemed likely that their chief would dare to assail - at such a forbidding season - a powerful fortress in the presence of a field army which only a few weeks before he had been unable to contain.

But Wellington was no longer outnumbered. The Guadiana fevers of the summer had run their course, his hospitals were almost empty, and reinforcements, including for the first time large numbers of cavalry, had been flowing into Lisbon throughout the autumn. There were now 38,000 British and 22,000 Portuguese facing Marmont's depleted army in the north. In their bones the men knew that something was going to happen. Despite the rain, the cold, the miserable, dirty villages and wolf-haunted mountains among which their lot was cast, they were in magnificent health and spirits. Their very privations had become a matter of pride to them. "Ours," wrote Johnny Kincaid of the Rifles, "was an *esprit de corps* - a buoyancy of feeling animating all which nothing could quell. We were alike ready for the field or for frolic, and when not engaged in the one, went headlong into the other." Coursing, fox-hunting, the chase of wolf and wild boar with the Commander-in-Chief himself in the field and a score of ragged, cheering riflemen acting as beaters, greyhound matches and boxing contests, football and donkey races with "every Jack sitting with his face to the tail and a smart fellow running in front with a bunch of carrots," were the characteristically English prelude to the adventure which was to knock Napoleon out of Spain. Straight across country and no flinching was the rule in all their contests; a favourite sport was for two officers to wager that

* Fortescue, VIII, 343-5; Oman, IV, 584; Gomm, 239; Grattan, 108.

each would reach a distant church-tower by a given time, where-upon off they would go with the entire Mess at their heels, stopping for nothing on the way - swamp, wall or ravine. At night there were theatricals in barns or gay, unconventional balls with the local señoritas and village girls joining uproariously in bolero, fandango and waltz to an improvised band of flute and guitar, and a supper of roast chestnuts, cakes and lemonade to follow. If sometimes the more squeamish of the ladies left early, no one minded so long as the rest remained. The avidity and delight of it all, wrote an officer in after years, was beyond the power of words to convey. "We lived united as men always are who are daily staring death in the face on the same side and who, caring little about it, look upon each new day added to their lives as one more to rejoice in."*

Foremost in that gallant company - in sport as in war - were the men of the Light Division. They were the very embodiment of the offensive spirit which now permeated the army. In one corner of Europe at least the cycle of the twenty years' war had come full circle; it was the French who had fallen back, like the allies in 1794, on defensive fortifications, their adversaries who had learnt to rely on audacity. "A soldier who trusts to his firelock," wrote Charles Napier, the living repository of Moore's teaching, "never despairs while he can use it, but he who puts much faith in works, on seeing them forced, thinks all is lost."† "The first in the field and the last out of it," was the toast of the Rifles, "the bloody, fighting Ninety-fifth!" It was a long road that the gay, good-humoured riflemen and their comrades of the 43rd and 52nd had travelled since they marched behind their band of thirty bugle-horns to take boat at Dover in 1809. Their jackets were now patched and faded, their trousers in-discriminately black, blue and grey, and even parti-coloured, their shakos dented, for Wellington did not mind what his men looked like so long as they were well-appointed for battle and carried their sixty rounds of ammunition. But the silver-mounted bugle-horns still sounded their merry invocation of "Over the Hills and Far Away," and, for all their rags and tanned, weather-beaten faces, "the grace and intrepidity and lightness of step and flippancy of a young colonel with a rill of grasshoppers at his heels in their green coats"

* Kincaid, 95-6; *Random Shots*, 250-1; Bell, I, 12, 22; Smith, I, 50, 55; Schaumann, 326; Costello, 88-9; Simmons, 134, 137.
† Charles Napier, I, 158. See also Scott, II, 67.

had lost none of its power to bring "the dear little dark creatures with their sweeping eyebrows," running with fluttering handker-chiefs and clapping hands to the windows and roadside.*

*   *   *

In the first days of 1812 Wellington drew his sword from the scab-bard. If Napoleon was bound that summer for Moscow, he would go with his merry men to Madrid. His adversary had sent 16,000 troops to Valencia, and to encourage him in his folly the British Commander-in-Chief sent a thousand of his - from the Cadiz garrison - by sea to Cartagena. The remainder of the French Army of Portugal, deceived by his carefully studied attitude of winter in-activity, was strung out on account of supply difficulties from Sala-manca to Toledo. Ciudad Rodrigo was Wellington's for the taking.

Early on January 4th the orders to march reached the waiting regiments in their cantonments. Before it was light they were on their way. It was a terrible day of sleet and rain. The snow from the hills drifted over the roads and made every village a sea of mire; the troops went through the Agueda with water up to their shoulders and with arms linked to save themselves from being swept away by the current. Next day five men of the 3rd Division died from the cold, though one stout Irishwoman of the 88th was delivered of a child by the wayside and continued the march with her new-born infant in her arms.

By January 7th the fortress was closely invested. The garrison was not expecting an attack, and when the British on the morning of the 8th appeared under its towering rocks and medieval walls, the French officers, treating the affair as an elaborate jest, stood on the ramparts and saluted. The day, they had been given to understand, had been specially appointed by their incomprehensible adversaries for a greyhound match; no serious attack at such a time of year could conceivably be intended.†

This was merely Wellington's cunning. That night three hundred picked men of the Light Division, commanded by the thirty-three-

---

* *Barnard Letters*, 196. See also Simmons, 5. "It is curious," recorded Kincaid, "that I never yet asked a nun or an attendant of a nunnery if she would elope with me that she did not immediately consent - and that, too, unconditionally." *Random Shots*, 224. In his humbler sphere, Rifleman Harris noted the same phenomenon. Harris, 14.

† Smith, I, 55; Kincaid, 101-3; Tomkinson, 122.

year-old Colonel Colborne, stormed the outlying redoubt of San Francisco without a preliminary bombardment. Within twenty minutes they captured or slew the entire garrison for a loss of six killed and twenty wounded. So carefully had Colborne rehearsed his men, and so swift and sustained was the covering fire from the edge of the glacis, that they were through the ditch and half-way up their scaling ladders before the French had time to fire a shot. In Napier's phrase the assailants appeared to be at one and the same time in the ditch, mounting the parapets, fighting on the top of the rampart and forcing the gorge of the redoubt.

Wellington did not waste an hour. That same night his engineers broke ground and commenced the first parallel. For the next five days the work was pressed on under a tempest of grape-shot and mortar shells, each division taking its turn with the spade in the trenches for twenty-four hours at a time. It was bitterly cold at night, but the fine, clear, frosty days aided rather than retarded operations, for, while it made the rocky, snow-covered ground harder, it forced the men to work to keep warm. The enemy, who had plenty of ammunition, soon had their range, and no one could move without provoking the deadly blast of the howitzers. But though casualties were high - more than 400 fell in just over a week - the attackers closed steadily in. By January 14th all the outlying suburbs and convents were in their hands.

On the same day, hearing that Marmont was hastily assembling his army fifty miles away, Wellington decided to carry the fortress by assault and not to wait till his heavy guns - many of them still moving up from Almeida - had completed the reduction of the walls. That night the first batteries opened fire, and for the next few days the earth shook and the far mountain valleys echoed with the roar of artillery. By the morning of the 19th, the eleventh day of the siege, two passable breaches had been made on the opposite side of the town to the Agueda river. Picton's 3rd Division was thereupon appointed to storm the greater breach on the right, and the smaller Light Division the lesser one on the left. Pack's Portuguese were to make a feint against the walls at another point, while the rest of the army was to stand by in support.

By all the accepted rules of war the decision to carry the fortress by storm before the counterscarp had been blown in was wrong. But Wellington had weighed the odds more carefully than he had

285

done at Badajoz in the summer. Not only were his engineers and gunners more efficient, but the garrison - less than 3000 - was too small to hold such extensive fortifications. The price of a frontal attack on narrow breaches might be high, but it was not likely to be greater than that of a sustained siege and was almost certain to be less costly than a prolongation of the stalemate on the frontier. It was a time for boldness, and, as against the Mahrattas nine years before, Wellington had made up his mind to be bold. The fate of Europe depended on it.

His orders were laconic: "Ciudad Rodrigo *must* be stormed this evening." The troops received them with enthusiasm: it was death or glory this time, wrote Lieutenant Simmons; a golden chain or a wooden leg. They had boundless confidence in their chief and complete assurance in themselves. "Give me sixty scaling ladders and two hundred volunteers with a supporting column," Charles Napier had pleaded nine months earlier, "and the British standard should fly in Almeida in two hours."* Now his brother George to his unspeakable joy was given three hundred volunteers from the Light Division and told to crack a far harder nut.

Grattan of the 88th saw them a few hours later marching at the head of the Light Division to their action stations while the band of the 43rd played the march that was sweeping England, "The Downfall of Paris." "They were in the highest spirits, but without the slightest appearance of levity in their demeanour—on the contrary, there was a cast of determined severity thrown over their countenances that expressed in legible characters that they knew the sort of service they were about to perform, and had made up their minds to the issue. They had no knapsacks - their firelocks were slung over their shoulders - their shirt-collars were open, and there was an indescribable *something* about them. In passing us each officer and soldier stepped out of the ranks for an instant as he recognised a friend to press his hand - many for the last time. Yet, notwithstanding this animating scene, there was no shouting or huzzaing, no boisterous bravadoing, no unbecoming language; in short, everyone seemed to be impressed with the seriousness of the affair entrusted to his charge, and any interchange of words was to this effect: 'Well, lads, mind what you're about tonight'; or, 'We'll meet in the town by and by'; and other little familiar phrases, all expressive

* Charles Napier, I, 170.

of confidence. The regiment at length passed us, and we stood gazing after it as long as the rear platoon continued in sight; the music grew fainter every moment, until at last it died away altogether. They had no drums, and there was a melting sweetness in the sounds that touched the heart."*

The men of the 3rd Division, asking the bitter question - Were they to be left behind? - had not long to wait. A few minutes later the word, "Stand to your arms," passed along the ranks. After the Forlorn Hope had been detailed under Lieutenant Mackie of the 88th and a storming party of five hundred volunteers under Major Russell Manners of the 74th, the whole division moved off towards the trenches in front of the grand breach. Before each regiment marched, General Picton spoke a few words, which were listened to with silent earnestness. "Rangers of Connaught," he told the 88th, "it is not my intention to expend any powder this evening. We'll do this business with the cold iron."† The announcement was greeted with a storm of cheering.

As soon as it was dark the storming parties and the troops who were to cover them with their fire from the glacis while they crossed the ditch, moved into position. It was bitterly cold and the frost lay crisp on the grass. The guns of both sides were now still. Presently the moon emerged from the clouds, revealing the glitter of bayonets on the battlements. The joyous animation of the afternoon had passed, and on the faces of the Rangers Grattan noted an expression of severity and even savagery which he had never seen before. Some distance to the left under a Convent wall, General Craufurd was addressing the storming party of the Light Division, and in the silence his voice was more than ordinarily clear and distinct. "Soldiers! the eyes of your country are upon you. Be steady - be cool - be firm in the assault. The town must be yours this night. Once masters of the wall, let your first duty be to clear the ramparts, and in doing this keep together."‡

* Grattan, 144-5.
† Grattan, 147-8. The storming party of the Light Division also moved off to the attack unloaded. Asked why by one of the Staff, their commanding officer replied, "Because if we do not do the business with the bayonet, we shall not be able to do it at all." At which Wellington murmured, "Let him alone; let him go his own way." George Napier, 215.
‡ Costello, 95-6. The chief English authorities for the assault other than Oman, Fortescue and Napier, are Grattan, 133-55; George Napier, 209-18; Kincaid, 101-14; *Random Shots*, 252-5, 261-4; Burgoyne, I, 137, 153-64; Gomm, 244-8; Simmons, 217-22; Donaldson, 230-5;

Just before seven o'clock the signal-rocket sounded from the ramparts, and the whole place became bright as day with French fireballs. On the right the 3rd Division rushed the 300 yards which separated it from the glacis through an iron hail from guns charged to the muzzles with case-shot. Despite heavy losses, the storming party covered the ground with astonishing swiftness, leapt from the glacis into the eleven-foot ditch and, under a smashing discharge of musketry and grape, began to swarm up the breached walls. Others, including the 5th or Northumberland Fusiliers and the 94th - the heroes of El Bodon - after silencing the French on the ramparts with their fire, attempted to scale the *fausse-braye* with twenty-five-foot ladders. Those leading the attack were blown to tatters, their bodies and brains splashing amongst their comrades, but others following continued to advance till the whole breach was piled high with corpses. Just as the head of the column, pressing furiously upwards, reached the top, a magazine on the ramparts exploded, killing about three hundred defenders and assailants, including Major-General Mackinnon, who was directing the attack. At that moment only one officer - Major Thomson of the 74th - remained alive on the breach, while a single gun, served by five heroic Frenchmen, kept firing into the mass of struggling redcoats across a crevice of fallen stone.

Meanwhile the Light Division had gone forward with its usual dash and efficiency on the left. Craufurd was one of the first to fall under the hail of canister, grape, round-shot and shell - a tragic loss for England. George Napier at the head of the storming party lost an arm; Major-General Vandeleur and Colonel Colborne were both wounded. But nothing could stay the rising tide of British courage in the breach. Two-thirds of the way up there was a check as the leader fell and a tendency on the part of some of the men to snap their muskets; then Napier, with his shattered elbow, cried out, "Recollect you are not loaded, push on with the bayonet!" and the whole mass with a loud shout swept over the head of the breach. Promptly fanning out as they had been ordered, they dispersed along the ramparts to left and right. A party under Captain Ferguson took the

Knowles, 44-50; Bell, I, 22-3; Moorsom, 150-3; Smith, I, 58-9; Seaton, 166-72; Charles Napier, I, 184; Tomkinson, 121-5; Lynedoch, 622; Weller, 192-8; *Peninsular Sketches*, I, 225-66; and Wellington's Dispatches of the 9th, 15th and 20th January 1812.

defenders of the main breach in the flank and helped to open a way for the 3rd Division. There, as resistance began to weaken and new supports arrived, every officer simultaneously sprang to his feet, while three devoted Irishmen of the 88th flung themselves with their unscrewed bayonets on the French gun crew beyond the ditch. There was a thrilling cheer and the breach was carried, the victors trampling the dead and dying under foot as they rushed forward.

Within half an hour of the assault, and while storming-parties were still advancing through the narrow streets with shouts of "Victory!" "England for ever!", the Governor, who had just sat down to dinner, surrendered his sword to Lieutenant Gurwood,* leader of the Light Division's Forlorn Hope. Soon afterwards all resistance ceased. The attackers, however, separated from their officers, continued firing in the darkness. As they converged on the central cathedral square a number of Italian soldiers ran out crying that they were *poveri Italiani*. But some of the British, who had conceived a strong dislike for their race, merely answered, "You're Italians, are you? Then damn you, here's a shot for you!"† For the redcoats, enraged by some foolish Spaniards who had been shooting indiscriminately into the streets, were completely out of hand, shouting and firing madly at one another and into every door and window.

The storm of a fortress by night was something new in British military experience. The officers, many of whom had been killed or wounded in the assault, had not visualised the immediate consequences of their victory. Their rough men, used as living weapons in place of the heavy guns and sapping implements their country had failed to provide, had seen their comrades blown to pieces before their eyes; they were parched with thirst and almost frantic with excitement; their faces were scorched and blackened with powder and gore. As in the retreat to Corunna, the mystic bonds of discipline suddenly snapped; those who a few minutes before had been heroes became momentarily demons or lunatics. Lost in the blazing streets

---

* Afterwards editor of Wellington's Dispatches.

† Kincaid, 114. Elsewhere, however, those who surrendered were scrupulously spared. "It is a remarkable feature in the history of this siege," wrote Captain Gomm, "that the loss of the besiegers doubles that of the besieged. . . . The milk of human kindness was flowing richly through the veins of these Englishmen who stopped to draw breath in the breach and gave terms there to Frenchmen and such Frenchmen." Gomm, 247. See also Grattan, 154.

of an unfamiliar town, they broke into the houses and liquor-shops in search of drink and plunder. Guided by the baser inhabitants and the light of blazing houses, they quickly found what they sought. For the rest of the night, until the light of dawn enabled the harassed provost-marshals to restore order, Ciudad Rodrigo became a hell on earth, where officers, hoarse from shouting, drew their swords on their own men in an attempt to save the persons of terrified citizens and where packs of drunken soldiers ran from house to house in diabolical rage. Few lives were lost, but the town was completely sacked. "John Bull, though heartily fond of fighting, is not a man of blood," wrote a spectator, "but he is a greedy fellow and he plundered with all the rapacity of one to whom such liberty was new."* It was the first time a British army had so disgraced itself since Cromwell stormed Wexford. When the Light Division marched out next morning it was scarcely recognisable. The men were decked out in Frenchmen's coats and cocked hats, with hunks of beef, tongues and hams stuck on their bayonets, while others, remembering their waiting wives in the camp, staggered under swathes of clothes, strings of shoes, birdcages and even tame monkeys. They looked for all the world, as they moved singing over the bridge, like rag-fair on the march.

But Ciudad Rodrigo had fallen. With Marmont's relieving army still twenty miles away, the door of northern Spain had been forced. General Brennier, 78 officers and 1700 men - all that remained alive after the storm - had been made prisoners for a British loss of 553 casualties in the trenches and 449 in the breaches. At the same time the entire siege-train of the Army of Portugal, including a hundred and fifty heavy guns, had been captured. A great feat of arms - one of the greatest in the whole war - had been achieved. The British now felt ready for anything. Kincaid, who led the storming detachment of the Rifles, declared as he stood on the ramparts that night that, had the ghost of Jack the Giant-Killer passed that way, he would have given it a kick in the breech without the slightest ceremony. As the Rangers fell in under the ramparts of the captured fortress on the morning of the 20th, General Picton rode by. Some

* Gomm, 247. See also *idem*, 245; Burgoyne, I, 159. "What the devil, sir, are you firing at?" Kincaid shouted at one soldier. "I don't know, sir," he answered, "I am firing because everybody else is." *Random Shots*, 262. See also Grattan, 155-63; Donaldson, 236; Bell, I, 23; Fortescue, VIII, 363; Tomkinson, 125; Simmons, 222-3; Costello, 102; Kincaid, 119-20.

of the men, still a little above themselves, cried out, " Well, General, we gave you a cheer last night; it's your turn now!" Smiling, he took off his hat and called to them, "Here, then, you drunken set of brave rascals, hurrah! we'll soon be at Badajoz!"*

Five weeks later the army with all its guns was on the move again towards the south; Wellington was wasting no time. At the moment that Napoleon had turned his face eastwards, thinking his rear safe, the British general had kicked open one of the two gates into Spain; now before the spring came, he was going to smash through the other. Before his tramping, singing columns lay the towers of Badajoz, the plains of Salamanca, and the defiles of Vittoria and the Pyrenees. The men knew nothing of these; it was enough for them that they were marching to victory. The morrow promised to be bloody, but they cared little for the morrow, and the song and the jest went round as usual.†

Far away in England the mail-coaches drawn up on the parade outside the General Post Office in Lombard Street were decked - men, horses, carriages - with laurels and flowers, oak-leaves and ribbons. Presently the lids thundered down on the mail-bags and the waiting horses pawed the ground, the guards sounded their horns, and the news of the fall of Ciudad Rodrigo went radiating outwards down a dozen great trunk roads, through cheering towns and villages where every heart leapt for an instant in the glow of a single common pride.

*   *   *

That spring of 1812 every road across Germany was thronged with horses, guns and wagons bound for Poland. The ditches were strewn with dead horses, farms stripped of livestock, villages commandeered and looted. More than half a million troops were marching east. The Emperor's aim was to drive back Russia into her Asian steppes and open a way to world empire. Europe, he announced, was an old prostitute who must do his pleasure; an unwieldy, medieval realm of barbarous serfs and wandering Asian tribes could not hope to resist him. Britain would inevitably fall when he had destroyed her influence at St Petersburg. The Continent would become a single state and Paris its capital.

* Grattan, 166. See also Bessborough, 220; Donaldson, 198.
† Kincaid, *Random Shots*, 250.

Napoleon was the embodiment of the dreams of a hundred years. He was the child of nature, the personification of reason and energy, the irresistible Figaro who, always triumphing, proved the force of natural genius. This stern, plump, iron-faced little Italian, with his aquiline nose and eagle eye, his sword, sash and laurel-wreath, had shattered the pretensions of mankind's "legitimate" rulers. Strong as tempest, swift as lightning, he had only to will and strike.

Yet, just because Napoleon shared this view of himself, he was doomed. Having risen by observing natural law, he had come to suppose himself above it. He acknowledged no morality but his own appetite and will. He cheated, lied, bullied and exploited until in the end no one who had had dealings with him trusted him. "I never was a believer in him," said Wellington, "and I always thought that in the long run we should overturn him."[*] Viewing treachery as inherent in human nature, he betrayed and was betrayed. He even denied arithmetic. Believing from repeated success that he could do anything, that the word *impossible* existed only in the dictionary of fools, and that he alone was exempt from folly, he essayed that summer what he himself had declared the greatest of military follies: a campaign against a desert. No one was better able to assess the arithmetical impossibility of supporting half a million men and their horse-borne transport in the Russian wastes. Yet with all the intensity of his passionate nature he was resolved to make the diversionist crawl, and when the Czar Alexander, sooner than do so, called on his God and the valour of his people, Napoleon turned his back on the Europe he had conquered and strode to destruction.

As he did so, the little British army, whose fighting power he despised, struck again in his rear. Before the end of February it had left its winter quarters in the lonely Beira mountains and begun the long southward march to Badajoz - a place which Napoleon had repeatedly declared it would never dare attack. "You must think the English mad," he had written to Marmont, "if you suppose them capable of marching there while you are at Salamanca and able to reach Lisbon before them." But, as so often in his correspondence

[*] "Even in the boldest things he did there was always a mixture of apprehension and meanness," Wellington said to Croker. "I used to call him *Jonathan Wild the Great*, and at each new *coup* he made I used to cry out 'Well done, Jonathan,' to the great scandal of some of my hearers. But, the truth was, he had no more care about what was right or wrong, just or unjust, honourable or dishonourable, than *Jonathan*, though his great abilities, and the great stakes he played for, threw the knavery into the shade." *Croker Papers*, I, 340.

with his distant Marshals in Spain, the Emperor overlooked the facts. For, in obedience to his own earlier orders, half Marmont's army was on the far side of Spain helping Suchet to capture Valencia, while the British, exploiting the fact, had possessed themselves of the Spanish frontier fortress which barred Marmont's road to Lisbon. With Ciudad Rodrigo in his hands, Wellington could for the moment ignore the French Army of Portugal and concentrate against Badajoz. So long as the French held that great fortress, with its towers dominating the Guadiana and the southern road to Spain, the British could neither advance into Estremadura nor concentrate against Marmont in the north without exposing southern Portugal to Soult's Army of Andalusia. But with both frontier-fortresses his, Wellington would be able to take the offensive. Napoleon's arrogance in supposing him incapable of a winter campaign had already given him Ciudad Rodrigo. If he could now take Badajoz before the summer, the Peninsular War could take a new turn.

When their destination became known, the British, fresh from their triumph at Ciudad Rodrigo, broke into cheers. Twice in the previous summer they had laid siege to Badajoz and, for lack of proper battering and sapping equipment, had thrown themselves at its half-breached defences; twice they had had to draw off as Soult's and Marmont's armies marched to its relief. Now, with his hands tied by his master's orders and his troops scattered in the interior, Marmont was left to watch the bolted door into northern Portugal, while Soult, unaware of the sudden threat to his Estremaduran bastion, was far away in Andalusia, holding down his wide province and laying interminable siege to sea-guarded Cadiz. "Proud" Badajoz, with its fever-laden mists, its rich, collaborating *alfrancesados*, its record of disaster to the Allied cause, was at Wellington's mercy.[*]

While the long, winding columns of men and mules followed the two-hundred-mile mountain-track along the frontier, the guns of the siege-train moved eastwards from Lisbon, sliding up the Tagus to Abrantes and jolting over rough unmetalled roads behind bullock teams, while hundreds of peasants followed bearing shot and shell. In every wooded valley climbing into Spain, droves of mules, laden with food and ammunition, converged on Badajoz, their bells mingling with the shouts of muleteers and the screeching ox-wagons. For Britain's power to strike in that barren land of sierras

[*] Grattan, 175; Gomm, 249-50; Bessborough, 221; Tomkinson, 145.

and far horizons depended on her ability to feed and supply; to purchase stores from neutral Morocco, America and Turkey, to carry them across the seas to Lisbon and Oporto and distribute them over mountain, gorge and forest to the fighting columns on the frontier. The commissaries in their travel-soiled cocked hats, the hardy, active muleteers with their bright trappings and guitars, the ragged, muddy escorts marching beside them with musket and pack, the bucking mules and patient bullocks, the wicker-sided, wooden-wheeled country carts piled with provender, were England's life-line and the conduit along which her power ran. So were the transports and merchantmen courting the winds as they followed their ocean courses to Tagus, Mondego and Douro. And guarding them, far away, the battleships which had fought under Nelson and St Vincent still kept their vigil outside the ports of Napoleon's closed empire. On Pellew, Collingwood's successor in the Mediterranean, watching Toulon and Venice; on Lord Keith, Commander-in-Chief of the Channel Fleet guarding Rochefort, Brest and Cherbourg; on William Young – "stiffo Rumpo" to the Navy which had bred him since his tenth birthday – blockading Antwerp and the Texel; on Saumarez in the Baltic; and on the rough, hard-used men who served under them, the fortunes of England and the world continued to revolve. Without them Wellington's eight fighting divisions would have counted for as little on the battlefields of Europe as they did in Napoleon's computation. It was maritime power which magnified their strength.

That, and the patient genius of their commander. Though contemptuously called a Sepoy general by Napoleon, who had never crossed swords with him, Wellington had already outmatched his finest lieutenants. Masséna, Soult, Victor, Jourdan, Marmont, Ney, Junot and Kellermann had all in turn tasted the iron he administered. Repeatedly on the point of being driven into the sea, he stood at the end of four campaigns undefeated on the Spanish frontier with a liberated Portugal behind him and an expectant Spain ahead. And by opening a fifth campaign in the depth of winter, he had raised the temper of his troops to the highest expectancy. They felt sure now he would always "out-manœuvre Johnny"; of the impossibility of his suffering defeat.*

* Granville, II, 147. See also Bessborough, 221; Kincaid, 196; Simmons, 183; Oman, *Wellington's Army*, 38; Smith, I, 93-4.

Yet he was not a commander who readily inspired emotion. He never embraced his veterans like Napoleon, spoke of them as comrades or wasted fine words on them. He had, as one of them put it, a short manner of speaking and a stern look. Save for an occasional brisk, "Now, my lads," when he required some more than ordinary effort, he confined his communications to general orders of the most sparing kind. These, however, never admitted of misunderstanding. Everyone knew where they stood with him, and though this may not have generated enthusiasm – a quality he suspected – it engendered a steady growth of confidence. His men did not love him, but they relied on him; they knew that, while he commanded them, their sacrifices would not be wasted. "Whare's ar *Arthur*?" asked one fusilier of another as, under Beresford's blundering command, they had tramped up the blood-stained hill of Albuera. "I don't know, I don't see him," replied his comrade. "Aw wish he wore here."[*]

For, little sentiment though he spared them, no commander ever took greater pains to deserve his men's confidence. He was as frugal with their lives as with his words. He looked after what they most valued – their stomachs. Regard to what he called regular subsistence was his first article of war. "The attention of commanding officers," ran one of his bleak, laconic orders, "has been frequently called to the expediency of supplying the soldiers with breakfast." Of all generals he was the most commissariat-minded. Having done most of his fighting in deserts, he had learnt to be.

He once defined the key to victory as the pursuit of all means, however small, which might promote success. He, therefore, left undone no duty which might enable his men to do theirs. He rose at six, applied himself in the absence of a trained staff to every detail of administration, and only rested when he had done the work of the day, falling asleep with the same ease, regularity and promptitude as he did everything else. It was characteristic of the man that he called himself, shaved himself and brushed his own clothes. "If anything went wrong," wrote an officer who served under him both in India and the Peninsula, "he vented his spleen at once, and, it must be confessed, in no very measured terms; but, as far as regarded himself, there was an end of it. He had, what I have rarely seen in any one, the power of dismissing a subject from his mind whenever he chose; so that, in the most difficult situations, he could

[*] S. Cooper, *Rough Notes of Seven Campaigns*, 63.

converse on familiar topics; or, while ordinary minds were fretted to death, he could lie down and sleep soundly under the most trying circumstances."*

As with all great soldiers, action worked on him like a tonic, sharpening the edge of his cool, incisive mind. In the field his temper grew calmer as storms arose. Then his strong common sense acquired the quality of genius. It was this which enabled him to forecast with such accuracy his enemies' movements; to guess what was "on the other side of the hill"; to do what he defined as the main business of life – finding out what he didn't know by what he did.

Having once or twice faced disaster through the failure of his allies and having, like most British commanders, suffered disappointment at the miscarriage of his plans through his country's failure to supply what he had a right to expect, he shunned projects built on grandiose anticipations. He relied only on what he was sure he could count on, and adapted his ends strictly to his means. The French Marshals, he once said, planned their campaigns like a splendid set of harness which answered very well until it got broken: after that it was useless. "Now I," he added, "made my campaigns of ropes. If anything went wrong, I tied a knot and went on."

He was a man without enthusiasms or illusions. He saw life and men very much as they were, and this enabled him to steer a steady course amid the passions, stratagems and treacheries of a war-racked, Revolutionary land. He put little trust in others and tended to do everything that was vital himself. Of his generals he only really confided in Hill and Graham. This was sometimes costly for, when he was not there himself, his subordinates were afraid to act. Yet, when they blundered, he took full responsibility and indulged in no public reproaches. No part of his character was more admirable and more rare, wrote a member of the Government which supported him, than his temper and fortitude under great disappointments arising from the weakness and neglect of others.†

Though a stern disciplinarian who would order a man five hundred lashes or string him up on the gallows without mercy if he thought

---

* Blakiston, II, 316. On a visit to Cadiz in 1812 he astonished his hostess by his simple habits. When her servants called him at seven they found him fully dressed and packing his shaving apparatus. Leslie, 24; Gronow, I, 213. See also Stanhope, 37, 47; Larpent, I, 85; Lady Shelley, I, 46; Fraser, 27, 33, 149.

† H. M. C.; Bathurst, 216.

it necessary, his troops bore him no ill-will for it. "Atty," they called him among themselves; "the ould chap that leathers the French!" When they saw, silhouetted against the tawny landscape, the familiar equestrian figure with the trim grey cloak, oilskin cocked hat, telescope and neatly buckled boots, or found themselves under the unrelenting scrutiny of those high-arched inquiring eyes, they cheered till the rocks rang. "Here he comes with his long nose, boys," they cried, "now you may fix your flints!" Once in an exposed spot an emotional Irish sentry, finding his Commander-in-Chief had forgotten the countersign, brought his musket to the salute with a "God bless your crooked nose; I would sooner see it than ten thousand men!"*

For between leader and led—though he gruffly called them "they" and, in his worse moments, the scum of the earth—there had grown a confidence that could not be shaken. Horse and rider were one, and in that lay a priceless asset for their country. And if the rider was acknowledged now by all Europe, the steed he rode was worthy of him. It was a very different force from that which, gallant but raw, had landed in Portugal in 1808. Though its staff was still a trifle amateur and its engineers, as befitted the men of an island race, lacking in knowledge of Continental fortification, and its cavalry over-apt to dash after the enemy like a field of fox-hunters, "as if," in Wellington's words, "incapable of manoeuvre except on Wimbledon Common," its infantry were the finest in the world. Again and again its patiently-husbanded volleys had halted the French columns at the moment of triumph; again and again Napoleon's advancing, cheering veterans had wavered, huddled together and broken before its terrible musketry. Being accustomed to operating with little support from other arms, it had evolved a combination of fire-power and movement perfectly fitted to the stony hills of the Peninsula. "We cracked them out with our muskets," wrote their Commander-in-Chief.

Three and a half years of campaigning had produced a wonderful synthesis between the men of four nations. Shepherds from the Dorset hills, rollicking blades from Cashel and Clonmel who had enlisted for drink and a fight, sober Nottinghamshire weavers, breechless giants with flaming hair from the Highlands, wastrels

* Bell, I, 34, 79. See also Cooke, 47-8; Bessborough, 221; Greville (Suppl.), I, 457; Kincaid, 196; Guedalla, 209; Simmons, 183.

297

from London gaols and sponging-houses, prudent Lowland Scots who had learnt their Latin at Aberdeen Grammar School or Glasgow Academy, were blended, under the command of country squires, fox-hunters, grizzled captains too poor to buy promotion, and eager boys fresh from school, into an entity that represented as nothing else at that moment the national spirit. Since they had sailed from England, cooped up in minute, leaky, rat-infested hulks, they had shared short commons, discomfort and danger. They had slept on arctic sierras and drenched fields, marched under blazing suns, weighed down by knapsack, firelock and ball-cartridge, with stiff leather girdles round their throats and as many belts as would harness a donkey, cantoned for years among poor, stinking mountain villages where the houses were so full of vermin that if a man lay down he was certain to rise bitten from head to foot.* When they fell sick or wounded, they had to endure a hell unimaginable by gentlemen in England, jolting in open bullock-carts with solid wheels or lying under clouds of flies with their wounds crawling with maggots while the surgeons went their round with cauterising iron and dripping knife. "No ventilation, twenty sick men in the room, of whom about eighteen died," ran the diary of a wounded sergeant. "Shirt unchanged and sticking to my sore back, ears running with stinking matter, a man lying close on my right side with both his legs mortified nearly to his knees and dying." Those who survived had small hope of pension or gratuity. Even their pay, thanks to the Treasury, was usually months in arrears.

Yet these hard-used men were filled with a burning love of their country and a resolve which no odds or injustice could daunt. They went into battle with shouts of "Hurrah for old England!" and drums playing "The British Grenadiers" or "Garryown," wild for a dash at the French. Their pride in their corps was a religion; when, at Albuera, two-thirds of the Gloucesters had fallen and all their officers, one of the latter, finding he could still stagger, hobbled back

---

* Larpent, I, 21. See also *idem*, 12, 17; Grattan, 223; *Johnny Newcome*, 40, 54; Kincaid, 89. Young Sir Thomas Styles of the 1st Foot Guards, who as a small boy at Eton had thrashed the poet Shelley, was bitten so badly on his way through Portugal to join his unit that he committed suicide. The girls in the Portuguese villages on the road made high jest of his sufferings, shaking the fleas out of their petticoats over pails of water and shouting with laughter. Gronow, II, 205-6. See also Bell, I, 5-7; Anderson, 4-5; Grattan, 2; Gomm, 130; Blakeney, 15; Boothby, 11, 134-5; Dyott, I, 268; *Johnny Newcome*, 11.

into the fight. " 'Twas the system," he explained, "of the Old Slashers." A soldier of the 43rd, that glorious regiment, dying on a straw palliasse, refused to lie still when a badly wounded superior was borne in; his nature would not let him die in peace when an officer was laid beside him on the stones. This was not servility but the spirit of proud subordination which makes an army. So was the sacrifice of the private of the Royal Artificers who exclaimed, when Masséna was sweeping towards Lisbon and a temporary bridge over the Murcella failed to blow up, "It shall not fail, they shall not pass," and standing on the structure, held the match to the mine. It was conscience, not fear of the lash, which kept men like these to the sticking-point. "I heard an old soldier," wrote a newcomer after his first engagement, "answer to a youth like myself who inquired what he should do during the battle, 'Do your duty!' "*

Under their rough exteriors these men were philosophers and humorists. Before a fight jokes and quips ran through the ranks; "Ah! if me poor mother saw me now!" the men of the 28th would shout when things went awry, rocking with rude laughter at the time-honoured sally. In the same spirit, when the famous rub-a-dub of the French *pas de charge* was heard, the riflemen called out to one another from behind the boulders, "Holloa there! Look sharp! for damme, here comes Old Trousers!"

Among the Irish, who crowded the ranks of almost every regiment, this joking spirit was often carried to the point of riot. "A parcel of lads that took the world aisy," they tended to turn their surroundings into a Donnybrook Fair. They nearly drove Wellington's Provost Marshals mad with their plundering; a few minutes after they bivouacked, the sheep and hens would start bleating and cackling for miles round. Nor, though their escapades sometimes brought them to the gallows, were they ever at a loss for an answer. "And I know you, sir, and the 'boys of Connaught' know you too," replied a Connaught Ranger whom General Picton had observed from the far side of an unfordable river making off with a goat, "and I'd be sorry to do anything that would be displaising to your honour; and, sure, iv you'd only let me, I'd send your sarvent a leg iv him to dhress for your dinner, for, by my sowl, your honour looks cowld and angry - hungry I mane." After which, this experienced cam-

* Grattan, 21. See also *idem*, 87, 123-5, 128, 136-8; Blakeney, 18-19, 165; Schaumann, 23, 202; Leslie, 97.

paigner, knowing himself safe, held up the old goat by the beard and shook it genially at the general's aide-de-camp.*

No discipline could wholly tame such inveterate plunderers. "I have no fear of your conduct in face of the enemy," Wellington told an Irish regiment, "I know you. You are where you wish to be, leading the army. But if I hear of any straggling or irregularities in pursuit, I'll punish you as severely as the worst corps in the army, and *you know me*." Upon which there arose from the rear rank an agonised cry of "Glory be to God! there'll be no plundering, after all!" The "Patlanders'" wives, who did the army's washing, were as incorrigible. "Bad luck to his ugly face - the spy of our camp!" cried Mrs Skiddy of the 34th after one of her brushes with the Provost Marshal, "may he niver see home till the vultures pick his eyes out, the born varmint!" Bestriding the rocky hill-tracks on her celebrated donkey, "the Queen of Spain," the little, squat, turtle-backed woman, with her uncontrollable tongue and invincible courage, was the type of all her ragged race. She and her sisters were always ready to risk their lives to be in at the bivouac before their husbands and "have the fire and a dhrip of tay ready for the poor craythers after their load and labour."

For fighting's sake these "Teagues" would endure without complaining an almost Roundhead discipline. In the whole army no corps was so severely drilled as the Connaught Rangers, the celebrated 88th - a regiment, as one of its veterans wrote, whose spirit it was impossible to break. If a man coughed in the ranks, if the sling of his firelock left his shoulder when it should not, if he moved his knapsack when standing at ease, he was punished. "Yet, if it came to a hard tug and we had neither rations nor shoes," wrote Captain Grattan, "then indeed the Rangers would be in their element and outmarch any battalion in the Service! Without shoes they fancied themselves at home, without food they were nearly at home." An officer of another regiment has left us a picture of them as they passed him in a moment of crisis, merry as larks, singing and cracking their jokes, with bronzed faces and frames hard as nails, and as eager for the fight as for a ration of rum. Danger seemed to inspire them; George Napier recorded how one worthless, drunken

* *Journal of a Soldier*, 22, 24. See also Donaldson, 211; Bell, I, 26-7, 83; Charles Napier, I, 163-4, 172; Blakeney, 204; Grattan, 112; Gomm, 226; Simmons, 80, 134, 249; Bessborough, 221.

dog ran up to a thirteen-inch shell which had dropped into a crowded trench and, knocking off its spluttering fuse, presented it to him with a "By Jasus, your honour, she'll do you no harm, since I knocked the life out of the cratur!"

With its "hard cases," inveterate drunkards, and gaolbirds—one colonel reckoned the criminal element at from fifty to a hundred men in every battalion—the British Army was no school for saints. The recruiting sergeant took what he could get. Yet nearly all were game-cocks in a fight; as one of their officers said, there never was such an army. And many of these rough men displayed at times a touching affection and kindness. George Napier, when wounded, was visited by an Irish private of his company who, after having his arm amputated, walked seven miles to assure himself of his captain's safety. His brother, William Napier, related how John Hennessy of the 50th, a drunken, thieving brute, several times flogged for his evil ways, who was captured with him at Corunna, tramped two hundred miles on his return home in order to deliver to Napier's sister a silver spur entrusted to his charge.

The British soldier's incurable vice was drink. An old woman of Pontalegre, after four years' acquaintanceship with Wellington's army, always assumed, when an Englishman asked a question, that he was after wine. To obtain it, he would commit every species of depredation; rob a house, plunder a church, steal from his comrade and strip his own dead officer after death. Sergeant Donaldson of the 94th, who wrote an account of life in the ranks, thought that the craving for liquor was often pathological - the result of harsh usage and brutal punishment. Soldiers had to endure so much and had so few normal pleasures that they turned automatically to drink when they relaxed. Men who could take three or four hundred lashes without a groan, chewing a musket ball or a bit of leather to keep themselves from crying out while the blood ran down their backs, were scarcely likely to restrain themselves when they got into a wine vault.

Yet Wellington's remark that the bulk of his men enlisted for drink concealed the representative character of his army. Though poverty was its recruiting ground, many of its soldiers were thoughtful and serious men of refinement and education. One Scottish private related how he found a comrade on guard reading Cromek's *Remains of Nithsdale and Galloway Song*; another how the eyes of himself and his comrades filled with tears as they sang the songs of their native land before a battle.* And running through the tough fibre of the rank and file was a strain of chivalry. Foul-mouthed, obscene, irreligious, they would yet give their last bit of biscuit to a starving Portuguese peasant or shoulder the burden of a woman or child. When he was sober and his blood not roused, the British soldier, so fierce and implacable in battle, could show an almost childlike tenderness towards an enemy: would tear the shirt off his own back to bind his wounds, carry him to safety or share with him the contents of his flask. Having never known invasion at home, he seldom evinced the revengeful spirit of his German and Iberian allies. A Scottish sergeant who was shot at by a wounded Frenchman for whom he had gone to fetch a drink, after a moment's reflection with raised firelock quietly went on with his mission of mercy. A private of the same race, finding a Portuguese muleteer robbing a peasant girl, faced his knife with his bare fists and knocked him down.

Among the officers this chivalrous sense of honour was more than an instinct; it was a code. They were almost too ready to take on a bully or punish a cheat; Charles Napier flattered himself that his leg was as straight a one as ever bore up the body of a gentleman or kicked a blackguard. He regarded the treatment of women as the measure of civilisation; tenderness towards the helpless and adherence to one's word constituted for him the tests of a gentleman. A man who broke his parole was beneath contempt; George Napier held it up to his children as the unforgivable offence – that and cowardice. One rode straight, spoke the truth and never showed fear. There was little outward religion in Wellington's officers; skylarking and often uproariously noisy, they were like a pack of schoolboys. Yet under the surface was a deep fund of Christian feeling; their *beau idéal* was a man like John Colborne of the 52nd – upright, fearless and gentle – or John Vandeleur, whom his friends never heard speak harshly of any man. "The British Army is what it is," Wellington said long afterwards, "because it is officered by gentlemen; men who would scorn to do a dishonourable thing and who have something more at stake than a reputation for military smartness."†

* Donaldson, 180; *Journal of a Soldier*, 115-6.

† Fraser, 207; Charles Napier, I, 316; Gomm, 375; George Napier, 55, 76, 174-5, 218, 221; Grattan, 57, 229, 303; Kincaid, *Random Shots*, 288; Tomkinson, 222; Blakeney, 178, 281-2; Leslie, 193-4, 198; Bessborough, 231; Oman, V, 453; Anderson, 14; *Journal of a Soldier*, 106; Boothby, 159; Costello, 74; Donaldson, 200; Bell, I, 42, 83-4; Smith, I, 46-7.

It was this which kept them so staunch at the testing time. They fought, not for public applause, but for an inward satisfaction that each man bore in his soul. "I should never have shown my face again," wrote one of them after a bout of fever, "had I applied for sick leave." They took their knocks as they came, believing that nothing mattered so long as they were true to code and comrade. "How did you sleep?" asked a young officer of a newcomer after a night in the clouds on the march to Arroyo-Molinos. "Slept like a fish," came the reply, "I believe they sleep very well in water." "Bravo," said he, "you'll do!" "Begin to like my trade," wrote the same apt novice a few weeks later, "seeing all my comrades as jolly and fearless as if they were fox-hunters."*

The Prussian rigidity, which the Horse Guards with pipeclay and lash had imposed on the eighteenth-century Army, had long been shed. Wellington's force was as knowing, adaptable and individualistic as a field of fox-hunters. After four years' campaigning in the toughest country in western Europe, it could, he claimed, go anywhere and do anything. Its courage was the cool, resourceful kind of men with complete confidence in their own skill. "Now, my lads," said Colonel Colborne, "we'll just charge up to the edge of the ditch, and, if we can't get it, we'll stand and fire in their faces."† Alert and wiry veterans as the French were, they had met their match. "Their soldiers got them into scrapes," Wellington replied when asked to explain his success, "mine always got me out." They were up to every trick of the game and, like their hardy adversaries, able to make themselves comfortable anywhere. Captain Leslie of the 29th and Kincaid of the Rifles have each described the scene at their nightly bivouac: the rough sedge-mats spread under a tree, the accoutrements hanging on the branches, the parallel trenches dug on festive occasions to form a table with candles stuck in the sockets of upturned bayonets, the soup made from stewed ration-beef and vegetables; the partridges and hares roasting on a turning thread suspended from a tripod of ramrods; the rough wine of the country cooled under moist cloths in canteens hung from the trees. Then

---

* Bell, I, 13-14, 22. See also Simmons, 193; Tomkinson, 22. "I knew no happier times, and they were their own reward." Kincaid, *Random Shots*, 252.

† *Random Shots*, 273. "I am confident if Colborne was suddenly woken out of his sleep and told he was surrounded by treble his numbers, it would only have had the effect of making him, if possible, still more calm and collected." George Napier, 220-1.

with a bundle of fine branches to lie on and a green sod or saddle for pillow, the young victors would sleep in their cloaks till reveille. "The bugles sounded," wrote Ensign Bell, "I rolled my blanket, strapped it on my back, and waited for the assembly call."

It was not the French now who hunted the British, but the British the French - "to pot them, kill them and cook them in their own fashion." "Damn my eyes," the men shouted to one another when on short rations, "we must either fall in with the French or the Commissary today; I don't care which!" "It was like deer-stalking," wrote another, "a glorious thing to whack in amongst a lively party with their flesh-pots on the fire of well-seasoned wood, a chest of drawers, perhaps, or the mahogany of some hidalgo in the middle of the street blazing away and the crappos calling out, '*Bonne soupe, bonne soupe!*'" Officers and men were always thinking out new ways of surprising and harrying the enemy; Captain Irvine of the 28th taught himself to sling stones with such accuracy that, if he encountered two or three Frenchmen, he would bowl one over with a well-placed rock, flatten another with his firelock, and petrify a third with a shout, tripping him up or, if he bolted, pelting him with pebbles - a spectacle which never failed to delight his men.*

It was this offensive spirit - itself the outcome of perfect training, fitness and team-work - that made Wellington's army so formidable. It was always on its toes; healthy, collected, well-provisioned, wary, impudent and out to make trouble. Apart from the old Scots champion, Sir Thomas Graham, and Picton, who was fifty-three, the average age of its divisional commanders in the spring of 1812 was slightly under forty. Stapleton Cotton, who commanded the cavalry, was thirty-eight; Alexander Dickson of the Artillery thirty-four; George Murray, the Quartermaster-General and Chief-of-Staff, forty.

Of those they led, the crown and exemplar was still the Light Division - capable, as Harry Smith claimed, of turning the tide of victory any day. "There perhaps never was, nor ever again will be," wrote Kincaid, "such a war brigade as that which was composed of the 43rd, 52nd and the Rifles." Its officers, who took a pride in being

* Bell, I, 163. See also *idem*, I, 24, 64, 81-2; Grattan, 176; *Johnny Newcome*, 170; Tomkinson, 137; Kincaid, 33, 42-8, 60, 211; *Random Shots*, 87-90; Leslie, 83-5; Donaldson, 206-7; Simmons, 15-16, 57.

gay of heart, were always ready to enter into whatever amusement was going - a practical joke, a hare- or fox-hunt, an impromptu donkey-race, a day after the partridges, a dance with guitar, cakes and lemonade in some draughty, candlelit barn where the raven-haired, garlic-scented village señoritas, screeching with excitement, pinned up their dresses for *bolero* and *fandango*. At the head of this famous Division went the green-jacketed Rifles - "the most celebrated old fighting corps in the Army" - who in the whole war never lost a piquet. And the scarlet-coated 43rd and 52nd—that beloved corps of George Napier's, "where every officer was a high-minded gentleman and every private a gallant and well-conducted soldier"—were their equals. "We had only to look behind," wrote Kincaid, "to see a line in which we might place a degree of confidence equal to our hopes in Heaven; nor were we ever disappointed." Grattan of the 88th - though a member of the rival 3rd Division - acknowledged the 43rd to be the best regiment in the army.*

There were many competitors: the peerless Fusilier regiments which snatched victory out of defeat at Albuera; the Guards with their grace and nonchalance and unbreakable discipline; the fiery Highlanders; the great, undemonstrative regiments of the Line - the 28th, the 29th, the 45th, the 48th, the 57th. On their capacity to rise, when called upon, to the highest capacity of human endurance and valour, their commander, though he seldom misused it, knew he could rely. "Ah," he said during a near-run fight to an officer who informed him that he had placed the Royal Welch in a dangerous gap, "that is the very thing!"

Pride in the continuing regiment - the personal individual loyalty which each private felt towards his corps - gave to the British soldier a moral strength which the student and administrator ought never to under-estimate. It enabled him to stand firm and fight forward when men without it, however brave, would have failed. To let down the regiment, to be unworthy of the men of old who had marched under the same colours, to be untrue to the comrades who had shared the same loyalties, hardships and perils were things that the least-tutored, humblest soldier would not do. Through the dusty, tattered ranks the spirit of companionship

* Grattan, 120; Bell, I, 12, 37, 54-5, 156; George Napier, 207-8; Kincaid, 96, 153-4, 179; *Random Shots*, 16; Simmons, XXI, 279; Smith, I, 185, 190; Schaumann, 339; Larpent, I, 89, 102; Costello, 148; Cooke, 71-2.

ran like a golden thread. "Years of hard fighting, fatigues and privations that we now wonder at," wrote Grattan, "had a charm that in one way or another bound us all together; and, all things considered, I am of opinion that our days in the Peninsula were amongst the happiest of our lives." "You may laugh at me," wrote George Napier after leading a storming party, "but it made me cry with pleasure and joy to find myself among the men and to see their rough, weatherbeaten countenances look at me with every expression of kindly feeling."

There was little outward pageantry now about Wellington's army - little except the bronzed faces, the level eyes, the indefinable air of resolution and alertness. The dandified uniforms of peace-time England, the powder, pipeclay, brilliant colours, shining brass-work, had become things of the past. Wellington cared little for these; provided his men brought their weapons into the field in good order and sixty sound rounds of ammunition, he never asked whether their trousers were blue, black or grey.* Their jackets were faded and ragged, their breeches patched with old blankets, their shakos bleached by sun and twisted into fantastic shapes. When an officer, returning wounded from Portugal, saw the Portsmouth garrison in their smart white small clothes and black gaiters, they seemed to him like the troops of another nation. And the Life Guards, arriving in Spain from England, mistook the Rifles from their dark clothing and sunburnt visages for Portuguese. The slouching gait, the motley wear, the alert, roving gaze of the Peninsular men were as far removed from the Prussian gait of the barrack square as was the fustian of Cromwell's Ironsides. Only their firelocks were always bright and clean.

*   *   *

Yet, as they assembled in the March of 1812 before Badajoz, there was no mistaking their power. On the 17th - the day after the city was invested - they paraded before Wellington, their bullet-ridden colours, bare and faded, floating in the wind and the band of each

---

* Grattan, 50. "There is no subject of which I understand so little. . . . I think it indifferent how a soldier is clothed provided it is in a uniform manner, and that he is forced to keep himself clean and smart as a soldier ought to be." Wellington, *Supplementary Despatches*, VII, 245. See also Oman, *Wellington's Army*, 296; Kincaid, 203-4; Fraser, 154.

regiment breaking into the march, "St Patrick's Day." That night the work of entrenching began under heavy fire from the fortress and in icy rain. The men had to dig up to their knees in slime under continuous bombardment; for the next week, while the rest of the army covered the siege, they spent sixteen out of every twenty-four hours in the trenches. At one moment floods swept away the pontoon bridge that linked them with headquarters at Elvas. Every morning of that anxious week as Wellington waited for news of Soult's army beyond the Sierra Morena, the Portuguese Governor of Elvas and his Staff in full uniform solemnly waited on him to ask, with a wealth of old-world compliment, how he had passed the night.*

On the afternoon of March 24th the weather cleared. Next night five hundred volunteers of the Light and 3rd Divisions stormed Fort Picurina, an outlying bastion on the south-east of the town. As the last stroke of the cathedral bell tolled eight, the storming detachments rose from the trenches and raced towards the glacis. Two hundred fell, but, before the enemy could recover, they were swarming up the ladders, the men of the 3rd Division crying out to their old rivals: "Stand out of the way!" to which the latter, shoving fiercely by, shouted back, "Damn your eyes, do you think we Light Division fetch ladders for such chaps as you to climb up!"†

The capture of Picurina enabled the breaching batteries to begin the bombardment of the south-eastern corner of the city wall which the engineers had selected as its weakest point. It was now a race between the British guns and Soult's troops. Fortunately, Marmont, who in the previous summer had successfully marched to the relief of Badajoz, had been expressly commanded by Napoleon to invade Portugal in Wellington's absence – a futile demonstration as he well knew, since, not only did Ciudad Rodrigo bar the road to Lisbon, but he had no means of supporting his army in the Portuguese hinterland.

By April 4th, the day Soult emerged from the Sierra Morena, two breaches had been made. Next day, every gun was directed to making a third in the curtain wall between. By the rules of siegecraft, no assault should have been made until the batteries had blown in the

---

* Stanhope, 327.
† Smith, I, 62. See also Grattan, 188; Bell, I, 28; Tomkinson, 143; Blakeney, 261; Fortescue, VIII, 286; Oman, V, 239-40.

counterscarp. But as this was beyond Wellington's power, an un-military Parliament and parsimonious Treasury having failed to provide him with trained sappers and miners, he had to use his infantry to do the work of mine and shell. "It is inconceivable," he had written to the Secretary of State after the storming of Ciudad Rodrigo, "with what disadvantage we undertake anything like a siege for want of assistance of this description. There is no French *corps d'armée* which has not a battalion of sappers and a company of miners. But we are obliged to depend . . . upon the regiments of the line; and, although the men are brave and willing, they want the knowledge and training which are necessary. Many casualties among them consequently occur, and much valuable time is lost at the most critical period of the siege."*

Badajoz was held by nearly 5000 veteran troops under General Phillipon, a past-master of fortification. Faced by Napoleon's threat to shoot the Governor of any fortress who surrendered before it had been stormed—a defiance of the eighteenth-century convention which allowed the Governor of a besieged town to yield as soon as a practicable breach had been effected so as to avoid casualties and the horrors of a sack—he had sealed off the breaches with tiers of trenches and strewn the unbridged ditch before them with thousands of mines, iron harrows, crows' feet and *chevaux de frise*. Believing the rest of the city's defences to be impregnable, he had then concentrated half the garrison at the point and armed every man with eight loaded muskets.

It was Wellington's plan that of the four divisions besieging the town, the 7500 men of the 4th and Light should storm the breaches. At Picton's eleventh-hour entreaty, the 3rd Division on their right had been given the supplementary task of trying to take the main castle by *escalade* - a feat apparently impossible, for part of its walls rose a hundred feet sheer above the ditch and the Guadiana. Mean-while, on the other side of the town, which was known to be heavily mined, General Leith's 5th Division and some Portuguese were to pin down as many of the garrison as possible by a demonstration. At the last moment a few ladders had been allotted to them to at-tempt the ramparts of the San Vincente bastion at the extreme north-west corner of the town.

By the afternoon of April 6th, the third breach had been made.

* To Earl of Liverpool, February 11th 1812, 232.

The order for the assault was immediately given. Though it was certain that there would be terrible losses, the troops received it with grim satisfaction. Even officers' servants insisted on taking their places in the ranks. The gaiety of the southward march had now been succeeded by something in the men's bearing which told that, though during the siege they had made no complaint of their fatigues and had seen their comrades fall without repining, they smarted under the one and felt the other. Their expression of anxiety to seize their prey was almost tiger-like.*

As evening approached a hush fell on the camp. The men sauntered about, many for the last time, while bands played airs which recalled distant homes and bygone days. The time for the assault had been fixed for seven-thirty, but owing to various mishaps it was postponed till ten, giving the enemy several further hours of darkness in which to sow the ditch and breaches with explosives. Ghostlike sheets of mist rose from the Guadiana, hiding the lanterns of the working-parties; only the rippling waters, the croaking of frogs along the bank and the sentinel's cry on the ramparts broke the silence. Grattan has left a picture of the waiting columns: the men without knapsacks, their shirts unbuttoned, trousers tucked to the knees, tattered jackets so worn as to make the insignia of regiment and rank indistinguishable, the stubby, keen-set faces, the self-assurance, devoid of boast or bravado, which proclaimed them for what they were—an invincible host.

Soon after nine the order was given to move to the storming positions, and without a word and in pitch blackness the men went forward. Those approaching the castle were discovered shortly before zero hour by the light of a flaming carcass thrown from the ramparts. Immediately every gun opened up. In front of the breaches the storming parties, creeping up to the glacis, had already begun to descend into the ditch. As the first fireball rose, the scene was lit up like a picture; the ramparts crowded with dark figures and glittering arms, and, below, the long red columns coming on "like streams of burning lava." Then there was a tremendous crash, and the leading files were blown to pieces as hundreds of shells and powder-barrels exploded.

For an instant, wrote an officer, the men stood on the brink of the ditch amazed at the sight; then, with a shout, flew down the ladders

* Grattan, 193-7; Kincaid, 130; Bell, I, 27.

or, disdaining their aid, leaped, reckless of the depth, into the gulf below. Hundreds fell, but their comrades, trampling over them, pressed forward through a storm of grape-shot and canister. The ditch became a writhing mass of dead and wounded, across whose bodies fresh assailants struggled through flame and darkness towards the breaches. Many were shot or burnt; some, losing their bearings in the darkness, stumbled into the flooded part of the ditch and sank beneath the waters. Others were blown to pieces by the exploding grenades, mines and powder-barrels. Yet still little groups of men forced their way through that surf of fire and "went at the breach like a whirlwind. . . . Hundreds fell, dropping at every discharge which maddened the living; the cheer was forever on, on, with screams of vengeance and a fury determined to win the town; the rear pushed the foremost into the swordblades to make a bridge of their bodies rather than be frustrated. Slaughter, tumult and disorder continued; no command could be heard, the wounded struggling to free themselves from under the bleeding bodies of their dead comrades; the enemy's guns within a few yards at every fire opening a bloody lane amongst our people, who closed up and, with shouts of terror as the lava burned them up, pressed on to destruction - officers, starting forward with a heroic impulse, carried on their men to the yawning breach and glittering steel, which still belched out flames of scorching death."* All the while the bugles continued to sound the advance.

But, though the breaches were three times cleared by the bayonet, none penetrated them. There were soldiers who, in the frenzy of attack, thrust their heads through the hedge of swords at the summit and allowed the foe to smash them with the butts of their muskets, or, enveloped in streams of fire, died trying to tear with lacerated hands the blades out of the *chevaux de frise*. All was in vain. No troops could have passed through that curtain of death.

Yet, "though valour's self might stand appalled," the British refused to withdraw. They stood sullenly facing that terrible fire until some officer, rallying fifty or a hundred tired men, led them forward once more, only to meet the same inevitable fate. For two hours the slaughter continued until a third of the Light Division had fallen. The 95th alone lost twenty-two officers.

About midnight Wellington, who was waiting in a neighbouring

* Bell, I, 30-1.

quarry, called off the attack. His face, lit by the flame of a candle, was grey and drawn, and his jaw fell as he gave the order. In that bitter hour he ordered one of his aides to hasten to Picton and tell him that he must try at all costs to succeed in the castle. He was unaware that the castle had already fallen. While the buglers on the glacis before the breaches still sounded the retreat and the stubborn survivors of the 4th and Light Divisions began to fall back to the quarries, an officer galloped up with the news that Picton's men were inside the walls. For by their refusal to admit defeat the men of the breaches had given their comrades the chance to achieve the impossible. Those struggling to breast the castle's towering cliffs had, too, suffered terrible casualties, and, baffled by a murderous cross-fire from the bastions and shells, stones and logs thrown from the ramparts, had fallen back in defeat. But Picton, who never did things by halves, wounded though he was in the groin, returned to the ditch and formed up his entire division, 4000 strong, at the base of the wall. Though ladder after ladder was flung down by the defenders and the rungs were slippery with blood, those below took the places of those who fell so swiftly that in the end a lodgment was made, the ramparts cleared, and, after nearly a fifth of its numbers had fallen, the 3rd Division swarmed into the fortress. Among the casualties was Colonel Ridge of the 5th Fusiliers - the third to reach the summit. " No man," wrote Napier, " died that night with more glory - yet many died, and there was much glory."

By capturing the castle, and with it the enemy's reserves of food and ammunition, Picton had made the fall of Badajoz certain. He could not alter the immediate situation in front of the breaches because the castle gates leading to the ramparts had been bricked up, and only a single postern, hastily closed by the enemy, gave access to the town. But while his men were dragging up a gun from the embrasure to blow it in, Wellington, still waiting in the quarries near the breaches, thought he heard the sound of an English bugle in the tower of San Vincente at the far side of the town. Here, though the walls were more than thirty feet high and the ladders too low, a detachment of General Walker's brigade of Leith's 5th Division, consisting of men of the 4th and 44th Regiments, managed in the darkness to secure a foothold on the under-manned ramparts.They had at once gone to the assistance of their comrades below, and by midnight, had lifted the whole brigade into the town. Though there was fierce fighting on the walls and Walker himself was wounded, Leith brought up the rest of his division with such speed that the enemy was given no chance to recover. It was the appearance in the rear of the breaches of a detachment of this force, marching in haste through the deserted streets, which caused the French to collapse. Unable to imagine how their foes had entered, they threw down their arms or fled. The exhausted survivors of the Light and 4th Divisions, returning to the attack, found the breaches deserted. Badajoz had fallen.*

What followed tarnished the night's glory. The men, separated in the darkness from their officers, parched with thirst and half-mad from the fury of the attack, broke into the cellars and wine-shops. By dawn they had become a mob of fiends. They had been promised, in accordance with the rules of war, that, if the garrison resisted after the breaches had been made, the city would be given up to sack; they did not now mean to lose a prey so hardly won. The worst horrors were the work of the scoundrel minority of an army recruited in part from the jails, and of the Spanish and Portuguese camp followers. For two days and nights packs of drunkards rushed from house to house, blowing in doors, firing through windows, and looting everything. Women were dragged screaming from hiding holes and raped, wine casks were broached in the streets, and satyrs with blackened faces drank till the liquor ran from their mouths and ears. No officer could control them. It was not till the third day that Wellington, marching in fresh troops and erecting a gallows in the square, restored order.

Yet even during these scenes soldiers risked their lives to stay the tumult. Groups of officers fought their way through the streets escorting women to the church of St John's where a guard was mounted; others kept watch over Spanish families and drove back the mobs who assailed them. Down at the camp below the town, where the British wounded lay in thousands, two young officers, standing at their tent door on the day after the attack, saw two Spanish ladies approaching, the elder of whom, her ears torn and bleeding from the grasp of drunken savages, confided to their protection her sister, a girl of fifteen. Such was her faith in the British character,

---

* Weller, 198-204; Glover, 175-80; Smith, I, 64-5; *Peninsular Sketches*, I, 339-56; Blakeney, 270-8; Grattan, 158, 208, 210-16; Gomm, 202; Costello, 120-1; Bell, I, 33-4; Tomkinson, 146; Simmons, 233; Kincaid, 139; *Random Shots*, 285; Stanhope, 49; Napier, IV, 430-1.

she declared, that she knew the appeal would not be in vain. Two days later Juanita Maria de los Dolores de Leon was married to Captain Harry Smith of the Rifles. The Commander-in-Chief gave her away, and she became the darling of the Army, henceforward sharing all its adventures and hardships.*

When the sun rose on the morning after the attack. the ditch before the breaches was a lake of smoking blood. Visiting the glacis where so many of his men had fallen, Wellington could not hold back his tears at the sight of the massed dead. Later, when gallant, foul-mouthed Sir Thomas Picton of the triumphant Third Division came to his headquarters to congratulate him, he broke down. "I bit my lips and did everything I could to stop myself," he told Mrs Arbuthnot afterwards, recalling that bitter memory, "for I was ashamed he should see it, but I could not; and he so little entered into my feelings that he said, 'Good God, what is the matter?' and I was obliged to begin swearing and cursing the Government for giving me no sappers and miners as an excuse for my agitation."† Nor could he conceal his feelings – and his indignation – in the report he sent on the same day to the Secretary of State. "The capture of Badajoz affords as strong an instance of the gallantry of our troops as has ever been displayed, but I anxiously hope that I shall never again be the instrument of putting them to such a test as they were in last night. . . . When I ordered the assault I was certain I should lose our best officers and men. It is a cruel situation for any person to be placed in, and I earnestly recommend to your lordship to have a corps of sappers and miners formed without loss of time."‡

* Many years later, when her husband, the victor of Aliwal, had become the hero of Victorian England and Governor of the Cape, she gave her name, Ladysmith, to a South African town destined to become the scene of another famous siege.

† Arbuthnot, I, 143 (February 17th 1822). "The Duke . . . said that he could never enjoy any of his successes for several days after the battle, the melancholy scenes he witnessed having always made so much impression upon him."

‡ To the Earl of Liverpool, April 7th 1812. "The assault was a terrible business, of which I foresaw the loss when I was ordering it. But we had brought matters to that state that we could do no more, and it was necessary to storm or raise the siege. I trust, however, that future armies will be equipped for sieges with the people necessary to carry them on as they ought to be; and that our engineers will learn how to put their batteries on the crest of the glacis, and to blow in the counterscarp, instead of placing them wherever the wall can be seen, leaving the poor officers and troops to get into and cross the ditch as they can." To Major-General George Murray, May 28th 1812.

Chapter Twelve

SALAMANCA SUMMER

Who, then, shall refuse to admire the undaunted firmness, the
unwearied temper and vigilance, the piercing judgment with
which he steered his gallant vessel, with a flowing sail, unhurt
through that howling storm of passion, this tumultuous sea
of folly?

SIR WILLIAM NAPIER

THE price of Badajoz had been 5000 British and Portuguese casualties, 3500 of whom, the flower of the army, fell in the assault. Yet it had been worth the sacrifice. The key fortress of western Spain with nearly 5000 prisoners was in Wellington's hands. So for the first time in the war was the initiative. Possessing Badajoz as well as Ciudad Rodrigo, he could now concentrate against either of the two French armies barring the road to Spain. With the use of interior lines, he could attack Marmont in the north or Soult in the south before either could come to the other's aid. Nor could either, with the Spanish frontier fortresses in their way, effectively invade Portugal in his absence. On Napoleon's orders, Marmont had attempted to do so during the siege of Badajoz, but though his marauding troops, helped by a panic among the Portuguese militia, had penetrated fifty miles, they were quickly forced back starving to their base at Salamanca. Three weeks later, after returning to the north, Wellington sent Hill's corps of observation in Estremadura to seize Almaraz - Soult's last bridge across the Tagus below Toledo. Thus all direct communication between Soult and Marmont was lost, and the two Marshals could henceforward only communicate through Madrid. Simultaneously, as there was not sufficient timber in the neighbourhood to repair Trajan's demolished bridge, Wellington's Engineers improvised a suspension-bridge of ropes and cables - the first of its kind in Europe - across the Tagus gorge at Alcantara, so giving him direct north-to-south communication along the frontier. It was for this he had been campaigning for the past year.

Yet Napoleon could still make Spain secure. He had a quarter of a million troops in the Peninsula to Wellington's 45,000 British and 25,000 Portuguese regulars. He had only to call off his attack on Russia to reinforce these to a point beyond which they could not be challenged by so few. But the flaw in his character which Wellington had always seen gave England her chance. Instead of regarding the loss of Badajoz as a warning, the Emperor greeted the news with one of his famous fits of rage, and then, forbidding all reference to it, behaved as though it had never happened. Turning his back on Wellington, he marched on June 24th into Russia with half a million men.

By that time Wellington was himself across the frontier. As in 1809, the outbreak of war in eastern Europe enabled him to take the offensive. Throughout May he had been preparing magazines for an advance towards the Douro. True to his unchanging strategy of doing nothing to distract Soult from his selfish preoccupation with his Andalusian viceroyalty, and leaving a token force under Hill to watch the Tagus and the road over the Sierra Morena, he concentrated against the northern highway from Ciudad Rodrigo to Salamanca and Valladolid. It was the road Moore had followed when he struck at Napoleon's communications. It offered a greater strategic prize than an advance through Badajoz towards Madrid or Seville, since if he could reach Burgos - two hundred miles to the north-east - Wellington would cut off both these places from south-western France and dominate the whole of Spain except the eastern coast. Between him and his goal lay Marmont's army, which, when assembled, equalled his own. Beyond it, holding down the country, were three other armies almost as large.

Yet, though numerically inferior, Wellington had certain advantages; it was his genius as a commander that, seeing the war whole and steadily, he never lost sight of any of them. One was that, so long as he could keep it supplied, his entire force was free for field operations, while the French were preoccupied in garrisoning a vast, turbulent country. Neither General Caffarelli's Army of the North, nor Marshal Suchet's Army of the East, nor King Joseph's and Marshal Jourdan's Army of the Centre, still less Soult's Army of Andalusia, could reinforce the Army of Portugal without abandoning a large part of Spain to the guerrillas and the Spanish hill armies. Here Wellington's second asset operated: that, thanks to Napoleon's system of ruling by division, no one of his Marshals trusted any other or would willingly send troops from his own domain to help the common cause. His third asset was that the Peninsula was almost surrounded by sea over which his country enjoyed complete mastery. Her ships could succour the Spanish guerrillas at any point and keep the French in continual alarm and uncertainty. Because of this, Caffarelli in Biscaya, Suchet in Catalonia and Soult in Andalusia instinctively faced, not westwards towards Wellington, but north, east and south towards the sea. Even Marmont, on Napoleon's orders, had had to send part of his army to the Asturias, where the Cantabrian guerrillas and the Spanish Army of Galicia were armed and supplied by the Royal Navy.

In planning his summer campaign Wellington made use of these factors. His object was to destroy Marmont while keeping the latter's colleagues busy elsewhere. The Spanish general, Ballasteros, with his raggle-taggle army in the mountains round Seville, supported by Hill's corps of observation in distant Estremadura, was to tie down Soult by threatening as many Andalusian towns as possible. In the east a British expeditionary force of 10,000 men, temporarily released from garrison duty in Sicily by the departure of Murat's Neapolitan army for Russia,* together with 7000 Spanish troops from Alicante and Majorca, were to be landed by the Mediterranean Fleet on the Valencian coast to harry Suchet's communications. And in the north, along the Atlantic cliffs, that erratic champion of amphibious war, Commodore Sir Home Popham, with two battleships, half a dozen frigates, a battalion of marines and a company of marine artillery was to keep the coastline from Gijon to the French frontier in an uproar. So sustained, the guerrillas of the Basque country and Navarre - the most serious of all the thorns in King Joseph's flesh - were to make it impossible for the harassed Caffarelli to reinforce Marmont. At the same time the Spanish army of Galicia was to take the offensive against the latter's northern wing, lay siege to Astorga and prevent even the Army of Portugal from concentrating.

On June 13th Wellington crossed the Agueda with 51,000 men, including 18,000 Portuguese and 3000 Spaniards. Marmont, with one division in the Asturias and the rest of his army dispersed, could offer little immediate resistance. Ordering a concentration,

* By April 1812 such was the concentration of troops for the impending march to Moscow, only one French division remained in Italy. Oman, V, 342.

he fell back across the Tormes. As the British entered Salamanca on the 17th, a surge of ecstatic humanity broke over the red-coated columns in the sun-bathed Plaza Mayor. It was the first Spanish city to be liberated in three years. Even Wellington, as he sat writing orders on his sabretache, was almost unhorsed by a charge of ladies.*

He remained, however, cautious. During the next ten days he blockaded three small forts which Marmont had built outside Salamanca. He made no attempt to bring the French to battle. Instead he covered the siege and awaited their attack in one of those innocent-looking but carefully chosen positions which had so often proved fatal to them. But Marmont, taught by experience, was cautious, too. After several half-hearted attempts at relief, he allowed the forts and their garrisons to fall.

Thereafter he fell back for thirty miles across the rolling Leon plain to the Douro. Here with his army concentrated and almost equal in size to Wellington's, and with ample reserves behind, he had only to hold the crossings from Toro to Tordesillas to bring the British offensive to an end. If he could stay there until the harvest was gathered, the French position in northern Spain would be secure for another year. For a fortnight at the beginning of July, while far away Napoleon's interminable columns drove through Lithuania into Russia, the two armies faced one another across the shallow, sunlit Douro. Then on the 16th, seeing nothing to stop him, Marmont recrossed the river at Tordesillas and feinted at Wellington's right flank. Next day, as the latter parried the stroke, he deftly shifted his forces eastwards and, crossing again at Toro, struck at his left. Like a true son of the Revolution and a Marshal of France, he was in search of glory: to survive he had to outshine his rivals.

To the disgust of his army Wellington promptly retreated. Unlike his adversary, who could live by plundering the country, he was dependent on his commissariat wagons. Rather than risk his communications with Portugal, he fell back towards the hillier and more barren *terrain* whence he had come and where he would have Marmont once more at a disadvantage. For the next six days the two armies, within easy striking distance of one another, marched and manoeuvred under a burning sun, steadily moving southwestwards as Marmont tried to cut off Wellington from his base and Wellington gave ground to prevent him. Both, like skilful fencers,

* Tomkinson, 162. See also Gomm, 272; Kincaid, 150; Oman, V, 360; Simmons, 236.

kept their forces closely concentrated, neither for a moment lowering his guard. On July 18th, when there was some skirmishing, and again on the 20th, the two armies marched within gunshot all day in parallel columns, their accoutrements glittering in the sunlight, while swarms of vultures cruised overhead.*

The French, who were slightly the better marchers, reached the Tormes first, crossing the river at the ford of Huerta, ten miles east of Salamanca, at midday on the 21st. Wellington recrossed the river the same evening about two miles above Salamanca. Marmont was driving straight for his communications, and, though the gloom of the liberated city now surpassed its esctasy of a month earlier, the British commander resolved that night to abandon it and retire on Ciudad Rodrigo. Without a major blunder by his opponent he could not hope for a decisive victory or for one without losses which he could not replace. The two armies were by now almost equal, the French having 50,000 men with a marked superiority in guns to the 48,500 Anglo-Portuguese and 3000 uncertain Spaniards. And thanks to the guerrillas' interception of French dispatches Wellington, unlike Marmont, knew that 15,000 men under King Joseph and Jourdan were hastening to Marmont's aid from Madrid. He had also learnt that the British Commander-in-Chief in Sicily had failed to make a diversion on the Valencian coast and was contemplating instead an expedition to Italy. Faced with the possibility of Suchet also reinforcing Marmont, there seemed nothing for it but to abandon the offensive for another year. He could not afford to be cut off from Portugal or to fight a battle which he was not reasonably sure of winning.

To those whose lives he was so prudently husbanding Wellington's decision to retreat came as a bitter disappointment. Their confidence in their own prowess, the warmth of their welcome from the Spanish people, the hopes of diving deeper into the romantic land before them, had ended in the old way. To add to their humiliation, that night as they lay tentless and hungry in the open fields they were assailed by a fearful thunderstorm. Flashes lit the blackness of the plain, horses broke from their pickets and galloped into the enemy lines, and the earth threw up multitudes of drowning worms. The summer dawn of the 22nd found the British soaked, aching and sullen.

* "I was frequently impressed with the horror of being wounded without the power to keep them off." Tomkinson, 190.

In Marmont's mind Wellington's iron self-restraint had by now established the idea that he was incapable of any but a defensive rôle. It had even eradicated the painful impression of British invincibility forced on the French consciousness by the battles of the past four years. It caused the Marshal to throw all caution to the winds. On the morning of July 22nd he saw his chance - the greatest of his career. Before the elusive British could slip away again to the Portuguese mountains, he would treat them as his master had treated the Austrians and Prussians. By reverting to the *élan* of Revolutionary tradition, he would do to the stiff-necked redcoats what Junot, Victor, Soult, Ney, Masséna, even Napoleon had failed to do.

With this intention the Marshal resumed his westward march on the morning of the 22nd, edging as he had done before round the right flank of the mainly invisible British, while his guns maintained a brisk cannonade against such of their positions as he could see. Presently, mistaking adjustments in Wellington's dispositions for signs of an immediate retreat westwards, he resolved to hasten the pace of his march towards the Salamanca-Rodrigo highway. He therefore ordered his advance-guard - the left flank of the line he presented to the British - to hurry ahead to envelop their right and cut their communications. By so doing he extended his force in the presence of an enemy still concentrated.

The British Commander-in-Chief, guardian of the only army England possessed, had told his Government that he would never risk a general encounter at a disadvantage. But he had never said that he would not seize victory if it was offered him. Between two and three in the afternoon the leading French division, which was marching across his front along a low ridge about a mile away, began to race ahead. Seeing the gap between it and the more slowly moving centre widen, Wellington dropped the chicken leg he was eating and seized a telescope. Then, with a quick, "My God! that'll do," he sent off aides with orders to his divisional commanders, and, outdistancing the rest of his staff, galloped three miles across the stony fields to the village of Aldea Tejada where, about two miles north of the point on which the French advance-guard was moving, he had posted the 3rd Division in reserve. Here he bade his brother-in-law, Edward Pakenham, move forward, take the heights in his front and drive everything before him. Then, before the colours could be encased and the men receive their orders to prime and load, he was on his way back to his position in the British centre. He had three hours of daylight and a chance which might never recur.

Before him the French army was spread out on a series of low rolling hills, moving in column of march in a great semi-circle westwards and on a scattered front of more than five miles. It was a sight not dissimilar to that which confronted Nelson at Trafalgar. The marching columns had their right flanks towards him. Because of the rolling and wooded nature of the country and the skill with which he had placed his own formations out of sight, they seemed unaware of the compact force which they were so hopefully passing and attempting to encircle. Indeed, misled by the westering movement of Wellington's baggage-train on the Salamanca-Rodrigo highway, Marmont was under the impression that the British army had already begun its retreat. Between his leading division, that of Thomières, and those of Maucune, Clausel and Brennier in his centre there was a gap of more than a mile, while another of equal size separated the centre from the four scattered divisions following.

Wellington, as always in an enemy's presence, had his force closely in hand. While his left, consisting of the 1st and Light Divisions and Bock's German cavalry - just over 10,000 men - faced eastwards, the bulk of his army, which in view of the French encircling movement he had earlier in the day wheeled towards the south, was grouped around the little village of Arapiles. Here 14,000 British infantry of the 4th, 5th, 6th and 7th Divisions, most of Cotton's cavalry, nearly 14,000 Portuguese and España's 3000 Spaniards - a force of some 34,000 - were drawn up in line of battle within a mile of the 18,000 marching men of Marmont's centre. Farther to the west another 6000 British and Portuguese under Pakenham, were moving up from Aldea Tejada to strike at the head of Thomières's strung-out advance-guard of 4500 infantry and attendant cavalry. The rest of the French army, more than 24,000 strong, was still coming up from the east.

Marmont, as Wellington had remarked to his Spanish liaison officer, General Alava, was lost. Supported by D'Urban's Portuguese cavalry, the 3rd Division, suddenly emerging from woods on its flank, cut across Thomières's line of march, in Napier's phrase, like a meteor. As it reached the summit of the plateau, it deployed and opened fire. The French were caught strung out on the march, surprised and at a hopeless disadvantage. Thomières was killed, half

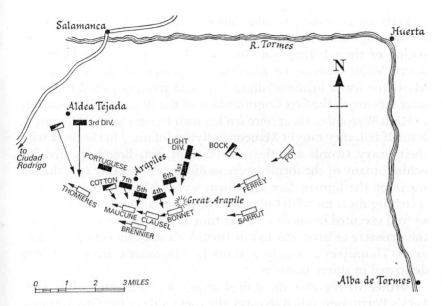

The Battle of Salamanca

his division mown down and all its guns captured. The survivors were driven back into the ranks of those following behind.

Here the British 4th and 5th Divisions, with their flanks covered by Bradford's Portuguese and Cotton's cavalry, had been moving in line across a shallow depression towards the French centre. As soon as Marmont had seen the British coming up over the opposing ridge, he had realised his mistake: Wellington was not a purely defensive general after all. But it was too late to retrieve it; a few minutes later, while galloping forward, he was struck down by a shell. Though his artillery, with 78 guns to the Anglo-Portuguese 60, raked the oncoming scarlet lines, nothing could break that confident advance; it came on like the bore of a tidal river. Behind, in support, followed the 6th and 7th Divisions. For some reason Maucune's men awaited the attack in square, a little in rear of the crest along which they had been moving. They could not have chosen a more disastrous formation. The 5th Division, marching with review precision, breasted the ridge and, at an order from General Leith, fired a tremendous volley. Then, through the smoke and darkness, it charged the shattered French squares with the bayonet.

As the latter broke, a terrible fate overtook them. At that moment on Wellington's orders the first of Cotton's cavalry brigades, consisting of the 5th Dragoon Guards and the 4th and 5th Dragoons under Major-General Le Marchant, appeared on the sky-line. Le Marchant was a brilliant officer who had recently joined the army after serving as the first Commandant of the Royal Military College at High Wycombe. He at once led his men to the charge. Though he himself fell, they caught Maucune's flying infantry in the flank with their heavy swords and then drove right into Brennier's division behind; many of the former were so disfigured by sabre cuts that all traces of the human face and form were obliterated. Wellington, watching the scene with Cotton, declared he had never seen anything so well executed in his life. By the time Leith's infantry had finished the massacre as little was left of Brennier's and Maucune's divisions as of Thomières's. Nearly a third of Marmont's army had been destroyed in thirty minutes.

Farther to the east the Allied attack was less successful. Here Pack's Portuguese failed to carry the rocky side of the Great Arapile knoll which, dominating the battlefield at the point where the original British line turned northwards, had been occupied by Bonnet's division as a pivot for the French enveloping movement. Charged by the defenders when gallantly trying to scramble up its steep side, the Portuguese were thrown back with serious loss. Their repulse exposed the left flank of Cole's 4th Division which, after breasting the ridge, found itself assailed on two sides by Clausel's and Bonnet's men. It, too, was forced back in confusion.

For a moment it seemed to Clausel, who had succeeded to the command, that the battle might be retrieved. While the remnants of the French left were flying into the woods, the right centre, consisting of his own and Bonnet's divisions, with Ferrey's in support, struck boldly at the ridge from which Wellington's attack had been launched. But as they pursued Cole's and Pack's retreating men, they encountered Clinton's 6th Division coming up in an unbroken line, with the 1st and 7th Divisions on either flank. As so often before, the unexpected appearance of Wellington's carefully husbanded and directed reserves was decisive. In twenty minutes Bonnet's and Clausel's men were as badly beaten as their comrades.

It was left to Ferrey's and Sarrut's divisions, forming line across the edge of the forest to the south-east, to cover the escape of the

French army. For half an hour in the failing light they fought with splendid steadiness, inflicting the heaviest British casualties of the day on Clinton's men who were trying to dislodge them* As at Talavera, the dry grass was kindled by the fire of the guns, so that the British, fighting up the slope towards the forest, seemed to be attacking a burning mountain. As darkness fell, the heroes of the French rearguard, almost naked and besmeared with blood and dust, withdrew, still firing, into the woods.

Throughout the day Wellington had personally directed each phase of the action, galloping from division to division and giving his orders in his usual calm, clear and curt staccato. At one moment he was struck by a spent bullet which went through his cloak and holster. "Our chief was everywhere," wrote his brother-in-law, Edward Pakenham, "and sadly exposed himself; in his preservation our little prayers were heard most surely. . . . He surpassed himself in the clearness and energy of his instructions; there never lived such a warrior, you may be assured." William Napier, commanding the 43rd, saw him at the end of the day. "He was alone, the flush of victory was on his brow and his eyes were eager and watchful, but his voice was calm and even gentle. . . . He seemed only to accept this glory as an earnest of greater things to come."

Without the failure of a Spanish officer whom he had placed in the castle of Alba to guard the crossing of the Tormes, scarcely a Frenchman would have got away. Believing the bridge there to be securely held, he assumed that the only escape for the French was to the northeast by Huerta, and sent the unused Light Division and Ponsonby's cavalry to seize the ford there. But with the incorrigible individualism of his race, the commander at Alba had not only abandoned his post, but omitted to inform his British chief that he had done so. And it was across the bridge which he had left open, eight miles south-east of the battlefield, that the demoralised survivors of the French army fled. As a result Wellington was robbed of a victory as complete as Ulm or Jena.†

---

* Two British regiments, the 11th and the 61st, lost 340 out of 516 and 366 out of 546 men. Oman, V, 462.

† "I hope you will be pleased with our battle, of which the dispatch contains as accurate a report as I can give you," he wrote to the Secretary of State for War. "There was no mistake; everything went on as it ought, and there was never an army so beaten in so short a time. If we had had another hour or two of daylight, not a man would have passed the Tormes. And, as it was, they would all have been taken if Don Carlos de España had left

Yet though more than 30,000 of Marmont's men escaped, they did so without cohesion and with no immediate hope of being able to re-form as a fighting force. As Foy, commander of the only undamaged division, confided to his diary, the catastrophe of the Spanish war had come. With the Army of Portugal's rout the balance of Napoleon's dispositions in the Peninsula had been destroyed. So had the legend of French invincibility. Suffering 15,000 casualties to Wellington's 5000, the French left in his hands two eagles, six colours, twenty guns and 7000 prisoners. Their Commander-in-Chief and four divisional commanders were among the casualties. The battle, Foy thought, raised Wellington almost to the level of Marlborough. "Hitherto," he wrote, "we had been aware of his prudence, his eye for choosing a position, and his skill in utilizing it. At Salamanca he has shown himself a great and able master of manoeuvres. He kept his dispositions concealed for almost the whole day; he waited till we were committed to our movements before he developed his own. . . . He fought in the oblique order - it was a battle in the style of Frederick the Great."* Not since the victor of Blenheim supped with two captive Marshals of France in his coach had a British army won such glory.

* * *

Wellington's pursuit was not the spectacular affair which followed Napoleon's victories. He had only 3000 cavalry; his tired men had fought three major engagements in six months, and many of his regiments were gravely depleted. Sweeping gestures and risks were beyond his means. Apart from his German, Portuguese and Spanish auxiliaries, he had still less than 40,000 troops in the Peninsula. Unlike Napoleon he could not look to conscriptions to fill his ranks;

---

the garrison in Alba de Tormes as I wished and desired, or, having taken it away (as I believe before he was aware of my wishes), he had informed me that it was not there." To Earl Bathurst, July 24th 1812.

* Foy, 178, cit. Oman, V, 472. The sources used for the account of the battle are Oman, V, 418-74; Fortescue, VIII, 480-98; Wellington's *Dispatches*; Napier, Book XVIII, Ch. iii; Colonel A. H. Burne's *The Art of War on Land*; Weller, 206-30; Glover, 129-41; Gomm, 272-80; *Dickson Papers*, II, 685-97; Granville, II, 437, 450; Simmons, 241-2; Grattan, 238-60; Greville, I, 75; Vere, 31-7; Tomkinson, 168-89; Lynedoch, 236-7; Leith Hay, II, 46-58; *Peninsular Sketches*, I, 339-56; *Croker Papers*, II, 120, 235; Ellesmere, 108.

he was the servant of a parsimonious Parliament. And there were still four other French armies in Spain.

Except for two regiments of Foy's rearguard, who were annihilated in square by a brilliant charge of German cavalry on the day after the battle, the retreating French received little injury from their pursuers. They moved too fast for them. The British commander was more concerned to feed his advancing columns and to prevent King Joseph's army from Madrid from joining and rallying Clausel's fugitives.

Only when he learnt that Joseph was withdrawing again across the Guadarramas, did Wellington push on to Valladolid where he took another 17 French guns and 800 sick on the 29th. Here he waited a week till he was satisfied that the shattered Army of Portugal, falling back on Burgos, was not being reinforced by Caffarelli's Army of the North. Then, finding that the latter was fully occupied by Popham's coastal operations, he turned his face to the south. On August 5th, a fortnight after Salamanca, leaving Clinton with the 6th Division to watch Clausel, he marched with 36,000 troops towards Segovia and Madrid. His resolution was reached after learning that the British expedition from Sicily had arrived after all on the Mediterranean coast. Reckoning that this would keep Suchet from reinforcing his colleagues, he decided to seize the Spanish capital before Soult's 45,000 troops from Andalusia could come to the rescue of Joseph's outnumbered Army of the Centre. For its liberation would not only hearten the Spaniards, stiffen the Russians in their resistance and suggest to a restless Europe that French power was on the wane, but would give the British the advantage of interior lines in any future operations against Soult. With the whole Tagus valley and both ends of the Madrid-Badajoz highway in his hands, Wellington then could bring up Hill's 21,000 men from Estremadura more quickly than Soult could attack him. He would also gain the main French arsenal in Spain.

In glorious weather the army crossed the Guadarramas and began to move on Madrid. Never had Spain shown such a welcoming face. In every village were bands of music, girls with streamers and laurel crowns to shower kisses on the victors, shouts of " *Viva el gran Capitan*," and " *Viva los Heroes Ingleses los Salvadores*." The rough, battle-worn men responded in character to this romantic Iberian flattery, and for once, though there were many opportunities for

325

drink, drunkenness was almost unknown. At the royal summer-palace of San Ildefonso there was a fête in the gardens under the blue mountains; bands played in the walks, and the waterworks threw up glittering cascades. At twilight, as Wellington, surrounded by generals and grandees, entered the gardens, every band broke into "See the Conquering Hero Comes," and thousands swelled the chorus, while hundreds of ladies saluted and embraced him as their saviour.*

Meanwhile in Madrid Joseph's satellites prepared for flight. All night carriages and carts rolled out of the city on the southern road, laden with household goods and terrified collaborators flying from their countrymen's ferocious patriotism. As there was no news of Soult, who was still ignoring all orders to quit his beloved Andalusia, the King, after probing the strength of Wellington's army, abandoned the capital. To have fought the victor of Salamanca with only 15,000 men would have been madness. Once more summoning the disobedient Duke of Dalmatia to join him, he set out across the high barren hinterland for Valencia.

Next day, August 12th 1812, Wellington entered Madrid, with every bell pealing, palms waving, fountains flowing wine, and women casting shawls before his horse. Everyone was shouting "God save King Ferdinand!" "Glory to the English Nation!" "Long live Wellington!" Ballet-dancers pirouetted before the columns; the ranks were broken by householders with gifts and wine; soldiers were dragged into doorways and feasted. All night the triumph continued, and even next day when the 3rd Division, still followed by an immense and excited multitude, advanced against the Retiro; as the troops moved up to the attack, every roof-top within sight of the fortress resounded with *vivas*. Fortunately the French commander, recognising that his defences were untenable, surrendered after a few shots, leaving the victors possession of nearly 200 cannon, 20,000 stands of arms and 2500 more prisoners. After that the city gave itself up to a round of fêtes, balls and bull-fights, while blissful parties of ill-looking patriots roamed the streets, breaking into houses and dragging off to dungeons and midnight executions anyone who was believed to have held a post under King Joseph.

---

* Those present remembered it as one of the most intoxicating nights of pleasure they had ever known. "When the shrill note of the bugle aroused us from our sleep all that had passed seemed but as a dream." Grattan, 261-4; Granville, II, 454-5; Simmons, 247; Kincaid, 176; Bell, I, 55.

"I am among a people mad with joy for their deliverance from their oppressors," Wellington wrote to John Malcolm in India. "God send that my good fortune may continue and that I may be the instrument for securing their independence and happiness."*

No Spaniard, however, seemed to give a thought to making any preparations for further military operations. That was left to the British and the mountain guerrillas. "What can be done for this lost nation?" the Commander-in-Chief asked his diplomat brother, Henry, now Ambassador to the Spanish Regency. "As for raising men or supplies or taking any one measure to enable them to carry on the war, that is out of the question. Indeed, there is no one to excite them to exertion or to take advantage of the enthusiasm of the people or of their enmity against the French. Even the guerrillas are getting quietly into the large towns and amusing themselves or collecting plunder, . . . and nobody looks forward to the exertions to be made, whether to improve or secure our advantage."†

Wellington did not, therefore, remain in Madrid, though during his brief triumphal but uneasy sojourn there, he found time to sit to the great painter, Francisco Goya, for an equestrian portrait, diplomatically and romantically clad in a blue Spanish cloak. He moved three divisions south to the Tagus to counter any move by Soult, and quartered the remainder of his troops at the Escorial, twenty miles to the north. Then, on the last day of August, learning that Soult was still lingering in Andalusia and that no attack from the south was likely for four or five weeks, he marched north again with half his army to rejoin Clinton at Valladolid, ordering Hill in Estremadura to reinforce Madrid if Soult moved against it. His object was to take the fortress of Burgos, eighty miles beyond Valladolid on the road to France, and so pin the Armies of Portugal and the North beyond the upper Ebro. For if he could barricade them out of central Spain and return to Madrid in October, he might, with Hill's aid and interior lines, be able to fend off Soult and Joseph, especially if the Spanish Army of Murcia and the British expedition from Sicily, which had now landed at Alicante, continued to keep Suchet occupied.

Yet he was under no illusions. With less than 80,000 troops of mixed nationality, half of them operating north of the Guadarramas

---

* *Supplementary Despatches*, VII, 384.
† To the Hon. Sir Henry Wellesley, August 23rd 1812.

and the other half a hundred and fifty miles away on the Tagus, he had to face an attack before the winter by two French armies from the north, and two - possibly three - from the south. For his very success had exposed him to the danger he had hitherto contrived to avoid - a concentric movement of all the French forces in the Peninsula. Beyond that lay a still worse threat: the return of Napoleon and a victorious *Grande Armée* from Russia. The news from the east was ominous: the Emperor, overcoming all resistance, was driving towards Moscow at tremendous speed to compel the Czar's surrender before the winter. "Though I still hope to be able to maintain our position in Castile and even to improve our strength," Wellington wrote to his brother on August 23rd, "I shudder when I reflect upon the enormity of the task which I have undertaken, with inadequate powers myself to do anything and without assistance of any kind from the Spaniards. . . . If by any chance I should be overwhelmed or should be obliged to retire, what will the world say? What will the people of England say?"

On September 16th, having marched another hundred and sixty miles, he appeared before Burgos with four of his eight divisions. Two days earlier Napoleon had entered Moscow after defeating the Russians in a great battle at Borodino. About the same time Soult, who had at last abandoned Seville and his lines before Cadiz, sulkily set out from Granada with 45,000 troops to join King Joseph and Suchet in Valencia. Meanwhile the guerrilleros, intoxicated by their successes, began to congregate in the liberated cities to plunder and murder collaborators. Their pressure on the French, therefore, relaxed.

The attack on Burgos castle did not go as Wellington had intended. Despite the lessons of Ciudad Rodrigo and Badajoz, he had underestimated the strength of the place - possibly deceived by the ease with which he had taken the Salamanca forts earlier in the summer with siege guns far too light to make much impression on the far stronger fortifications of Burgos. The sappers for whom he had repeatedly asked had not yet reached him from England; he had only five engineer officers and eight artificers in all. As before, therefore, he had to use storming parties to do the work of guns and mines. Yet, shaken by the casualties of Badajoz, he did not dare to use them decisively. The Governor of the castle - "a very clever fellow," as Wellington called him - was a master of the techniques of siege warfare and though the assailants gained the outer walls, countered their every attempt against the inner ring wall and the keep. And the weather, instead of being dry and sunny as might have been expected in a Spanish October, was cold and abysmally wet. Shivering and exposed in the trenches, the troops found their setback hard to bear after the triumphs of the past nine months.

So did their commander. Fortune, which at one time had been so grudging and fickle, had showered gifts on him that year. After the capture of Ciudad Rodrigo, he had received an earldom, and his Talavera pension of £2,000 p.a. had been doubled; after Salamanca, Parliament had voted him £100,000 for the purchase of an estate, and the Prince Regent had made him a marquess. As a landless younger son he had been grateful for the money, for his allowance as Commander-in-Chief of ten pounds a day - reduced by income tax to eight guineas - barely covered his entertaining and other expenses. For titular dignities he cared less—"what," he asked, "is the use of making me a marquess!" Ready cash to pay his troops would have been far more acceptable. "The difficulties under which we labour here are but little known in England," he wrote to Colonel Torrens, the Military Secretary at the Horse Guards. "There is no soldier in the army who has at present been paid to a later date than April 24th for want of money. . . . If a soldier has been in hospital since the month of March last, at which time the soldiers had not been paid later than January and the pay for March not received till June or July, I should like to know how it is possible for any officer to come to a settlement by a correspondence with one officer who has to settle the accounts of probably 500 men going to England at the same moment? It is quite impossible, and the consequence is that the poor men are detained here three, four or five months . . . till the correspondence respecting their accounts is finished, during which time many settle all accounts with the world. . . . There is no point in the Service to which I have at all times paid so much attention as the settlement of the soldiers' accounts. I account early settlements to be essential to discipline."*

Under the strain of the siege Wellington's usually equable temper grew a little sharp. It was a time when, as his senior medical officer, Dr James McGrigor wrote, everything was going wrong for him and when, at his morning reception of the heads of his departments,

* To Lieut-Colonel Henry Torrens, September 13th 1812.

they and, in particular, his chief engineer, had little but unfavourable reports to give. On October 8th, in an attack on an outpost he suffered what was for him, as well as for the army, a terrible loss in the death of a brilliant young Intelligence officer, Major Somers Cocks, a son of Earl Somers and a dedicated soldier of outstanding qualities, of whose future he had formed the highest hopes. Colonel Frederick Ponsonby recalled how the Commander-in-Chief entered his room on that fatal day and, after walking up and down in silence, uttered the words, "Cocks is dead!" and left as abruptly as he came; he remembered, too, the despair on his face at the funeral.* Wellington did not wear his heart on his sleeve like Nelson; but those who knew him best sometimes caught a glimpse of it and realised its intensity.

After losing two thousand men in five minor assaults he was forced on October 21st - Trafalgar Day - to abandon the siege. By that date not only were the French armies of Portugal and the North - half again as strong as his own - marching to the fortress's relief, but Soult and Joseph with 60,000 men were threatening Madrid from Valencia. The British seemed in danger of being crushed between the upper and nether mill-stones.

In victory Wellington had displayed some of the weaknesses of his country. He had been a little too easy-going and sanguine, and had shown signs, most unusual in him, of preferring to hope for, rather than to ensure, success. But when the storm broke he acted with wonderful resolution and presence of mind. Years later, when asked what was the test of a great general, he replied, "To know when to retreat and to dare to do it." Withdrawing both the besiegers and his covering army in a deep silence in the night, he gained a day on the relieving army before the French were aware that he had gone. Yet, with 6000 cavalry to his own 1300 dragoons, they were able to press him very hard. The weather, too, remained persistently adverse, making muddy rivers of the primitive Castilian roads. His men were weakened by sickness and sulky at having to withdraw; in the little wine town of Torquemada 12,000 of them broke into the wine vaults with the usual disgraceful results. None the less, he brought them back with few casualties to the Douro in five days.

* "The painful expression of his face was so marked that no one . . . presumed to approach him. After a considerable time passed in silence, he said: 'D'Urban, had Cocks outlived the campaigns, which from the way he exposed himself was morally impossible, he would have become one of the first generals of England.' " Tomkinson, 217.

Here he intended to stand, facing northwards across the river, while Hill, a hundred miles to the south on the other side of the Guadarramas, faced southwards across the Tagus to keep Joseph and Soult from Madrid. With 55,000 Anglo-Portuguese and 25,000 Spaniards operating on interior lines, there seemed at least a hope of being able to hold the summer's gains and prevent the 50,000 men of the French armies of Portugal and the North from uniting with the 60,000 of the armies of the South and Centre.

But that autumn Wellington's star was not in the ascendant. He failed to hold the Douro because, during the evening of October 29th, a party of French volunteers with splendid daring swam across what was thought to be an impassable reach near the shattered bridge at Tordesillas and surprised and routed a regiment of German infantry, thus enabling Foy's sappers to get a pontoon bridge across the flooded stream. And Hill was unable to hold the Tagus because the autumnal rains which had set in with such violence north of the Guadarramas had still to fall in New Castile. Not only did the rivers south of Madrid fail as a result to bar Soult's and Joseph's advance, but General Ballasteros, the erratic commander of Spain's southern army, omitted, in a fit of sulks, to make his promised move against the French flank in La Mancha. Both halves of the British army were thus forced into the open, and both, being outnumbered - particularly in cavalry - were left with no alternative but retreat.

Ordering Hill to blow up the Retiro and cross the Guadarramas to join him, Wellington prepared to fall back on Salamanca. On the last day of October the British marched out of Madrid, watched by reproachful multitudes. Then, knowing there was an end to peace and pleasure so long as a Frenchman remained in Spain, the men, bronzed and strapped under their packs, swung out in the familiar columns towards the snow-capped mountains. " A splendid sight it was," wrote eighteen-year-old Ensign Bell of the 34th Foot,* " to see so grand an army winding its way zig-zag up that long pass so far as the eye could see. The old trade was going on, killing and slaying and capturing our daily bread." On either side of the track lay dead beasts and murdered peasants, slain no one knew how or by whom. And all the while the skilful Wellington, with an inferior force, parried every move of his opponents of the armies of Portugal and the North, as he gained time for his southern lieutenant to reach safety. " I

* Afterwards General Sir George Bell, KCB.

fairly *bullied* the French into remaining quiet upon the Douro for seven days," he wrote, "in order to give him time to make his march. . . . I have got clear, in a handsome manner, of the worst scrape I was ever in."

As soon as Hill was through the Guadarramas, Wellington resumed his retreat, their roads converging. By November 9th 30,000 British and Germans, 20,000 Portuguese and 25,000 Spaniards were concentrated on the Tormes in front of Salamanca, while 50,000 Frenchmen under Souham moved cautiously against them from the north-east and 60,000 under Soult from the south-east. With perfect judgment Wellington had brought the two halves of his army back two hundred miles in the face of a superior enemy without losing a gun and hardly a prisoner. It would have been possible for him at that moment to throw his united force against either of his still divided adversaries. There was not a man in the British ranks who did not hope and believe he would. But without counting the Spaniards who were still almost impossible to manoeuvre, Wellington had not sufficient men to win a decisive victory over either French army – to one of which, without the Spaniards, he was inferior, and to the other about equal. And in the event of victory over one adversary, he would still, with depleted ranks, have had to encounter the other; while, had he failed, he must have been crushed between their approaching pincers. True, therefore, to his unchanging Peninsular principle, he avoided needless risks and, allowing the French to join armies—that grand concentration which he had so long and successfully avoided—awaited their attack in one of his usual well-chosen positions. As they were a third again as strong as his own force, he had every reason to expect one.

But the French, remembering Salamanca, were taking no risks either. Pursuing the same strategy as Marmont, Soult crossed the Tormes on the 14th and began to work his way southwards and westwards round Wellington's southern flank, while Souham's Army of Portugal faced him from the east. But, unlike Marmont, who had tried to envelop Wellington by cutting straight across his front, Soult took so broad and cautious a sweep that his adversary was never in any danger of being encircled at all. And as it was clear that the French were not going to attack him on his own ground but were merely hoping, without an encounter, to cut his communications with Portugal, the British commander resolved to fall back to his base at Ciudad Rodrigo. It meant abandoning Salamanca, but there was nothing now to be gained by remaining there for the winter.

On the afternoon of November 15th, therefore, he gave the order to retreat, so bringing the campaign of 1812 to an end. Though he had been forced to relinquish his gains in Castile and Leon, it had proved more profitable than any he had yet undertaken. Twenty thousand French prisoners had been sent to England and 3000 guns had been taken or destroyed, the fortresses of Ciudad Rodrigo, Badajoz, Almaraz and Alcantara were in his hands, and Santander and the Asturian coast ports had been won by Popham and the guerrillas as a sea base for future operations. A British force from Sicily was established at Alicante in the east, and Estremadura and the whole of the south had been liberated. Indeed, the very concentration of French armies which had driven Wellington from Madrid and Valladolid had given to the Spanish guerrillas and patriot armies the control of vast new areas. With the Cortes installed at Seville instead of being penned in Cadiz, Joseph's pretence of being King of Spain was almost at an end. His very capital, though he did not know it, had been reoccupied as soon as his troops left by the guerrilla chief, El Empecinado.

Still, it was humiliating for the British to have to retrace their steps and withdraw from the scene of their triumphs to the bleak hills of the Portuguese frontier. On the day their retreat began, the equinoctial gales set in with an intensity of cold and rain unprecedented at that season. Within a few hours every stream and watercourse was a torrent and the roads rivers of icy mud which, rising to men's ankles and sometimes to their knees, sucked the boots off their feet. For four days, until the Agueda could be reached, there was no prospect of any bivouac but the drenched ground. That night it became known that there was small hope of food either.

For through an administrative blunder the rations had gone astray - a misfortune common enough in the French army, which in any case lived off the country, but so rare in an army commanded by Wellington as to seem to his hungry troops like some monstrous reversal of nature. In pursuit of time-honoured formulas of transfer and promotion the Horse Guards, with an Olympian disregard of his wishes, had posted an inexperienced nominee of its own in place of his highly experienced and efficient Quartermaster-General,

George Murray, while the latter was on leave in Ireland. This officer, Colonel Willoughby Gordon, on receiving orders to retire to Ciudad Rodrigo, sent off the supply-train by a route twenty miles to the north of the army's line of retreat on the assumption that the road farthest from the enemy was the safest. By forgetting that his first business was, not to preserve his stores, but to feed his troops, he inflicted greater suffering and loss on them than the concentration of four French armies. Had it not been for the excessive caution of Soult's pursuit – a legacy of Corunna and Albuera – they might have had to fight without the strength to do so.

For four dreadful days, as they fell angrily back, the men were without rations. Not knowing why, they assumed that some terrible military disaster had occurred and that the French, in some unaccountable way, had outmanoeuvred them and won a bloodless victory. For the veterans the retreat revived memories of the race to Corunna. No coat could keep out the wet and icy wind from hungry bodies; soaked, footsore, their old wounds aching and their teeth chattering with ague, weighed down with heavy packs and arms, the frostbitten men trudged across that bitter upland without comfort or hope. At night they bivouacked in drenching woods and fed on acorns or raw carrion cut from dead bullocks and on such unmilled wheat as the harassed commissariat officers could find. Kincaid confessed he was so sharply set he could have eaten his boots.*

On the second night an encounter with a herd of swine in a forest provided an unexpected dinner for several thousands. But the greater part of the army remained without rations for four days. As a result more than three thousand men fell by the way out of sheer exhaustion and were gathered up by the French.

Though in many of the regiments, especially those fresh from England, discipline temporarily failed, in others the flame of courage shone only the more brightly. For those covering the retreat it was kept so as well by Wellington's presence. "Our illustrious chief," Costello of the Rifles recalled, "was generally to be found where danger was most apparent. Seeing us come, puffing and blowing up to our column, he called out to us in a cheering voice, 'Be cool, my lads, don't be in a hurry!'" Famished, with bleeding feet, racked with

* Bell, I, 66-7, 73-4; Kincaid, 186-7, 192. See also Gomm, 290; Grattan, 291-4, 304-6; Larpent, I, 20, 29, 42; Bessborough, 231; Kincaid, 187-8, 194; Simmons, 255-6, 265; Costello, 142; Oman, VI, 143-8, 159. *Peninsular Sketches*, II, 20-7; Long, 233-6.

ague and dysentry, men still had the heart to make light of their
lot. Courage, pride and comradeship kept the best of the army together. In the rearguard, formed by the Light Division, the rough
veterans of the 95th offered their precious biscuits to the 18-year-old
son of Lord Spencer as he sat pale and shivering over the acorns he
had gathered: in such times, wrote Costello, lords found they were
men and men that they were comrades.*

In those four disastrous days, the loss of men fallen by the way or
captured by the enemy proved half again as great as the casualties
sustained before Burgos. To Wellington it seemed the culminating
penalty for what he regarded as the worst of all military crimes - disobedience and neglect of orders. It had occurred at all levels—from
the drunkenness which had disgraced the army† in its retreat
through the wine-towns of Old Castile and the more recent
massacre of grazing herds of swine in the beechwoods, to the deliberate disregard of their marching instructions by three of his
generals who, while he slept, had held what he called a "council of
war" and directed their troops by a shorter and supposedly easier
route which he had expressly forbidden them. The result had been
that they had been brought to a full-stop, as he had foreseen, by a
river in flood and beside which he subsequently found them. "If the
French had known our circumstances," he told Croker, recalling the
incident, "they might have caught these two divisions in this trap
and the whole army would have been in consequence irretrievably
lost."‡ "What did he say?" someone asked Lord Fitzroy Somerset,
Wellington's Military Secretary, who was with him when he came
upon his disobedient generals. "O, by God, it was far too serious to
say anything," was the reply.§

How necessary it was for Wellington to enforce discipline in his
army, at all levels, can be seen from the journal kept by the new

---

* Costello, 142-3; Grattan, 293.

† Private Wheeler of the 51st, who was in the retreat, wrote of it, "It is impossible for
any army to have given themselves up to more dissipation and everything that is bad as
did our army. The conduct of some men would have disgraced savages; drunkenness had
prevailed to such a frightful extent that I have often wondered how it was that a great part
of our army was not cut off. It was no unfrequent thing to see a long string of mules
carrying drunken soldiers to prevent them falling into the hands of the enemy." Wheeler,
105-6.

‡ *Croker Papers*, II, 308-9.

§ "You see, gentlemen," was the indignant Commander-in-Chief's comment when he
finally spoke, "I know my own business best." Longford, 297-8; Weller, 244.

Judge-Advocate-General, Francis Larpent, who came out from England that autumn to help the harassed Commander-in-Chief manage his courts-martial. There were something like a hundred of these pending, some of them of more than two years' standing. One was against a lieutenant-colonel with six charges and thirty-seven witnesses, another against a commissary for deliberately burning down a house in a drunken frolic, another of a man for shooting and killing a Spanish girl because she would not give him some chestnuts, another of an Irishman charged with robbery who, while awaiting trial, declared that, since he did not know whether he was to be hanged or flogged this time, if the latter he would take good care next time there should be no witness to tell what he did. "There never were known so many courts-martial . . . as at this moment," wrote Larpent, "I really scarce know where to turn. . . . I suppose people think I have some weight in Lord Wellington's decision, but that is by no means the case. He thinks and acts quite for himself; *with* me if he thinks I am right, but not otherwise. . . . He is reasonable enough, only often a little hasty in ordering trials when an acquittal must be the consequence." On one occasion Wellington complained to Larpent that his whole table was covered with details of robbery and mutiny, and with complaints from all quarters, in all languages, and that he was nothing but a general of courts-martial. He spoke bitterly about the difficulty of procuring convictions and the lenity of the Courts; "how can you expect," he asked, "a Court to find an officer guilty of neglect of duty when it is composed of members who are all more or less guilty of the same?"*

After the disorderly retreat to the Portuguese frontier, holding, as he did, that there was only one way to command a British army, which was "to have a hand of iron," the disgusted Commander-in-Chief issued on November 28th a memorandum to all general officers, heads of Staff departments and colonels commanding brigades.

> "I must draw your attention in a very particular manner to the state of discipline of the troops. . . . I am concerned to have to observe that the army under my command has fallen off in this respect in the late campaign to a greater degree than any army with which I have ever served, or of which I have ever read. Yet this army has met with no disaster; it has suffered no privations

* Larpent, I, 36, 52-3, 73, 84, 87, 91-3, 94, 100-1, 110, 123, 143-4.

which but trifling attention on the part of the officers could not have prevented, and for which there existed no reason whatever in the nature of the service. Nor has it suffered any hardships excepting those resulting from the necessity of being exposed to the inclemencies of the weather at a moment when they were most severe.

"It must be obvious, however, to every officer, that from the moment the troops commenced their retreat from the neighbourhood of Burgos on the one hand, and from Madrid on the other, the officers lost all command over their men. Irregularities and outrages of all descriptions were committed with impunity, and losses have been sustained which ought never to have occurred. Yet the necessity for retreat existing, none was ever made in which the troops made such short marches; none on which they made such long and repeated halts; and none on which the retreating armies were so little pressed on their rear by the enemy....

"I have no hesitation in attributing these evils to the habitual inattention of the officers of the regiments to their duty, as prescribed by the standing regulations of the Service, and by the orders of this army.

"I am far from questioning the zeal, still less the gallantry and spirit, of the officers of the army.... Unfortunately, inexperience ... has induced many to consider that the period during which an army is on service is one of relaxation from all rule, instead of being, as it is, the period during which of all others every rule for the regulation and control of the conduct of the soldier, for the inspection and care of his arms, ammunition, accoutrements, necessaries, and field equipments, and his horse and horse appointments; for the receipt, issue and care of his provisions; and the regulation of all that belongs to his food and the forage for his horse, must be most strictly attended to by the officers of his company or troop....

"These are the points then to which I most earnestly intreat you to turn your attention, and the attention of the officers of the regiments under your command.... The Commanding Officers of regiments must enforce the orders of the army regarding the constant inspection and superintendence of the officers over the conduct of the men of their companies in their cantonments; and they must endeavour to inspire the non-commissioned officers with a sense of their situation and authority, and the non-commissioned officers must be forced to do their duty by being constantly under the view and superintendence of the officers. By this means the frequent and discreditable resource to the authority of the provost, and to punishments by the sentence of courts martial, will be prevented, and the soldiers will not dare to commit the offences and outrages of which there are too many complaints, when they well know that their officers and their non-commissioned officers have their eyes and attention turned towards them.

"The Commanding Officers of regiments must likewise enforce the orders of the army regarding the constant, real inspection of the soldiers' arms, ammunition, accoutrements, and necessaries, in order to prevent at all times the shameful waste of ammunition, and the sale of that article and of the soldiers' necessaries. With this view both should be inspected daily.

"In regard to the food of the soldier, I have frequently observed and lamented in the late campaign, the facility and celerity with which the French soldiers cooked in comparison with those of our army. The cause of this disadvantage is the same with that of every other description, the want of attention of the officers to the orders of the army, and the conduct of their men, and the consequent want of authority over their conduct. Certain men of each company should be appointed to cut and bring in wood, others to fetch water, and others to get the meat, etc to be cooked. . . . If this practice were daily enforced, and a particular hour for seeing the dinners and for the men dining named, as it ought to be, equally as for parade, . . . cooking would no longer require the inconvenient length of time which it has lately been found to take, and . . . soldiers would not be exposed to the privation of their food at the moment at which the army may be engaged in operations with the enemy. . . .

"I repeat, that the great object of the attention of the General and Field Officers must be to get the captains and subalterns of the regiments to understand and perform the duties required from them, as the only mode by which the discipline and efficiency of the army can be restored and maintained during the next campaign."[*]

[*] *Dispatches*, IX, 574-77.

Unfortunately this confidential document, addressed to senior officers, became public and even appeared in English newspapers. Its sweeping and indiscriminate condemnation of the entire army caused deep resentment; it was even whispered that the strain of the past few weeks had been too much for the Commander-in-Chief's mind. "The officers asked each other," one of them wrote, "how or in what manner they were to blame for the privations the army had endured. Their business was to keep their men together and, if possible, to keep up with their men on the march. Many were mere lads, badly clothed and without a boot to their feet, some attacked with dysentery, others with ague, others with a burning fever running through their systems. They had scarcely strength to hobble on in company with their more hardy comrades, the soldiers. Nothing but a high sense of honour could have sustained them."*

* * *

When the news of the retreat and its sufferings reached England it seemed like a defeat. Those four days of famine and cold had temporarily reduced a victorious army to an assemblage of famished tramps. Though food in plenty was waiting on the Agueda, it was long before the hospitals could restore to the ranks the thousands laid low by typhus, enteric and ague. Until the end of January the death-rate averaged five hundred a week, and a third of the army was on the sick list.

Yet Wellington had not been alone in November 1812 in having to retreat across a desert. After waiting five weeks in a burnt-out Moscow for a Russian surrender which never came, Napoleon had set out on October 18th for Kaluga and the warmer lands of the Ukraine with 115,000 fighting troops, 20,000 sick in wagons and 40,000 camp followers. But the Russian army under Kutusof, heartened by the news of Wellington's liberation of Madrid, had barred his way at Malo-Jaroslavitz, and, after a bitter fight, had forced him back on the more northerly route by which he had come. Here the countryside had been completely stripped by his advance—one of the most destructive even in the annals of Revolutionary war—and partisans from the forests were already harrying the long lines of communica-

* Grattan, 307, 311-12; Simmons, 265; Bell, I, 73-4, 77; Costello, 144; Fortescue, IX, 100; Larpent, I, 6, 19, 54, 74, 127; Oman, VI, 181; Weller, 243; Sherer, 305-7; Long, 237-8.

tion. Apart from what it carried, there was nothing for the *Grande Armée* to eat until it reached its advance magazines at Smolensk, two hundred miles to the west.

As the starving host retraced its steps through charred villages, the immensity and savage gloom of the Russian landscape struck a chill in every heart. The germs of typhus were already in men's veins; near the battlefields of Borodino, where thousands of corpses lay unburied, gangrenous cripples from the hospitals, fearful of Russian vengeance, fought for places on the plunder-laden wagons. Vast numbers, unable to obtain food, fell by the wayside; hundreds of baggage-carts and ammunition wagons were left abandoned with the horses dead in the shafts.

On November 5th, when they were still a few days short of Smolensk, the first cold set in. Prisoners had warned the French that when it came their nails would drop from their fingers and the muskets from their hands. A deadening and penetrating fog rose from the ground; then out of the darkness the snow began to fall. As it did so a terrible wind swept out of the north, howling through the forests and piling the snow in the path of the blinded invaders. Famished and exhausted, the vast predatory army lost hope and cohesion, began to disintegrate and dissolve.

When at the beginning of December Napoleon abandoned the remnants of his broken army, he blamed everyone and everything but himself for his Moscow débâcle. Wellington blamed only himself for his setback at Burgos. "I see that a disposition exists to blame the Government for the failure of the siege," he wrote to the Prime Minister on November 23rd; "it was entirely my own act." If he expected unquestioning obedience from his army and stood no nonsense when it was lacking, he took full responsibility for whatever it did or failed to do. And if he scarified his military subordinates for their faults, he pointed out to his political superiors, with equal force and clarity, the defects in their system which had caused those faults. "In respect to recruiting the Army," he wrote to Colonel Torrens at the Horse Guards, "my own opinion is that the Government have never taken an enlarged view upon the subject. It is expected that people will become soldiers in the Line and leave their families to starve, when, if they become soldiers in the Militia, their families are provided for. . . . What is the consequence? That none but the worst description of men enter the regular Service. The omission to provide for the families of soldiers operates particularly upon recruiting in Ireland. It is the custom for the lower orders to marry when very young and it will be found that in the Irish Militia nearly every soldier is married. But when they volunteer from the Militia to the Line they lose the provision for their families; the women, therefore, always object to the volunteering, and none but the worst members of society ever offer their service. This is one of the causes of the increase of desertion in the army on foreign service, and of the frequency and enormity of the crimes committed by soldiers."*

Nor was it only with deficiencies of the rank and file that Wellington had to make do. "I have received your letter," he wrote on another occasion to Colonel Torrens, – "announcing the appointment of Sir William Erskine, General Lumley and General Hay to this army. The first I have generally understood to be a madman; I believe it is your own opinion that the second is not very wise; the third will, I believe, be a useful man. . . . Colonel Sanders, . . . who was sent away from Sicily for incapacity and whom I was very glad to get rid of from hence last year, has lately come out again. I have been obliged to appoint him a Colonel on the Staff because he is senior to others and I wished . . . to prevent him from destroying a good regiment. . . . Then there is General Lightburne, whose conduct is really scandalous. . . . When I reflect upon the characters and attainments of some of the General Officers of this army and consider that these are the persons on whom I am to rely to lead columns against the French generals and who are to carry my instructions into execution, I tremble; and, as Lord Chesterfield said of the generals of his day, 'I only hope that when the enemy reads the list of their names he trembles as I do! Sir William Erskine and General Hay will be a very nice addition to this list! However, I pray God and the Horse Guards to deliver me from General Lightburne and Colonel Sanders."†

According to the administrative practices of the time, the senior

---

* To Lieut-Colonel Henry Torrens, January 28th 1811. "The country has not a choice between Army and no arms, between peace or war. They must have a large and efficient Army, one capable of meeting the enemy abroad, or they must expect to meet him at home; and then farewell to all considerations of . . . greater or lesser expense, and to the ease, the luxury and happiness of England. God forbid that I should see the day on which hostile armies should contend within the United Kingdom."

† To Lieut.-Colonel Henry Torrens, August 29th 1810.

members of Wellington's Headquarters Staff, were also chosen for him in England—his Adjutant-General and Quartermaster-General, through whom he issued his orders, by the Horse Guards; the Commissary-General, who provided and paid for transport, food and forage, by the Treasury; the Officer Commanding the Royal Artillery and the Commanding Royal Engineer by the Board of Ordnance in the Tower of London, which was a separate Department of State and maintained by a separate vote of Parliament; and the Inspector General of Hospitals by the Medical Board. It was, like so many things British, an illogical, not to say absurd, system. But, though the most logical-minded of men, with his still stronger common sense Wellington, instead of vainly attempting to change things, made the best of them by moulding his departmental assistants, like his generals, to his own will. Remote functionaries in England, acting by rule of thumb, might appoint them, but the Commander-in-Chief, relying on his mandate to command, saw to it that, in all matters vital to the success of his campaigns, they obeyed him implicitly. "I assembled my officers and laid down my plan," he said, "and it was carried into effect without any more words."*

Provided they did this he left them to manage the detailed administration of their departments in their own way, for he believed in delegating authority provided there was no question as to where ultimate authority lay. If any dared question that, they quickly found out their error. On one occasion he reduced his Adjutant-General, Brigadier-General Stewart—son of the Marquis of Londonderry and brother of the Secretary of State, Lord Castlereagh—to tears because that proud and petulant aristocrat claimed, by virtue of his office, an exclusive right to interrogate prisoners and, because one of the Commander-in-Chief's ADCs had done so, refused to perform his duty of feeding and looking after them. "This was too much," Wellington said, "so I sent for him into my room. We had a long wrangle, for I like to convince people rather than stand on mere authority. But I found him full of the pretensions of this Department of his, although he and it and all of them were under my orders and at my disposal. ... At last I was obliged to say that if he did not at once confess his error and promise to obey my orders frankly and cordially I would dismiss him *instanter* and send him to England in arrest. After a great deal of persuasion he burst out crying

* Maxwell, II, 194.

and begged my pardon and hoped I would excuse his intemperance."*

On another occasion—it had happened in Madrid while Goya was painting his portrait—the new Inspector-General of Hospitals, James McGrigor, reported to him that he had dispatched the wounded and their supplies to the base hospitals in Portugal by a more expeditious route than that which he had ordered. "I shall be glad to know," Wellington thundered at him, "who is to command this army, I or you? I establish one route, one line of communication for the army; you establish another and order the commissariat and the supplies by that line. As long as you live, Sir, never do so again; never do anything without my orders." Yet the rebuke ended with an invitation to McGrigor - an admirable man whom Wellington increasingly respected and trusted - to dine with him that night, when he placed him next to himself and treated him, as the doctor gratefully recalled, with "unusual civility and marked attention."†

For, when what one who loved him called "his devil" was not aroused, Wellington could be most human and, in his dry way, surprisingly kind. When during the retreat of the army that autumn a young soldier of the king's German Legion deserted for love because his officer had ordered away a Spanish girl who had been most honest and faithful to him in very trying scenes, the Commander-in-Chief, after finding from the evidence that the lad had no intention of going over to the French, pardoned him for the good character of his regiment. And when the furious wife of a Portuguese nobleman, whose daughter had been run away with by an English officer, arrived at army headquarters at Frenada, Wellington, after first saying he would hand the offending lover over to the laws of Portugal, refused, after the latter had married the girl, to interfere at all.‡ "It is impossible not to feel for the unhappiness of the young lady which you have so well described," he replied on another occasion to an influential correspondent's request for the release on

* *Croker Papers*, I, 346. See also Ward, 35-46.

† McGrigor, 302. In 1814, when he was demobilising the army, Wellington turned to McGrigor and said, "Mac, we are now winding up all arrears with the Government; I have asked them how you are to be disposed of, and I am told you are to be placed on half-pay, but I consider your peculiar circumstances will entitle you to a specific retirement." He was as good as his word and secured him a knighthood and a retirement pension of £3 a day. McGrigor, 357-8.

‡ Larpent, I, 70, 83, 126.

compassionate grounds of one of his officers at a critical moment when he was facing the joint armies of Soult and Marmont, "but it is not so easy as you imagine to apply the remedy. It appears to me that I should be guilty of a breach of discretion if I were to send for the fortunate object of this young lady's affections, and to apprise him of the pressing necessity for his early return to England. The application for permission to go ought to come from himself; and at all events, the offer ought not to be made by me, and particularly not founded on the secret of this interesting young lady. But this fortunate major now commands his battalion, and I am very apprehensive that he could not with propriety quit it at present, even though the life of this female should depend upon it; and, therefore, I think that he will not ask for leave.

"We read, occasionally, of desperate cases of this description, but I cannot say that I have ever yet known of a young lady dying of love. They contrive, in some manner, to live and look tolerably well, notwithstanding their despair and the continued absence of their lover; and some even have been known to recover so far as to be inclined to take another lover, if the absence of the first has lasted too long. I don't suppose that your protégée can ever recover so far, but I do hope that she will survive the continued necessary absence of the major, and enjoy with him hereafter many happy days."*

Confronted by real suffering and sorrow this seemingly bleak Commander-in-Chief could show a surprising delicacy and tenderness. "I am sorry to tell you," he wrote to Lady Sarah Napier after the storming of Ciudad Rodrigo, "that your son George was again wounded in the right arm so badly last night . . . that it was necessary to amputate it above the elbow. He, however, bore the operation remarkably well; and I have seen him this morning, quite well, free from pain and fever and enjoying highly his success before he had received his wound. When he did receive it, he only desired that I might be informed that he had led his men to the top of the breach before he had fallen. Having *such* sons, I am aware that you expect to hear of those misfortunes which I have more than once had to communicate to you."† Shortly after Wellington wrote this letter, his senior ADC, Colonel Alexander Gordon, told a friend in England how, at dinner one night, a guest mentioned that he had just returned

---

* To ――――, June 27th 1811. Brett-James, 217-18.
† To Lady Sarah Napier, January 21st 1812.

from a place where a number of sick and wounded soldiers had been lying without shelter, exposed to the weather. Immediately dinner was over, Wellington ordered his horse, and, taking Gordon with him, set off for the post in question, some thirty miles away, arriving there at midnight. Finding a great number of sick lying in the open, he immediately knocked up the commanding officer who replied that there was no accommodation for them in the place. "Be so good," the Commander-in-Chief said, "as to show me this house," and, after inspecting it, he ordered Gordon to move 150 of the sick into it. He then went to the next officer in rank and so on until he had accommodated the whole of the sick. After warning the offending officers that he would make an example of anyone who presumed to consult his own convenience or luxury when a single sick man remained unsheltered, he returned to his headquarters before dawn without anyone realising he had been away. Next evening he told Gordon that he suspected, from the sulky manner in which his orders had been received, that they were not being obeyed. Accordingly the two again set out on another sixty mile ride through the night. When they arrived they found the sick were back in the open air, and the officers comfortably reposing in their old quarters. They were at once placed under arrest for disobedience and ordered to be cashiered.*

It was through such personal contacts, and through the eyes of his young ADCs—all mounted, like himself, on the finest thoroughbreds of matchless speed and stamina—that Wellington kept in touch with his troops. Like Field-Marshal Montgomery in a later war, he exercised an elastic control of both campaign and battlefield by using, as antennae, members of his personal staff, appointed by himself and chosen almost exclusively from the cadets of the great aristocratic families with whom, as an aristocrat himself, he felt most at home. Most of them were still in their teens, and even his senior ADC, Colonel Alexander Gordon - a brother of the Earl of Aberdeen - was only 26, while his Military Secretary, Lord Fitzroy Somerset† was under 23 when in 1809 he succeeded to this most confidential of all posts. In the company of these gay and spirited lads, whose mentor and hero he was and between him and whom there was complete

---

* Bland Burgess, 324-5.
† A younger son of the Duke of Beaufort and destined, as Lord Raglan, to command the British army in the Crimea.

confidence and trust, he felt free, not only to express himself frankly and forcibly—a valuable safety-valve for a sternly repressed and lonely man bearing an almost intolerable load of responsibility—but to relax and be gay. His "champions" he laughingly called them; and their loyalty and devotion were absolute. "How would society get on without all my boys?" he remarked to Lady Shelley, as they together watched them dancing at a ball at Carlton House when the war was over and he and they were about to be parted and to return to civilian life. Asked by her how he would manage without them, he replied, "Oh yes, I shall, but I must always have my house full. For sixteen years I have been at the head of an army, and I must have these gay fellows round me."*

But if Wellington's personal, as distinct from his administrative, staff was drawn from the *haute monde* to which he himself, though at a remove, belonged, nothing could have been more unostentatious than the appearance either of himself, his entourage or his headquarters. "Is that Lord Wellington," exclaimed a Spaniard accustomed to the glittering cavalcade which accompanied the generals of the French and Spanish armies, "sitting so meekly there in a grey coat with only one officer at his side?"† "Everything was strikingly quiet and unostentatious," reported the German commissary, Schaumann, of his village headquarters on the Portuguese frontier, "No one could have suspected that he was quartered in the town. There was no throng of scented staff officers with plumed hats, orders and stars, no main guards, no crowd of contractors, actors, valets, cooks, mistresses, equipages, horses, dogs, forage and baggage wagons as there is at French or Russian headquarters. Just a few aides-de-camp, who went about the streets alone and in their overcoats, a few guides and a small staff guard; that was all!" Occasionally Wellington himself might be seen, as once an onlooker saw him, holding the hand of a small peasant girl as she led him submissively to a sweet-stall in the market place at Frenada.‡ "The village presented the veriest piece of still-life . . . that I ever saw," wrote a visitor to an earlier headquarters at Fuente Guinaldo. "In the market-place were some half dozen Spanish women sitting in a row, selling eggs and cabbages, and half a dozen soldiers in their undress were their buyers. Now and then an officer in a plain blue coat would cross the

plaza on foot or on horseback and this was all that met the eye."
The Commander-in-Chief's daily routine was described by an
officer of his escort:

"He rises at six every morning and employs himself till nine -
the breakfast hour - in writing. After breakfast he sees the heads
of departments, viz Quartermaster- and Adjutant-General, Commissary General, Commander of Artillery and any other officers
coming to him on business. This occupies till 2 or 3 p.m. and
sometimes longer, when he gets on his horse and rides till near
six. . . . At nine he retires to write again or employs himself until
twelve, when he retires for the night. His correspondence with
England and the Spanish and Portuguese Governments is very
extensive."*

When not actually campaigning—as happened during the winter
months in cantonments after the retreat to the Portuguese frontier
in November 1812 until the spring of 1813 brought green forage for
the tens of thousands of horses, mules and oxen without which the
army could not march—Wellington, despite the prodigious quantities of work and correspondence he got through, contrived to take
a great deal of exercise and recreation. There were three packs of
hounds of a kind at Frenada, of which the best, known as "the
Peer's," consisted of sixteen couple of foxhounds. Though,
according to Judge-Advocate Larpent who kept a journal of his day-
by-day life at headquarters, Wellington knew nothing of the science
of the sport, he was very fond of it in his own way, rode hard and
loved a good gallop. "He hunts every other day almost," wrote
Larpent, "and then makes up for it by great diligence and instant
decision on the intermediate days. He works till about four o'clock;
and then, for an hour or two, parades with any one whom he wants
to talk to, up and down the little square of Frenada (amidst all the
chattering Portuguese) in his grey greatcoat."† The Quartermaster-
General told Larpent that on hunting days he could get almost
anything done, as Lord Wellington stood whip in hand ready to
start and soon dispatched all business. But after some of his lieutenants
had taken advantage of their Commander-in-Chief's impatience to

* Tomkinson, 108; Longford, 304; Buckham, 43-4.
† Larpent, I, 78, 85.

get him to agree in a hasty way to things he did not intend, he remarked to General Murray, "Oh damn them, I won't speak to them again when we are hunting." On another occasion, when he had been kept in by rain on a hunting day, he made up for it next morning by setting out before dawn to ride twenty-eight miles by 10 a.m. to attend a review of one of his outlying divisions, and returned to dinner at headquarters by four that afternoon. "This is something like vigour," Larpent commented, "and yet I think he overdoes it a little; he has, however, a notion that it is exercise makes Headquarters more healthy than the rest of the army generally is, and that the hounds are one great cause of this."*

*   *   *

At the close of the year 1812, which had seen the triumphs of Ciudad Rodrigo, Badajoz and Salamanca, the reverse of Burgos and the retreat to Portugal, accompanied only by his Military Secretary, Lord Fitzroy Somerset, and his Spanish liaison officer, General Alava, Wellington paid a visit to Cadiz. Here he was accorded a tremendous popular triumph, addressed the Cortes in Spanish and was invested with the command of the Spanish armies—conferred on him that autumn, together with the Dukedom of Ciudad Rodrigo, after his liberation of Madrid. He was now at long last undisputed commander of all the allied forces in the Peninsula. He was not very optimistic as to what he could make of his new charge; "I want to see," he had written to General Beresford, the trainer of his fine Portuguese soldiers, "how far I can venture to go in putting the Spanish army in a state to do something. In your life you never saw anything so bad as the Galicians, yet they are the finest body of men and the best movers I have ever seen. God knows the best prospect of success from this journey of mine is not bright, but still it is best to try something."

He returned to Frenada at the beginning of February 1813, travelling light and covering the last lap of his journey from Lisbon in five days and riding, on the last of them, fifty miles between breakfast and dinner. He was in high spirits and good humour with everyone, declaring that he would take the field in the spring with

* Larpent, I, 78, 85, 150, 168. See *Barnard Letters*, 208; Maxwell, I, 298; Blakiston, II, 158; Costello, 88-9.

150,000 troops of one sort or another, including his hard core of 40,000 British. Having asked his Spanish hosts what the military rules and laws of his new armies were, he had said to them, "Well, that is very good; now mind and see that they are put in force, and remember, it is not I, but your law orders this. I have only to see your laws executed, which are very good, and they must be obeyed."[*] As a compliment to his allies, and in gratitude for his Spanish title, he gave a grand dinner, ball and supper in the ruins of the fortress town which he had liberated a year before at such cost and whose name he now bore. "The whole went off exceedingly well," wrote Larpent, "except that it was excessively cold, as a few balls during the siege had knocked in several yards of the roof of the ballroom, and it was a hard frost at the time. Lord Wellington was the most active man of the party, but yet I hear from those about him that he is a little broken down by it. He stayed at business at Frenada until half-past three and then rode full seventeen miles to Rodrigo in two hours to dinner, dressed in all his orders etc., was in high glee, danced himself, stayed to supper, and at half-past three in the morning went back to Frenada by moonlight and arrived here before daybreak by six, so that by twelve he was ready again for business." In the English country dances which followed the *bolero* and *fandango*, Larpent noted, "the Spanish ladies were a little more twisted about and handled than our own fair ones would like." But no one fell through a large shell hole in the ballroom floor - guarded by a sentry - and, at the end of the proceedings, only a few silver spoons and forks were missing.[†]

When Wellington had returned to his headquarters after his trip to Cadiz, where he had been given the greatest of Spanish orders, the Golden Fleece, he learnt that the Prince Regent had conferred on him the Garter and the Colonelcy of the Blues. "I ought to have somebody behind me," he confided to a friend, "to remind me that I am but a man. I believe that I have been upon the whole the most favoured of God's creatures, and, if I don't forget the above mentioned, think I may yet do well."[‡]

---

[*] Muriel Wellesley, 260-2; *Dispatches*, IX, 60a; Larpent, I, 50, 66, 80, 112.
[†] Larpent, I, 113-17; Gleig, 186-8.
[‡] Longford, 302; *Dispatches*, IX, 609.

Chapter Thirteen

NEPTUNE'S GENERAL

He rode a knowing-looking thorough-bred horse, and wore a
grey overcoat, Hessian boots and a large cocked hat.
GRONOW

THE Peninsular campaign of 1813 was planned against the background of a new war beyond the Pyrenees and Alps. In the last days
of the old year, while the remnants of the *Grande Armée* were trying
to rally on the Vistula, General Yorck, in command of its Prussian
contingent, concluded an armistice with the Russians. Though at
first repudiated by King Frederick William, who was still mesmerised by Napoleon, it was received with wild enthusiasm by every
patriot. Six weeks later the Prussian king, surrendering to popular
clamour, signed an alliance with the Czar at Kalisch. On March 4th,
Cossacks entered Berlin as the French fell back to the Elbe. Twelve
days later Prussia declared war on France. On the 25th, in a joint
proclamation, the Russian and Prussian sovereigns summoned all
Germany to rise.

Meanwhile Napoleon had called up half a million more conscripts.
Many were lads of sixteen: France was reduced to its last man and
horse. But, though the possessing classes had lost all faith in him,
the Emperor's resolution rallied the nation for one last great throw.
He rejected his Austrian father-in-law's offers of mediation, refused
to withdraw his troops from a single fortress in eastern Europe and
made it clear that he would accept nothing less than his full former
authority.

To provide cadres for his new army Napoleon again ignored
Wellington. In the teeth of the evidence, he chose to assume that the
latter had only 30,000 British troops. By recalling the remaining
units of the Imperial Guard and drafts of veteran non-commissioned
officers and men from every regiment in Spain, he reduced his forces
there to little more than 200,000 effectives. The only reinforcements

350

he sent to Spain to replace the heavy casualties of 1812 were boys. Many of them, unable to stand the hardships of the march, died on the road.

Already, though the British had scarcely fired a shot since the autumn, King Joseph was in trouble. So strong was the guerrilla stranglehold on his communications that the news of the retreat from Moscow took a month to travel from the Pyrenees to Madrid; Napoleon's return to Paris on December 18th only became known to Joseph on February 14th. After Wellington's triumphs of the previous summer the Spanish partisans were past holding. They behaved no longer as outlaws but as men certain of victory, and the whole country was either behind them or terrorised into acquiescence. In Navarre the great guerrillero, Mina, levied taxes and maintained a personal army of eight thousand; in February, with the help of guns landed from British ships, he forced the French garrison of Tafalla to surrender. One of his detachments stormed the castle of Fuentarrabia on the frontier, threw its armament into the sea and made a funeral pyre that was visible far into France. Every village along the trunk roads had to be garrisoned, every church and farm made a fortress. To reach its destination a French dispatch needed a regiment, sometimes a brigade in escort.

On March 17th 1813, Uncle Joe - "the King of the Bottle" - left Madrid for ever. On Napoleon's orders he took up his headquarters at Valladolid and dispatched half his field-forces to hunt down guerrillas in the valleys of Biscaya and Navarre. Clausel with the Army of the North and almost the entire infantry of the Army of Portugal was sent to chase Mina out of Navarre, Foy with another corps to pacify the Biscayan coast. In their attempts to restore their communications, Joseph and his master reduced the forces facing Wellington to little more than 50,000 men.

The British army had no guerrillas to hunt: the people of Spain were its friends. And with the centre and south now liberated, it was all concentrated in the north within fifty miles of the Leon plain. Thanks to the fine work of James McGrigor, the chief of the Medical Staff in emptying the hospitals, there were more men with the colours than there had ever been before. All that winter and spring the roads to Portsmouth and Plymouth had been full of troops bound for the Peninsula: jangling Household Cavalry with splendid accoutrements and fresh, beefy faces, the spoilt "householders" of army jest; reserve battalions marching to join their consorts; detachments of rosy-cheeked militiamen under raw young ensigns "in fine new toggery," the drums and fifes playing before them and the village boys running beside, while housewives at their cottage doors mourned over the poor lambs going to the slaughter, and the confident young soldiers, not knowing what was coming to them, jested back. Thence, drawn by the invisible strings of Wellington's design, they crossed the Bay and saw for the first time the barren, tawny shores of the Peninsula, felt the stones and smelt the stink of Lisbon town, and marched out of Belem barracks on the long mountain track to the frontier. When, bug-bitten, footsore and dusty, they found themselves among the tattered, cheery veterans who were to be their comrades, their education began. "Do you see those men on the plain?" barked old Major O'Hara of the Rifles to the latest batch of "Johnny Newcomes" as they looked down from their rocky fastness. "Es, zur." "Well, then, those are the French and our enemies. You must kill those fellows and not allow them to kill you. You must learn to do as these old birds do and get cover where you can. Recollect, recruits, you come here to kill and not be killed. Bear this in mind; if you don't kill the French, they'll kill you!"* Every fresh arrival was ruthlessly probed by the old hands for weak points; if he was game and survived their rough chaff, he was accepted; if not, he was dealt with unmercifully.

By the end of April 1813, Wellington was in command, not of the 30,000 British troops Napoleon supposed, but of 52,000, together with 29,000 well-disciplined Portuguese – a striking-force of over 80,000 men. To these, following his appointment as Generalissimo of the Spanish Armies, were now added 21,000 Spaniards under his direct command and discipline, and, for what they were worth, another 50,000 irregulars operating independently in the mountains of the north. He was still, however, unable to get regular rations and pay for them out of the jealous, quarrelling Regency and Cortez.

During the winter he had made many improvements in his army. The defects of the previous campaign had been carefully corrected. The former Chief of Staff, George Murray, was back at his post; tents were issued for the first time; portable tin kettles

* Costello, 70. See also *Johnny Newcome*, 16, 18, 30, 151; Bel l, I, 3-5, 79; Simmons, 124 232; Grattan, 311-12; Kincaid, *Random Shots*, 238.

substituted for heavy iron vessels; every soldier equipped with three pairs of shoes and a spare set of soles and heels in his knapsack. Discipline, too, had been tightened, for Judge-Advocate Larpent had spent the winter speeding up courts-martial, hanging deserters and flogging plunderers. Even a small corps of trained sappers had arrived from England, and a properly organised siege-train.

With a force embodying the accumulated experience of five years' campaigning and with his adversary facing a war on two fronts, Wellington was more hopeful than he had even been before. "I propose," he wrote, "to take the field as early as I can and to place myself in Fortune's way." Of his plans for doing so, however, he said little, even in his dispatches to the Secretary of State. They depended on surprise and on the use of sea-power. Instead of a frontal attack against the broad and easily defensible Douro as in 1812, he proposed to outflank that river by secretly transferring the bulk of his troops while still in Portugal to its northern bank and sending them, first north and thence east, to cross its mountain tributary, the Esla, and appear in the rear of the enemy's defences. To do so, with their guns and supplies, they had first to negotiate a wild and almost roadless region on the borders of northern Portugal and Spain. But for months Wellington's engineers and commissariat officers had been probing the Tras-os-Montes, and he was satisfied that it could be done.

Once across the mountains and the Esla, the British commander planned a further surprise - one which the Royal Navy's capture of Santander had made possible. While threatening the French communications by driving round their right or northern flank towards the Bayonne trunk road, he would put it out of their power to threaten his own supply-lines by switching these from Portugal to the Bay of Biscay. For Lisbon and Oporto he would substitute Santander and later, perhaps, Bilbao and Passages. In doing so he would shorten his communications with England by four hundred land-miles and as many sea-miles. Instead of advancing away from his supplies, he would move towards them. And with every mile he drove into the north-east, edging nearer the sea from which his strength came, his communications would become, not more exposed, but safer. Scarcely ever had the offensive use of sea-power on land been more clearly envisaged by a soldier. Being England's, he was Neptune's general.

In the utmost secrecy and under pretence of equipping the Spanish Army of Galicia, Wellington assembled supply-ships, guns and ammunition in Corunna for transference to Santander Bay, two hundred and fifty miles to the east. The operation was attended by difficulties. For the war with the young American Republic, begun in the previous summer, had taken an unexpected course. While the long-impending American attack on the defenceless Canadian frontier had been thwarted by a few hundred regulars, American frigates, more heavily manned and gunned than their British counterparts, had triumphed in three spectacular duels which, though of little strategic importance, caused an immense sensation in both countries. Thus encouraged, American privateers had begun to appear on the Portuguese coast in search of Wellington's supply ships. The menace was never serious, for the strength of the Royal Navy was immense and the United States had not even a single capital ship. But during the early months of 1813, as the campaign which was to decide the fate of Spain took shape in his mind, Wellington waxed very bitter over naval slackness and inefficiency.

He possessed, however, another asset. Thanks to the guerrillas he knew the enemy's dispositions while having his own concealed. When the campaign started, 55,000 men under King Joseph and Marshal Jourdan were strung out across a front of nearly two hundred miles from the Douro to the Tagus. Far behind them, as many more were hunting partisans in the tangled mountains near the French frontier or garrisoning fortresses and blockhouses. And four hundred miles away, on the east coast, cut off from the rest of Spain by mountain and desert, Marshal Suchet with 68,000 troops was holding down Valencia and Catalonia. To make sure that no reinforcements from this quarter should reach Joseph through the Ebro valley, Wellington made a further use of his country's command of the sea. In April he ordered Lieutenant-General Sir John Murray, who had just successfully repulsed Suchet at Castalla, to embark his force of 18,000 Britons, Germans, Italians and Spaniards for an attack on Tarragona two hundred miles up the coastal road to the north. Confronted by such a threat to his communications, as well as by the unpredictable movements of the Spanish Army of Murcia and the guerrillas of Catalonia and Aragon, Suchet, a selfish man at the best of times, was unlikely to spare any help for his colleagues.

Yet everything depended on the British striking quickly. Clausel and Foy were bound before long to disperse the northern guerrillas and rejoin King Joseph. And events in Europe might soon release far larger French forces. On April 15th Napoleon had left Paris to join his army on the Rhine; on the 24th he reached Erfurt, intending to fall on the Prussians and Russians before the Austrians could intervene. It was, therefore, irritating for Wellington to be delayed by a late spring and consequent lack of green forage*; it had been a bitter winter all over Europe, and in London the Thames had been frozen for eight weeks. Accidents, due to fraudulent contractors, had also held up the pontoon bridge on its way from Tagus to Douro. And with a succession of rivers to cross, Wellington's plan depended on pontoons.

During the second week of May the main British army began its northward march through the Tras-os-Montes. To distract the enemy's attention, Wellington and Hill with the remaining 30,000 moved on the 22nd on Salamanca. As he crossed the frontier the British Commander-in-Chief turned in his stirrups and bade farewell to Portugal. He and his men were leaving forever the rocky upland villages, the stunted trees and stony fields, the boggy woods and heaths; the smoky, flea-ridden billets, the dances with ivory-teethed peasant girls in bat-haunted, windy barns, the hunts and horse-races among the vineyards and olive trees, the days after partridge, snipe and hare; the gallina and garlic sausages, the black bread and sour country wine, the rain and mountain wind in the desolate square of lonely Frenada.†

The French were taken completely by surprise. On May 25th, Hill's troops drove in their outposts before Salamanca. The single French division in the neighbourhood of the town, after losing two hundred prisoners, withdrew towards the Douro. Everything pointed to a British advance in that direction, and orders were given

---

* Larpent wrote on April 4th, 1813, from Headquarters at Frenada, "We have again a clear north wind and hot sun, and not a blade of grass growing – without the latter we cannot stir. If the rains will but come soon and bring grass, we may, perhaps, move in the first week of May, but not before. . . . How little you know in England about the real state of things here, and the requisites for moving in a campaign! You forget our ten or fifteen thousand animals for baggage and for food, besides the cavalry and artillery." Larpent, I, 131.

† Simmons, 277-8, 281; Costello, 148; Kincaid, 89, 203-4; Schaumann, 317-18; Tomkinson, 22; Grattan, 223; Gronow, II, 205-6; Larpent, I, 12, 17, 21, 44, 63, 75; Boothby, 162-3; *Johnny Newcome*, 40.

at Joseph's headquarters to meet it, between Toro and Tordesillas, as Marmont had done in the previous summer.

On reaching the Tormes, however, Wellington and Hill halted. Screened by their cavalry, they remained there for a week, while to the north the main body under Graham completed its two-hundred mile outflanking march through the Tras-os-Montes. Guns had to be lowered over precipices by ropes, and the infantry had to climb at times on hands and knees. But by May 28th the entire force was across the frontier and marching in three columns on the Esla. They reached the river on the 29th and 30th, and, finding it in flood, crossed it on the last day of the month, partly by pontoons and partly by fords wading chin-deep. Except from a few scattered cavalry patrols, there was no resistance. Next day the advance-guard entered Zamora. Before Joseph and his Chief of Staff could realise what had happened, their entire line had been taken in flank.

By that time Wellington himself had joined the northern wing of his army. Leaving Hill to direct the southern part, he had left Salamanca at dawn on the 29th, ridden all day, and crossed the swollen Douro at Miranda in a basket slung from ropes. Everything was happening as he had intended. The French now knew that his army was across the Esla, but it was too late for them to do anything about it. On June 2nd, realising that their Douro defences were useless, they evacuated Toro. Here on the following day, covered by Graham, Hill's 30,000 also crossed the river. By June 4th the whole Allied army, 81,000 strong, was concentrated north of the Douro.

It at once set out north-eastwards towards the Carrion and Pisuerga. For the next ten days it marched without a halt in parallel columns across the great corn plain of Old Castile - the waving Tierra de Campos - its cavalry screen interposing between it and the retreating French. "The sun shone brilliantly," wrote an officer, "the sky was heavenly blue, the clouds of dust marked the line of march of the glittering columns. The joyous peasantry hailed our approach and came dancing to meet us, singing and beating time on their tambourines; and when we passed through the principal street of Palencia the nuns, from the upper windows of a convent, showered down rose-petals upon our dusty heads."* Thanks to

* *Peninsular Sketches*, II, 37. See also Tomkinson, 239; Schaumann, 371; Oman, VI, 352-3; Smith, I, 93-4; Gomm, 301; Simmons, 285-6; Fortescue, IX, 147; Blakiston, II, 179-202;

Murray's staff work supplies were plentiful. All was cheerfulnes s and anticipation.

Against this unexpected march the French were powerless. They had either to retreat or be cut off. Valladolid was evacuated on June 2nd, Palencia on the 7th, Burgos itself on the 12th. Fear of hunger sped their steps, for, unlike the rich corn-lands of the Douro, the country along the royal *chaussée* to the north-east was a desert. Though their fighting troops still mustered less than 60,000 they were impeded by a vast host of useless courtiers, officials, and refugees as well as by thousands of wagons laden with ladies of pleasure and loot. "We were a travelling bordel," a French officer complained.

On June 13th, the British were awakened by a tremendous explosion reverberating through the mountains. It was the end of Burgos castle, which the retreating French had blown up in despair. Yet, even had it been defended, it could no longer have stopped Wellington. For, having outflanked the Douro and its tributaries, he had already turned north again to encircle the French defences in yet another river valley, the Ebro. His staff, seeing they had covered more than two hundred miles from the Portuguese frontier, were in favour of a halt; the French were falling back on reinforcements, and the news from Germany was bad. On May 2nd Napoleon had defeated the Russo-Prussian army at Lützen on the Saxon plain; on the 8th he had entered Dresden, and, two days before Wellington set out from Portugal, had won a second, though not decisive, victory at Bautzen. The possibility of another Continental peace was in every mind; in fact, though the news had still to reach the Peninsula, a five weeks' armistice had already been signed at Plaswitz. Yet Wellington knew that, whatever happened on the Elbe, time must elapse before its effect would be felt on the Ebro. His safest plan now was to go forward. For once on the Pyrenees, whatever the French might do he would have an easier front to defend than a Spanish river.

Without a halt, therefore, the advance continued. Once more the army struck out across desert and mountain. Only the cavalry screen remained in the neighbourhood of the Burgos-Bayonne highway to deceive and shadow King Joseph. Wellington's plan was to cross

Croker Papers, II, 307. For a rhymed description of this wonderful march, see *Johnny Newcome*, 213-15.

the headwaters of the Ebro between Rocamonde and Puenta Arenas, and thence, turning eastwards, to strike the road at Vittoria twenty miles in rear of the French defences. By this sweep to the north he would link up with Giron's Galicians and Longa's guerrillas and open his new communications with Santander and the Bay of Biscay.

For the next three days the footsore, dusty army toiled northwards through iron-bound hills and defiles which no artillery had ever passed. Again the guns had to be brought down precipices by hand with locked wheels; the sweating infantry, spoiling for a fight, muttered that they would make the French pay for it. By the 14th, the marching columns found themselves looking down from the stony plateau to the green and wooded valley of the infant Ebro. By nightfall tents were rising among the cherry trees and the men were garlanded with blossom by dancing peasant girls. Next day, having crossed the river, they turned once more into the east, marching in torrential rain through richly cultivated valleys and along the base of forest-clad mountains. They had covered three hundred miles through hitherto enemy territory and had scarcely fired a shot. "It was a most wonderful march," wrote Harry Smith, "the army in great fighting order, and every man in better wind than a trained pugilist."*

On June 17th, two days after crossing the Ebro, the army regained touch with the French. The men, in high spirits, began to fix their flints, for they could smell, they said, the frog-eaters' baccy and onions. Next day the Light Division directed by Wellington in person, was in action with an outlying French division at San Milan. As the French, with a loss of 400 casualties and all their baggage, fell back, Jourdan, still waiting for Clausel twenty miles to the southwest, ordered a general retreat. The line of the Ebro had gone the same way as those of the Douro, Carrion and Pisuerga.

On the 20th the French army, 66,000 strong, with 20,000 useless followers, came pouring into the valley of Vittoria. Here the river Zadora, winding between mountains, made a miniature plain twelve miles by seven, tapering towards its eastern end into a bottleneck where the little twin-spired town of Vittoria nestled under the spurs of the Pyrenees and the great high-road to France ran into the hills. Here a number of lesser roads met, one going eastwards to

---

* Smith, I, 97; Tomkinson, 256. See also Bell, I, 82-3; Kincaid, 209-10; Simmons, 305; Gomm, 306; *Pakenham Letters*, 211-14.

Salvatierra and Pamplona – the only way of escape left the French should the Bayonne *chaussée* be cut.

The British did not stay for the attack. They meant to destroy Joseph before he could get his baggage-train through the guerrilla-haunted mountains and before Clausel, still labouring in the Navarrese defiles, could join him. They waited a day in the Bayas valley to collect their forces; then at dawn on June 21st advanced for battle. They came out of the west in three columns, close on 70,000 Anglo-Portuguese with 7000 Spaniards. The southernmost under Rowland Hill crossed the Zadora and Madrid highway eight miles below Vittoria and in the clear morning sunlight climbed the rocky Puebla ridge that enfiladed Joseph's lines to the south. Ever since his first fight against them at Roliça, Wellington had realised the sensitiveness of Napoleon's intelligent and imaginative infantry to any threat to their flanks. And, as he intended, Hill's eastward feint along the ridge drew off their reserves in that direction.

It was not till the early afternoon that the main British attack developed on the other side of the valley. It was directed partly against the French centre over the bridges of the winding Zadora, and partly four miles further east where Graham, with the 1st and 4th Divisions and Longa's Spaniards, some 20,000 men, was driving along the Bilbao-Vittoria road towards the vital highway to France with orders to cut it but only to attack the main enemy force when contact had been obtained with the other allied columns. Unfortunately both Graham and the four divisions attacking in the centre were delayed by the rough ground they had to cover between the Bayas and their battle stations. The difficulty of Wellington's convergent attack – forced on him by the character of the terrain – was its timing; inter-communication between his widely separated columns was almost impossible, and they had to be guided mainly by the sound of one another's fire.

But for the resource of the British commander and the speed of the Light Division, one of whose brigades under Major-General·Kempt crossed an unguarded bridge over the Zadora unseen and took up a position in the very heart of Joseph's lines, and the fiery spirit of General Picton, the attack in the centre might have come too late. Lord Dalhousie, who had recently arrived from England to command the 7th Division and who was to have led the attack, failed to bring up his men in time, and, though aide-de-camp after aide-de-camp arrived with orders, the assault on the bridges hung fire. Picton, who alone had reached his station punctually, waited till he could stand it no more. Conspicuous in a blue frock-coat and a broad-brimmed top-hat,* he rode up to one of Wellington's messengers to ascertain his orders. On hearing that they were for the 7th Division to attack the Mendoza bridge, he shouted back, "Then you may tell Lord Wellington that the 3rd Division under my command shall in less than ten minutes attack that bridge and carry it!" Upon which he set his men in motion towards the valley, calling out with customary oaths as he rode beside them, "Come on, ye rascals! Come on, you fighting villains!"

Supported by the 4th and the remainder of the Light Division, and aided by an attack on the French guns by the brigade already across the Zadora, the Fighting Third crossed the river and broke the enemy's centre. Though the ground was suitable for defence - vineyards, woods and standing corn, interspersed with ditches and villages - the French infantry did not fight well that day. They were depressed by their long retreat, had lost confidence in their leaders and knew that the British for once, though only slightly, outnumbered them. And as the threat to their flanks grew, they began, commanders and privates alike, to look over their shoulders.

Thereafter the end was certain. About five o'clock Longa's guerrillas on Graham's left flank cut the Vittoria-Bayonne *chaussée* at Durana, two miles beyond the town. The direct line of retreat to France was gone. Only the valour of General Reille's two divisions—the last to retain their morale—in delaying Graham's advance prevented a complete encirclement. Holding the last high ground before Vittoria, their muskets flashing like lightning and the guns shaking the earth as the gunners bounded to and fro through the smoke, the remnants of the old Army of Portugal kept back the left prong of Wellington's pincers until the rest of the French could escape to the east.

But they did not go as an army or stand upon the order of their going. Hitherto they had retired with their guns and train; now they went without. A mile beyond Vittoria, on the narrow road to Pamplona, the treasure-wagons and carriages of King Joseph's Court were blocked in indescribable confusion. As the British shot

* To protect an inflamed eye. He swore, wrote his admirer Kincaid, as roundly as if he had been wearing two cocked ones. Kincaid, 222. See also Picton, II, 195-6.

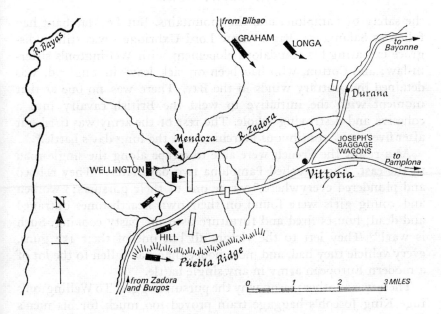

The Battle of Vittoria

crashed overhead and pursuing cavalry appeared on the skyline, panic broke out. Soldiers and civilians cut the draft-horses' traces and rode off, leaving their vehicles to the victors: ladies were thrown off their mounts or flung from their carriages; sacks of dollars and jewels were torn open by the retreating infantry and spilt about the road. Among those carried away in the tumult were King Joseph and Marshal Jourdan; the latter's baton was picked up by a British hussar, and sent to the Prince Regent. When the latter replied, it was to award Wellington the highest rank to which a soldier can aspire. "You have sent me," he wrote, "among the trophies of your unrivalled fame, the staff of a French Marshal, and I send you in return that of England."

The battle of Vittoria was over. As the victorious columns moved forward across the plain and the artillery galloped to the front, the sun began to sink behind the western hills, gilding the helmets of thousands of horsemen. Before them the French empire in Spain was dissolving. Had the pursuing cavalry been led by Cotton, Paget or Le Marchant, few of the enemy would have reached the safety of Pamplona and the mountains. But Le Marchant had fallen at Salamanca, Paget - now Lord Uxbridge - was still in disgrace expiating his scandalous elopement with Wellington's sister-in-law; and Cotton, who had been on sick leave in England, was detained by contrary winds in the Bay. There was no one at that moment with the initiative to weld the British cavalry into a cohesive and destroying whole. The rest of the army was tired out after five weeks' continuous marching and the long day's battle.*

As a result the French were able to escape along the single road to the east. They reached Pamplona two days later. "They robbed and plundered everywhere," wrote one of their pursuers; "women and young girls were found on their own hearthstones outraged and dead; houses fired and furniture used for hasty cooking. Such is war!"† They left to the victors all but one of their 152 guns, every vehicle they had, and more booty than had fallen to the lot of a modern European army in any single battle.

There was another reason why the pursuit flagged. To Wellington's rage King Joseph's baggage train proved too much for his men's discipline.‡ Around it the soldiers of three nations, with powder-blackened faces, fought one another for boxes of dollars, rummaged state papers, pictures, and furniture, dressed up in fine clothes, and feasted on the wines and foods of a luxurious court. "Come, boys," shouted an Irish grenadier, "help yourselves wid anything yez like best, free gratis and for nothing at all! The King left all behind him for our day's trouble. Who'll have a dhrink o' wine?" For miles the Pamplona road was strewn with the plunder of six years' predatory war: here the personal baggage of a king, there the decorations of a theatre, war stores and china, arms,

---

* The account of the battle is based on Oman, VI, 384-450; Fortescue, IX, 152-87; Longford, 309-16; Graham, 269; Napier, Book XXX, Ch. viii; Weller, 255-69; Bell, I, 83-91; Tomkinson, 243-54; Schaumann, 374-81; Kincaid, 217-26; *Johnny Newcome*, 223-32; Simmons, 289; Gomm, 304-6; Costello, 157-65; Smith, I, 95-102; Blakiston, II, 206-10; Jourdan, *Mémoires*; Maxwell, II, 40-3; Leith Hay, II, 10-208; Picton, II, 195-200. *Peninsular Sketches*, II, 41-54; 103-11; Ellesmere, 146-7.

† Bell, I, 96-8. See also Simmons, 291; Smith, I, 102-3. "The seat of war," wrote the latter, "is hell upon earth."

‡ "About dusk, the head of our column came suddenly on some wagons which had been abandoned by the enemy. Someone called out, 'They are money tumbrils!' No sooner were the words uttered than the division broke as if by word of command and, in an instant, the covers disappeared from the wagons and in their place was seen nothing but a mass of inverted legs." Blakiston, II, 216. See Sherer, 331-2; *Barnard Letters*, 228.

drums, trumpets, silks, jewellery and plate; "wounded soldiers, deserted women and children of all ages imploring aid and assistance - here a lady upset in her carriage - in the next an actress or a *femme de chambre*; sheep, goats and droves of oxen roaming and bellowing about, with loose horses, cows and donkeys." That night the abandoned carriages were turned into the stands of an impromptu torchlit fair. When next day the pursuit was resumed, the victors were so gorged and laden they could scarcely move.

It was the indignant Commander-in-Chief's old problem of discipline again. In battle his troops acquitted themselves like lions, yet, under Britain's parsimonious and libertarian method of recruitment, there were so many gaolbirds, ne'er-do-wells and drunken Irish peasants among them that when, in the hour of exhaustion after a victorious battle or siege, the bonds of command momentarily relaxed and liquor - never far to seek in a wine-producing country - became easily accessible, a large proportion of the army relapsed into a kind of Donnybrook or Bartholomew Fair orgy. "We started with the army in the highest order," he wrote to the Secretary of State, "and on the day of the battle nothing could get on better. But that event has, as usual, totally annihilated all order and discipline. The soldiers of the army have got among them about a million sterling in money. . . . The night of the battle, instead of being passed in getting rest and food to prepare for the pursuit of the following day, was spent by the soldiers in looking for plunder. The consequence was that they were incapable of marching in pursuit of the enemy and were totally knocked up."*

Three days later, in a further letter, Wellington continued his complaint. "It is quite impossible for me or any other man to command a British army under the existing system. We have in the service the scum of the earth as common soldiers; and of late years we have been doing everything in our power, both by law and by publications, to relax the discipline by which alone such men can be kept in order. The officers of the lower ranks will not perform the duty required from them for the purpose of keeping their soldiers in order. . . . As to the non-commissioned officers, as I have repeatedly stated, they are as bad as the men, and too near them in point of pay and situation . . . for us to expect them to do anything to keep the men in order. It is really a disgrace to have anything to say to

* To Earl Bathurst, June 29th 1813.

such men as some of our soldiers are." And as evidence of what he had to suffer from what he called his "vagabond soldiers," he cited the fact that, while before the battle the total of British and Portuguese in arms was 67,036 rank and file and 58,694 twelve days later, the 4186 lost in the battle were almost equalled by the 4156 lost in plundering and desertion since.*

* * *

Yet, though as a result only 2000 prisoners were taken, and more than 50,000 French escaped by Pamplona and the Pyrenean passes to France, Vittoria was one of the decisive battles of the war. It liberated Spain, exposed France to invasion and heartened Europe to make the final effort to break its chains. When on the night of June 30th the news reached the Allied camp on the Silesian border, Count Stadion broke into Prince Metternich's bedroom with a shout of "*Le roi Joseph est – en Espagne!*"† At that moment Austria's attitude and the prolongation of the armistice were in the balance. Next day Napoleon, who had been on the point of taking the field again against the still inadequately equipped Russians and Prussians, agreed to a conference and a six weeks' extension of the truce. It was the period the Austrians needed to complete the mobilisation of their army. For a moment Britain became the idol of resurgent German youth; in Vienna Beethoven wrote a symphonic piece on the theme of "Rule Britannia," and even the Russians sang, for the only time in their history, a *Te Deum* in gratitude for a foreign victory.

---

* "They are not in the hospitals, nor are they killed, nor have they fallen into the hands of the enemy as prisoners. . . . I believe they are concealed in the villages of the mountains." To Earl Bathurst, July 2nd 1813. Speaking long afterwards on this subject, Wellington said of the difference between the discipline of the Napoleonic conscript army in the Peninsula and the British voluntary one: "The conscription calls out a share of every class; no matter whether your son or my son, all must march – but our friends – I may say it in this room – are the very scum of the earth. People talk of their enlisting from their fine military feeling – all stuff – no such thing. Some of our men enlist from having got bastard children – some for minor offences – many more for drink; but you can hardly conceive such a set brought together, and it really is wonderful that we should have made them the fine fellows they are." Stanhope, 18. See also *Idem*, 13-14.

† *Croker Papers*, I, 336.

Chapter Fourteen

ACROSS THE PYRENEES

Beating from the wasted vines
Back to France her banded swarms,
Back to France with countless blows,
Till o'er the hills her eagles flew
Beyond the Pyrenean pines,
Follow'd up in valley and glen
With blare of bugle, clamour of men,
Roll of cannon and clash of arms,
And England pouring on her foes.
Such a war had such a close.

TENNYSON

BEFORE Napoleon had signed the extension of his truce with the eastern Powers Wellington's men were on the Pyrenees. Graham with the left wing reached the sea and Bidassoa on June 25th. The centre and right, stretching south-eastwards along the frontier, rested on the mountain passes of Maya and Roncesvalles. "We fired our last shots into the *parlez-vous*," wrote Bell, "as we slashed them over the hills into their own country, while they carried along with them the curses of a whole kingdom." It was five years since Canning had predicted that one day Europe would see a British army looking down on France from the Pyrenees.

Napoleon was not the man to brook invasion of his territories. He reacted to the news of Vittoria with passionate rage. Forbidding all reference to it in his closed Press, he put Joseph and Jourdan under house arrest and replaced them by the man whose disobedience had been the cause of half their troubles. On July 1st Soult left Dresden for Bayonne with orders "to re-establish the imperial business in Spain." He reached the headquarters of the demoralised army on the 12th and at once set to work to restore its morale. A superb organiser and, when driven to it, like all the great Revolutionary leaders, a dynamo of energy, the big, bullying Marshal completed his task in less than a fortnight. After five years of sulkily serving under others, he had at last achieved his ambition. In a flamboyant proclamation he told his troops that they had been expelled from Spain through

365

the incompetence of their leaders and that under his command they would annihilate the enemy's "motley levies."

At that moment Wellington was occupied with the reduction – by storm or starvation – of the two remaining Spanish fortresses in French hands behind his lines. Profoundly distrustful of the armistice in Germany and of his country's new allies, he had no intention of advancing into France without securing his rear. His front, extending for fifty miles into the mountains, necessitated the division of his force into a number of isolated posts along the frontier passes. His left under Graham, who was in charge of the operations against St Sebastian, was on the coastal plain; his centre under Hill in the mountain *massif* called the Bastan; his right under Picton and Lowry Cole on the high Roncesvalles road from Pamplona to St Jean Pied de Port in France. His strategy, for the present a defensive one, was to hold the passes with small delaying forces against any French thrust until his main strength could be concentrated to give battle behind them. It meant reposing more trust in his scattered subordinates than he cared for, but Pyrenean geography left him no alternative. His own headquarters was at the hill village of Lesaca, half-way between St Sebastian and the Bastan. It was far nearer his ocean left than his mountain right, but it was at the former, where the main road from France crossed the Bidassoa, that he expected trouble. He had ordered St Sebastian to be stormed at once and he believed that Soult would try to relieve it. Reports of French movements towards the passes in the south he regarded as feints to distract his attention from the coastal sector.

In this he was wrong. Soult's plan, a most daring one, was to throw 35,000 bayonets – two-thirds of his force – against the Allied right at Roncesvalles, while D'Erlon with the remainder stormed the Maya pass to the north and, dominating all roads through the Bastan, interposed himself between Wellington and his threatened right in front of Pamplona where 5000 veteran troops and the main French artillery park were besieged by the Spaniards. Once the fortress was relieved, the whole army was to drive towards Tolosa or Vittoria in Wellington's rear, so turning on him the tables of his own campaign and forcing him to retreat. It was a gamble, for, being without transport since its defeat, the French army was bound to starve unless it could reach Pamplona and capture its besiegers' stores within four days. But it was helped by the existence of a lateral

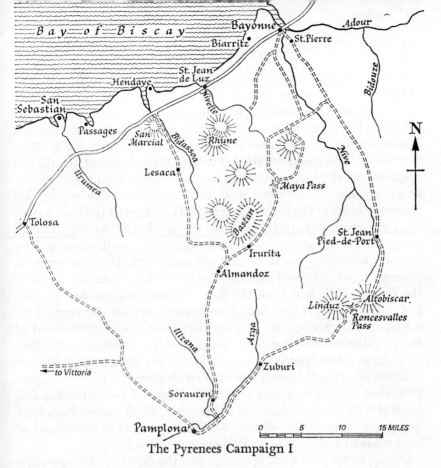

The Pyrenees Campaign I

road system on the French side of the Pyrenees that was lacking on the other, and by the fact that Wellington, being about to storm St Sebastian, was expecting Soult to strike in the north to relieve it.

At dawn on July 25th Graham's storming parties moved against St Sebastian. By midday Wellington, listening in Lesaca churchyard to the guns ten miles away, knew that the attack had failed. But hardly had he left Lesaca for the coast to discuss the next move with Graham, when heavy gunfire was heard from the opposite direction. Here D'Erlon had launched his attack on the Bastan against Hill's outposts in the Maya pass. A further twenty miles to the south-east 6000 British, Portuguese and Spaniards under Major-General Byng had been defending the defiles of Altobiscar and Linduz since dawn against 35,000 assailants.

Despite the odds against them Byng's men had held their positions before Roncesvalles without difficulty, for Soult's columns, strung

367

out along narrow mountain roads, had no room to deploy. But at five that evening a dense fog fell, and Sir Lowry Cole, the commander of the 4th Division, fearful for his flanks, decided against orders to fall back along the Pamplona road on Picton and the 3rd Division behind him. Nearer Wellington, in the Bastan, Sir William Stewart's two brigades repulsed D'Erlon's three divisions, thanks to a desperate stand by the 92nd Highlanders. "They stood there," wrote an eyewitness, "like a stone wall, until half their blue bonnets lay beside those brave Highland soldiers.... I can see now the line of their dead and wounded stretched upon the heather."* At nightfall all the ground lost was regained by a sudden attack on the French flank by two battalions from Lord Dalhousie's 7th Division under a young brigadier named Barnes. Yet here, also, what the pluck of the rank and file had held, the fears of their commanders yielded. For, with the Maya pass sealed once more against the French, Sir Rowland Hill arrived with news that Cole was overwhelmed at Roncesvalles and that a retreat was necessary to straighten the line. So it came about that on the morning of the 26th, both Soult and D'Erlon found to their surprise the British gone and the passes open. Instead of having to admit failure, the Duke of Dalmatia was able to send a flamboyant dispatch to Dresden which caused Napoleon, going one better, to announce that Pamplona and St Sebastian had been relieved and the British decisively defeated.†

Owing to his visit to St Sebastian and the failure of his subordinates to send prompt warning of what was happening, Wellington only learnt of the French attack late that night. At four o'clock next morning he set out post-haste for the Bastan where he found Hill and Stewart with 9000 men at Irutita, ten miles south of the abandoned Maya pass. As they were now strongly posted and as there was no sign of D'Erlon, he continued his journey southwards along the wooded mountain tracks, ordering a general concentration of reserves on Pamplona. After travelling all day he learnt at eight in the evening that Cole had abandoned Roncesvalles on the previous

---

† "You had better," wrote the Emperor to his Foreign Secretary, "circulate the news that in consequence of Marshal Soult's victory on July 25th, the siege of St Sebastian has been raised and 30 siege guns and 200 wagons taken. The blockade of Pamplona was raised on the 27th; General Hill, who was in command at that siege, could not carry away his wounded and was obliged to burn part of his baggage. Twelve siege guns were captured there. Send this to Prague, Leipzig and Frankfort." *Lettres de l'Empereur Napoléon, non inserées dans la Correspondance*, 3.   * Bell, I, 104.

night and had fallen back to join Picton at Zuburi, twenty miles north-east of Pamplona. He at once sent Picton orders to hold his ground at all costs, promising to join him next day.

Yet Picton had already abandoned Zuburi without a fight. This fine soldier, who normally could never bridle his ardour in the presence of the French, had joined Cole at Linzoain that morning. At the sight of his tall hat and umbrella the men had supposed their retreat at an end. "Here comes old Tommy," they cried, "now, boys, make up your minds for a fight!" But, after consulting Cole, Picton, paralysed by the responsibility, decided that it was not safe to stand in a defile where his flanks might be turned. He ordered instead an immediate retreat to the foothills north of Pamplona. By doing so he needlessly abandoned a further ten miles of difficult country and placed the relief of the fortress almost within Soult's reach. It was this which caused Wellington to write to the Prime Minister that all his victories had not yet given his generals confidence in themselves, and that, though heroes when he was present, they were like children in his absence. "There is nothing I dislike so much," he added, "as these extended operations which I cannot direct myself."

In the race to reach Pamplona before the British, Soult had gained the initial advantage. By the morning of the 27th - two days after he started - there were only six hilly miles and 19,000 British and Spanish troops between him and his goal. But at dawn Wellington had resumed his southward ride at Almandoz, half-way down the Maya-Pamplona road. Ten miles farther on, at Ostiz, he learnt of Picton's retreat and of what was happening ahead. Out-distancing all his staff but his military secretary, he galloped the remaining four miles to Sorauren village, reaching it just before Soult's outposts. Here he could see Cole's men spread across the heights with the French skirmishers moving towards them. He had just time before the enemy cut him off to scribble orders for Fitzroy Somerset to take back to his chief-of-staff, following far behind, for a general concentration on the spot. Then, as the French entered one end of the village, he galloped on to join Cole and Picton. It was, as he said, "a close run thing."*

At the sight of the erect, lithe figure on the thoroughbred, the

* Larpent, II, 12-16, 40, 71-3, 144-5; Weller, 289-94. See also Oman, VI, 658-62; Fortescue, IX, 269-72; Glover 161-70; Bell, I, 106-7; Blakeney, 297-8; Smyth, *History of the XXth*, 396; H.M.C. Bathurst, 234.

Portuguese light infantry broke into a shout of "Douro! Douro!" Soon the whole ridge was cheering; everyone knew that there would be no more retreat. It is possible, as Napier suggests, that the familiar sound, reverberating up the mountain valleys, caused Soult to postpone his attack until the morrow. Since Albuera, Soult, or General Salt as the British called him, had always hesitated in the immediate presence of the redcoats. There was an Achilles-heel in this fine strategist's armour which became apparent on the day of battle, when his magnificent self-assurance always temporarily deserted him.* With Pamplona only two hours' march away and his adversary for the moment outnumbered by two to one, he shrank from an immediate attack. Instead, he took his siesta and waited till next day.

By then it was too late. Wellington had made his dispositions, his staff, after a long detour through the hills, had rejoined him, and four British divisions – one, at least, certain to arrive during the day – were marching on the battlefield. He had won the race after all. Within twenty-four hours he would outnumber the enemy; till then he had only to hold his position and trust to his men's proved steadiness. Soult's ensuing attack was like Busaco, with the Allied line drawn up behind the skyline of a series of ridges. As so often before, when the dense columns reached the summit they encountered the concentrated fire of an extended two-deep line, till then invisible – first a shattering volley from the whole line overwhelming the leading files, then a continuous sequence of rolling volleys by successive platoons which made any recovery or deployment impossible. As always, Wellington, anticipating the enemy's movements, was at the precise spot where each attack was to fall, and, though at the start outnumbered by two to one, he contrived by his skilful dispositions to bring twice as many muskets as his adversaries to bear at every decisive point.

By four o'clock the battle of Sorauren was over. It had been, as the victor remarked, "fair bludgeon work," but his lines had held. Several of his staff, including the Adjutant General and his deputy, had been struck by spent balls or bullets, and the young Prince of Orange had had a horse shot under him while carrying an order.

---

* Maximillien Lamarque, II, 182. "He loved vigorous enterprises," wrote one of his aides, "provided they did not involve too much personal danger." *Memoires de St Chamans*. See also Lemonnier-Delafasse, 219, cit. Oman, VI, 590-1, 663; Cooper, 24.

"I escaped as usual unhurt," Wellington wrote to his brother, "and I begin to believe that the finger of God is upon me."[*]

The French, who had lost nearly 4000 to the Allies' 2600, had shot their bolt. They had failed either to relieve Pamplona or capture supplies. They had now either to retreat or starve. In an effort to save something from the wreck, Soult ordered a march across Wellington's flank towards the Pamplona-Tolosa road, hoping to raise the siege of St Sebastian. By doing so he gave his adversary, whom he had already presented with a Busaco, the chance of a Salamanca. During the last two days of July Wellington struck at his rearguard and all but annihilated it. Famished and demoralised, Soult's troops abandoned all pretence of order and ran for safety. Nearly a quarter of his total force was lost. Scarcely half regained France with their colours.

Had Wellington chosen to pursue he could probably have reached the Garonne. But the truce in Germany was still continuing and, for all he knew, might already have culminated in a peace, freeing Napoleon's full strength for operations against him. At that moment his was the only Allied army actively engaged. It amounted, after its Vittoria and Pyrenean casualties, to little more than 80,000 men, of whom 25,000 were ill-fed and ill-disciplined Spaniards. To have invaded France with the latter—unpaid by their politicians and burning with savage desire to revenge themselves on their country's oppressors—might have provoked a partisan resistance which the British commander was resolved to avoid. He therefore forewent his chance of glory and halted his army once more on the summit of the Pyrenees.

For more than two months, throughout August and September 1813, Wellington awaited events in the north, while his besieging troops reduced St Sebastian and Pamplona at either end of his extended mountain lines along the frontier, the one by battery and storm, the other by starvation. With Soult's army temporarily out of action he was now able to take his time and await the arrival in the little Basque port of Passages of fresh siege artillery and ammunition from England. Though suffering from lumbago, brought on by the hardships of his hard-won victory in the Pyrenees, he rode almost every day from his headquarters at Lesaco to St Sebastian

[*] Longford, 330; Bell, I, 107-8; *Barnard Letters*, 230; Long, 285-7; Maxwell, I, 336-8; Weller, 296-302; Oman, VI, 667-80; Fortescue, IX, 275-80; Larpent, II, 20-1.

on the coast twenty miles away to supervise operations there. One of his officers, who was billeted in a village on the route, has left a picture of that daily pilgrimage and of the "indefatigable Commander of the Forces working with an energy which often threatened his life. He rode so much one week that he was confined for several succeeding days to his bed; and I have seen his fifteen valuable chargers led out by the groom to exercise with scarcely any flesh on their bones – so active and vigilant was their noble rider, and so much were his horses used. Every day. . . . I saw him, unattended by his staff, riding by my window, in a narrow street of Renteria, on his way to the besieged fortress, accompanied by an old artillery or engineer officer, . . . and dressed in a plain grey frock, white cravat, and cocked hat, evidently intent on matters of the siege. This was upwards of thirty miles a day for a *ride*, between breakfast and dinner; but he has often rode double that distance, over the worst roads and in the worst of weather."* A young English merchant, employed in northern Spain, who also saw him at this time, compared him to a centaur, seeming part of his horse and sleeping " as soundly in his saddle as if in his bed.†

By the end of August, the preparations were complete for a second assault on St Sebastian. On the last day of the month, while Wellington in the hills above the Bidassoa parried Soult's attempts to relieve it, Graham's men stormed the fortress. The casualties were appalling; one British brigade lost more than half its number, another a third, and another a quarter. But by the early afternoon, after the artillery had opened fire on the curtain only a few feet above the heads of the stormers, the little fortress town, blazing to the stormy summer sky, was in British hands. "Such was the ardour and confidence of our army," wrote one of its officers, "that if Lord Wellington had told us to attempt to carry the moon we should have done it." Next day, having lost nearly 4000 men in his attempt to raise the siege, Soult fell back across the Bidassoa.

Again the Fabian Commander-in-Chief refrained from following up his success. He was still awaiting news from the North and for the fall of Pamplona. His difficulties were many; disease and con-

* William Maginn, *Military Sketch Book II*, 157-8.
† Bowring, 105. Wellington himself recalled that in the last letter he received from the Mahratta chieftain, Holkar, the latter wrote, "My house is the saddle on the horse's back." Stanhope, 311.

tinuous bad weather making quagmires of roads and billets; Biscayan storms wrecking transports and holding up supplies from England; above all, constant trouble with his Spanish troops and their rulers, who failed to supply them with either rations or pay. But, despite lumbago—so severe at times that he could hardly rise from bed or table—he remained in good humour and high spirits. His active busy mind, his Advocate-General, Larpent, thought, was always looking to the future, and he had too much of everything and everybody always in his way to let it dwell long on his troubles.* At his headquarters, the same eyewitness noted, everyone under his system and all-seeing eye worked hard and did his business, attending to the substance and not the form. "The maxim of our Chief," he wrote, "is, 'Let everyone do his duty well, and never let me hear of any difficulties about anything', and that is all he cares about."† Occasionally even he was overwhelmed by the multiplicity of business; once when, after five days' absence at the front, he returned to be confronted by his Advocate-General with a vast bundle of evidences for courts martial, some running into eighty or ninety pages, he put his hands before his eyes and said, "Put them on that table, and do not say anything about them now or let me look at them at all."‡

More usually, between furious bouts of activity—rising in the small hours and riding like an express, when anything needed his special attention or investigation—he was in a pleasant and relaxed mood, and ready, when business was not too pressing, to talk with members of his military household about legal matters, the Poor Laws, the state of Ireland, or the Catholic question, as if he had nothing else upon his mind at all. When at dinner the Spanish general, Castanos, asked him how Madame Gazan—the wife of an elderly French general who had been captured in the rout at Vittoria—was faring in captivity, since she was accustomed to a considerable number of lovers, the British Commander-in-Chief, looking across the table rather drolly at his Advocate-General, remarked that she had been treated, he believed, very properly and respectfully.§

Despite the discomforts of an unhealthy, smelly Pyrenean village, oppressively in the clouds, swarming with fleas and flies,¶ and

---

* Larpent, II, 39, 48-9, 52, 56, 73.   † *Idem*, 212.   ‡ Larpent, II, 227, 234.
Larpent, II, 5-6, 7-8, 145-6, 171, 248-9, 70.
¶ "Writing all day with fleas up to the middle, from the floor and all over me during the

crowded with sutlers, mules, muleteers and ragged Spanish soldiers so quick-fingered that nothing was safe from their depredations from a horse to a biscuit, Wellington's headquarters, with its gay young A D Cs grouped around their adored chief, somehow remained a remarkably cheerful place. "Theirs," he recalled in after years, was "such an active and merry life, all in high spirits and confident of victory." His fame had now brought him a constant stream of visitors,* and he had taken to celebrating the anniversaries of his past victories by dinner-parties with tables set for thirty or forty, good claret, well-cooked food and regimental bands and, perhaps to round off the evening—for it was a sententious age much given to histrionics—a rendering of his favourite song, "*Ah Marmont, onde va Marmont?*" Larpent, who preferred the smaller parties when fewer grandees were present, less was drunk and Wellington talked more, feared that his victories would ruin him in wine and eating, since his calendar of feasts was now likely to become as full with red-letter days as the Romish one.

During September, while he was waiting for the surrender of Pamplona to release the besieging force and Hill's covering army for operations on the frontier, news arrived that Austria had joined with Russia and Prussia in war against France. Napoleon having refused to accept the Rhine frontier, the ten weeks' armistice had ended.

Without further delay, Wellington decided to invade France. Though nothing would induce him to risk his army needlessly, he knew that a concentric attack on Napoleon could only succeed if pressure was simultaneously exerted at every point on the circumference. He therefore prepared for an assault on Soult's mountain defences. He had to face the price of his earlier prudence: the time given to the Duke of Dalmatia to reorganise his troops and defence. For weeks that officer had been constructing an immense line of redoubts running southwards from the sea - a substitute for the offensive spirit his men had lost and a strange reversion for a Revolutionary general to eighteenth-century practice. But they were too extended; all but 8000 of his 47,000 infantry had to be

---

night; flies biting and whizzing all round me from daylight to dark. . . . They eat up all my wafers . . . and spot my letters all over if left one day on the table. . . . I am half eaten up by fleas." Larpent, II, 69-70, 120. *Idem*, 28, 46, 47, 50.

* "The curiosity is very great about Lord Wellington as one of the great men of the age." Larpent, II, 107; Arbuthnot, I, 212; Larpent, II, 4-5, 50-2, 181, 214.

strung along them, leaving too small a reserve to repel a concentrated attack. In this Soult was the victim of his country's political system; he dared not shorten his lines by a withdrawal because he knew that Napoleon would visit his wrath on any subordinate who retreated or gave up anything. He was also afraid that his troops, accustomed to living on the countryside, would provoke a rebellion in France by their excesses.

Wellington's plan was to attack the seaward end of the enemy line and, by pinching out a westward bulge on Spanish soil, capture the frontier town of Hendaye on the lower Bidassoa and advance his line to the Nivelle. By doing so he hoped to secure the little port of St Jean de Luz for his supply-ships. His objectives, as always, were carefully attuned to his resources – a fact which assisted his project, since Soult, who attributed to him the more daring designs he himself would have favoured, had concentrated his reserves at the other end of his line to guard against an enveloping drive from Roncesvalles to the sea. As a result, only 10,000 men were holding the mouth of the Bidassoa.

During the early days of October, Wellington unobtrusively moved unit after unit to his seaward flank until more than 25,000 were concentrated near the river. At dawn on the 7th the light companies of the 5th Division opened the battle of the Bidassoa by wading, armpit deep, across the estuary. They reached the northern bank before the French were even aware of what was happening. When Soult arrived from the other end of his long line, the British were firmly established inside the frontier. Farther inland the Light Division and Freire's Spaniards simultaneously assaulted the mountain bastion of the Grande Rhune. By the evening of the next day all Wellington's objectives had been gained, and the French right was in retreat to the Nivelle. The operation, giving him possession of a whole chain of carefully prepared entrenchments,* had cost less than 1500 casualties.

Though the French had shown little of their old spirit and had abandoned the strongest positions as soon as their flanks were turned, Wellington again made no pursuit. He was still waiting for more certain news from Germany and for the fall of Pamplona to release

---

* "We found the soldiers' huts very comfortable; they were built of trees and furze and formed squares and streets, which had names placarded up such as Rue de Paris, Rue de Versailles, etc." Gronow, I, 4; Blakiston, 279-84; Weller, 313-18.

more troops. He contented himself, therefore, with consolidating the rocky ledge of France he had won and preparing for the next move.

Looking down from the Pyrenean heights in those days of waiting, the way ahead – the final straight of the long race begun twenty years before – was already visible to the British. To the right ran a great wall of peaks stretching into the remote distance towards the Mediterranean: to the left the Bay of Biscay, with the warships of the Royal Navy perpetually on the move. In front lay France. "From these stupendous mountains," wrote Simmons of the Rifles, "we had a most commanding view of a vast extent of highly cultivated French territory, innumerable villages, and the port and town of St Jean de Luz. We could also see our cruisers sailing about near the French coast which gave an additional interest to the view before us. . . . One morning one of our ships was observed to be chasing a brig of war and got between her and the shore. As the boats from the English went to board her, the Frenchman got into theirs and made for the shore. A short time after she was one mass of fire and blew up. It was a beautiful morning and some thousands of veteran Englishmen, having a bird's-eye view of the whole affair, took a lively interest in the manner our brave tars performed their duty."

Had the vision of the watching soldiers been able to penetrate the October horizon, they would have seen beyond the Biscay bay the sails of British battleships in the swell off Brest and Lorient; the transports bearing men and supplies to feed the battlefields; the ocean merchantmen coming and going with the tribute of trade which sustained their country's alliances; the smoking chimneys of the North Country towns and Midland forges; the tax-collectors gathering their harvest and the moneylenders at their ledgers; the politicians debating in the forum at Westminster; the semaphore watchers on the Admiralty roof gazing across the river to the wooded Surrey heights. And far away in the north-east beyond the Alps they might have seen, amid the wooded folds of great rivers serpentining across the Saxon plains, the steely glint of marching armies set in motion by British faith and fortitude and paid by British gold, as they converged from north and east and south on the city of Leipzig, where Napoleon, clinging to his conquests, stood at bay with an army of veteran marshals and young, sickly conscripts.

For on October 16th 1813, three hundred thousand Russians,

Austrians, Prussians and Swedes, with more than 1300 guns, closed
in on a hundred and ninety thousand Frenchmen, Italians and Saxons
under the man who for the past seventeen years had been thought of
as invincible and the greatest captain of all time. Three days later
the battle of Leipzig ended with the desertion of Napoleon's last
German allies and the utter rout of his army, scarcely a third of it
escaping. Britain's part in the victory was confined to the doings
of a single battery of Congreve rockets, commanded by a young
officer who a generation later was to fall fighting against his country's Russian allies. Yet, though its scale made the battles of the
Peninsular War seem insignificant, it was the redcoated watchers
on the Pyrenean heights and their sea-going comrades in the Bay
who had laid its foundations.

Three weeks later, as the first authentic news of Leipzig chilled
the hearts of France's southern army, the British stormed the heights
of the Nivelle and broke into the Gascony plain. Pamplona, reduced
to its last rat, had surrendered at the end of October; early in November a spell of cold and storm was succeeded by brilliant sunshine.
The French, brought by conscript drafts up to 62,000 men, were
holding the hilly south bank of the Nivelle, their redoubts and
entrenchments bristling with guns. Confident in this wall of rock
and iron, which was reputed as strong as the Lines of Torres Vedras,
Soult boasted that it would cost the attackers a third of their force to
dislodge him. But Wellington, unbending over the port, told his
generals that he meant to prod the fat Marshal till he came to terms.*
"Those fellows think themselves invulnerable," he remarked, "but
I will beat them out with ease."

Once again the French were holding lines longer than they
could man, and the British commander could bring a force against
any point greater than they could concentrate to meet it. And he
had an instrument with which to do so which, as he said, could go
anywhere and do anything: "the finest army," in the words of one
of its officers, "in better order, better discipline, in better health
and more effective than any British one on the Continent ever was
before." On November 10th, a month after the battle of the Bidassoa,
he put it to the test as "the two gamecocks of England and France"
grappled all day on the hills to the south of the Nivelle. The British
columns, which had moved up to their stations overnight, waded

* *Blackwood's*, December 1946. "A Gallant Pack," by Peter Carew. No. 1574, Vol. 260,

the river in the half-light of dawn and, scaling the heights, broke through the redoubts of Soult's centre like a screen of reeds. "Nor did we ever meet a check," wrote Harry Smith, "but carried the enemy's work by one fell swoop of irresistible victory." There is a lyrical quality in all the eye witness accounts of that day; in no engagement of the war was the supremacy of Wellington's army shown more clearly than in that of the Nivelle. "The fierce and continued charge of the British was irresistible," recalled one who, wounded in the heather, watched his comrades storm the incredible crags of the Petite Rhune; "onwards they bore nor stopped to breathe, rushing forward through glen, dale and forest. . . . The star of three united nations shone victorious on the summits of the lofty Pyrenees, gilding the tall pines which capped their heads and foreboding downfall to Imperial France."* By sundown the British spearheads were many miles behind the French lines, pressing after the fugitives with a running fire till nature could do no more, when the tired men stretched their limbs on the sod, pulled out their captured rations of cheese and onions and went to roost.

Once the chain of Soult's line was broken, no link could hold. Units in almost impregnable fortresses, finding themselves surrounded, surrendered without a shot; others, fearful for their flanks, fell back leaving their comrades isolated. The morale of France's southern army could no longer withstand the attack of the British infantry.† Only the shortness of the November day saved Soult's right between the hills and the sea. It fled from encirclement towards Bayonne, leaving the port of St Jean de Luz, over fifty guns and 1200 prisoners in the attackers' hands. The latter's casualties, which Soult had expected to number 25,000, were less than half the defenders."

*   *   *

The tidings of these victories set the hearts of the British people rocketing. From the Prince Regent, who hugged the Speaker when he announced the news of Sorauren, to the smock-frocks around the ale-house fire, they were kept that winter in a state of continuous excitement. The guns sounded for triumphs in France, Germany and

* Blakeney, 320-3. See also Weller, 319-25; Bell, I, 119-25; Granville, II, 471-8; Smith, I, 145-6; Simmons, 321-5; Larpent, II, 155-7; Smith, I, 125-6, 142-54; MS. *Diary of Robert Blak.*, 5-6; Schaumann, 390-4; William Napier, I, 132; Kincaid, 272.

† "They always met us like lions, but in the end it was like hares." Bell, I, 151.

Italy; day after day the clanging bells of the mails, as they dashed by in a bower of laurel branches, set country folk along the highways cheering. On October 18th a chaise-and-four with a flag waving from the window dashed on to the Horse Guards Parade with the news of Wellington's crossing of the Bidassoa; a fortnight later the Tower salvoes proclaimed the victory of Leipzig. Boney, men told one another, was back on the Rhine; his routed army, dripping with typhus, was crawling like a dying beast from the Europe it had ravaged. On November 4th the Allied Sovereigns entered Frankfurt; a few days later German troops reached the Rhine. Even the Dutch, who had placidly borne the conqueror's yoke for twenty years, caught the infection and drove the feeble French garrisons from their cities. A Prussian army stormed Arnhem, liberating Cossacks clattered over the cobbles of Amsterdam, and the Guards, repeating their initiating act of twenty-one years earlier, marched through cheering streets to embark for Holland.

Yet the war was not over. Napoleon was still set on conquest. When on the day before the battle of the Nivelle the Allied Sovereigns from Frankfurt offered him the "natural frontiers" of Rhine, Alps, Pyrenees, he refused to consider such terms. "The word peace is ever in my ears," he told his Council of State, "when all around should echo with the cry. War! Peace! No peace till Munich is in flames!" The Corps Législatif, who petitioned him to declare that he was only fighting for the independence of France, were denounced as traitors in the pay of England. Regardless of the cost, the Emperor meant to win back all he had lost. He might lose his throne, he assured Metternich, but he would bury the world in its ruins.

Everything, therefore, depended on the hunters holding together. In their failure to do so, as Napoleon knew, lay his one hope. Three times a European Coalition had dissolved before him; once again divisions in the victors' councils might save him. It was England who cemented Europe's wavering purpose. She was already underwriting the Grand Alliance by maintaining nearly a quarter of a million Russian, Austrian and Prussian troops. She now reminded those who were taking her subsidies of the purpose for which they had been granted. England would consent to no peace that did not give solid securities for a permanent settlement. Though prepared for the sake of one to surrender the greater part of her colonial conquests, she demanded the independence of Holland, Spain, and

379

Portugal, the demilitarisation of Antwerp and the mouth of the Scheldt, and the freedom of the seas. To ensure these the Foreign Secretary, in the last week of the year, set out for Allied headquarters in southern Germany.

Long before Lord Castlereagh, travelling across a Continent gripped by frost, reached his destination, Wellington had resumed his advance. The Pyrenean roads were sodden with rain, but on December 9th, having learnt of Napoleon's losses at Leipzig, he struck once more. To break out of the restricted triangle between the mountains and the Lower Adour and Nive, he threw four of his eight divisions under Hill across the latter. It was a daring move, for until the flooded river could be bridged, it enabled Soult, whose force was concentrated round Bayonne, to hit back with superior numbers at either half of the British army. Yet Wellington, who never took risks without weighing them, felt complete confidence in his men's ability to beat off any assault the French might make.

The event proved him right. With nearly 50,000 troops Soult attacked, first Hope's 30,000 between the sea and the Nive on December 10th and 11th, and then Hill's 14,000 on the right bank of the Nive at St Pierre on the 13th. He was held in both cases until the arrival of Wellington's reserves. In the second battle the British were nearly overwhelmed; one nervous colonel, fresh from England, withdrew his indignant men from the slaughter: another - a braggart - was found behind the lines attending to the wounded. But the rank and file and rosy-faced " Farmer" Hill, their commander, rose gloriously to the occasion; it was almost the only time the latter had ever been heard to swear. For three hours the "thin red line of old bricks" stood between the cheering French columns and a victory which seemed at last within their grasp; "dead or alive," cried Colonel Brown of the Gloucesters, "we must hold our ground." And they did. The field was so thickly strewn with corpses that Wellington said afterwards that he had never seen its like. General William Stewart of Albuera fame - " auld grog Willie," as the men called him - had every member of his staff struck down: "a shell, sir, very animating!" he remarked as one exploded at his feet, and went on with his conversation. The battle ended with a counter-attack by the 92nd Highlanders, who went into the fight with tossing plumes and a piper with a broken leg playing "Hey! Johnny Cope." "This," wrote Bell, recalling the blue bonnets' advance, "was to understand war." As the French began to stream back to Bayonne, the victors threw up their caps and gave "a long, thrilling cheer."*

Having established himself on the east bank of the Nive, a new prospect opened before Wellington. By remaining in his intrenched camp at Bayonne, the enemy could still bar his road to Bordeaux and the north, but only at the expense of leaving unguarded a broad and fertile expanse of France stretching eastwards for more than two hundred miles. On this Soult depended not only for his supplies— for the country north of Bayonne was mainly sand and pines—but for his communications with Suchet, who was still trying to hold the Catalonian fortresses.

Before he could advance Wellington had to win a victory of another kind over his own army. For, if it was to retain numerical superiority in the field, he could spare no troops to hold down territory in his rear. While the midwinter rains temporarily bogged down the armies, he devoted himself to winning the goodwill of the civilian population. In this he was helped by his opponents who, after twenty years of pillage, rape and arson abroad, could not deny themselves these pleasures in their homeland. This had the effect of making the invaders appear as liberators instead of conquerors. There was a little difficulty at first in imposing this conception on them; one private, tried and hanged for a rape, explained that, as he was now in France, he thought it must be in order. But realising what a hornets' nest would be aroused if he loosed an undisciplined army on a land where, after twenty years of conscription, every civilian was a trained soldier, the British Commander-in-Chief was inexorable in punishing every case of plunder and outrage. "Lord Wellington," wrote his Advocate-General, "never attends to individual hardships but to the general good," and against all offences against person or property he was merciless, disciplining the gaolbirds in his army† by sending a strong force of military

---

* Bell, I, 126-41; Gomm, 331; Larpent, II, 223; Gronow, I, 19-21; Fortescue, IX, 469-72; Oman, VII, 223-81; Weller, 325-41; Blakiston, II, 306-17.

† There were many. When, having occasion to coin money for the occupied territories, Wellington called for a return of professional forgers, he was supplied with enough to man a mint. Oman, VII, 289. See also *Idem*, VII, 215-19; Weller, 326-7; *Dispatches*, XI, 288-9, 296, 306; Larpent, II, 5, 43, 106-7, 161, 164-5, 167, 226, 240; III, 36, 68; Gronow, I, 12-13; Bell, I, 131-3, 153; Smith, I, 150; Simmons, 329; Bessborough, 237-8; George Napier, 251-2; Fortescue, IX, 443; Schaumann, 394-5; Brett-James, 270.

police up and down the columns with orders to string up on the spot every man found pilfering. "I do not care," he wrote, "whether I command a large or a small army; but large or small, I will be obeyed and I will not suffer pillage."

For this reason, though it meant reducing his army from more than 100,000 men to little more than 60,000, he sent back to their native land all but 4000 of his Spanish troops, and this despite the fact that, if he failed to prevent a junction between Soult in south-western France and Suchet in Catalonia, he would be heavily outnumbered. But though the Spaniards had fought with great gallantry defending the San Marcial ridge above the Bidassoa in October, their general state of indiscipline was such that, except for a small force under General Morillo, it was impossible either to rely on them or control them. "Our success and everything depends upon our moderation and justice," Wellington wrote to the Secretary of State justifying his self-denying action, "and upon the good discipline of our troops. I despair of the Spaniards. They are in so miserable a state that it is really hardly fair to expect that they will refrain from plundering a beautiful country into which they enter as conquerors, particularly adverting to the miseries which their own country has suffered from its invaders. Without any pay and food, they must plunder, and if they plunder, they will ruin us all."[*]

Wellington's manner of making war much astonished the French. They could scarcely believe their eyes; an innkeeper veteran of Napoleon's Italian campaign was speechless when Brigadier Barnard of the Light Division asked him how much he owed for his dinner. Having long repudiated the idea of gentility, the people of south-western France found themselves quartering an army of gentlemen. It was worth a dozen victories to the Allies. The British Commander-in-Chief even invited the *maires* of the towns where he stayed to his table: a thing undreamt of in a French Revolutionary general. Those who had fled came flocking back to their homes: the British, it was said, only waged war against men with arms in their hands. What was more, they paid for all they needed. Before long the inhabitants were coining money: fowls were selling at 14s apiece and turkeys at 30s. The Commissariat was inundated with cattle, grain and fodder. Even bankers offered the British cash and credit.

* To Lord Bathurst, November 21st 1813; Weller, II, 308-11, 326-7; Larpent, II, 120, 127-8, 160, 166-7, 240, 270, 273, 289, 305.

If this, wrote an English officer, was what making war in an enemy country was like, he never wished to campaign in a friendly one again. This wise humanity increased the size of Wellington's striking force by at least two divisions. Lines-of-communication troops were rendered needless. Men and supplies could travel about the country unescorted, while the wounded could be billeted and nursed in French households. In vain Soult circulated proclamations exhorting the people to raise partisan bands; they declined to do anything so unprofitable. The only partisans were disgruntled conscripts who took to the hills and fought, not the British, but the Emperor's recruiting officers. Instead, the people of Aquitaine looked on their nice, orderly conquerors as harbingers of peace and prosperity who had come to put an end to conscriptions and war taxes. Some even expressed a wish to be governed by them permanently.*

* * *

By the second week in January 1814, Wellington knew that his fears of a premature peace were groundless and that the Austrians, Russians and Prussians had crossed the Rhine and invaded France. He did not approve of their dispersed line of advance in Napoleon's presence - a system, he said, on which he would not have marched a corporal's guard; his own advice would have been to "run in upon him" by a concentrated drive on Paris. None the less, he was resolved to give them what support he could, and on February 12th, after a week's sunshine had dried the roads, he resumed his offensive. Napoleon had drawn off 14,000 of Soult's men for his own campaign in the north, so partly offsetting the Spanish divisions which had had to be left behind on the frontier. As usual, the Marshal, facing south across the Adour and digging himself in, had taken up too wide a front. This gave Wellington the initiative. Dividing his army, he left 30,000 men under Sir John Hope in front of Bayonne and struck eastwards into the interior with the remaining 45,500. By doing so he caused the defensive-minded Soult to sup-

* Larpent, III, 42. See also *idem*, II, 181, 211, 221-2, 231; III, 30, 35, 44, 76-7, 90-1; George Napier, 241-2; Simmons, 342; Lynedoch, 610-11; Oman, VII, 286, 291-2, 390; Fortescue, X, 1819; Smith, I, 166; Bell, I, 150-1; Gronow, I, 12; Simmons, 335; Schaumann, 402; Bessborough, 237-8.

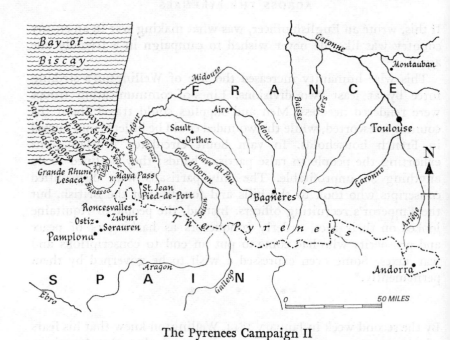

The Pyrenees Campaign II

pose that the line of the Adour was about to be attacked at its eastern end and to draw away his reserves from Bayonne.

Instead, however, of turning north against the line of the Adour, Wellington continued his eastward march. The country east of the Nive was an open plateau, crossed by five swift Pyrenean rivers – Joyeuse, Bidouze, Saison, Gave d'Oloron and Gave de Pau – running from south to north and joining the Adour in its long westward reach above Bayonne. By using his slight superiority in numbers to maintain a strong flanking column under Hill to the south, Wellington turned the defence lines of each river without a fight and compelled the French to fall back ever farther eastwards. As was his wont, he guarded against a counter-blow by keeping a strong reserve under his own command behind his marching columns. Then, having by February 19th driven Soult's field army as far east as the Gave d'Oloron, forty miles from Bayonne, he halted and, while his opponent tried to anticipate his next move, proceeded to do the one thing he was not expecting. On the 23rd, instead of attempting to cross the Adour above Bayonne, he threw

Hope's 18,000 men across it at its broadest point between the fortress and the sea. Wellington had returned to St Jean de Luz on the 19th to supervise this delicate operation. But the gunboats which were to have bridged the estuary being delayed by a Biscay gale, he had been forced to return to his main army on the Gave d'Oloron, leaving the task to Sir John Hope. Undeterred by the continuance of the gale and the non-appearance of the flotilla, this gallant Scotsman succeeded on the morning of the 23rd in shipping five companies of the Guards and two of the 60th in rowing boats to the north bank of the Adour. Here they maintained their position under the noses of 14,000 Frenchmen. In this feat they received unexpected help from a battery of the new Congreve rockets which, at the instance of the Prince Regent, had arrived from England, and about which, on account of their erratic aim, both Wellington and the Army had been very scornful.* The frightful noise they made and their capacity for setting things on fire kept the French from investigating the crossing too closely. By the evening of the 24th, when the British naval vessels at last forced the bar and came up the river, Hope had contrived to get the bulk of the Guards Division across. By the 26th the bridge of boats was complete and 15,000 British troops were beyond the Adour encircling Bayonne and its garrison.

On the day the fortress was invested - February 27th - Wellington, sixty miles away, struck at Soult on the Gave de Pau, the last river line that barred his advance into the central plain of southern France. Having been driven from the Gave d'Oloron by yet another march of Hill's flanking column, the Marshal had concentrated 36,000 men to dispute the crossing at Orthez. Though the attacking force only numbered 7000 more, Wellington again divided it, sending two of his seven divisions to cross the river above the town and threaten the French line of retreat. Since his victories on the Nive he no longer feared Soult's counter-attacks. He knew that the latter lacked resolution and his men fighting spirit: he knew, too, of what his own army was capable.

The battle took place, not in front of the town, where the river was impassable, but to the west of it, where the British left wing under Beresford had crossed on the previous day while the French

* "I don't want to set fire to any town and I don't know any other use of rockets." Wellington's *Dispatches*. See also Larpent, II, 256-8; Fortescue, IX, 485.

cavalry, expecting a repetition of Hill's out-flanking movement, had been watching the fords on the other side of Orthez. Soult's position was one of great natural strength, not dissimilar to those from which Wellington had repulsed so many attacks in the past. But, instead of, like the latter, keeping a strong reserve in hand and using it for counter-blows, he hoarded it to cover a withdrawal. Retreat from the start was his dominating idea. Throughout the six hours' fight the initiative remained with the British, who, attacking with inferior numbers, even after their first assault had failed, were able to renew it elsewhere without interference. As so often before, when the battle hung in the balance, a modification by Wellington of his flexible dispositions proved decisive. The day's crowning achievement was an attack by the 1st battalion of the 52nd Light Infantry, which at a critical moment deployed and, supported by a cloud of sharpshooters, drove with review precision up a bullet-swept height; Harry Smith thought it the most majestic advance he had ever seen.

The battle ended, as Wellington had reckoned when he sent Hill's two divisions on a flanking march against Soult's communications,* with the French scurrying to the bridge of Sault, ten miles to the north-east. Had the country been favourable for cavalry the French might have suffered a major disaster. As it was, their losses were over 4000, including 1350 prisoners: casualties almost double those of the attackers. During their retreat they lost as many more from desertion.

While he was re-aligning his troops after the repulse of his first attack—"walking his horse quietly and chatting with some of his staff just as if nothing of consequence was going on"—Wellington was struck by a spent bullet which drove his sword-hilt into his thigh, temporarily unhorsing him and much alarming his entourage; as one of them put it, "all our prospects here would vanish with that man." One of his favourite aides-de-camp, Lord March, son of his old chief, the Duke of Richmond, had been dangerously wounded by his side - it was feared at the time fatally. On the second night after the battle, despite the pain he was in,

* "The cry, 'We are cut off, the enemy is across the road,' began to be heard in our ranks!" Lapene, 264. See also Fortescue, IX, 498-514; Oman, VII, 282, 343-75; Weller, 345-50; Beatson, *Orthez Campaign*; Larpent, III, 37; Smith, I, 163-5; Bell, I, 147-8; Foy, 238-42; *Narrative of a Soldier*; Brown, 259-60; Seaton, 201-2; Cooper, 110-11; Blakiston, II, 327-30; Colonel A. Burne, *The Enigma of Toulouse* (*Army Quarterly*, January 1927).

the Commander-in-Chief rode back alone to the hospital at St Sever, where the young man was lying. "About the middle of the night," George Napier* of the 52nd recorded, "as Dr Hare was sitting dozing in a chair opposite Lord March's bed, who had fallen asleep, the door of the room gently opened and a figure in a white cloak and military hat walked up to the bed, drew the curtains quietly aside, looked steadily for a few seconds on the pale countenance before him, then leaned over, stooped his head and pressed his lips on the forehead of Lord March, heaved a deep sigh and turned to leave the room. When the doctor, who had anxiously watched every movement, beheld the countenance of *Wellington*, his cheeks were wet with tears."

* * *

During February, while Wellington, having crossed the Adour and invested Bayonne, was advancing eastwards towards the central plain of southern France, the war in the north had taken a dramatic and unexpected turn. At the beginning of the month, having over-run more than a third of France, the Allies were moving on Paris in two great armies, 60,000 Prussians and Russians under Blücher in the Marne valley and 100,000 Austrians and Russians under Prince Schwarzenberg along the Seine, while to the north a third army under Bernadotte—the renegade French Marshal who had become Crown Prince of Sweden—having overrun Flanders, had occupied Laon, Rheims and Soissons. Antwerp was closely besieged and a British force under Sir Thomas Graham was investing Bergen-op-Zoom, while in Germany the last surviving French garrisons, left far behind by the tide of war, faced starvation. The morale of Napoleon's troops, outnumbered by three to one, was visibly disintegrating, and hordes of deserters were pouring towards a silent and appalled Paris, while Cossack patrols, spreading far across the country, had penetrated as far as Orleans and had even threatened the imperial palace at Fontainebleau.

Yet Napoleon's genius never shone more brightly than at that moment. As Wellington—who gave it as his considered opinion that he could hardly conceive of anything greater than Napoleon

* Afterward General Sir George Napier. He had lost an arm leading the storming party at Ciudad Rodrigo. George Napier, 246-7; Muriel Wellesley, 300-1.

at the head of a French army—once said of him, there never was a general in whose presence it was more dangerous to make a false step. Field-Marshal Blücher, in his zeal to be the first to reach Paris, did so, allowing his army to become dangerously strung out. Taking advantage of the leisurely pace of the Austrian army down the Seine valley, the French Emperor drove his famished and exhausted men northwards and unexpectedly appeared at Champaubert on the morning of February 10th. Here, after annihilating a Russian division, he cut across Blücher's line of march; then turning westwards towards the head of his column, defeated another of his corps commanders at Montmirail on the 11th, another at Chateau-Thierry on the 12th, and Blücher himself at Vauchamps on the 14th. In four swift battles which seemed to reach back across the years to Rivoli, in every one of which he brought superior numbers against the enemy's isolated columns, he inflicted 20,000 casualties and took fifty guns. Then, having flung back Blücher towards Chalons, he hurried back to the Seine where Schwarzenberg's army had driven to within fifty miles of Paris. At Nangis on the 17th and Montereau on the 18th he inflicted a further 5000 casualties on the leading German and Russian corps. Appalled by the successive tidings of disaster, the Austrian Commander-in-Chief ordered a general retreat. By the 21st the Allies were back at Troyes; three days later, after a council of war, they began to retire - like Brunswick's army twenty-two years before - towards the Vosges. Against all probability Napoleon had saved his capital. His decision, speed and the legend of his name had snatched victory from defeat. He had beaten the Austrians, Prussians and Russians - three different armies - always with the same troops, and as Wellington commented: "I have had experience enough to know how very exact a man must be in his calculations and how very skilful in his manoeuvres to be able to do that."*

The Coalition was saved by Castlereagh's firmness from the folly and division which had destroyed its predecessors. Pitt's successor reminded his allies of their overwhelming superiority in numbers; even, after their losses of the past fortnight, they commanded within or near the borders of France, more than half a million men. He was supported by Blücher who, despite his recent drubbing, was all for trying again and marching on Paris. On March 1st, after Napoleon, threatening to carry the war to Munich, had rejected terms which

* Stanhope, 12. See also *Idem*, 8-9, 30, 81.

would have given him the frontiers France had enjoyed under her
ancient kings, the massive Allied advance on the French capital was
resumed.

*   *   *

Meanwhile, Wellington, unaware of what was happening in the
north, was exploiting his victory. The French rearguard made a
show of standing at Aire on March 2nd but disintegrated when
attacked. " It was all in vain," wrote Bell of the 34th, " the blood of the
old bricks was up and we drove them into and right through the
town." A few nights later he slept in a bedroom, with damask drap-
ery, mirrors and polished furniture; it was the first time he had
been in a bed since the occupation of Madrid two summers before.
The campaign had suddenly become a picnic, with fowls to roast at
the camp-fires, wine at fifteen *sous* a bottle, and riflemen slicing
slabs of bacon on their bread like English haymakers.*

By his retreat eastwards Soult left the road to the north open.
More than a hundred miles up the Atlantic coast from besieged
Bayonne lay the great city of Bordeaux, the third in France and
the capital of Gascony. While his field army halted its eastward
march to consolidate its communications, the British Commander-
in-Chief extemporised a flying force under Beresford to seize the
city and secure the Gironde estuary for his transports. Reports had
reached him that its merchants, ruined by the blockade, were talking
of a Bourbon restoration, and, though scrupulously anxious not to
encourage any Frenchman to a step which might prove fatal in the
event of an Allied peace with Napoleon, he could not afford to ignore
a civil movement so favourable to his operations. On March 12th
Beresford reached Bordeaux with two regiments of hussars. The
mayor met him at the gates and, tearing off his tricolour scarf,
trampled it in the mud with cries of "*A bas les aigles!*" " *Vivent les
Bourbons!*" Subsequently, ignoring the delicate negotiations at
Chaumont, he proclaimed, to Wellington's embarrassment and
indignation, that he had been authorised by the Allies to conduct
the administration of the city in King Louis's name.

For under its own momentum the war was gathering speed at a

* Bell, I, 151-8; Smith, I, 175; Larpent, III, 32-3, 46, 75, 87-9; Gronow, I, 24-5; Pellot,
Guerre des Pyrénées. cit. Alison, XIII, 33.

rate transcending sober political calculations. Faced by the recoil upon itself of the Revolutionary maxim of making war support war, and bled white by successive conscriptions and taxations, Napoleonic France was disintegrating. Her people could not take the medicine they had so often inflicted on others. Everywhere, save in her Emperor's immediate presence, her soldiers were on the run, watched by apathetic civilians who made no response to his proclamations enjoining them to emulate the Spanish guerrilleros and fall on the invaders' rear. The only result of his injunctions in the south was the formation of local guards to protect villages from the depredations of these hypothetical partisans. On March 20th, two days after Wellington resumed his eastward advance against Toulouse, Lyons, the second city of France, fell to an Austrian column advancing from the Jura while the French, unsupported by the countryside, withdrew hastily before it.

As the British swept forward, in sunshine at last, after Soult's scarecrow army, across a flat, water-logged meadow-country of orchards, vineyards and trout-streams, the people flocked out of their houses to greet them. At Bagnères Spa, even before the first redcoat appeared, the National Guard turned out to present arms to a party of English civilians. When Wellington reached the outskirts of Toulouse on March 26th, he had less than a battalion guarding the two hundred miles that separated him from his ships in the Bay of Biscay. The reinforcements which should have reached him from England had been deflected by the politicians, who, in their excitement at the news from the Continent, had forgotten their hard-earned lessons and sent every available man to Holland to enable Graham to capture Bergen-op-Zoom and Antwerp—places which were bound to fall in any case if the French armies were defeated in the field. But, since Wellington's discipline enabled him to dispense with lines-of-communication troops, it mattered little, except to Graham's unfortunate soldiers who were repelled from Bergen with heavy loss on March 8th.

Meanwhile Napoleon had made his last throw and lost. As Wellington had always said, he lacked the patience for defensive operations. His army was by now a horde of famished desperadoes in ragged greatcoats and bare feet, its guns and wagons worn out, its units inextricably confused. More than 70,000 veterans who might have brought its depleted ranks up to strength were locked up in fortresses beyond the Rhine which Napoleon, in his insane desire to retain the unretainable, had refused to relinquish. Even Blücher's army was now twice the size of his own. And along the Seine valley, the Austrian host, stirred into activity by the expostulations of Castlereagh, was moving once more on Paris. On March 20th Napoleon, marching in haste to intercept it, fell on its flank at Arcis-sur-Aube and was again repulsed. Henceforward, while it pursued its way towards the capital, he was left to roam, furious but impotent, across its lines of communication with an army of ghosts; still sending hourly messages to Paris and his Marshals to resist, still summoning to his aid armies that had ceased to exist, still breathing threats of vengeance against Rhineland, Danube and Vistula. He was now no more interested in what was arithmetically possible than he had formerly been in what was morally so.

On March 28th, ignoring his futile demonstrations, the two main Allied armies joined hands at Meaux, less than thirty miles from Paris. Two days later, while Napoleon, with his men dropping in hundreds by the roadside, desperately marched by way of Fontaine-bleau to rescue his capital, 180,000 invaders stormed its northern heights. That afternoon, with the Allied artillery commanding its streets, Paris surrendered.

But the war was not quite over. Six hundred miles away to the south, on the Languedoc plain, the British army was still fighting. Its commander did not yet know that Napoleon had abdicated, though he had learnt of the occupation of Paris. Soult, whose love of digging-in had become an obsession, had got his troops behind the walls of a fortified city with a flooded river between them and the British, and, in a dissolving world, it seemed as safe a place as any he could hope to find. Wellington would have preferred to have advanced northwards from Bordeaux through the traditionally royalist Bocage to the Loire, so carrying the war which he had begun on the circumference of Napoleon's empire to its heart. By doing so and making Nantes his base, he would have drawn, as in his march to the Bay of Biscay in the previous summer, towards his sea-borne supplies.* But with the reinforcements he should have received sent by the Cabinet to besiege fortresses in Holland, he had not the men both to advance towards the Loire and contain Soult in the east. The latter might at any time be joined by Suchet who,

* See his conversation in Stanhope, 21.

at last, was withdrawing from Catalonia; and, though the two Marshals hated each other, they would together constitute a formidable force.

As Wellington also feared that Napoleon might try to prolong the war by marching south to join his last two armies, and, as the capture of Toulouse might precipitate a royalist rising throughout Languedoc, he resolved to drive Soult out of the town. It involved a grave risk, for he was in an enemy country far from his base, only slightly superior in numbers, and without any siege-train. Before he could even reach the city and attack its eastern and only superable side, he had to move the bulk of his troops across the Garonne – swollen by floods to a width of over 500 feet. "How the devil," asked the cheery Patlanders, "are we to get over that big strame of a river or leather them vagabones out o' that!"

It proved an operation of great difficulty. The troops had to trudge barefooted through knee-deep clay; at one point on the road six oxen and four horses, in addition to its own six mules, had to be fastened to Wellington's travelling carriage to drag it through the quagmires. The first attempt to cross the river below Toulouse failed owing to the inadequacy of the pontoon bridge; a second, made by Hill's corps a mile lower down, was abandoned owing to the state of the roads. But Wellington, with the resilience that always came to his aid when thwarted, chose a new crossing-place above the town, withdrew Hill's troops, and on the stormy night of April 4th renewed his attempt. While the operation was only half completed the bridge was broken by floods, and for three days 18,000 British troops under Beresford were isolated and exposed to the attack of more than double their numbers. Yet Soult refused to attack. "You do not know what stuff two British divisions are made of," he is reported to have said; "they would not be conquered so long as there was a man left to stand." Instead, he continued to dig himself in.

On three sides, where the walls were surrounded by water defences, Toulouse was impregnable. Its weakness lay in a 600-foot ridge named Mont Rave to the east from which a besieger's artillery could dominate the city. It was this that Soult had been so busy fortifying. Here, behind his field-works, he had concentrated nearly half his 42,000 troops on a two and a half-mile front, with a strong reserve behind. As Toulouse was the chief magazine of southern France, he had been able to re-equip them with plentiful arms and ammunition. In artillery he out-gunned the British - a fortnight's march from their nearest base - by two to one. Thus, with 49,000 troops - only 7000 more than the defenders - Wellington had to attack a fortified city from the side farthest from his communications and with a flooded river dividing his army. His own headquarters at Grenade were guarded by less than twenty men with a French garrison at Montauban only an hour's ride away.

Yet he never hesitated. His moral ascendancy over the enemy was now complete. As one of his officers put it, six years of almost uninterrupted success had engrafted a seasoned confidence into his soldiers that made them invincible. Leaving sufficient forces to contain the defenders round the city's circumference and to act as a reserve, Wellington at dawn on April 10th - Easter Day - moved up two British and two Spanish divisions against the eastern heights. To reach their assault stations at the south end of the ridge the British had to march, or rather flounder, through three miles of swamp under heavy fire from Mont Rave, closely crossing the enemy's front with an unfordable river behind them. There was only one thing to prevent Soult descending from the hill to destroy them: his fear, founded on repeated experience, of what would happen if he did.

Before Beresford's British divisions could deploy, the Spaniards, who had begged to be allowed to share in the glory of the day, rashly attempted to storm the northern end of the ridge without waiting for orders. During the ensuing rout, as Wellington hastily plugged the gap in his line with the Light Division he remarked that he had never before seen ten thousand men running a race. "There they go," he said, "off to Spain, by God!"* Their absence till they could be re-formed for another attack gave Soult two hours to complete his preparations for dealing with the British, who were still plodding across his front through the marshes. Bringing up his reserve to the south end of the ridge, he concealed it in almost Wellingtonian fashion behind the skyline, ready to fall on Cole's 4th Division - the men of Albuera - as they came toiling in

* Blakiston, II, 361. On the following day, passing the spot, he called out to Colonel Colborne of the 52nd, "Well, Colborne, did you ever see anything like that?" To which he replied, "Oh, I don't know. They ran to the bridge I believe." To this came the retort, "to the bridge, indeed. To the Pyrenees! I dare say they are all back in Spain by this time." Booth, 48.

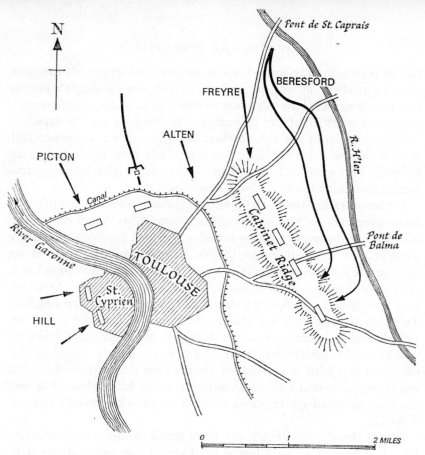

The Battle of Toulouse

a thin, extended line up the slope. But instead of driving them in
rout down the hill, Soult's charging columns were stopped dead
in their course. Closing their ranks and forming square on either
flank, against cavalry the English regiments, though taken by surprise, riddled their assailants with volley after volley. The French divisional commander fell pierced by three bullets; his men, as the redcoats resumed their advance, fled up the hill. Their panic spread to the
garrison of the Sypière redoubt on the summit. Within a few minutes
the British were in possession of the southern crest of the ridge.

During the remainder of the day Beresford's two divisions,
exploiting their success, fought their way northwards along the
ridge, enfilading successive redoubts. Though the French fought
fiercely back, repeatedly counter-attacking, the issue was never in
doubt. The battle ended with a magnificent charge by General

394

Pack's 42nd and 79th Highlanders with the 91st in support. By five o'clock, twelve hours after the first shot, the whole ridge was in British hands. Though the guns had still to be brought up, Toulouse was at Wellington's mercy. Of the attackers 4568 had fallen, to the French 3236, the Black Watch alone losing more than half and the Camerons nearly half their strength. Four hundred of the casualties were needlessly contributed by Picton, who, haunted by the memories of his achievement at Badajoz, disobeyed his orders and converted a sham diversion against the city's water defences into a real attack.*

On the following evening Soult began the evacuation of the city, withdrawing southwards, to the immense relief of its inhabitants, to join Suchet along the only road remaining open. He left behind 1600 wounded and half his guns. Next day Wellington entered amid scenes of, to him, rather distasteful jubilation. When at dinner the leading royalists of the place hailed him as the Liberator of Spain, France and Europe, he bowed shortly and called for coffee. His troops, on the other hand, were charmed with their reception as they marched in their tattered coats through the city, their colours flying, drums beating, and the ladies waving to them from the balconies and throwing garlands. They supposed, after their victory that they were now to enjoy this garden of Eden with its flowers and pretty girls. A smirking aide-de-camp in a cocked hat soon undeceived them, and by nightfall they were marching along the Carcassone road after the old familiar stink of tobacco and onions. It appeared that, having boxed them round the compass, they had now to chase the *parlez-vous* back to Spain.

But that evening Colonel Frederick Ponsonby of the 12th Light Dragoons galloped into the town with dispatches from Bordeaux. He found Wellington in his lodgings pulling on his boots. "Ay, I thought so," he said, as Ponsonby broke the news, "I knew we should have peace." "Napoleon has abdicated." "You don't say so, upon my honour. Hurrah!" And, spinning on his heel, the British Commander-in-Chief snapped his fingers.†

* The account of the battle is based on Oman, VII, 465-95; Fortescue, X, 79-80; Weller, 355-9; a brilliant article by Colonel Alfred Burne, *The Enigma of Toulouse*, in *The Army Quarterly* for January 1927. See also Lapéne, 370-85; Bell, I, 164-9; Seaton, 205; Booth, 48; George Napier, 257-9; Vidal de la Blache, *L'Evacuation de l'Espagne et l'invasion dans le midi*.

† Broughton, I, 189-90. See also Oman, VII, 498; Bell, I, 170; Larpent, III, 137; Fortescue, X, 91.

Yet even now it was not quite over. After a day or two of argument, Soult laid down his arms. His rival, Suchet, had already done so. Bayonne alone held out till April 26th when the French Governor condescended to do as the rest of the world had done and made peace.

Thereafter the British army took its ease. The cavalry, by arrangement with the new Bourbon Government, rode home across France to Boulogne and Calais, feasting off champagne at a shilling a bottle and delighting in a countryside unravaged by war. The infantry marched to Bordeaux to await transportation to England or America, where war with the United States was still continuing. As the troops tramped the sunny roads of southern France or glided in barges down the silver stream, a new world of peace seemed to be opening before them and mankind: a world in which there should be no more parades and piquets no more midnight alerts, no more broken bones, no more slaying and being slain. After hard commons for so long they found it difficult to accustom themselves to down beds and no danger; an officer of the Rifles, who had never lost a piquet in six years' campaigning, woke in a cold sweat in his château bed with dreams of sentries unposted and lines surprised.[*]

*   *   *

At the end of April while the fallen Emperor embarked at Fréjus for the tiny island kingdom of Elba to which his conquerors had consigned - and assigned to - him, Wellington travelled to Paris to discuss the affairs of Spain with the British Foreign Secretary, at that time conferring there with the Allied sovereigns. On the way he stopped at Cahors to visit his old adversary, General Foy, who was convalescing from his wounds and was much touched by the warmth with which his magnanimous victor repeatedly wrung his hand. "His countenance," Foy wrote, "is full of distinction, simplicity and kindness, just as one pictures our great Turenne." At Paris, where he learnt he had been made a duke, Wellington appeared at a victory parade of the Allied troops, wearing among a glittering throng of potentates, not regimentals, but a blue civilian coat. For, his work as a soldier being done, Castlereagh had proposed that he should serve the State in that other capacity in which, both in India and the Peninsula he had shown, like Marlborough before him,

* Smith, I, 189-90; Costello, 183, 186; Bell, I, 173-4.

such superlative skill - that of diplomat and pacificator. "I have not declined," he wrote to his brother, Henry. "I must serve the public in some manner or other, and, as under existing circumstances, I could not well do so at home, I must do so abroad."*

After a week's stay in Paris, a preliminary to taking up his duties as Ambassador to the restored Bourbon court, he left for Madrid to try to adjust matters between the ultra-liberal Cortes and the far from liberal Spanish king, Ferdinand, now released from French captivity and back on his uneasy throne. On his way he broke his journey at Toulouse, looking, Larpent thought, thin and rather worn, and suffering from a cold. Here, at his old headquarters - now about to be dissolved - he was, the Advocate-General recorded, "absolutely overwhelmed with business" with "every department . . . at work in a sort of confusion and hurry that has never happened before." However, he seemed gay and in excellent spirits, and gave a splendid ball and supper where he received, according to Larpent, "the kind attentions of the fair ones with whom he is a universal favourite."†

Then, early on May 17th, he left for Madrid, travelling back over the road along which he had fought his way so painfully - Orthez, Nive, Nivelle, Bidassoa, Vittoria, Burgos. During his twelve days' stay in the Spanish capital, trying by his diplomacy to reconcile the irreconcilable, he succeeded in preventing an outbreak of civil war which might have seriously prejudiced the negotiations for a European peace settlement shortly to be held in Vienna.

On June 8th Wellington left Madrid, spending a last five days with his Peninsular army at Bordeaux, where it was in process of dispersing, part to America to bring, as it was hoped, war with the United States to a victorious conclusion, and part to England, half-pay and disbandment.

Here at the camp of Blanquefort, among fruit, flowers, wines,

* Five months before, on December 2nd, after his victories of the Nivelle and Nive, Lady Anne Barnard—the authoress of the ballad *Auld Robin Gray*—had written to her husband Colonel Sir Andrew Barnard of the Rifle Brigade: "I protest I should not be surprised if after a little more fighting Lord W. should return to this country so crowned with triumphs and popularity that the Regent would try to make him convert his sword into a plough-share and be the Minister of this country to settle on and plan the ten thousand new things which it will require a different ability to settle, but of which I have been told he displayed a great deal in India. A man of so much clearness and decision on one set of things is likely to possess equal sense and decision in another." *Barnard Letters*, 237.

† Larpent, III, 206-8.

and friendly people, the veterans who had begun the liberation of Europe bade farewell to one another and, as an army, dissolved. Their skill and comradeship and hard-won experience were no longer needed. They left behind the bones of their companions and the memory of their victories, of their invincible endurance in adversity, and their magnanimity and good conduct in triumph. When the time came for them to sail, the host of one subaltern - a worthy Bordeaux merchant - took his bronzed, youthful lodger aside and, with tears in his eyes, offered to lend him any money he might need, adding that he had every confidence in the word of an Englishman, and expressing a desire that their two countries might henceforward live together in peace. Then he accompanied him to the ship, kissed him on both cheeks and parted from him forever.*

In his last General Order, issued on June 14th, 1814, Wellington took leave of his troops:

"1. The Commander of the Forces, being upon the point of returning to England, again takes this opportunity of congratulating the army upon the recent events which have restored peace to their country and to the world.

"2. The share which the British Army has had in producing those events, and the high character with which the army will quit this country, must be equally satisfactory to every individual belonging to it, as they are to the Commander of the Forces; and he trusts that the troops will continue the same good conduct to the last.

"3. The Commander of the Forces once more requests the army to accept his thanks.

"4. Although circumstances may alter the relations in which he has stood towards them for some years so much to his satisfaction, he assures them that he will never cease to feel the warmest interest in their welfare and honour; and that he will be at all times happy to be of any service to those to whose conduct, discipline, and gallantry, their country is so much indebted.†

"The commands of the great man who had so often assembled them at his beck," wrote Captain Grattan of the Rangers, "now separated them for ever." Guided by his genius, at a cost of some

* Bell, I, 185-7.
† *Dispatches*, XII, 62.

36,000 casualties, in less than six years they had driven the enemy from Portugal and Spain, invaded France before any European soldier had set foot on her soil and inflicted on her armies losses many times greater than their own.

On June 23rd—the day on which the visiting Allied sovereigns concluded a two weeks' round of victory celebrations in the British capital—Wellington landed in England after an absence of more than five years. At Dover he was seized by the crowd and borne shoulder-high to the Ship Inn; all the way to London, through the Kentish hayfields, where old men in white smocks stood bareheaded to see him pass, the cheering and fêting continued. "It was quite refreshing," wrote Mary Mitford, who saw him driving in an open carriage without the slightest affectation of bowing, "after all those parading foreign emperors." He took the lionising calmly, as he had taken worse things, rode about London in a plain blue coat with a single groom, and made it clear that, while promiscuous pawing might do for an Emperor, it was too much for an English gentleman. In the Commons, after the Government had proposed to vote him £300,000 to buy an estate, the leader of the Opposition tabled an amendment increasing the grant to £400,000. "When the will of Heaven and the common destinies of our nature," the Speaker told him as he sat, in Field-Marshal's uniform, within the bar of the House, "shall have swept away the present generation, you will have left your great name and example as an imperishable monument, exciting others to like deeds of glory and serving at once to adorn, defend and perpetuate the existence of this country among the ruling nations of the earth."

EPILOGUE

What a happy consummation of his story it would be to put
the last hand to the destruction of Bonaparte's power in direct
conflict with Bonaparte himself.

CANNING TO CASTLEREAGH
April 28th 1815

I look upon Salamanca, Vittoria and Waterloo as my three best
battles – those which had great and permanent consequences.
Salamanca relieved the whole south of Spain, changed all the
prospects of the war, and was felt even in Prussia. Vittoria freed
the Peninsula altogether, broke off the armistice at Dresden,
and thus led to Leipzig and the deliverance of Europe; and
Waterloo did more than any other battle I know towards the
true object of all battles – the peace of the world.

WELLINGTON

INTERLUDE

*Although, with his usual self-abnegation where public duty was concerned,
the Duke of Wellington offered to go to Canada to command the small-scale
forces engaged in the war against the young United States,* he was employed during the autumn and early winter of 1814 as British Ambassador
to the restored Bourbon court in Paris. Here he bought for his country from
Napoleon's sister, the Princesse de Borghese—complete with its furniture
and at a most advantageous price—the beautiful 18th-century house in the
Rue du Faubourg St Honoré, which has ever since been the British Embassy.
It seemed that at forty-five his soldiering days were over forever. Then at
the end of January, alarmed in the increasingly disturbed state of France
by threats to assassinate the man who had done so much to defeat her, the
Government appointed him to succeed the Foreign Secretary, Lord Castlereagh, as Britain's representative at the Congress of Vienna, where the
statesmen of monarchical Europe were engaged in re-drawing the frontiers
of the world. While there, he brought to a successful conclusion the international negotiations for the gradual abolition of the Slave Trade for which,
since the previous autumn, both he at Paris and Castlereagh at Vienna had*

---

* "I see that the public are very impatient about the want of success in America, and I
suspect that they will never be quiet till I shall go there." To Lord Bathurst, November 4th
1814. H.M.C., Bathurst, 303.

been contending as the prize above all others which Britons wished their representatives to bring back from the peace congress.

On the night of March 7th 1815, a great ball was held in the Austrian capital. During the evening a courier arrived at Metternich's house with dispatches from Genoa. The Chancellor was tired from too much business by day and revelry by night. After resting for a while on his couch he opened the dispatch. Napoleon had escaped. In its well-bred inefficiency, the ancien régime had let out the Corsican ogre.

Thereafter events moved at a terrible speed. On March 10th, evading all attempts by the Bourbon authorities to arrest him, Napoleon appeared at Lyons, announcing that he had come with the violets to save the French from degradation and that his eagles would soon alight on the spires of Notre Dame. Unit after unit of the royal army went out to stop him, and, on meeting that familiar, grey-coated figure at the head of his daring few, threw down their arms and welcomed him in a tempest of emotion. On the 14th he was joined by Marshal Ney, who had promised King Louis he would bring him back to Paris in an iron cage. Six days later he reached Fontainebleau, where less than a year before he had abdicated and bade farewell to his veterans. That night he slept at the Tuileries, the king with a handful of courtiers tearfully scampering before him across the Flemish frontier. France had gone about again and the Revolution militant was once more enthroned.

The Sovereigns of Europe assembled at Vienna refused to accept the outrageous fait accompli. On March 18th they proclaimed the escaped prisoner an outlaw and "disturber of the peace of the world." Thereafter they called for an immediate mobilisation of the Continent's armies, noting with high satisfaction—for, despite malicious rumours put about by his political enemies that he had seldom much exposed himself to danger in the Peninsula, Wellington's military prestige was second only to Napoleon's—the former's appointment by the Governments of Great Britain and the Netherlands to command their joint forces in the Low Countries. Here, with a Prussian army, they were to act as an advanced-guard until the hosts of Austria and Russia could be mobilised. "It is for you," the Czar said to the victor of Vittoria, "to save the world again."*

Wellington arrived in Brussels to take up his command on April 5th. He found a situation, both military and diplomatic, as unsatisfactory as any he had faced in his bleakest early Peninsular days when, as he told his friend, George Chad, "everyone was raw" and he "had to teach them all their

* Fraser, 40.

business down to the most trifling details" and when the Horse Guards, as he put it, " sent me out such people sometimes."* His British force consisted of twenty-five battalions of infantry and six regiments of cavalry, some 14,000 men in all, of whom half were raw recruits who had never seen a shot fired. The flower of his old Peninsular army - what remained of it after demobilisation - was in America or on the high seas returning from that country. For, as was habitual after her wars, Britain, having built up an army second to none, had proceeded to get rid of it as fast as possible in the belief that, victory having been won, further war was unthinkable. Even now though, unlike the Whig Opposition which was all for peace and trusting Bonaparte, the Government was wholly committed to war, it refused to call out the Militia.†

As for the Dutch-Belgian forces which constituted the other half of the Duke's army, these were as little dependable as the Portuguese had been before good officers, discipline and regular subsistence had turned them into first-class soldiers.‡ The Catholic French-speaking or Belgian part - formerly the Austrian Netherlands - of the newly-created Dutch, Belgian and Flemish kingdom under the now restored House of Orange, had accepted its forcible incorporation by Revolutionary France twenty years before with something approaching enthusiasm and strongly resented its transfer by the peace-makers to the rule of a Dutch Protestant monarch. Those of its people who were used to arms had all served in the Napoleonic armies and were only too likely, given the chance, to desert to the Eagles. Such of the Dutch-Netherlander troops as had experience of war, though far less favourably disposed to the French under whom they had suffered, had also learnt their soldiering as part of Napoleon's Grand Armée when Holland was ruled by his brother, Louis Bonaparte. Commanding the new kingdom's polyglot forces were the young princes of the Dutch royal family - the twenty-three-year-old Prince of Orange, who had served on Wellington's staff in the closing year of the Peninsular War and, in consequence, thought he knew all there was to be known of war, and his eighteen-year-old brother, Prince Frederick, who, though without other qualifications, at least did not suffer from this - as it was twice to prove on the battlefield - fatal delusion.

---

* "During which I remember the Duke quoted several instances of utterly incompetent persons sent out to him." Chad, 18.

† Weller, *Waterloo*, 30-3.

‡ Wellington, talking of the Portuguese to Larpent in July 1813, had said, "It was extraordinary ... to observe their conduct – that no troops could behave better, that they never had now a notion of turning and that nothing could be like their forwardness now and willing, ready tempers." Larpent, II, 3. See also *Idem*, 70.

With his customary energy, industry and good sense, Wellington set himself to overcome these handicaps. Within six days of his arrival, he had issued orders by which his polyglot army, formed into three corps, was cunningly strengthened, so far as it proved politically possible—for the King of the Netherlands was bitterly opposed to anything which derogated from his authority over his artificial kingdom—with a stiffening of British or King's German Legion troops in every major unit. He could not transform into reliable soldiers the Belgian or Dutch peasants or raw German mercenaries from the petty Teuton principalities who were sent in the ensuing weeks to swell his numbers. Yet by dint of common drill, organisation and, above all, the immense morale-raising prestige of his name and the personal attention he gave to every unit of his command, irrespective of nationality, he did everything possible to blend his force into a single international whole accustomed to working together.

Gradually, as spring gave place to summer and Napoleon assembled and equipped his armies for the coming conflict with the Teuton and Slavonic hosts which were moving slowly towards Rhine, Moselle and Meuse, Wellington built up the strength of his army from the 40,000 international rag, tag and bobtail with which he started to 60,000 by the end of April and over 90,000 by the middle of June. But it was anybody's guess whether Napoleon, who was expected by some to have 600,000 men in arms by the end of the summer, would wait to try issues with the hosts of eastern Europe or strike first at Wellington and the Prussian army under Blücher who were now together holding the line of the Sambre until the joint forces of the dreaded Emperor's enemies were ready to converge on his capital. It was Wellington's view that Napoleon's wisest plan would be to remain on the defensive and, as in his wonderful 1814 campaign in France, strike first at one ally, then at another, till their internal divisions compelled them to fall back. But he also knew that the Emperor, for all his genius, lacked the patience for defensive warfare. And with their forces strung out along the French-Belgian frontier for more than a hundred miles from Tournai to Liège—for Napoleon could strike at, at least, three different points— Wellington and Blücher could not be strong everywhere. But they took counsel to ensure swift mutual support in every contingency, and each established a liaison staff at the other's headquarters. As the weeks passed and the strength of the two armies grew, the likelihood of a Napoleonic invasion of Belgium seemed to recede.

While—as his interminable letters, dispatches and general orders on every branch of organisation and training reveal—Wellington worked that

403

spring and summer as even he had seldom worked before, he displayed to the world a confidence, gaiety and calculated insouciance which suggested to army and civilian populace alike that he hadn't the slightest doubt of his ability to withstand the former conqueror of Europe if he chose to try conclusions with him. There is a charming picture of him, a few days after he arrived in Brussels to resume his old profession of soldiering, in the letters of Spencer Madan, tutor to the Duke of Richmond's children who were living with their parents in the Belgian capital at that time. He was in the highest spirits, full of fun and drollery, when he dined with them and seemed to young Madan to unite the extremes of character which Shakespeare had given to Henry V—" the hero and the trifler":

"*You may conceive him at one moment commanding the allied armies in Spain or presiding at the conferences at Vienna, and at another sprawling on his back or on all fours upon the carpet playing with George. His judgment is so intuitive that instant decision follows perception, & consequently, as nothing dwells for a moment upon his mind, he is able to get thro' an infinity of business without ever being embarrassed by it or otherwise than perfectly at his ease. In the drawing-room before dinner he was playing with the children, who seemed to look up to him as to one on whom they might depend for amusement and when dinner was announced they quitted him with regret, saying, 'Be sure you remember to send for us the moment dinner is over,' which he promised he would do and was as good as his word.*"[*]

Three months later, when Napoleon's veteran army was massing on the Belgian frontier, Wellington remained to outward appearance the very life and soul of the gay cosmopolitan society of Brussels, giving a ball or fête champêtre every week, attending every party and looking as though he hadn't a care in the world. The moral effect of this was tremendous and gave confidence to everyone. He took Lady Jane Lennox, the seventeen-year-old sister of his favourite young aide-de-camp, Lord March, to a cricket match at Enghien, Madan reported on June 13th, " and brought her back at night, apparently having gone for no other purpose than to amuse her."[*] Nor was he much concerned as to the company he entertained, so long as it was amusing. " The Duke of Wellington," wrote one strait-laced English lady that June, " has not improved the morality of our society, as he has given several things and makes a point of asking all the ladies of loose character. Everyone was surprised at seeing Lady John Campbell at his house, and

[*] *Spencer and Waterloo, 95-6.*

one of his Staff told me that it had been represented to him her not being received, for that her character was more than suspicious. 'Is it, by—;' said he, 'then I will go and ask her myself.' On which he immediately took his hat and went out for that purpose." He was still "amusing himself with humbugging the ladies, particularly the Duchess of Richmond," wrote the same censorious correspondent, Lady Caroline Capel - sister of the commander of his cavalry, Lord Uxbridge - on June 11th, a week before the battle which, as yet unknown to him or anyone else, was to decide the fate of the world.

* *Spencer and Waterloo*, 102-3; *Capel Letters*, 102, 106-7.

THE LAST BATTLE

DURING the afternoon of Sunday, June 18th 1815, the city of Brussels was in a state of panic. Since three o'clock a stream of fugitives had been pouring in from the plain beyond the forest of Soignes where, twelve miles to the south, Wellington, with 25,000 British and 42,000 Germans and Netherlanders - most of them inexperienced or unreliable - and 156 guns, was barring the way of a victorious French army of 74,000 veterans and 246 guns commanded by Napoleon himself. Most of the British visitors who had invaded the city in the wake of their army had already fled to the north and were crowding the roads and waterways to Antwerp, where, on Wellington's orders, a state of siege had been proclaimed and crowds waited all day in the rain for news. But hundreds more, unable to obtain transport in the panic - for everything on wheels had been requisitioned - remained in the city without hope of escape. Every few minutes fugitives from the battlefield kept galloping into the town, shouting that all was lost and that the French were at their heels. Once a whole regiment of Hanoverian cavalry poured in through the Namur gate with swords drawn and foam-flecked horses and rode through the town towards the north, upsetting everything in the streets on their way. There were other fugitives with bloody and bandaged heads, cartloads of wounded, and occasionally, towards evening, an officer of high rank, British or Belgian, extended upon a bier borne by soldiers. As the dreadful afternoon advanced and the distant cannonade grew in intensity, the rumour spread - possibly circulated by French sympathisers, of whom there were said to be many - that Napoleon had promised his soldiery the sack of the city. Every woman knew what that meant. "I never saw such consternation," wrote Fanny Burney. "We could only gaze and tremble, listen and shudder."

Yet three days earlier Brussels had seemed as securely held by British wealth and the martial power of united Europe as London.

For weeks it had been a scene of gaiety and military pageantry, with the brilliant aristocracy of Britain flooding the city in the wake of her army and spending money with a profusion never matched by its successive Spanish, Austrian, French and now Dutch rulers. The nearest French vedettes had been forty miles away beyond the Sambre, and between them and the Belgian capital two great armies had guarded every road on a hundred-mile front, growing daily in strength and commanded by the two most famous soldiers of the European alliance which had defeated and dethroned Napoleon. The Prussian host of around 113,000 men—almost as numerous as the largest striking force Napoleon could be expected by then to raise from an exhausted and divided France—had entered Belgium under Blücher to hold the frontier from the Ardennes to Charleroi, while a smaller joint British, Netherlands, Hanoverian and Brunswick army guarded it from Mons to the North Sea. Soon the young, understrength battalions sent out in haste from England were expected to be joined by the veteran regiments which had driven the French from Spain and which were now returning from America. Elsewhere more than half a million men, mobilised by the Sovereigns of Europe, were on the march, their vanguards already closing in on the French frontiers. The danger to Brussels and the Low Countries, so great three months before, seemed to have passed. Though no official state of war existed—Napoleon being merely treated as an outlaw under the new international system of collective security—it had been known that an invasion of France was to begin in July. It had even seemed likely that the French, republicans or royalists, would themselves throw out the returned usurper and so avoid the necessity of invasion.

On the night of Thursday, June 15th, there had been a ball in the city. It had been given by the wife of a British milord of fabulous wealth - the Duchess of Richmond - and the principal officers of the British and Allied army had attended it, including the Duke of Wellington, most of his generals and the leader of the Netherlands forces, the Prince of Orange. But during its course, and even before it had begun, it had become known that something was amiss. Several times Wellington had been interrupted by messages and was seen to write orders, and at an early hour many of his officers took their leave. During the small hours of the 16th the squares and streets of Brussels had filled with troops as trumpets sounded and drums beat to arms. Presently the troops - green-jacketed Riflemen, scarlet-clad infantry of the Line and Highlanders, blue-coated Belgians, and Brunswickers in black - had moved off, laughing and joking in the early morning sunshine, and asking one another what all the fuss was about. The stolid Flemish country folk, rolling into the city in their carts, had watched them with curious eyes as they marched out down the Charleroi road. Everyone in command had seemed very composed and quiet; old Sir Thomas Picton, commander of the British 5th Division, with top-hat and reconnoitring-glass slung over his shoulder, cheerfully accosted his friends as he rode through the streets.

Elsewhere - at Enghien, Ath, Grammont, Nivelles, Oudenarde, and even as far away as Ghent - other troops, British, German and Netherlander, roused from their cantonments, had assembled to the sound of trumpets and bugles and, marching off along the hot, dusty high-roads southwards and eastwards, had begun to converge on the assembly point. It had been a day of intense heat. As they emerged from the beech forests on to the great corn plain which fringed the Sambre to the north, the tramping infantrymen and jingling cavalry and gunners heard a dull, sullen sound like distant thunder and saw on the horizon columns of smoke arising.[*]

* * *

For at dawn on June 15th, after one of his incredibly swift and secret concentrations, Napoleon had sprung like a tiger across the Sambre and driven in the outposts of Blücher's army not far from the point where its right touched the left of Wellington's equally scattered force. With 124,000 men he had placed himself, as he hoped, between them. His object was to defeat the Prussians before they had time to concentrate, forcing them back eastwards on their Rhine communications and then, brushing aside Wellington or driving him back towards the sea, to enter Brussels as a conqueror. Thereafter, he believed, the Belgian common people would rise against the Dutch, the war-weary French take heart and unite behind him, the Tory

---

[*] "There they go, shaking their blankets again," said the old soldiers. Leeke, I, 11; *Near Observer*, 2-4; Becke, 49-5; Bessborough, 240-1; Costello, 190; *Creevey Papers*, I, 223, 226-7, 229-30, 232; Lynedoch, 756; D'Arblay, III, 341-2, 347-8; Frazer, 520-4, 529-30, 536, 544, 572; Jackson, 6, 14-18; Kincaid, 153-6; Mercer, I, 47, 53-5, 103-4, 156-7, 198-202, 217-19, 230-9, 242-3, 284; Siborne, 3, 23; Simpson, 16-17; Smith, I, 226.

Government in London fall, and his Austrian father-in-law, deprived of British subsidies, sue for peace.

It was not true, as is sometimes said, that Wellington had been caught off his guard. Neither he nor Blücher could have known at what point on the French-Belgian frontier Napoleon would choose to strike. Of the three main roads to Brussels one, through Charleroi, crossed the Prussian sector, the other two, through Mons and Tournai, the Anglo-Dutch. But though that through Mons was the shortest and, therefore, constituted the greatest threat to the Belgian capital—Napoleon's political objective—until that past-master of strategic surprise and sudden, concealed movement showed his hand, it was guess-work which he would take. Wellington had therefore had to be equally ready both to resist an advance along either of the roads crossing his own sector and to hasten eastwards to join the Prussians if they were attacked first. True, therefore, to his unchanging principle of so disposing his forces as to be able to respond to any move of an enemy, instead of keeping them strung out and exposed he placed them in commanding positions well back from the frontier whence they could march to one another's or their allies' aid in the shortest possible time. Two thirds of them could be assembled at any point within twenty-two hours and the whole in not more than forty-eight.*

As, however, the French had struck at the Prussian outpost line and not his own, Wellington was dependent on his ally for information of their initial direction and strength. And, owing to defective Prussian staff work, no authentic news of what was happening reached the British Commander-in-Chief till the middle of the afternoon and then many hours too late and out of date. Even then it was not clear whether the reported attack was a feint to draw off forces from some real danger-point elsewhere. It was not till after dark that, just before he left for the Duchess of Richmond's ball, Wellington learnt that it was something more than an affair of outposts and that Napoleon had thrown his whole weight against the Prussians. Only then had he felt justified in ordering an immediate concentration of his entire army at Nivelles, a few miles west of the Charleroi-Brussels road.

When at midnight he arrived at the ball—which, like Drake before the Armada, he insisted on attending lest a panic flight of civilians

* Weller, *Waterloo*, 42-4; Fraser, 267; Ellesmere, 193-4; Greville, I, 82.

from the Belgian capital should precipitate a pro-French rising—his troops were already marching. An hour later, just as supper was being served, an ADC arrived with news that a brigade of Nassauers under Prince Bernhard of Saxe-Weimar had made contact with French patrols at Quatre Bras where the road from Nivelles to Namur crossed the Charleroi-Brussels highway. Before retiring at 2 a.m. to snatch three hours sleep before setting out to the south, Wellington, therefore, issued further orders to make Quatre Bras— essential for keeping open communications with the threatened Prussians—the assembly-point for his entire army.*

*   *   *

All afternoon on Friday 16th—the day after the French had crossed the Sambre—the people of Brussels had heard, through the hot airless haze, the sound of cannonading from Quatre Bras, where twenty miles to the south of the Belgian capital Marshal Ney, commanding the left wing of Napoleon's advancing army, was trying to brush aside a still weak but growing British and Netherlands force from the cross-roads which preserved communication between the two allied armies and alone prevented him from falling on the flank of the Prussians whom Napoleon was assailing frontally at Ligny a few miles to the east. When at 10 a.m. that morning, after passing on the road his Reserve Corps, which he had sent off at dawn from Brussels with Picton's British division in the lead, Wellington had arrived at Quatre Bras, he had found all quiet and a Dutch-Belgian division of 8000 men under the young Prince of Orange strongly placed at the crossroads. Having already made dispositions for an early concentration of his army at this vital point, he had ridden over to Sombreffe on the nearby Plain of Fleurus to take counsel with Blücher who was awaiting Napoleon's attack in a position which did anything but inspire him with confidence. "If they fight here," he had remarked to Colonel Hardinge, his liaison officer at Prussian headquarters, "they will be damnably mauled."†

---

* Weller, *Waterloo*, 45-9; Glover, 196-8; Ellesmere, 185-6, 194-9, 224-7, 237; Becke, 49-52.

† "I told them so myself, but of course in different terms. I said to them, 'Everybody knows their own army best; but, if I were to fight with mine here, I should expect to be beat.' . . . They were dotted in this way – all their bodies along the slope of a hill, so that no

When, shortly before 3 p.m., the Duke had returned to Quatre Bras he had found that the French about to attack the Dutch-Belgian lines there. The latter were strongly posted, but as soon as the enemy's offensive developed, they gave way. There was a moment when, but for Wellington's timely arrival, there would have been a disaster, as the young Prince of Orange had completely lost his grip on the situation and assumed that a wood full of advancing French troops was held by his men. "It is all over," he had assured the Duke, "they are driven back!" "Over, but what are those in that wood?" "They are Belgians." "No, by God, but they are French and the wood is full of them!"* Fortunately the head of Picton's British division was then just arriving on the field, headed by the veteran 1st battalion of the Rifles, probably the most resourceful and versatile fighting unit in any of the three armies. For the next hour or two, under the Duke's tactical command, a British infantry force of divisional strength, without cavalry and at first only partially deployed, had held off three veteran French divisions under one of Napoleon's greatest marshals, supported by 4000 horse. Reckoning, as at Assaye, that in an apparently hopeless situation boldness is the best policy, and relying on the fact that reinforcements were on the way, the British commander, directing every action down to battalion and even, at times, company level, hit back wherever possible and gradually gained the breathing-space he needed to hold the vital crossroads. At one moment, while trying to rally a force of Dutch-Belgian and Brunswick light horse, he was all but surrounded by French lancers and only reached safety by putting his horse at a ditch lined by the 92nd Highlanders and jumping clear over their heads and bayonets. By a miracle of tough, confused fighting in which Picton's veteran Scottish and English regiments, though suffering heavy losses, covered themselves with glory and the Duke of Brunswick fell at the head of his troops, Wellington for six hours clung to a weak but essential strategic position and then, as his numbers little by little rose from 7000 to 36,000, took the offensive

---

cannon-ball missed its effect upon them; they had also undertaken to defend two villages that were too far off, only within reach of cannon-shot. Now here is a general rule. Never attempt to defend a village that is not within reach of musketry." Stanhope, 109. See also Ellesmere, 127, 186.

* Retailing this conversation to George Chad nine years later, Wellington observed, "By God, if I had come up five minutes later, the battle was lost." Chad. 7.

and drove back Ney's 20,000. By doing so, he saved the Prussian army from an assault on their western flank which would have involved them in utter disaster.* As it was, by nightfall—though as yet unbeknown to him—63,000 French veterans under the Emperor, attacking with magnificent *élan*, had beaten 80,000 Prussians at Ligny and inflicted on them between 15,000 and 20,000 casualties. Their gallant septuagenarian commander, Blücher, only narrowly escaped capture after being ridden over by French cavalry.

Yet Napoleon's victory had not been as complete as he had hoped. Owing to Wellington's success in withstanding and defeating Ney, and the failure of a French corps which, through the Marshal's and Napoleon's contradictory orders, had marched and countermarched all day between the two battlefields without taking part in either, the Prussians had escaped annihilation and had been able to withdraw northwards in tolerable order into the night. Next day, when, after detaching 33,000 troops under Marshal Grouchy to follow them, the victorious Emperor threw the rest of his army against Wellington, the latter, retaining contact with his defeated ally, fell back in good order up the Charleroi-Brussels highway. And though Napoleon had meant to drive the Prussians eastwards on their communications, Blücher, in loyalty to Wellington, and contrary to the advice of his Chief of Staff, Gneisenau, had retreated northwards towards Wavre on a road parallel to the British and only a dozen miles to the east. The Allied armies thus remained in touch, and, though the Emperor had reduced their numerical superiority and shaken their morale, he had not, as he supposed, divided them. And, though the people of Brussels had expected all day to see the victorious French emerge from the Forest of Soignes, the British withdrawal on the afternoon of the 17th, brilliantly directed by Wellington, had not been in the least precipitate. Covered by Lord Uxbridge's cavalry and horse artillery, by nightfall he had concentrated his entire army on the ridge of Mont St Jean twelve miles south of the city. During the late afternoon the retreat of the cavalry rearguard and Napoleon's pursuit were delayed by torrential thunderstorms which converted the Charleroi *chaussée* and the fields on either side into quagmires. It

---

* There are excellent detailed accounts of Quatre Bras in Jac Weller's *Wellington at Waterloo*, Elizabeth Longford's *Wellington, The Years of the Sword*, Volume X of Fortescue's *History of the British Army*, and A. F. Becke's *Napoleon and Waterloo*.

had seemed, recalled one officer, as if water was being tumbled out of heaven in tubs.*

The two armies had spent a most uncomfortable night. The rain fell almost continually, with flashes of lightning and violent gusts of wind. The ground on which the men lay, drenched to the skin and shaking with cold, was sodden with wet crops. A few old campaigners made themselves tolerably comfortable by smearing their blankets with clay and making pillows of straw. Few of the newcomers to war, who in the Allied army by far outnumbered the old hands, got any sleep at all.

*   *   *

The ridge, or rather rolling plateau, on which the British army had halted was one which the Duke had long marked as a favourable position for the defence of the Belgian capital. It crossed the highroad from Brussels to Charleroi a mile and a half south of the village of Waterloo and the Forest of Soignes. It was named after the farm of Mont St Jean which nestled by the roadside in one of its northern folds. In the course of riding and hunting expeditions, Wellington had carefully studied its gentle undulations and contours.† It was here that twenty-one years before, when he was a young lieutenant-colonel, his chief, the Duke of York, had urged the Austrian General-issimo, Coburg, to give battle to Jourdan's levies after Fleurus. But Coburg had chosen to fall back eastwards on his communications, leaving Brussels to its fate and the British to shift for themselves. It was because, after a generation of disaster and servitude, a Prussian Field-Marshal had learnt the necessity of unselfish co-operation between allies, that Wellington was able to take his stand here. For, though his only reliable troops were outnumbered by two to one and though the French had nearly double his weight of artillery, he knew that he had only to hold his ground with one wing of an international army until the other under Blücher, who had given him his assurance that he would so do, could reach the battlefield. For while

* Hamilton of Dalzell MS., 46-8, 77. See Weller, *Waterloo*, 53-77; Simmons, 364; Stanhope, 244; Tomkinson, 286-8; Ellesmere, 230-1; Anglesey, 128-32; Howarth, 20.

† "If the Prussians are beat, which I think is very probable," he told the Duke of Richmond on the night of the ball, "that is the spot"—pointing on the map—"where we must lick those fellows." Lady Shelley, I, 171. For a first-hand confirmation of this story, see Granville, II, 538. See also Mercer, I, 194.

neither the British nor the Prussians, acting alone, were strong enough to defeat Napoleon's army, together they were too strong for him. To keep them together was, therefore, the basis of Wellington's strategy, and to do so he was ready to sacrifice temporarily, if necessary, both the Belgian capital and his communications with England. For if he and Blücher could unite, on the morrow their joint forces could take the offensive and sweep Napoleon back to France.*

Unlike Blücher at Ligny, who, in the normal Continental manner, had drawn up his army in view of Napoleon, Wellington - the greatest master of defensive tactics in Europe - had chosen a position where his infantry could inflict the utmost damage on the attackers while suffering the least themselves. Its reverse or northern slopes, in whose undulations he concealed his forces, gave him precisely the cover and field of fire needed for an active defence. Behind it lay the forest which, stretching for miles on either side of the Brussels highway, constituted, with its open pines and beeches and freedom from undergrowth, an excellent temporary refuge into which to withdraw inexperienced troops if they proved unable to withstand Napoleon's attack. Once inside it, he remarked, he would have defied the Devil himself to drive him out.† But as, like his ally, he was thinking in ultimate terms, not of defence but of offensive action, he gave battle on the open plain where the full strength of the Prussian and British armies could later be brought to bear on Napoleon.

Until then, however, Wellington knew that his rôle must be strictly defensive. At least half the foreign troops under his command could not be trusted to manœuvre. Kincaid of the 95th drew the picture of a detachment of them at Quatre Bras, behaving for all the world like the comedian, Mathews's ludicrous sketch of the American Militia; whenever, after a careful explanation of their rôle, they were given the word to march, they had started blazing away at the British skirmishers ahead of them. "We were at last," Kincaid wrote, "obliged to be satisfied with whatever advantages their appearance would give, as even that was of some consequence where troops were so scarce." Later in the day, he admitted, when they got used to the

---

* See Fraser, 265, 268, 270.

† "It is not true that I could not have retreated. I could have got into the wood and I would have defied the Devil to drive me out." Arbuthnot, I, 235. See also Cotton, 303; Fraser, 264.

sensation of being fired at, they behaved quite well. Having fought for Napoleon when Belgium, Holland and Western Germany formed part of his empire, however, they had little stomach for fighting against him. Many more were boys and raw Landwehr, though, in the case of the Brunswickers, with good officers and NCOs. Few were adequately equipped or trained.* Of the 42,000 foreign troops in Wellington's army only the 5500 men of the veteran King's German Legion - an integral part of the British Army - could be described as first-line troops.

Wellington was, therefore, forced to do as he had done in early Peninsular days; to stiffen his foreign formations with redcoats. In the teeth of opposition, particularly from the King of the Netherlands, he had tried to make his force as international in organisation as possible; to this end he had not only worn the national cockades of all the Allies in his hat but had forbidden the playing of "Rule Britannia" at regimental concerts. As at Talavera, the most immobile troops of all he stationed among buildings and behind walls. Fortunately one of the features of his position was the presence of villages and farms on either flank of his two-and-a-half-mile front - Smohain, Papelotte, La Haye and Frischermont to the east, and Merbe Braine and Braine l'Alleud to the west. In these he placed some rather uncertain Nassauers - who, however, defended them bravely - Chassé's Belgian division and the youthful Brunswickers who had suffered so severely at Quatre Bras. They thus served - an old device of Wellington's - both as flank guards and reserves.

The backbone of his polyglot, and what for this reason he afterwards described as his "infamous army,"† were its 21,000 British regulars—of whom more than 2000 had arrived from Ostend only that morning—and their comrades of the King's German Legion. Yet of this vital 26,500 - a smaller British force than any he had commanded since his first Portuguese campaign - only about half had ever been under fire. Several of its units were weak second-line battalions, scarcely out of the goose-step. Even most of the eighteen infantry battalions which had fought in Spain had been brought up to strength by recruiting from the plough before they left England. Probably not more than 12,000 of his men had served in the incom-

---

* Lynedoch, 764; Ellesmere, 216-18; Fortescue, 238, 243-7; Gomm, 363-4; Jackson, 10; Kincaid, 325, 329; Mercer, I, 93-4, 197-8, 281.
† Stanhope, 221.

parable army which had marched from the Douro to Toulouse, and of which he had said that he could have done anything.

Compared with his Peninsular army, Wellington's force was relatively stronger in cavalry than infantry. Its 7000 British and King's German Legion horse, though far outnumbered by Napoleon's cuirassiers and lancers, made an imposing spectacle, superbly uniformed and caparisoned - the Prince Regent saw to that - and mounted on the finest horses in the world. They could ride across country like a field of high-metalled foxhunters, for they came from a land where horsemanship was a passion. At a review they left Blücher speechless with admiration. "It did one's heart good," wrote a Rifleman, watching them on the retreat from Quatre Bras, "to see how cordially the Life Guards went at their work; they had no idea of anything but straightforward fighting and sent their opponents flying in all directions." Their chief, the Earl of Uxbridge, was the Lord Paget who had commanded Moore's cavalry so brilliantly during the Corunna campaign, but whose service in the Peninsula had been cut short by an elopement with the wife of Welington's brother, Henry. Apart from his amatory exploits,* he was an excellent officer, quiet and incisive, though, like his command, rather too dashing.

What the British cavalry lacked, except for the King's German Legion and a few fine Peninsular regiments like the 23rd Light Dragoons, was experience of war and, in their high-spirited younger officers, discipline. Too many of the latter held their commissions, not because they wanted to be professional soldiers, but because a few years in a crack cavalry mess was a mark of social distinction. Their courage and dash were indisputable; their self-control and staying-power less certain.† The troopers, magnificent fighting material, were what the officers—so much less experienced and realist

---

* When someone mentioned to Wellington that Lord Uxbridge had the reputation of running away with everybody he could, he replied, "I'll take good care he don't run away with me." In this anecdote, Fraser adds, he was compelled to soften "the vigorous vernacular of the Duke." Fraser, 186. See also Frazer, 520. Anglesey, 119-24.

† "The real truth was that our cavalry never had much to do before this sanguinary battle; and the officers were, and always have been, very inferior to that of the infantry, being generally composed of country gentlemen's sons from the hunting counties of England. Such persons have no particular inclination for fighting but enter the Army as a genteel business, the oldest son being the squire, the second the parson, the next the dragoon." *Hamilton of Dalzell* MS., 80. See also Kincaid, 161; Stanley, 105; Tomkinson, 296, 318.

than their humbler infantry colleagues—made or failed to make of them. The same witness of the Lifeguards' charge during the retreat noticed with amusement that, whenever one of them got a roll in the mud, he went off to the rear as no longer fit to appear on parade.*

In artillery, though he acknowledged it only sparingly, Wellington was brilliantly served. Its mounted branch was magnificently horsed,† and, Horse and Field Artillery alike, officers and men were animated by the highest professional spirit. Only 96 of the 156 guns opposed to Napoleon's 266 pieces were British or King's German Legion, but they were probably better handled than any guns even on a battlefield where one of the commanders was the master gunner of all time. They were lighter metalled than the French guns, many of which were the dreaded twelve-pounders. Yet, thanks to the foresight of Sir Augustus Frazer, their commander, three of the seven mounted batteries had recently substituted nine-pounders for the normal six-pounders. There were also some howitzers.

The weakest branch of the army was its staff. "I command," Wellington had written to a friend a few weeks before Napoleon crossed the frontier, "a very small British army with a very large British staff," and to another, "I have more generals and officers of all nations than I know how to employ." "To tell you the truth," he told the Secretary of State, "I am not very well pleased with the manner in which the Horse Guards have conducted themselves towards me. It will be admitted that the army is not a very good one and, being composed as it is, I might have expected that the generals and staff formed by me in the last war would have been allowed to come to me again. But, instead of that, I am overloaded with people I have never seen before, and it appears to be purposely intended to keep those out of my way whom I wished to have." "However," he added, with his customary philosophy of obedience, "I'll do the best I can with the instruments which have been sent to assist me."‡

Of these by far the best were his British and King's German Legion

* "I thought at first that they had all been wounded, but on finding how the case stood, I could not help telling them that theirs was now the better situation to verify the old proverb, 'The uglier, the better the soldier.' " Kincaid, 334.

† "Mein Gott," said Blücher, after inspecting Mercer's battery, "dere is not von 'orse in diss batterie wich is not goot for Veldt Marshal." Mercer, I, 217.

‡ To Earl Bathurst, May 4th 1815.

infantry; on them in the last resort everything depended. There were too few of them, and far too few with battle experience; as he carefully sent them off on the retreat from Quatre Bras before the rest of his troops, he remarked, "Well, there is the last of the infantry gone, and I don't care now." A few weeks earlier, Thomas Creevey, encountering the Duke in a Brussels park, had asked him his view of the military prospects. He had stopped and said in the most natural manner, "By God, I think Blücher and I can do the thing." "Do you calculate," Creevey asked, "upon any desertion in Bonaparte's army?" "Not upon a man," he replied, "from the colonel to the private in a regiment - both inclusive. We may pick up a marshal or two, perhaps, but not worth a damn." Then, seeing a private of one of the Line regiments who was gaping at the statues in the park, he added, "There, it all depends upon that article whether we do the business or not; give me enough of it, and I am sure."

He therefore placed his thirty-five under-strength British and King's German Legion infantry battalions where he thought the danger was greatest, but left no part of the battlefield without them. He had received in the small hours of the morning, Blücher's assurance that he would join him in the course of the day with not less than two corps - a force as large as his own. His anxiety was, therefore, for his right rather than his left. Believing it to be to Napoleon's interest to shift the battle away from the Prussians' impending flank-march and so separate the two allied armies, he expected him to incline to the west, possibly even striking as far as the Mons-Brussels road to seize the Belgian capital in his rear. For this reason he had posted at Hal and Tubize, some ten or twelve miles to the west, 15,000 Dutch and Hanoverian and 3000 British and King's German Legion troops to guard the Mons-Brussels road, protect the capital, and keep open his communications with Ostend, where more veterans from America were expected. In the event of the battle shifting to the west this force might have an important effect, either against a French offensive move or in pursuit of a French retreat towards Maubeuge or Lille.* For, since Wellington was unaware that his world-famous adversary, having beaten the Prussians, had not taken the trouble to verify their subsequent

---

* "It was my business to be prepared for all events." *Gascoyne Heiress*. See also Stanhope, 280; Ellesmere, 104-5, 183, 234; Fortescue, X, 351, 355; Fraser, 264-5, 269-70, Greville, I, 82-3; Tomkinson, 297; Glover, 200.

movements but had assumed – merely because he wanted to – that they had retreated eastward towards Liège instead of, as Wellington knew, northwards on Wavre, it would have been flying in the face of all military common sense and prudence not to have guarded against the probability of Napoleon manœuvring to the west to separate him from his ally instead of committing his army to a frontal attack against a well-defended position where, by the afternoon, he would have to fight both allied armies instead of only one. For this reason also, Wellington placed his main reserve behind and beyond his right or western flank under his most experienced and reliable corps commander, General-"Daddy"-Hill.

There was another reason why Wellington felt anxious about his right. The unobtrusive but fine defensive position he had chosen had one flaw – a narrow, winding, shallow depression which, passing under the walls of a country house called Hougoumont in the plain below the ridge, afforded an approach by which a column could climb round the west shoulder of the plateau out of direct gunfire and debouch on to the reverse slope where his army was drawn up. For this reason he placed near the danger spot on the right of his front line the First or Guards Division, and behind it, in reserve and *en potence*, Clinton's fine 2nd Division which, with its two brigades of veteran British and King's German Legion infantry, was the nearest he possessed to his old Peninsular Light Division – a force which could manœuvre quickly. Beyond it he stationed at Merbe Braine and Braine l'Alleud his less mobile reserve of Bruns-wickers and Chassé's Belgians. In addition, since the winding hollow which his experienced eye had perceived could be commanded by musketry fire from Hougoumont, he adopted the, for him, unusual but, under the circumstances, necessary expedient of fortifying and garrisoning an outpost nearly a quarter of a mile in advance of his main position on the ridge. With its château, barns, orchards, gardens, park and woods, the estate of Hougoumont formed a 500 yards square whose wooded southern border extended almost to the ridge occupied by the French. Without its possession Napoleon could neither move a column up the concealed hollow nor, unless he divided his army in the presence of his enemy's best troops, envelop the Allied right. Wellington, therefore, placed seven hundred Hanoverians and Nassauers in the Hougoumont woods, and four light companies of the Guards, detached from the Guard's Division on the ridge behind, to hold the house, gardens and orchard and command the sunken way. To the west, defending the avenue to the house from the Nivelles road, he stationed Mitchell's British brigade with some light cavalry in rear. Thus garrisoned, the Hougoumont estate outflanked from the west the plain between the rival armies; if it could be held till the Prussians arrived, Napoleon's position would ultimately become untenable. In the meantime it would gravely delay and impede his attack.

Having secured his right, Wellington strengthened the remaining two miles of his front in his usual way by placing his formations, except for the guns and skirmishers, on the reverse slopes of the ridge. They were thus out of sight, though not out of range, of the enemy's cannon. They were deployed in broken and staggered lines so as to present single rather than double targets for the enemy's round-shot. The artillery, save for the reserve batteries, Wellington placed along the summit of the ridge, with orders to keep its fire for the enemies' columns and not to waste ammunition in duels with his guns. The skirmishers and riflemen were stationed on the forward or southern slope, concealed, as were all his troops, in the corn which, almost shoulder-high, covered the entire battlefield. By this arrangement the French masses would have to advance through three successive zones of fire – the rifle fire of picked marksmen, the round-shot and grape of the guns, and, as they came over the crest, the musketry volleys of deployed and, till then, invisible infantry.

Apart from Hougoumont on the west, Smohain, Papelotte and La Haye on the east, and the little farm of Mont St Jean just behind the centre of the British lines, there were no buildings on the open ground Wellington had chosen for battle except the farm of La Haye Sainte. This lay a hundred yards or so down the slope on the southern side of the ridge, abutting on to the straight-paved *chaussée* from Charleroi to Brussels which, ascending the hill here through a cutting, intersected it and the British line at right angles. Here Wellington placed a battalion of the King's German Legion under Major Baring with close by, in an adjoining gravel-pit, part of the 1st battalion of the 95th Rifles, the remainder of which lined a sunken road and hedge on the ridge above. This sunken road crossed the Charleroi-Brussels road at right angles and, following the crest from west to east, joined, north of Hougoumont, another highway that fanned out of the Brussels road at Mont St Jean and ran through a cutting south-westwards towards Nivelles. This road, like the orchards and woods of Hougoumont, had the effect of constricting the frontage on which the French could assail Wellington's right. It helped, too, to form those lateral communications by means of which, in all his chosen defensive positions, he could reinforce any point on the battlefield as circumstances dictated.

For the essence of Wellington's defensive tactics was freedom to manœuvre and the ability to react in strength to whatever the enemy might do. Before retiring for three brief hours of sleep in the village inn of Waterloo which was his headquarters, he was asked by Lord Uxbridge, whom, to his annoyance, the Horse Guards had sent him as commander of his cavalry and who, by seniority in the Army List, was his nominal second-in-command – an office he resented and ignored – what his plans for the morrow were. "Who," the Commander-in-Chief replied, "will attack tomorrow, I or Bonaparte?" "Bonaparte." "Well, Bonaparte has not given me any idea of his projects; and, as my plans will depend upon his, how can you expect me to tell you what mine are?" Then, as though to make amends for his terseness—for Uxbridge had only wanted to know what instructions to carry out in the event of his death—he laid his hand on his cavalry commander's shoulder, and said: "There is one thing certain, Uxbridge, that is, that whatever happens, you and I will do our duty."*

For the second night running Wellington rose at 3 a.m., for he had another twenty hours' day – the third in succession – before him. It may have been that he was woken by a letter from Blücher which is known to have reached him early on the 18th, informing him that two Prussian corps were setting out at dawn to march to his assistance.† There was no question now but that he and his men must fight where they stood, and, if necessary, to the death, for to retreat would be to expose these loyal allies to the full force of Napoleon's counter-attack. His only doubt was lest Napoleon, instead of attacking frontally, should strike westwards through Tubize and Hal and so force him temporarily to uncover the Belgian capital. For this reason Wellington wrote in the small hours of the morning several letters warning the British Ambassador at Brussels and others of this contingency. "Pray keep the English quiet if you can," he told the

* Fraser, 2-3.
† See also James, 200; Weller, 82; Longford, 444.

former. "Let them all prepare to move, but neither be in a hurry or a fright, as all will yet turn out well." One letter was a personal one to Lady Frances Webster, then *enceinte*—the neglected wife of one of Uxbridge's aides-de-camp and a great favourite of his.

> "Waterloo. *Sunday morning,*
> *3 o'clock.* June 18th 1815
>
> "My dear Lady Frances,
>
> "As I am sending a messenger to Bruxelles, I write to you one line to tell you that I think you ought to take your preparations to remove from Bruxelles to Antwerp in case such a measure should be necessary. We fought a desperate battle on Friday, in which I was successful, though I had but very few troops. The Prussians were very roughly handled, and retired in the night, which obliged me to do the same to this place yesterday. The course of the operations may oblige me to uncover Bruxelles for a moment, and may expose that town to the enemy; for which reason I recommend that you and your family should be prepared to move to Antwerp at a moment's notice."*

Whatever doubts Wellington may have had as to the issue—knowing that only half his army could be trusted to stand if attacked, he must have had many—he did not show them to his troops. When, in a deep gloom—feeling that his former chief was certain after the Prussian débâcle to be defeated by a veteran army numbering twice as many battle-worthy troops as his own and commanded by the great Napoleon himself whom Wellington had always said was worth 40,000 men on the battlefield—General Alava rode out early from Brussels to join him, he was greeted to his amazement by a smiling Commander-in-Chief who, instead of dwelling on his difficulties plied him with questions about Lady Charlotte Greville's latest party. From that moment, Alava recalled, he felt reassured.

Alava was not the only man on the battlefield who took courage and confidence that morning from Wellington's bearing. Dawn on the 18th was cold and cheerless; everyone was soaked and covered in mud from head to foot. Presently the thunder-clouds began to lift, and the men managed to get their camp-fires lit and to cook break-fast. Afterwards, on their officers' orders, they dried their am-

* Brett-James, 308-9.

munition and cleaned their arms. Later as the sun came partly out, Wellington rode round the lines with his glittering staff of aides and foreign attachés, looking, wrote a young Guards' officer, as gay and unconcerned as if they were riding to a meet in England. He was wearing a low cocked hat, bearing the four cockades of Britain, Spain, Portugal and the Netherlands, a white cravat and blue civilian coat, white buckskin breeches and a pair of Mr Hoby's - the famous St James's Street bootmaker's - shining top-boots, together with a blue cape which he was to put on and off repeatedly on that long day of showers, fog and mist.* To everyone, as he rode along the ridge, visiting every unit and outpost, he gave the impression that he knew what he was about and was confident of teaching the French another of his familiar lessons, Napoleon, his *Grande Armée* and Imperial Guard notwithstanding. "The very sight of him put heart into us all," wrote a young officer who saw him pass. Beside the *chaussée* above La Haye Sainte, Captain Kincaid of the Rifles had brewed a huge camp-kettle full of sweet tea, out of which the smiling Duke and his staff partook. "It was delightful," wrote Harry Smith of the same regiment, who was acting as Brigade-Major to General Lambert, whose brigade was stationed in reserve at Mont St Jean, "to see His Grace that morning on his noble horse, Copenhagen, in high spirits and very animated, but so cool and so clear in the issue of his orders that it was impossible not fully to comprehend what he said; delightful also to observe what his wonderful eye anticipated while some of his staff were of the opinion the attack was not in progress." For when one of his entourage remarked that he did not believe the French would attack that day, Wellington, who had been closely watching the opposing ridge through his telescope, replied, "Nonsense! The columns are already forming and I think I have discerned where the weight of the attack will be made. I shall be attacked before an hour." And he gave orders to Harry Smith to instruct General Lambert to be ready to reinforce General Picton's division half a mile ahead, where he could see the French main attack was likely to fall. Soon afterwards he turned to the Duke of Richmond who, with a sixteen-year-old son, had ridden out from Brussels that morning, saying, "As the father of ten children, you have no right to be here. You must go. You may go now, but a quarter of an hour or twenty minutes hence, you could not go - it would no longer be right." For,

---

* "I never get wet when I can help it." *Croker Papers*, II, 311.

with his experience of battles, he could foretell the storm that was coming. "It was only just beginning," he recalled afterwards, "but it was already quite clear that we should have a terrible day."*

For in the course of the morning it had become plain that the enemy advanced-guard, which had bivouacked during the night on the parallel ridge three-quarters of a mile to the south, was now being joined by the entire French army. Presently watchers could see long lines of massed troops, with their glittering helmets, cuirasses and arms, forming a magnificent spectacle on the ridge of La Belle Alliance - named after the solitary, red-tiled public house of that name. The spectacle was no doubt meant to intimidate Wellington's raw young soldiers and encourage his French-speaking Belgians to desert. At one moment there was a burst of cheering as a grey figure on a white horse, accompanied by a cavalcade, rode down the lines. For the French were not only intending to attack, but in their resolve to conquer, were partaking of a sacrament. Napoleon might not have France, or even all his anxious generals, behind him, but there was no question of the devotion of his fighting men. Between him and his old *moustaches* was a bond to be found in no other army on earth. For all his grandiloquent pretensions, he and they were familiars. Cam Hobhouse, watching him review the Imperial Guard just before the campaign began, had been amazed at the way he mingled with his troops, leaving the saluting base and marching in time beside each column; once he had gone up to a grenadier and affectionately pulled his nose. He might be prodigal of his men's lives, but, unlike Wellington, who was not, he valued his command of their hearts. It was the foundation of his fortunes. At that moment, as he rode along the lines amid shouts of " *Vive l'Empereur!*", Leipzig, the retreat from Moscow and the Abdication were as though they had never been.

Neither Napoleon nor his men doubted their ability to destroy Wellington's army and reach Brussels by nightfall. Their triumph over the Prussians two days before - achieved against superior numbers - had whetted their appetite for glory. They saw themselves, for all their difficulties, on the verge of a new Marengo. Nor was the urgent victory Napoleon needed the key only to political salvation.

* Smith, I, 270; Stanhope, I, 220; H. M. C. Bathurst; Bessborough, 242; Frazer, 546; Kincaid, 338; Smith, I, 268; Gronow, I. 68-9; Leeke, 187; Gomm, 363-4; *Hamilton of Dalzell* MS., 49-50; Jackson, 7-8.

It would be a revenge for all the humiliations the English had heaped on him. Wellington was the one commander with a European reputation whom he had never beaten, and the British the one army. "Because you have been defeated by Wellington," he told his Chief of Staff, Soult, who dwelt on the British capacity for recoil, "you think him a great general! I tell you that Wellington is a bad general, that the English are bad troops and that this will be a picnic!" His only fear was that they would vanish before he could attack them, as they had done on the previous day at Quatre Bras and seven years earlier under Moore on the Carrion. As, however, they now appeared to be calmly waiting for him, their doom was certain. "We will sleep tonight," he told his officers, "in Brussels."

Owing to the usual dispersal in search of food and plunder the last of the French only reached their battle stations at midday, three hours after the time originally ordered. Napoleon, however, was not hurrying, since to make full use of his superior artillery and cavalry, he wanted the soaked ground to dry. Despite warnings from those who had fought in Spain, he was quite sure that, once he struck in overpowering force, there would be little need to waste time in manœuvring. Most of Wellington's foreign auxiliaries, he reckoned, would bolt at the start, and the stiff redcoats would then break under the triple shock of his massed bombardment, veteran columns, and discharge of grape at close range. "I shall hammer them with my artillery," he announced, "charge them with my cavalry to make them show themselves, and, when I am quite sure where the actual English are, I shall go straight at them with my Old Guard."*

As for the Prussians, he was so convinced that they had retreated eastwards, as he wished, that he never considered the possibility of their appearance on the battlefield at all. After the hiding he had given them at Ligny they were manifestly incapable of further fight for the present. Having detached Grouchy to shepherd them out of Flanders, he felt he could discount them. They could be trusted, as in the past, to act selfishly and leave their allies to their fate. It had never been his habit to keep faith with anyone unless it suited him. That a Prussian commander should endanger his army and strain his communications to keep faith with Wellington never occurred to him.

The Emperor therefore decided to open his main attack at one

* Foy, 278-9, 345.

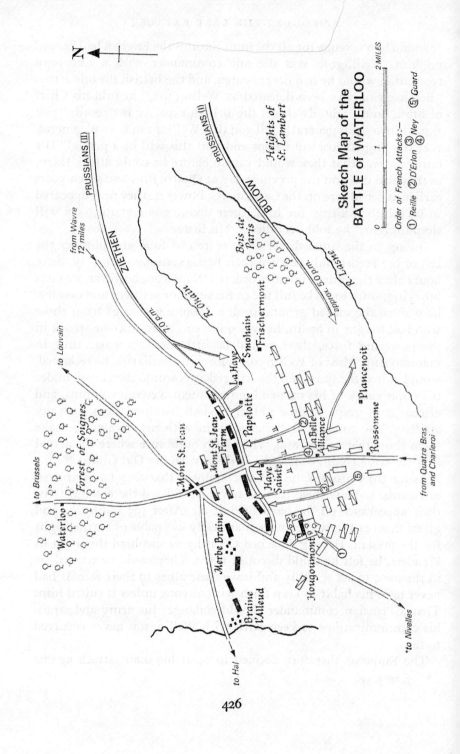

Sketch Map of the
BATTLE of WATERLOO

Order of French Attacks:—
① Reille ② D'Erlon ③ Ney ④ ⑤ Guard

2 MILES
1
0

N

PRUSSIANS (I)

Heights of
St. Lambert

BÜLOW

PRUSSIANS (III)

ZIETHEN

from Wavre
12 miles

R. Lasne

approx. 5.0 p.m.

R. Ohain

Bois de
Paris

Frischermont

Smohain

7.0 p.m.

La Haye

Papelotte

Plancenoit

Rossomme

La Belle
Alliance

Mont St. Jean

Mont St. Jean
Farm

La
Haye
Sainte

from Quatre Bras
and Charleroi

to Louvain

to Brussels

Forest of Soignes

Waterloo

Merbe Braine

Braine
L'Alleud

Hougoumont

to Hal

to Nivelles

426

o'clock. In the meantime, while he massed eighty field-pieces on a spur of high ground in the middle of the valley opposite and about 600 yards short of the British centre, he ordered the troops on his two flanks to engage the extremities of the defenders' line at Papelotte and Hougoumont in order to distract attention from his impending blow, and probably—though of this there can be no certainty - to clear a way for the use, at the decisive moment, of the sunken hollow leading to the heart of Wellington's right. In that case, however, he was unfortunate in his adversary.

The first shots of the battle were fired shortly before noon in front of Hougoumont where Prince Jerome's division had been massing for some time. Actually Wellington himself had already been under fire there, but not from the enemy. For when earlier he had ridden down to check its defences, a battalion of Nassauers, lining an outlying hedge, believing the French to be about to attack, had suddenly panicked, and when, after rallying them and calming their fears, he was riding away, some of them, whether deliberately or unintentionally, had opened fire on him.*

At midday, after a short preliminary bombardment, four battalions of Prince Jerome's division advanced against the wood to the south of the château. During the next hour they succeeded in driving out its German defenders. But they then went on to attack the gardens and mansion and, in doing so, came up against a far more formidable adversary, the four light companies of the British Guards under Lord Saltoun. The attackers, closely watched by Wellington, who had stationed himself on the ridge immediately above, suffered exceedingly heavy casualties—1500 in the first forty minutes —both from the aim of the British guardsmen, firing through embrasures in the walls, and from the accurate fire of Bull's howitzer battery stationed on the ridge. When the Guards counter-attacked and drove them back, Jerome threw another brigade into the assault and tried to gain a lodgment in the courtyard of the château. So furious was his attack that at one moment a detachment of his men broke open the great gate with an axe and swarmed in, only to be surrounded and destroyed inside, while four officers and a sergeant of the Coldstream closed the door behind them by main force. Once again the British counter-attacked with four companies of the Coldstream whom Wellington sent down from the ridge. "There, my

* Weller, *Waterloo*, 88; Hooper, 189; Longford.

427

lads, in with you," he said as they moved off, "let me see no more of you."

Jerome's answer, and that of the commander of the French left, General Reille, was to undertake—a quarter of an hour before Napoleon's main attack on the centre was due to begin—a third attack on Hougoumont with still larger forces. For every regiment they committed, the frugal Wellington staked no more than a company or whatever smaller force was necessary to hold the position. All the while his guns continued to shell the wood with such effect that, as one unending column of fresh attackers poured into it, another - of wounded - as continuously poured out.*

So far Napoleon had been only partially successful. His diversion to the east had made little effect on the Netherlanders in Papelotte and La Haye, while the more important one to the west, though occupying Wellington's attention, had failed either to by-pass or capture Hougoumont. It was now one o'clock, the hour at which the bombardment of the Allied centre was due to begin. But before its smoke enveloped the battlefield, Napoleon, watching the preparations from a knoll beside the Brussels road, observed through his telescope a suspicious movement on the high ground towards Wavre, five or six miles to the east. Wellington, who knew what it was, had earlier seen it. It might - at first it seemed to Napoleon that it must - be Grouchy, from whom he had just heard that the Prussians were retiring, not on Liège as both had thought, but on Brussels. Yet this was now scarcely likely, as Grouchy in his dispatch, dated at six that morning, had announced his intention of following them northwards on Wavre. And, as Grouchy, like Napoleon, had been wrong once about the Prussians' movements, there was another and less pleasant possibility.

At that moment this terrifying suspicion was confirmed. For a Prussian hussar—captured by a French vedette to the east of the battlefield—was brought to Napoleon bearing a dispatch from Blücher to Wellington which showed that the troops visible on the heights of St Lambert were Bülow's corps, advancing from Wavre, and that the rest of the Prussian army had spent the night around that town, only thirteen miles away.

Napoleon, in other words, had been "making pictures" - the crime

* Stanhope, 47. See also Ellesmere, 105-6; Frazer, 556; Gronow, I, 198-9; Greville (suppl.) I 83; Cotton, 51-7; Kennedy, 89-92; Houssaye, 187-9; Morris, 229-32.

against which he had always warned his subordinates. He had made his dispositions to fight under conditions that did not exist. Instead of having only the English and their feeble auxiliaries to contend with, if he proceeded with his attack, he would have to face before nightfall the intervention of another army. His attempt to separate Wellington's and Blücher's forces had failed, at least in any but the most temporary sense. He must either withdraw - the prudent course - shift his offensive to the west—as Wellington had anticipated when he placed a reserve force at Hal—or break through the British lines in the next three hours. For after that he would have to contend against two foes.

Being a gambler, and being, both politically and strategically, in desperate need of an immediate victory, Napoleon decided to proceed with his frontal attack. It still seemed unthinkable to him that the breach he was about to blast in the British centre could fail to defeat Wellington, and, with him out of the way, Blücher could be dealt with in turn. Indeed, with Grouchy in his rear and his army committed to the muddy defiles between Wavre and Mont St Jean, the old Prussian might end the day in an even worse disaster than Ligny. Napoleon, therefore, detached part of his reserve to delay the still distant Prussian advance and ordered the attack on the British to proceed.

The eighty-gun bombardment, which opened at one o'clock, fully came up to expectations. Twenty-four of the guns were Napoleon's great twelve-pounders, with a 2000 yards' range. It took away the breath of Wellington's young recruits and militiamen, and surprised even Peninsular veterans by its intensity. Captain Mercer, commanding a reserve battery of horse artillery in a hollow several hundred yards in rear of the British right flank, found, even in that sheltered position, the shot and shell continually plunging around him. One shot completely carried away the lower part of the head of one of his horses. Fortunately the ground was still wet and many shells burst where they fell, while the round-shot, instead of hopping and ricochetting for half a mile or more, frequently became embedded in the mud.*

But though very alarming, owing to Wellington's skilful dispositions the bombardment did comparatively little harm except

* Becke, 168; Cotton, 87-8; Fortescue, X, 360; Houssaye, 203; James, 223; Kennedy, 107; Kincaid, 341; Mercer, I, 294-6; Siborne, 327-8; Tomkinson, 297, 303.

to a brigade of Belgians, whose commander, General Bylandt, misinterpreting his orders, had drawn it up, in the Continental manner, on the forward slope of the ridge. During its half-hour of bombardment in this exposed position it lost one man in four, and, had it not been hastily withdrawn to a less conspicuous position, its loss might have been still greater. When, therefore, at half-past one, D'Erlon in charge of the French right moved his corps forward to the attack, with all the panoply and terror of a Napoleonic offensive - drums beating at the head of dense columns, bearded grenadiers marching four hundred abreast shouting at the top of their voices, and clouds of *tirailleurs* running and firing ahead - the customary conditions for success seemed to have been ensured. Four divisions of infantry - more than 16,000 men - each moving in close column of battalions at a quarter of a mile's distance, tramped down the slope and up the hill against the British centre and left through clouds of sulphurous smoke. Behind came companies of sappers, ready to turn the farm of Mont St Jean beyond the British centre into a fortress as soon as it was captured.

A hail of shot from the artillery on the crest greeted them. But it did not halt the men who had conquered at Wagram and Friedland. One column, supported by cuirassiers, swept round La Haye Sainte, encircling it and its German defenders and driving back the two companies of the Rifles - the most formidable marksmen in Europe - who were stationed in a sandpit on the opposite side of the *chaussée*. Another column, to the east, forced the Dutch out of Papelotte and La Haye and temporarily occupied Smohain. In the centre about 8000 men approached the summit simultaneously. As they did so, Bylandt's Belgians - raw troops who had endured to the limit of their capacity - fired one hysterical volley at the advancing, shouting column and took to their heels, carrying away the gunners of the reserve batteries behind. They never stopped till they reached the forest of Soignes, where they remained for the rest of the day.*

To Napoleon, watching from the knoll near La Belle Alliance, it seemed as though, as at Ligny, his adversary's centre was broken.

---

* "I peeped into the skirts of the forest, and truly felt astonished; entire companies seemed there, with regularly piled arms, fires blazing under cooking kettles, while the men lay about smoking as coolly as if no enemy were within a day's march. . . . General Müffling—Wellington's Prussian liaison officer—in his account of Waterloo, estimates the runaways hidden in the forest at 10,000." Jackson, 47

But it was not a Netherlander or even a Prussian army he had to dislodge, but a British. As the French bore down on the gap they had opened, Picton deployed Kempt's reserve brigade in their path. "The French came on in the old style," recalled Wellington—who was viewing their advance from his command-post beside an elm tree where the Charleroi road crossed the sunken lane—"and we drove them off in the old style." The 28th, 32nd, 79th Highlanders and the 95th Rifles - all veterans of Spain - held their fire till the head of the column was only twenty yards away. Then, from their thin extended line, they poured in their disciplined rolling volleys, and, as the leading French files tried, too late, to deploy, charged with the bayonet. At that moment Picton was struck in the head by a bullet and killed.*

Farther to the east, D'Erlon's two other divisions reached the summit. Here, after its heavy losses at Quatre Bras, Pack's brigade - Royals, 44th, 42nd and 92nd Highlanders - could only muster 1400 bayonets. Slowly, against odds, they began to give ground, while a brigade of French cavalry on their flank, having cut a Hanoverian battalion to pieces, swarmed on to the crest to the west of the Brussels-Charleroi *chaussée.*

At this point, Wellington, who had anticipated what was going to happen, intervened decisively. Forming the last infantry battalions behind the gap in his dented line into square, he ordered Lord Uxbridge to launch the Household Brigade of heavy cavalry at the intruders, he himself leading the Life Guards into line and sending them off with a brisk, "Now, gentlemen, for the honour of the Household Troops!" Leading the brigade in person, Uxbridge drove the astonished French cuirassiers into the ranks of the infantry behind, who, seeing the big, scarlet-coated Life Guardsmen slashing at them, turned and joined in the flight. It was the charge at Salamanca over again. Simultaneously the Union Brigade - consisting of Royal Dragoons, Scots Greys and Inniskillings - swept down on another French column to the east of the *chaussée.* Within a few minutes the flower of D'Erlon's corps was flying across the plain with 2000 British cavalry after it. "Hundreds of the infantry threw

* Becke, 195-7; Belloc, 171-3; Fortescue, X, 360-4; Gomm, 351, 358-9; Gronow, I, 188; Horsburgh, 249-51; Houssaye, 193-6; Jackson, 47, 88-92; James, 223, 228-9; Kennedy, 107-12; Kincaid, 344-6; *Random Shots,* 206, 273; Siborne, 19; Simmons, 365, 367; Smith, I, 270-1, 277; Stanhope, 221; James, 228-35; Cotton, 59-62; Weller, *Waterloo,* 95-100; Howarth, 83-93.

themselves down and pretended to be dead," wrote Kincaid, "while the cavalry galloped over them and then got up and ran away; I never saw such a scene in all my life." More than 4000 were cut down or taken prisoner. Many did not stop till they reached Genappe. Unfortunately the pursuers did not stop either. The secret of cavalry is iron discipline. It was a secret that the British cavalry, though superlative in dash, physique and horsemanship, had never wholly mastered. According to Hamilton of Dalzell of the Scots Greys, the troopers had been served with rum before the charge. They followed the French into the heart of Napoleon's position, sabring the gunners of his great battery and riding on to the ridge of La Belle Alliance itself as though they were after a fox. Having charged in the first line, Uxbridge was unable either to stop them or to bring up reserve cavalry in support. When the French cuirassiers and lancers counter-attacked in superior strength, the scattered, breathless men and horses were powerless and became themselves the pursued. The flower of Wellington's cavalry - the striking-force of his tactical reserve - having saved his centre, was itself needlessly destroyed. Sir William Ponsonby was struck down at the head of the Union Brigade, and nearly half the personnel of the six splendid regiments which had smashed D'Erlon's columns was killed or taken prisoner. Vandeleur's Brigade, which gallantly tried to cover their retreat, also suffered severely. Those who got back to the British lines were too few to intervene with real effect in the battle again.*

* * *

But for this unexpected advantage, there would have seemed little object in Napoleon's continuing the battle. It was now three o'clock. Not only had one of his two corps of front-line infantry become heavily committed to an increasingly costly and still unsuccessful struggle in front of Hougoumont, but the British, contrary to expectation, had repulsed and shattered the other which, untouched at either Ligny or Quatre Bras, was to have breached and pinned down Wellington's centre until Lobau's reserve infantry, Ney's

* Lynedoch, 760, 762-3; Fortescue, X, 365-7; Gomm, 351; Gronow, I, 78-80, 195-6, 204; II, 3; *Hamilton of Dalzell* MS., 50-3, 70-1, 77-8; Haydon, I, 311; Houssaye, 197-20; Kennedy, 110-11; Kincaid, 345; Picton, 78-80; Lady Shelley, I, 173-4, 183; Siborne, 7-10, 16-17, 43-4, 72, 77, 81-2; Tomkinson, 300, 304; Howarth, 93-102; Becke, 197-8; Weller, *Waterloo* 102-5.

cavalry and, at the end of all, the Imperial Guard, had destroyed him. Instead, Napoleon now found himself committed to an impending battle on a second front, to avert or postpone which he was forced to detach, under Lobau, the very reserve of infantry which was to have followed up D'Erlon's expected success. With the Prussians approaching from the other side, he dared not commit this now to a left-hook against the British centre, the vital approach to which was still untaken. Apart from the small portion of Reille's corps still uncommitted to the unending fight round Hougoumont, he had no infantry left for a new attack on the ridge except the twenty-four battalions of the Imperial Guard. And these, in view of the growing threat to his flank and the, to him, unexpected revelation of British defensive striking-power, he was not yet prepared to commit. For the Guard was the last card that stood between him and ruin. He kept it, 13,000 strong, the apple of his eye, unused beside him.

For about half an hour there was a pause in the battle, except at Hougoumont, where Jerome and Foy threw ever more troops into the inferno round the blazing but still defiant buildings. Wellington took advantage of the lull to readjust his dispositions. Pack's brigade took the place vacated by Bylandt's Netherlanders, Lambert's brigade came up from the second line to strengthen Picton's battered division, and two more companies of the King's German Legion were thrown into La Haye Sainte. The Prussians were taking far longer to arrive than the British commander had expected. There had been a delay in their start, aggravated by a fire in the narrow streets of Wavre and the fact that Bülow's as yet unused corps in the van had the farthest distance to march. After the rains, the cross-country lanes were almost impassable for transport, and Gneisenau, the Prussian Chief of Staff, was reluctant to attack Napoleon, with Grouchy's troops in his rear, until he knew for certain that Wellington was standing fast. Only Blücher's insistence—for the old man, oblivious of his injuries, was with Bülow's advanced-guard by midday—carried the tired and hungry troops forward through the soggy defiles of the Lasne and the dense woods which lay between it and the battlefield. "I have promised Wellington," he told them as they dragged the guns axle-deep through mire, "you would not have me break my word!"

Meanwhile the French gunners had taken up their position again on the central ridge and, soon after three o'clock, reopened their fire.

It was more intense than anything the oldest Peninsular veteran had experienced. The range was so accurate that almost every shot told, and after a quarter of an hour Wellington withdrew his infantry a hundred yards farther back from the crest. Under cover of the bombardment, La Haye Sainte in the centre was again surrounded. But Baring's handful of King's German Legionaries continued to hold the walls, and with Kempt's and Lambert's men standing firm on the plateau above, D'Erlon's mangled infantry refrained from pressing home their assault. They seemed to fear a renewal of the storm of cavalry which had struck their comrades.

Suddenly the battle took a novel and spectacular form. For, mistaking the partial withdrawal of Wellington's infantry for the beginning of a general retirement, Marshal Ney decided to take a shortcut to victory by sweeping the ridge with heavy cavalry. Of these – the finest in the world – his master had almost as many as Wellington's British infantry. He therefore ordered forward 5000 of them, including eight regiments of cuirassiers, drawing them up in the plain immediately to the west of the *chaussée* where the slope was easiest.

Wellington watched the splendid spectacle with amazement. It seemed unbelievable that the French would dare to assail a line of unbroken British infantry with cavalry alone. But such was plainly their intention, and, with his own heavy cavalry too weakened to counter-charge in strength, there was a danger that, if Napoleon was able to bring up infantry and guns behind them, the defenders, forced to remain in square, might be blasted out of existence by case-shot. The two divisions to the west of the Brussels road – the 3rd and 1st – were ordered to form battalion squares or oblongs* in chequer-wise pattern across the gently swelling, corn-covered plateau. They were aligned so that every face of every square had a field of fire free of the next. Until the attackers appeared over the crest, Wellington ordered the men to lie down. Behind the twenty squares his cavalry, including the remnants of the two British heavy brigades, were drawn up in support.

Between and a little in advance of the squares Wellington placed his guns, bringing up his last two reserve batteries of Horse Artillery

* The unusual but convenient formation chosen by young Captain Shaw Kennedy, a pupil of Moore and Craufurd, who was acting as chief-of-staff to Alten's third division. Kennedy, 98-102.

to inflict the utmost damage on the advancing cavalry. "Ah! that's the way I like to see horse artillery move,"* he said, as Mercer's men, on the order, "Left limber up, and as fast as you can!" galloped into the inferno of smoke and heat on the plateau. As they did so, they heard a humming like the sound of myriads of beetles on a summer's evening; so thick was the hail of balls and bullets, wrote their commander, that it seemed dangerous to extend the arm lest it should be torn off. Their orders, in the event of the enemy charging home, were to run for shelter to the nearest square, taking the near wheel of each gun with them.

Mercer disregarded this order - one that could only have been given to gun detachments of the highest discipline and training - not because he doubted his battery's morale, but because he believed that the young Brunswickers in square on either side of him, who were falling fast, would take to their heels if they saw his men run. As soon as the French appeared out of the smoke a hundred yards away - a long line of cuirasses and helmets glittering like a gigantic wave on the crest of the rye - he ordered his six nine-pounders, doubly loaded with round-shot and case, to open fire. As the case poured into them, the leading ranks went down like grass before a skilled mower. Again and again, when the French charged, the same thing happened, and the Brunswickers who, before the battery's arrival, had stood like soulless logs in their agony and had only been kept at their posts by the gallantry of their officers, recovered heart.

Elsewhere, where the gunners obeyed Wellington's orders, the French cavalry, crowded in a dense mass into the half-mile gap between Hougoumont and La Haye Sainte, rode over the abandoned guns and swept round the squares beyond. They did not gallop like English foxhunters, but came, as was their wont, at a slow, majestic pace and in perfect formation, their horses shaking the earth. As they appeared the British infantry rose at the word of command, their muskets at the ready and their bayonets bristling like gigantic *chevaux de frise*. If the cavalry of the Empire were Atlantic breakers, the British squares were the rocks of an iron coast. The men, many of them rosy-faced youngsters from the plough, were much impressed by the splendid appearance of the hordes of legendary horsemen who suddenly encircled them, and even more by their courage. But they were not intimidated by them, as Ney had intended.

* Mercer, I, 313.

As their experienced officers and NCOs seemed to regard the newcomers as harmless, in their stolid, unimaginative English way they did so too. The cuirassiers and lancers made a great deal of noise and glitter, brandishing their weapons like pantomime giants and shouting " *Vive l'Empereur*," but they seemed infinitely preferable to the continuous hail of shot and shell which had poured from the French batteries till they arrived on the ridge.

Short of impaling their horses on the hedges of bayonets, Ney's cavalry tried every device to break the squares. Occasionally little groups of horsemen, led by frantic officers, would dash for the face of one, firing off carbines and pistols and hoping to draw sufficient fire to enable their comrades behind to break in on a line of unloaded muskets. But the British and Hanoverian squares preserved perfect discipline, withholding their fire until they received the word of command and then, with their volleys, bringing down everything before them. The loss of horses was prodigious; the poor creatures lay dead or dying in hundreds, their riders, many of them wounded, making their way in a continuous stream back down the hill, or sprawling in their heavy cuirasses in the mud, looking, as Wellington afterwards recalled, like overturned turtles.*

Whenever he judged that the intruders were sufficiently worn down and wearied, Wellington endeavoured to push them off the plateau with his cavalry, or, in default, by edging forward his squares in échelon towards the abandoned guns. He did not hurry, for he was playing for time, and he could not afford to let his light British and King's German Legion cavalry encounter the heavier armed cuirassiers until the latter were too exhausted and reduced to retaliate. The foreign Horse which he had brought up from the flanks and reserve to take the place of Ponsonby's and Somerset's lost squadrons proved, most of it, worse than useless, refusing repeated appeals from Uxbridge to charge. One regiment of Hanoverian hussars, led by its colonel,† fled as far as Brussels.

---

* Someone once asked him whether the French cuirassiers had not come up very well at Quatre Bras. "Yes," he replied, "and they went down very well too." See also Becke, 202-9; *Croker Papers*, I, 330; Lynedoch, 759; Ellesmere, 98-9, 240; Fortescue, X, 370-6; Fraser, 558-9; Frazer, 559; Gomm, 373; Gronow, I, 69-73, 190-1; Houssaye, 204-14; Jackson, 48-51; Kennedy, 19, 20, 115-16; Mercer, I, 310-11; Picton, 81-2, 85-6; Siborne, 1-12; Tomkinson, 305.

† "The Aide-de-Camp . . . seeing that the Hanoverian would not advance, said, 'As you do not attend to the order given, I have another from the Duke of Wellington which is *that you fall back to the rear of the army*.' This the Hanoverian readily complied with, saying

Even the British cavalry showed a reluctance at times to charge home in the face of such overwhelming weight and numbers, though several regiments, particularly the 13th Light Dragoons and the 15th Hussars, behaved with the greatest gallantry. The shock felt by men encountering for the first time the sights and sounds of battle - and such a battle - had in the nature of things a more paralysing effect on cavalry than on infantry whose men in square had the close support of officers and comrades. Once Uxbridge, whose energy and initiative throughout this critical time was beyond praise, was driven into exclaiming that he had tried every brigade and could not get one to follow him, and then, as he rode up to the 1st Foot Guards, "Thank God, I am with men who make me not ashamed of being an Englishman."* One of the officers recalled how, while Wellington was sheltering in his square, the men were so mortified at seeing the cuirassiers deliberately walking their horses round them that they shouted, "Where are our cavalry? Why don't they come and pitch into these French fellows?" Such resentment failed to take into account the hopeless numerical inferiority of the Allied cavalry after its earlier losses, and was based on an incomplete view of the battle-field. All the hard-pressed infantrymen could see, amid clouds of thick, eddying smoke, was the outer face of the square on either side, and the hordes of encircling French Horse. They could not realise that the very presence of the decimated English squadrons in their rear helped to sustain the wavering morale of the Netherlanders and Brunswickers, and that the memory of their earlier and heroic onslaught accounted for Napoleon's failure to follow up his cavalry with infantry and subject their squares to case-shot at close range.

Five times in two hours the French horsemen were driven from the plateau; five times, after rallying in the plain they returned.

---

it was very considerate of the Duke when engaged in so much action to think of his corps with so much care. Accordingly this corps retreated, and it was from them that a report reached Brussels that the French had gained the victory." Farington, VIII, 19-20. See also *Hamilton of Dalzell* MS., 73; Frazer, 560-1; Siborne, 14, 18-19; Stanhope, 221; Tomkinson, 296.

* From a copy of a letter of Captain (later General) Horace Churchill of June 24th 1815, communicated by Brigadier C. E. Hudson, VC, CB, DSO, MC. "All that Churchill says in censure," wrote Napier of this letter, "was the common talk of the Army at the time." See *Hamilton of Dalzell* MS. for a cavalryman's criticism, and Gronow, I, 73; Tomkinson, 318. Lord Uxbridge afterwards wrote in glowing terms of the conduct of the British cavalry as a whole. Siborne, 12, 16-17.

Whenever they disappeared the British gunners ran out of the squares and reopened fire, while Napoleon's guns resumed their cannonade. Some time after five o'clock Ney brought up the last cavalry from the second line - Kellermann's two divisions of cuirassiers and the heavy squadrons of the Imperial Guard. At one moment more than 9000 Horse assailed the ridge in a compact phalanx. This immense body was packed in the 800 yards' front between the *chaussée* and the British bastion at Hougoumont, where the ground was a morass piled with dead horses. The front ranks, including most of the senior officers, were completely wiped out by the English batteries, and the weary mounts could only proceed at a walk. Yet they still continued to return.

Throughout this time and during the bombardments which preceded each assault the British infantry patiently endured their fate. They seemed in their steady squares to be rooted to the ground. Though it would have been hazardous in the extreme to have manœuvred with some of the young British and Hanoverian Landwehr battalions, they showed themselves, under their fine officers and NCOs, as capable of standing fire as the oldest veterans. Theirs, as Harry Smith said, was no battle of science; it was a stand-up fight between two pugilists, milling away till one or the other was beaten. Inside each suffocating square, reeking with the smell of burnt cartridge and powder, it was like a hospital, the dead and dying strewing the ground. The sufferings of many of the wounded were indescribable; one rifleman had both legs shot off and both arms amputated, but continued to breathe as he lay amid his comrades. Few cried out in their pain, and, when they did so, their officers immediately quieted them;* it was a point of pride with Englishmen of all classes to take punishment without murmuring. Their stoicism was equalled by that of the French cavalry, who won the ungrudging admiration of the entire British army.†

Nor was less courage shown by the defenders of Hougoumont. The flank companies in the burnt-out mansion among the charred

* "The rear man made a considerable outcry on being wounded, but on one of the officers saying kindly to him, 'O man, don't make a noise,' he instantly recollected himself and was quiet. This was the only noise . . . which I heard from any wounded man during the battle." Leeke, I, 33.

† "Never was such devotion witnessed as the French cuirassiers. . . . I could not help exclaiming when the mêlée was going on, 'By God, those fellows deserve Bonaparte, they fight so nobly for him.' " MS. letter of Horace Churchill, June 24th 1815.

remains of their comrades, the Coldstream lining the hedge and garden wall, the 3rd Guards in the orchard, all lived that day up to the highest tradition of the Brigade of Guards. They had made up their minds to die sooner than yield. Three times the wood was taken and retaken; every tree was riddled with bullets, and in the orchard alone more than two thousand bodies were crowded together. "You may depend upon it," said Wellington, "no troops could have held Hougoumont but British, and only the best of them."

* * *

The British Commander-in-Chief neither avoided nor courted danger, but, knowing that his presence was necessary to keep his young soldiers to the sticking-point, he showed himself, placid and unconcerned, wherever the fire was hottest. Riding up and down his hard-pressed lines "slowly and coolly," as Lieutenant Wheatley of the King's German Legion twice saw him that afternoon, with an ever-dwindling staff, and at one time without even a single aide, he seemed completely calm and oblivious of the storm of shot around him. Every now and then, with his raised telescope, he surveyed the battlefield, ready to anticipate the enemy's every movement. Whenever the French cavalry, swarming over the ridge, made it necessary, he withdrew into one of the squares. "Wait a little longer, lads," he called out to the men in one of them, as they begged to be allowed to avenge their sufferings with the bayonet, "you shall have at them, presently." Everywhere he infected men, near the limit of endurance, with courage and confidence.*

During the last hour of Ney's cavalry attacks the sound of Prussian guns had been audible on the British ridge in the lulls of firing, though few yet realised its import. By four o'clock, the two leading divisions of Bülow's corps had reached the western edge of Paris wood, just over two miles east of La Belle Alliance. Half an hour later, in view of the urgency of Wellington's messages, they went into action without waiting for their supports. Soon after five, when they had advanced to within a mile and a half of the Brussels road,

---

* "Not a private in the ranks but felt that the Duke of Wellington—the man of Wealth, Rank and Success with the world at his feet—was jeopardising his life to at least the same degree as the poor outcast who had become a soldier from starvation." Fraser, 252-3. See also D'Arblay, VII, 134; Lennox, *Three Years with the Duke*, 114-115.

Lobau counter-attacked and drove them back. But at six o'clock, two more Prussian divisions having emerged from the wood, Bülow again attacked, striking round Lobau's southern flank at Plancenoit, a village less than a mile from the French life-line.

The situation was growing grave in the extreme for Napoleon. His troops had been marching and fighting almost continuously for four days; their losses during the afternoon had been heavier than in any engagement of comparable scale in his career. Again and again they had seemed on the point of carrying the ridge and sweeping Wellington's international flotsam and jetsam down the Brussels road. Yet whenever the smoke cleared, the stubborn redcoats were seen to be still standing. The Prussian shot, already playing on the *chaussée*, brought home to the Emperor that, unless he could break Wellington's line in the remaining hours of daylight, his doom was certain.

Though, like his adversary, still in his middle forties, the Emperor had so far taken little active part in the direction of the assault. After a study of the battlefield in the early hours and the issue of orders for the attack, he had delegated tactical control to Ney. Exhausted by the exertions of the last three days and suffering from a severe attack of piles, he had spent part of the afternoon at his headquarters at Rossomme in what seemed to onlookers a coma, and had not even intervened to stay the impetuous Marshal's abuse of his cavalry. But he now roused himself, to snatch, as so often in the past, victory from defeat.

He had to fight on two fronts. To the south-east 30,000 Prussians were striking at his communications; to the north 20,000 Britons and as many or more Germans and Netherlanders were still barring the Brussels road. Despite his casualties he still had between 50,000 and 60,000 veteran troops, though of Grouchy's 33,000, wandering somewhere in space to the east,* there was no sign. To clear his flank and gain time for a further assault on the British, he dispatched eight Young Guard battalions of the Imperial Guard to reinforce Lobau and recover Plancenoit. Simultaneously he gave Ney peremptory orders to throw in infantry and capture La Haye Sainte.

Conscious that the crisis of the battle was at hand and that the interminable and futile attacks of the French cavalry must now be

* Unknown to him they were at that moment fiercely attacking the Prussian rearguard at Wavre twelve miles away.

followed up by infantry, Wellington had already reorganised his line. Taking advantage of the lull after the last charge, he had brought up Clinton's division of Peninsular veterans from its place in reserve to a point at which, standing between the defenders of Hougoumont and Maitland's Guards, they could enfilade any attack on his right. Feeling that Hougoumont was now secure and that, as a result, no threat could develop from that quarter, he also summoned Chassé's Netherlanders from Braine L'Alleud and placed them in rear of his centre. Simultaneously, seeing that Ney's force was spent, he deployed his shrunken battalions from square, forming them four-deep instead of in the normal two-rank line so as to give extended fire-power against infantry while preserving sufficient solidity to repel what remained of the French cavalry.*

Soon after six Ney attacked in the centre with two columns of infantry and cavalry. They were driven back by a terrific fire from the British guns. But the French were fighting magnificently and with the recklessness of despair, and the young Prince of Orange, in charge of the defenders at this point, was without experience of command. Repeating a mistake made at Quatre Bras, he ordered one of Ompteda's battalions of the King's German Legion above La Haye Sainte to deploy in the presence of cavalry, with disastrous consequences. Their comrades inside the farmhouse were now down to their last round of ammunition,† and at about six-thirty the key to the British centre was captured. Baring's remaining forty men fought their way back to the ridge with the bayonet. At about the same time the eight battalions of the Young Guard, sent to Lobau's aid, recovered Plancenoit.

This double success gave the French, at the eleventh hour, a chance of victory. Throwing sharpshooters and guns forward from the captured farm, they established themselves on the ridge and opened a destructive fire on the left of the 3rd Division and the right of the 5th. The Prince of Orange, who had by now completely lost his head,

* Becke, 211; Ellesmere, 207-9; Fortescue, X, 372, 378; Tomkinson, 308; Weller, *Waterloo*, 106-7 111-12.

† Through a failure on the Prince of Orange's part, and ultimately on Wellington's, to make adequate provision in time. "The Duke lamented the loss of La Haye Sainte from the fault of the officer commanding there, but immediately correcting himself, 'No, in fact it was my fault, for I ought to have looked into it myself.'" Stanhope, 245-6, 220. See also Ellesmere, 104, 208-9; Fortescue, 381-3; Kennedy, 122-3, 174-5; Siborne, 32-3; Tomkinson, 305.

deployed another of Ompteda's battalions in the presence of cavalry with the same disastrous result. A few minutes later Ompteda was killed. His shattered brigade and that of Kielmansegge's young Hanoverians had reached the limit of their endurance and were on the point of breaking. An immediate break-through the British centre was only averted by a timely charge of the 3rd Hussars of the Legion and the gallantry of the 1st Battalion of the 95th Rifles, whose accurate fire from the hedgerow to which they had fallen back from the adjacent gravel-pit after the capture of La Haye Sainte, alone prevented the enemy field-guns from establishing themselves on the summit and raking the defenders' entire line from close range.

Had Napoleon been on the spot to exploit the opportunity, he might have turned the gap in the British centre into a chasm. But when, still watching from La Belle Alliance three-quarters of a mile away, he received Ney's urgent appeal for more infantry, he only asked petulantly whether the Marshal expected him to make them. At the crisis of his gamble his moral courage faltered; he was not yet ready to stake everything. And while the twelve remaining battalions of the Imperial Guard waited, unused, Wellington, summoned from his position with the Guards Division above Hougoumont, galloped to the spot, calling up every remaining available unit.

The British Commander-in-Chief took the news of the disaster to his centre with his habitual calm and decision. Colonel Shaw Kennedy of the hard-pressed 3rd Division, General Alten's chief staff-officer who reported it to him, said that he received it " with a degree of coolness and . . . with such precision and energy as to prove the most complete self-possession. . . . From the determined manner in which he spoke, it was evident that he had resolved to defend to the last extremity every inch of the position which he then held. His Grace's answer to my representation was, 'I shall order Brunswick troops in reserve behind Maitland to the spot, and other troops besides. Go you and get all the German troops of the division to the spot that you can, and all guns that you can find.' "* Then, sending for Vivian's light cavalry brigade from its reserve position behind Papelotte, as nearly all the Allied leaders in the centre had by now been killed or wounded, he temporarily took over command there himself. Leading five young Brunswicker battalions into the full

* Kennedy, 128. See also Weller, *Waterloo*, 119-24.

storm of the French batteries, he rallied them when they broke under that hurricane of shot and brought them steadily back into line. Swarms of *tirailleurs*, formed from D'Erlon's broken divisions, were now everywhere infiltrating the ridge, keeping the long-tried British squares under continuous fire at close range—a thing which would have been impossible had Uxbridge's heavy cavalry not suffered such disastrous losses through their inability to control their own triumphant charge earlier in the day. But the *tirailleurs* were driven back when Vivian, anticipating Wellington's orders and seeing a new force of Prussians moving up from the east, arrived on his own initiative from the left of the ridge. Simultaneously Uxbridge galloped off to fetch Vandeleur's 11th, 12th and 16th Light Dragoons, and Somerset, with the wreck of the Union Brigade extended in single rank to make the utmost show, instilled confidence and pressure from behind into Chassé's Netherlanders.

Once again a desperate situation had been saved by Wellington's action. But the losses of the battered 3rd Division were desperate. When Sir Colin Halkett, two-thirds of whose brigade had fallen, asked if it could be temporarily relieved, Wellington replied to his message, "Tell him what he asks is impossible. He and I, and every Englishman on the field, must die on the spot which we occupy."*

The bombardment had now reached a new degree of intensity as Napoleon brought up every available gun to reinforce his massed batteries. All along the Allied centre men were going down like ninepins; close by the crossroads 450 of the 700 men of the 27th lay in square where they had fallen. In a neighbouring regiment - the 40th - both ensigns and fourteen sergeants had been killed or wounded round the tattered colours. The 5th Division, 5000 strong when the battle started, seemed almost to have dwindled to a line of skirmishers. Kincaid with the Rifles began to wonder whether there had ever been a battle in which everyone on both sides had been killed.† The stream of wounded and fugitives towards the rear was so great that a Prussian aide-de-camp, who rode up from Ziethen's oncoming corps to investigate, returned with a report that the British were defeated and in retreat. No one knew what was happen-

* Clinton, 421.
† Kincaid, 352. See also Ellesmere, 172-3; Fortescue, X, 396-7; Frazer, 139, 189, 219; Gomm, 359-60, 366; Gronow, I, 212; Basil Jackson, 75-6; *Autobiography of Sergeant Lawrence*, 239; Simmons, 375; Tomkinson, 308.

ing outside his own immediate vicinity, for in the windless, oven-like, smoke-filled air visibility was reduced to a few yards. Yet Wellington's grip on the battle never relaxed. Unlike his imperial adversary he was used to commanding comparatively small armies and to attending to every tactical detail himself. At one point, riding up to a square of the 1st Battalion of the Rifles which had lost its senior officers, he himself gave them the command, "95th, unfix your swords, left face and extend yourselves once more; we shall soon have them over the hill!" Then, according to the rifleman who recalled the incident, "he rode away on our right, and how he escaped being shot, God only knows, for all that time the shot was flying like hailstones."*

Lord Uxbridge, who had never before served under him, said after the battle that his coolness and decision in action surpassed anything he could have conceived; "I thought I had heard enough of this man," he told Lady Shelley, "but he has far surpassed my expectations. It is not a man but a god." "Cool and indifferent at the beginning of battles," Sir Alexander Frazer, his artillery commander, wrote of him, "when the moment of difficulty comes, intelligence flashes from the eyes of this wonderful man and he rises superior to all that can be imagined."†

Almost every member of his staff had by now fallen, his Quartermaster, General de Lancey, and his leading aide, Colonel Canning – both killed by his side – his military secretary, Fitzroy Somerset, dangerously wounded, and his beloved Alexander Gordon, companion of every Peninsular campaign, with his thigh fatally shattered by a cannon-ball as he helped him rally the Brunswickers. Yet though he looked thoughtful and pale, he betrayed no sign of anxiety.‡ Once, when chatting with the commanding officer of a square in which he had taken shelter, he was heard to say, "Oh, it will be all right; if the Prussians come up in time, we shall have a long peace." But occasionally he looked at his watch.

"Hard pounding this, gentlemen," he observed, "but we will see who can pound the longest." And when the smoke for a moment

* Booth, *Waterloo*, II, 275, (Letter of Rifleman Lewis) cit. Glover, 274.
† *Spencer and Waterloo*, 114-15; Lady Shelley, I, 106; Frazer, 560.
‡ Broughton, I, 103; Castlereagh, X, 383; Ellesmere, 172-3; Farington, VIII, 32; Frazer, 263, 276; Gronow, I, 69-70; Guedalla, 275-6; *Hamilton of Dalzell* MS., 56-60; Kennedy, 126-9, 176; Picton, 88-9, 106; Jackson, 42-4; Smith, I, 271; Stanhope, 183; Longford, 471-3; Weller, *Waterloo*, 121-4; Becke, 216-19; Muriel Wellesley, 370.

drifted away and the scanty lines of red were seen everywhere to be standing, a cheer went up from his tired countrymen that showed him to be justified. The hour for which he and they had endured so much was near. For streaming on to the east end of the battlefield from Smohain, driving the French from the environs of Papelotte and La Haye, where Bernhard of Saxe-Weimar's steady Nassauers had been holding their own all day, and filling in the two-mile gap between Bülow's men before Plancenoit and the left of the British line, came Ziethen's long-awaited Prussian corps. Recalled in the nick of time by General Müffling, who had galloped after it when, in the belief that the British were defeated, it had started to withdraw, its intervention—so long delayed—was far more decisive than Bülow's earlier, more distant attack on Plancenoit. As the Prussian batteries, adding their quota to the inferno on the ridge,* began to shell the ground near La Belle Alliance, Napoleon knew that the supreme crisis was at hand. Already from his right rear news had come that the Young Guard had been driven out of Plancenoit. The field was closing in as it had done at Leipzig, and the night was little more than an hour away.

Soon after seven, the Emperor took his final resolution. He sent two of the magnificent, untouched battalions of the Old Guard to recapture Plancenoit and prevent encirclement. Then, bidding his aides-de-camp announce that it was Grouchy, not the Prussians, who had arrived from the east, he ordered a general advance of all units. As its spearhead he brought forward the remaining battalions of the Imperial Guard, keeping only three as a last reserve. With the former he descended the plain, marching at their head towards the British ridge. As he did so the French guns again increased their tempo.

Fresh from its triumph at Ligny two nights before, the Guard advanced with a deeply impressive *élan*. Its men were conscious that they bore the destinies of the world. Such was their tremendous prestige that the two veteran battalions who had been sent to recapture Plancenoit did so in twenty minutes without firing a shot and in the face of 25,000 Prussians. Those advancing against the British were inspired by the personal presence of Napoleon. At the foot of the slope, in a sheltered hollow, he halted to let them pass, throwing open his greatcoat to display his medals and repeatedly

---

* Mercer's battery was almost cut to pieces by their fire. See also Mercer, I, 325-30; Siborne, 21-2.

crying out, " *A Bruxelles, mes enfants! à Bruxelles!*" They answered with shouts of " *Vive l'Empereur!*" and pressed forward with solemn tread and shouldered arms. In front of each regiment rode a general, Marshal Ney - "*le rougeaud*" - with powder-blackened face and tattered uniform, directing all. Cavalry moved on their flanks, and in the intervals between the battalions came field-pieces loaded with case-shot. Ahead went a cloud of sharpshooters. Simultaneously, closely observed by Wellington through his telescope, what remained of Reille's three divisions moved up for a new assault on Hougoumont, while to the east of the Brussels *chaussée* D'Erlon's regrouped corps massed for one last blow against the battered British left centre. Everything Napoleon possessed was being staked on a final culminating bid for victory.

The Guard went up the hill in two columns, the one moving obliquely up a spur from the Brussels road towards the centre of the British right, the other using, so far as Wellington's dispositions admitted, the sheltered ground between La Belle Alliance and Hougoumont. True to the tactical conception which had dominated the earlier attacks, the frontal blow was to be clinched by a left hook. But with Hougoumont firmly held and Du Plat's Hanoverians and Adam's brigade of Light Infantry deployed by the Duke across the hollow way between it and the ridge, the front on which the attackers could operate was narrower than ever. And, with his unerring tactical sense, Wellington was waiting at the very spot at which his adversary's main knock-out blow was aimed: on the right of the Guards Division where it touched the left battalion - the 2nd 95th - of Adam's brigade. Warned of the imminent approach of the Imperial Guard by a deserting royalist colonel, as well as by what he had seen through his field-glass before the marching columns disappeared into the declivity below the ridge and by the ominous, ever-nearing throbbing of the imperial drums, he had ordered his men to lie down in the corn until the French appeared; their long vigil of endurance, he told them, would soon be over.

Until the columns reached the summit Wellington's artillerymen, serving their exposed guns on the ridge till the last possible moment, drove swathes of death through them. In the general darkness and confusion, and because of the fire from the guns on the ridge, the leading battalions of the first column struck the British line at two points: where Halkett's battered brigade of the 3rd

Division was drawn up in front of Chassé's Netherlanders, and immediately to the west where Wellington was waiting with Maitland's 1st Guards. As the huge bearskins loomed suddenly out of the swirling mist and smoke, the Commander-in-Chief's voice rang out, "Now, Maitland, now's your time," followed by the order - taken up by officers and the sergeants along the ranks - "Stand up, Guards! Make ready! Fire!" Then the British sprang to their feet in the corn and, enfilading the advancing files from either side, poured from their extended lines a tremendous and shattering volley, following it up by the familiar rolling fire by platoons and half companies which had broken so many French columns. The "Immortals" tried to deploy but too late, and most of their leading officers were swept down. Then, while they were still in confusion, the British Guards charged.

But though the Imperial Guard recoiled, it did not yet break. Both parts of the main column re-formed and opened fire on the oncoming British, their field-guns supporting them with case. To the east the remnants of the 33rd and 69th were driven back by a smaller column and almost broke, but were rallied by Halkett and by Wellington himself, who galloped quickly to the scene. A Dutch battery, behaving with great coolness and gallantry, raked the French column, and Chassé's Belgians, 3000 strong, kept in position by Vivian's shepherding cavalry in their rear, came up in support. Gradually the attackers, isolated and without support behind them, began to give ground. Meanwhile those opposed to the 1st Guards, though driven back for some distance, had also rallied. Maitland ordered his Guardsmen back, but his voice could not be heard above the firing, and some of them, mistaking his intention, tried to form square. In the confusion the two British battalions withdrew in some disorder, only to re-form at the word of command, with flawless and habitual steadiness, on regaining their original position.

But before the battle between the rival Guards could be resumed, it was decided by the action of the most experienced regiment on the British side. Wellington always maintained that, if he had had at Waterloo the army with which he crossed the Pyrenees, he would have attacked Napoleon without waiting for the Prussians: "I should have swept him off the face of the earth," he said, "in two hours."[*]
The first battalion of the 52nd, commanded by John Colborne,

* Fraser, 38; Ellesmere, 106, 163; Kincaid, 356.

afterwards Lord Seaton, had served in John Moore's original Light Brigade; Colborne himself was Moore's finest living pupil. It had gone into action at Waterloo with more than a thousand bayonets, half of them veterans of the Spanish War, being one of the very few British battalions which was up to strength - "a regiment," wrote Napier of its Peninsular exploits, "never surpassed in arms since arms were first borne by men." Owing to the skilful way in which Colborne had placed and handled it during the French cavalry charges and the long hours of bombardment, its casualties had been extraordinary light.

As the second and westernmost column of the Imperial Guard after passing by Hougoumont pressed up the slope towards Maitland's unbroken line, the drummers beating the *rummadum, dummadum, dum*, of the *pas de charge*, Colborne, who was stationed in the centre of Adam's brigade to the right of the Guards, took a sudden decision. Without orders either from the Duke or any superior officer, he moved his battalion forward out of the line for a distance of three hundred yards, and then, as it drew level with the leading company of the advancing French column, wheeled it to the left as though on parade, with the order, "Right shoulders forward." He thus laid it on the flank of the French. By doing so he took the risk both of leaving a gap in the line behind and of having his men cut to pieces by cavalry - a fate he had experienced when, as one of Stewart's brigade commanders, he had moved up the hill at Albuera.

The reward of his daring was decisive. The Imperial Guard, taken by surprise, halted and poured a volley into the 52nd which brought down a hundred and forty of its men. But the British reply of this grave Roman battalion was decisive. It seemed as though every bullet found its mark. So heavy were the casualties in the dense column that the Imperial Guard did not wait for the 52nd to charge. It faltered, broke and fled. As it did so, the 52nd resumed its advance eastwards across, and at right angles to, the British front, with the two other battalions of Adam's brigade - the 95th and 71st - moving up on Wellington's instructions on either flank and firing devastating volley after volley into the recoiling veterans' ranks. A few hundred yards on, this magnificent brigade, so carefully husbanded for this decisive moment, encountered another French column re-forming, and dealt it the same treatment and with the same results.

Then, as with cries of "*La Garde recule!*" the disordered assailants of that impregnable ridge fell back once more, Wellington was seen to raise his hat high in the air and wave it three times towards the enemy. With the instinct of genius, he realised that the moment for which he and his men had waited had at last come. "Oh, damn it!" he was heard to say, "In for a penny, in for a pound!" One who was with him told Lady Shelley afterwards that the expression of his face at that moment was almost superhuman. Then, hat still raised high, he galloped westwards along the ridge from one tattered, enduring regiment to another. "Who commands here?" he shouted to Harry Smith, Lambert's brigade major. "Generals Kempt and Lambert, my Lord." "Desire them to form column of companies and move on immediately." "In what direction, my Lord?" "Right ahead, to be sure."* And when, uncertain whether to proceed farther in its daring march across the flank of the discomfited attackers, the 52nd halted for instructions, the Commander-in-Chief, spurring down to it, called out, "Well done! Go on, Colborne, go on! Don't give them time to rally! They won't stand!"

It was now nearly dusk. But, as the French cannonade ceased and the smoke began to drift from the ridge, the setting sun, breaking through the low clouds of that long day, cast a ray of light along the glinting British line, motionless no more, and on the accoutrements of the defeated columns in the plain. The whole French army was suddenly dissolving with the landscape: entire regiments leaving their arms piled and taking to their heels. From the east the Prussians were pouring in a great flood across the battlefield, and to the south, where the Old and Young Guard were still fighting fiercely to keep Napoleon's life-line open, Bülow's men had swept through Plancenoit and were approaching the *chaussée*. "I have seen nothing like that moment," wrote Frazer of the Artillery, "the sky literally darkened with smoke, the sun just going down and which till then had not for some hours broken through the gloom of a dull day, the indescribable shouts of thousands where it was impossible to distinguish between friends and foe."

---

* "I never saw his Grace so animated," Smith, I, 272-3. See also Becke, 222-30; Longford, 478-80; Weller, *Waterloo*, 149-50; Howarth, 182-3; Cotton, 125-35, 305-6; Ellesmere, 183-4; Fortescue, X, 391-2; Gomm, 361-2, 367-73; Gronow, I, 73, 89-90; Houssaye, 221-32; Jackson, 69-70; Kennedy, 140-50; Leeke, I, *passim*; Moorsom, 256-65; Robinson, 611-14; Siborne, *passim*; Tomkinson, 311-15; Chesney, 210-13.

In that final advance, with scattered units of British and French cavalry appearing out of the darkening gloom in charge and counter-charge, and little groups of French gunners and a few unbroken squares of the Old Guard fighting to give their Emperor time to escape, Lord Uxbridge, riding forward by the Duke's side, had his leg shattered by a shell. "By God! I've lost my leg," he said. "Have you, by God!" replied his chief as he dismounted and helped him to the ground. Then, as with stoic grandeur Uxbridge let himself be carried away, the Duke rode on, following the receding fight. Most of the British regiments were so exhausted that they halted in the plain. Only the cavalry and Adam's brigade, harrying the last retreating squares of the Imperial Guard, proceeded through the heart of what had once been the French position. "We are getting into enclosed ground and your life is too valuable to be thrown away," urged one of Wellington's entourage. "Never mind," he answered, "let them fire away. The battle's won; my life is of no consequence now."*

As Ziethen's Prussian cavalry from the east and Vivian's and Vandeleur's British from the north met at La Belle Alliance, the union of the armies, fought for so fiercely during three days and nights, was consummated. Somewhere between nine and ten o'clock the two men whose good faith, constancy and resolution had made it possible, met on the spot where Napoleon had launched his attack. They were both on horseback, but the old Prussian embraced and kissed his English friend, exclaiming, "*Mein lieber Kamerad*," and then, "*Quelle affaire!*" which, as Wellington observed, was about all the French he knew.

Then, having agreed on plans for the pursuit, in weariness and darkness Wellington turned his tired horse towards Waterloo and the ridge he had so long defended. He rode in silence across a battle-field in which 15,000 men of his own army, including a third of the British troops engaged, and more than 30,000 Frenchmen lay dead, dying or wounded. The sound of gunfire had ceased, but, to the south, trumpets could be faintly heard as the Prussian cavalry took up the pursuit of their inexorable enemies. As their infantry, many of whom had marched fifty miles in the past two days, debouched from Plancenoit into the Charleroi highway, where the 52nd, with its tattered colours, was halted by the roadside, they

* Longford, 81.

broke into slow time and their bands played "God Save the King."[*]

* * *

It was eleven o'clock before the victor dismounted outside the inn at Waterloo. As he patted the horse which had borne him so patiently all day, Copenhagen made his commentary on the terrible battle through which he had passed by suddenly lashing out and breaking free.[†] Inside the inn Wellington bent over the prostrate form of Colonel Gordon, the faithful aide-de-camps who had been with him ever since he sailed for Portugal in 1809 and whose leg had been amputated three hours earlier. "Thank God you are safe," Gordon whispered, as his life began to ebb. But the Duke, hoping for his recovery, ordered him to be carried to his own bed.

There were forty or fifty persons gathered for supper in the crowded inn, including several high-ranking prisoners, among them General Lobau and General Cambronne of the Imperial Guard who was to go down to history with the false legend of having defied surrender with the words, "*La Vielle Garde - qui meurt mais ne se rend pas.*"[‡] But though Wellington ordered them to be given some supper, as traitors to the King to whom they had sworn allegiance he declined to let them remain, saying, "*Messieurs, j'en suis bien fâché, mais je ne puis pas avoir l'honneur de vous recevoir jusqu'a ce que vous avez fait votre paix avec Sa Majesté Très-Chrétienne.*" His own table had been laid, as always in a campaign, for his personal staff, but there were only Alava and one or two others to share it with him. Whenever the door opened, he looked up in hope, but no more came to that silent feast of ghosts. Presently he held up his hands and said to Alava, "The hand of Almighty God has been upon

---

[*] Leeke, 67; Moorsom, 267; Jackson, 57-9; Tomkinson, 315; Gronow, I, 200; Simpson, 129; Stanhope, 245; Picton, 98; Gomm, 370-1, 375-6.

[†] It took a groom half an hour to catch him. "There may have been many faster horses," Wellington said of him, "no doubt many handsomer, but for bottom and endurance I never saw his fellow." Longford, 484.

[‡] " 'Never, certainly,' said the Duke, 'was anything so absurd as ascribing that saying to Cambronne.' " Stanhope, 172. See also *Idem*, 245. "There is not a word of truth in all this bombast. I have fought the French as often as anybody, and . . . I never saw them behave ill except at the end of the battle of Waterloo. Whole battalions ran away and left their arms piled, and as for Cambronne, he surrendered without a wound." Strathfieldsaye, March 31st 1820. Chad, 2; Ellesmere, 111.

me this day." Then he raised his glass and gave a single toast: "To the memory of the Peninsular War!" Immediately afterwards he lay down on a pallet on the floor and, exhausted, fell asleep.

Soon after 3 a.m. he was awoken by his surgeon, Dr Hume, who told him that Gordon was dying. He rose at once and went to him, but found him already dead. As the doctor, taking his proffered hand, read the list of those whose deaths had been reported during the night, he felt tears on his hand and, looking up, saw them coursing down the Duke's battle-grimed face. "Well, thank God I don't know what it is to lose a battle," he said when Hume had finished. "But nothing can be more painful than to gain one with the loss of so many friends."*

Then he rose, washed and dressed and sat down for an hour to begin his Waterloo dispatch to the Secretary of State. "It gives me great satisfaction," he began, "to assure your Lordship that the army never, upon any occasion, conducted itself better. The Division of Guards, under Lieut-General Cooke, who is severely wounded, Major-General Maitland and Major-General Byng, set an example which was followed by all; and there is no officer nor description of troops that did not behave well. . . ." But though his dispatch dwelt on the army's losses, there was little in it about victory and glory, and it was so laconic that, when it was published in London, the American Minister, Quincy Adams, at first believed it came from a defeated general whose army had been annihilated.†

So many of the staff and general officers had been killed or wounded that, with their places to fill and urgent orders to be given for the pursuit of the French, at 5 a.m. the Duke, with his dispatch unfinished, mounted his horse and rode to Brussels. Here all the bells were ringing and the reprieved people shouting in the streets.‡ Sitting at the open window of his hotel room, Wellington resumed his task. There was a crowd outside, including Thomas Creevey who recorded for posterity what happened. "Upon recognising me, he immediately beckoned to me with his finger to come up. . . . The first thing I did was to put my hand out and congratulate him upon his victory. He made a variety of observations in his short, natural,

---

* Longford 485; Stanhope, 84.

† *Dispatches*, XII, 484; Stanhope, 145.

‡ "What a contrast to six hours' plunder by the French which Napoleon had promised." Spencer Madan to Dr Madan, June 19th 1815. *Spencer and Waterloo*, 108.

blunt way, but with the greatest gravity all the time, and without the least approach to anything like triumph or joy. 'It has been a damned serious business,' he said, 'Blücher and I have lost 30,000 men. It has been a damned nice thing - the nearest run thing you ever saw in your life. Blücher lost 14,000 on Friday night, and got so damnably licked I could not find him on Saturday morning; so I was obliged to fall back to keep up communications with him.' Then, as he walked about, he praised greatly those Guards who kept the farm (meaning Hougoumont) against the repeated attacks of the French; and then he praised all our troops, uttering repeated expressions of astonishment at our men's courage. He repeated so often its being *so nice a thing - so nearly run a thing*, that I asked him if the French had fought better than he had ever seen them do before. 'No,' he said, 'they have always fought the same since I first saw them at Vimiero.' Then he said, 'By God! I don't think it would have done if I had not been there.' "*

As well as his dispatches the Duke wrote that day to those whose near relations had served on his staff and fallen. "I cannot express to you," he assured Lord Aberdeen, brother of his beloved Alexander Gordon, "the regret and sorrow with which I look around me and contemplate the loss which I have sustained, particularly in your brother. The glory resulting from such actions, so dearly bought, is no consolation to me, and I cannot suggest it is any to you. . . . But I hope that this last one has been so decisive . . . that our exertions and our individual losses will be rewarded by the early attainment of our just object. It is then that the glory of the actions in which our friends and relations have fallen will be some consolation for their loss."† In a similar letter to the Duke of Beaufort about Lord Fitzroy Somerset, he wrote, "The losses I have sustained have quite broken me down and I have no feeling for the advantages we have acquired." "The Duke," Georgina Capel reported from Brussels—a city now become a hospital "crowded with wounded wretches and with wagons filled with dead and dying"—"was never known to be in such low spirits as he was in consequence of the blood shed at Waterloo." "It was the most desperate business I ever was in," he told his brother, William. "I never took so much trouble about any battle, and never was so near being beat. Our loss is immense, partic-

---

* *Creevey Papers*, I, 23-67.
† *Dispatches*, XII, 488.

ularly in that best of all instruments, British Infantry. I never saw the Infantry behave so well."*

Three weeks after the battle, when his victorious troops had entered Paris, the Duke spoke again of his feelings to his friend, Lady Shelley. "I hope to God," he said, "that I have fought my last battle. It is a bad thing to be always fighting. While in the thick of it I am too much occupied to feel anything; but it is wretched just after. It is quite impossible to think of glory. Both mind and feelings are exhausted. I am wretched even at the moment of victory, and I always say that, next to a battle lost, the greatest misery is a battle gained. Not only do you lose those dear friends with whom you have been living, but you are forced to leave the wounded behind you. To be sure, one tries to do the best for them, but how little that is! At such moments every feeling in your breast is deadened. I am now just beginning to regain my natural spirits, but I never wish for any more fighting."†

His wish was granted.

* To the Hon. William Wellesley-Pole. Wellesley-Pole, 35.
† Lady Shelley, I, 102.

Abbreviations

List of Abbreviated Titles of Sources
given as references in the footnotes

As there is a wealth of excellent up-to-date Wellington bibliographies covering the period of Wellington's military career—notably in Elizabeth Longford's *Wellington, The Years of the Sword*, Jac Weller's *Wellington in the Peninsula* and *Wellington at Waterloo*, Antony Brett-James's *Wellington at War*, and Michael Glover's *Wellington*—I have confined myself to a list of abbreviated titles used as references in the footnotes.

In addition to the sources cited as references in the footnotes, an indispensable work not cited is *The Iconography of the 1st Duke of Wellington* by Lord Gerald Wellesley (now the 7th Duke of Wellington) and J. Steegman published in 1935. An admirable short biography, also not cited, is S. G. P. Ward's *Wellington*, 1963.

To save space and unnecessary repetition I have given only the date and name of the recipient when citing letters printed in the twenty-three volumes of Wellington's *Dispatches* and *Supplementary Despatches*.

ALISON.—Sir A. Alison, *History of Europe from the Commencement of the French Revolution to the Restoration of the Bourbons*, 1849.

ANDERSON.—Lt.-Col. J. A. Anderson, *Recollections of a Peninsular Veteran*, 1913.

ANGLESEY.—Marquess of Anglesey, *One-Leg, the Life and Letters of Henry William Paget, 1st Marquess of Anglesey*, 1961.

ANN. REG.—Annual Register.

ANTON.—J. Anton, *Retrospect of a Military Life*, 1941.

ARBUTHNOT.— *Journal of Mrs Arbuthnot* (ed. F. Bamford and the 7th Duke of Wellington), 1950.

ARTECHE.—General José Arteche y Moro, *Guerra de la Indepencia*, 1868-1902.

AUCKLAND.— *Journal and Correspondence of William Lord Auckland*, 1862.

AUSTEN.—J. H. and E. C. Hubback, *Jane Austen's Sailor Brothers*, 1906.

Barnard Letters.—The Barnard Letters (ed. A. Powell), 1928.

BARRINGTON.—Sir Jonah Barrington, *Personal Sketches of his own Times*, 1869.

BATHURST.—Bathurst MSS (Historical MSS Commission), 1923.

BEATSON.—Maj.-Gen. F. C. Beatson, *With Wellington in the Pyrenees*, 1914.

BECKE.—A. F. Becke, *Napoleon and Waterloo*, 1936.

457

BELL.—G. Bell, *Rough Notes by an Old Soldier*, 1867.

Berry Papers.—*The Berry Papers* (ed. L. Melville), 1914.

BESSBOROUGH.—*Lady Bessborough and her Family Circle* (ed. Earl of Bessborough and A. Aspinall), 1940.

BLAKENEY.—*Services, Adventures and Experiences of Captain Robert Blakeney*, 1899.

BLAKISTON.—Major John Blakiston, *Twelve Years' Military Adventure in Three-Quarters of the Globe*, 1829.

BLAND-BURGESS.—*Letters and Correspondence of Sir James Bland-Burgess* (ed. J. Hutton), 1885.

BOOTH.—Philip Booth *The Oxfordshire and Buckinghamshire Light Infantry*, 1971.

BOOTH, *Waterloo.*—*The Battle of Waterloo by a Near Observer*, 1817.

BOOTHBY.—C. Boothby, *Under England's Flag*, 1900.

BOWRING.—*Autobiography of Sir John Bowring*, 1877.

BRETT-JAMES.—Antony Brett-James, *Wellington at War*, 1961.

BRETT-JAMES, *Hundred Days.*—Antony Brett-James, *The Hundred Days*, 1964.

BROUGHTON.—Lord Broughton, *Recollections of a Long Life* (ed. Lady Dorchester), 1911.

BUCKHAM.—P. W. Buckham, *Personal Narrative of Adventures in the Peninsula*, 1827.

BURGHERSH.—*The Correspondence of Lady Burghersh with the Duke of Wellington* (ed. Lady Rose Weigall), 1903.

BURGOYNE.—*Life and Correspondence of Field-Marshal Sir John Burgoyne*, 1873.

Capel Letters.—*The Capel Letters* (ed. Marquess of Anglesey), 1955.

CASTLEREAGH.—*Memoirs and Correspondence of Viscount Castlereagh*, 1850-3.

CHAD.—*The Conversations of the First Duke of Wellington with George William Chad* (ed. 7th Duke of Wellington), 1956.

CHARLES NAPIER.—Sir W. Napier, *The Life and Opinions of General Sir Charles James Napier*, 1857.

CLINTON.—H. B. Clinton, *The War in the Peninsula and Wellington's Campaigns in France and Belgium*, 1878.

COLE.—*Memoirs of Sir Galbraith Lowry Cole* (ed. M. Lowry Cole and S. Gwynn), 1934.

COLEBROOKE.—Sir T. E. Colebrooke, *The Life of the Honourable Mountstuart Elphinstone*, 1884.

COOKE.—Captain Henry Cooke, *A Narrative of Events in the South of France*, 1835.

COOPER.—J. S. Cooper, *Rough Notes of Seven Campaigns*, 1869.

COPE.—Sir William Cope, *History of the Rifle Brigade*, 1877.
COSTELLO.—Edward Costello, *Adventures of a Soldier written by Himself*, 1852.
COTTON.—Sergeant-Major Edward Cotton, *A Voice from Waterloo*, 1913.
COWELL.—Lt.-Col. Sir John Stepney Cowell, *Leaves from the Diary of an Officer of the Guards*, 1854.
CRABB ROBINSON.—*Diary of Henry Crabb Robinson*, 1869.
CREEVEY, *Life and Times.*—*Creevey's Life and Times* (ed. John Gore), 1934.
Creevey Papers.—*The Creevey Papers* (ed. Sir H. Maxwell), 1903-5.
Croker Papers.—*The Croker Papers* (ed. L. J. Jennings), 1884.

D'ARBLAY.—*The Diaries of Madame D'Arblay*, 1854.
DE LANCEY.—*A Week at Waterloo in 1815: Lady de Lancey's Narrative* (ed. Maj. B. R. Ward), 1906.
Dickson Papers.—*The Dickson Papers* (ed. Maj.-Gen. J. Leslie), 1908-12.
D.N.B.—*Dictionary of National Biography.*
Dispatches.—*The Dispatches of Field-Marshal the Duke of Wellington*, 1834-8.
DONALDSON.—J. Donaldson, *The Eventful Life of a Soldier*, 1827.
DROPMORE.—Historical MSS Commission, *Report on the MSS of J. B. Fortescue*, preserved at Dropmore.
DUDLEY.—Lord Dudley, *Letters to "Ivy"* (ed. S. H. Romilly), 1905.
DUNCAN.—Capt. Francis Duncan, *History of the Royal Regiment of Artillery*, 1872.
D'URBAN.—*The Peninsular Journal of Major-General Sir Benjamin d'Urban*, 1930.
DYOTT.—*Diary of William Dyott* (ed. R. W. Jefferey), 1907.

EDGEWORTH.—*The Life and Letters of Maria Edgeworth* (ed. Augustus Hare), 1894.
ELERS.—*Memoirs of George Elers* (ed. Lord Monson and George Leveson Gower), 1903.
ELLESMERE.—*Personal Reminiscences of the Duke of Wellington by Francis, First Earl of Ellesmere* (ed. Alice, Countess of Strafford), 1903.

FARINGTON.—*The Farington Diary*, 1922-6.
FESTING.—J. Festing, *John Hookham Frere and his Friends*, 1899.
FORTESCUE.—Hon. Sir John Fortescue, *History of the British Army*, 1899-1930.
FOY.—*Vie Militaire de Général Foy* (ed. Girod de l'Ain), 1824.
FRASER.—Sir William Fraser, *Words on Wellington*, 1899.
FRAZER.—*Letters of Colonel Sir Augustus Simon Frazer* (ed. Maj.-Gen. Edward Sabine), 1859.
FULLER.—J. F. C. Fuller, *Sir John Moore's System of Training*, 1925.

Gascoyne Heiress.—Carola Oman, *The Gascoyne Heiress,* 1968.
GEORGE NAPIER.—*Passages in the Early Military Life of General Sir George Napier* (ed. W. E. E. Napier), 1884.
GLEIG.—G. R. Gleig, *The Life of Arthur, Duke of Wellington,* 1873.
GLOVER.—Michael Glover, *Wellington as Military Commander,* 1968.
GOMM.—Field-Marshal Sir William Gomm, *Letters and Journal,* 1881.
GORE, *Creevey.*—John Gore, *Creevey,* 1948.
GRAHAM.—Antony Brett-James, *General Graham, Lord Lynedoch,* 1959.
GRANVILLE.—*Private Correspondence of Granville Leveson-Gower, Earl Granville,* 1916.
GRATTAN.—W. Grattan, *Adventures with the Connaught Rangers,* 1847.
Greville Memoirs.—*The Greville Memoirs* (ed. H. Reeve), 1874.
GREVILLE.—*The Greville Diary* (ed. P. W. Wilson), 1927.
GRIFFITHS.—A. Griffiths, *Wellington, his Comrades and Contemporaries.*
GRONOW.—*The Reminiscences and Recollections of Captain Gronow,* 1892.
GUEDALLA.—P. Guedalla, *The Duke,* 1931.
GURWOOD.—Lt.-Col. Gurwood, *Selections from the Dispatches and General Orders of Field-Marshal the Duke of Wellington,* 1851.

H.M.C.—*Reports of the Royal Commission on Historical Manuscripts.*
Hamilton of Dalzell MS.—Manuscript in the possession of Lord Hamilton of Dalzell.
HARRIET GRANVILLE.—*Letters of Harriet, Countess Granville* (ed. F. Leveson-Gower), 1894.
HARRIETTE WILSON.—*Harriette Wilson's Memoirs* (ed. J. Laver), 1929.
HARRIS.—*Recollections of Rifleman Harris,* 1848.
HAYDON.—B. Haydon, *Autobiography* (ed. E. Blunden), 1927.
HAYDON, *Life.*—*Life of Benjamin Robert Haydon from his Journals* (ed. T. Taylor), 1853.
HESTER STANHOPE.—*The Memoirs of Lady Hester Stanhope,* 1845.
HICKEY.—*Memoirs of William Hickey* (ed. A. Spencer), 1913-25.
HOBHOUSE.—*The Diary of Henry Hobhouse* (ed. A. Aspinall), 1947.
HOOPER.—George Hooper, *Waterloo,* 1862.
HOUSSAYE.—H. Houssaye, *1815 Waterloo* (ed. A. Euan-Smith), 1900.
HOWARTH.—David Howarth, *A Near Run Thing,* 1968.

JACKSON.—Lt.-Col. Basil Jackson, *Notes and Reminiscences of a Staff Officer* (ed. R. C. Seaton), 1903.
JACKSON, *Diaries and Letters.*—Sir George Jackson, *Diaries and Letters,* 1872.
JAMES.—Lt.-Col. W. H. James, *The Campaign of 1815,* 1908.
JERNINGHAM.—*The Jerningham Letters,* 1896.
JOHNNY NEWCOME.—*The Military Adventures of Johnny Newcome,* (1904 ed.).

Journal of a Soldier.— *Journal of a Soldier of the Seventy-First Regiment*, 1822.

JOURDAN.—Marshal H. B. Jourdan, *Mémoires Militaires sur la Guerre d'Espagne*, 1899.

KAYE.—John William Kaye, *The Life and Correspondence of Major-General Sir John Malcolm*, 1856.

KENNEDY.—Gen. Sir James Shaw Kennedy, *Notes on the Battle of Waterloo*, 1865.

KINCAID.—J. Kincaid, *Adventures in the Rifle Brigade*, 1830.

KINCAID, *Random Shots*.—J. Kincaid, *Random Shots from a Rifleman*, 1835.

KNOWLES.—*The War in the Peninsula: Some Letters of Lieutenant Robert Knowles*, 1913.

LADY SHELLEY.—*The Diary of Frances, Lady Shelley* (ed. Richard Edgecumbe), 1912-13.

LAPÉNE.—E. Lapene, *Campagne de 1813-14 sur l'Ebre, les Pyrenées, et la Garonne*, 1834.

LARPENT.—*The Private Journal of Judge-Advocate F. S. Larpent*, 1835.

LAWRENCE.—*The Autobiography of Sergeant William Lawrence* (ed. G. N. Bankes), 1886.

LEACH.—J. Leach, *Rough Sketches of the Life of an Old Soldier*, 1831.

Leaves from the Diary of an Officer.—*Leaves from the Diary of an Officer.*

LEEKE.—W. Leeke, *The History of Lord Seaton's Regiment at the Battle of Waterloo*, 1866.

LEITH HAY.—A. Leith Hay, *Narrative of the Peninsular War*, 1879.

LENNOX.—*Life and Letters of Lady Sarah Lennox* (ed. Countess of Ilchester and Lord Stavordale), 1901.

LENNOX, *Three Years with the Duke*.—*Three Years with the Duke*, 1853.

LESLIE.—*Military Journal of Colonel Leslie of Balquhair*, 1887.

LONDONDERRY.—Marquis of Londonderry, *Narrative of the War in 1813 and 1814*, 1830.

LONG.—*A Peninsular Cavalry General:* The Correspondence of Lt.-Gen. Robert Ballard Long (ed. T. H. McGuffie), 1951.

LONGFORD.—Elizabeth Longford, *Wellington: The Years of the Sword*, 1969.

LUSHINGTON.—S. R. Lushington, *Life and Services of General Lord Harris*, 1840.

LYNEDOCH.—A. M. Delavoye, *Life of Thomas Graham, Lord Lynedoch*, 1880.

McGRIGOR.—*The Autobiography and Services of Sir James McGrigor*, 1861.

MAGINN.—William Maginn, *The Military Sketch Book*, 1831.

MAJOLIER.—*Memorials of Christine Majolier* (ed. M. Braithwaite), 1881.

461

MALCOLM.—*The Life and Correspondence of Maj.-Gen. Sir John Malcolm* (ed. J. W. Kaye), 1856.

Marlay Letters.—*The Marlay Letters* (ed. R. W. Bond), 1937.

MAXWELL.—Sir Herbert Maxwell, *The Life of Wellington*, 1900.

MERCER.—General Cavalié Mercer, *Journal of the Waterloo Campaign*, 1870.

MOORE.—*The Diary of Sir John Moore* (ed. Sir J. M. Maurice), 1904.

MOORSOM.—Capt. W. S. Moorsom, *A Historical Record of the Fifty-Second Regiment*, 1860.

MORRIS.—W. O'Connor Morris, *The Campaign of 1815*, 1900.

MÜFFLING.—Freiherr von Müffling, *Aus Meinen Leben*, 1855.

MUNSTER.—Lt.-Col. Fitzclarence (Earl of Munster), *An Account of the British Campaign of 1809 under Sir A. Wellesley*, 1831.

MURIEL WELLESLEY.—Muriel Wellesley, *The Man Wellington*, 1937.

NAPIER.—Sir W. Napier, *History of the War in the Peninsula*, 1834-40. (See also CHARLES NAPIER and GEORGE NAPIER.)

Near Observer.—*Battle of Waterloo by a Near Observer*, 1817.

NUGENT.—Lady Nugent, *Journal* (ed. F. Cunall), 1907.

OMAN.—Sir Charles Oman, *A History of the Peninsular War*, 1902-31.

OMAN, *Wellington's Army.*—Sir C. Oman, *Wellington's Army*, 1913.

PAGET.—*Letters and Memorials of Gen. The Hon. Sir Edward Paget* (ed. Eden Paget), 1898.

Paget Brothers.—*The Paget Brothers* (ed. Lord Hylton), 1918.

Paget Papers.—*The Paget Papers* (ed. Sir A. Paget), 1896.

Pakenham Letters.—*Pakenham Letters* (ed. Lord Longford), 1914.

Peninsular Sketches.—*Peninsular Sketches* (ed. W. H. Maxwell), 1845.

PETRIE.—Sir Charles Petrie, *Wellington, a Reassessment*, 1956.

PICTON.—H. B. Robinson, *Memoirs and Correspondence of General Sir T. Picton*, 1836.

PICTON, *Waterloo.*—G. W. Picton, *The Battle of Waterloo*.

Pitt and the Great War.—J. Hollard Rose, *William Pitt and the Great War*, 1911.

PLUMER WARD.—E. Phipps, *Memorials of the Political and Literary Life of Robert Plumer Ward*, 1850.

ROBINSON.—Maj.-Gen. C. W. Robinson, *Wellington's Campaigns*, 1911.

ROGERS, *Recollections.*—Samuel Rogers (ed. W. Sharpe), 1959.

ROSE.—*The Diaries and Correspondence of the Right Honourable George Rose*, 1860.

SALISBURY.—*A Great Man's Friendship* (ed. Lady Burghclere), 1927.

SCHAUMANN.—A. L. F. Schaumann, *On the Road with Wellington*, 1924.

SCOTT.—*The Letters of Sir Walter Scott* (ed. Sir H. C. Grierson), 1932-7.

SEATON.—*Life of John Colborne, Field-Marshal Lord Seaton* (ed. G. C. Moore-Smith), 1903.

SHAND.—A. E. Shand, *Wellington's Lieutenants*, 1902.

SHERER.—Moyle Sherer, *Recollections of the Peninsula*, 1825.

SIBORNE.—Maj.-Gen. H. T. Siborne, *Waterloo Letters*, 1891.

SIMMONS.—*A British Rifleman* (ed. Col. Willoughby Verner), 1899.

SIMPSON.—J. Simpson, *Paris after Waterloo*, 1853.

SMITH.—*The Autobiography of General Sir Harry Smith* (ed. G. C. Moore-Smith), 1901.

Spencer and Waterloo.—*Spencer and Waterloo, The Letters of Spencer Madan* (ed. B. Madan), 1970.

Standing Orders.—*Standing Orders as Given out and Enforced by the late Major-General Robert Craufurd for the Use of the Light Division* (ed. Campbell and Shaw), 1880.

STANHOPE.—Earl Stanhope, *Notes on the Conversations with the Duke of Wellington*, 1888.

Supplementary Despatches.—*Supplementary Despatches, Correspondence and Memoranda of Field-Marshal Arthur, Duke of Wellington*, 1858-64.

SURTEES.—W. Surtees, *Twenty-five Years in the Rifle Brigade*, 1833.

THIÉBAULT.—Baron Thiébault, *Mémoires* (ed. F. Calmettes), 1893-5.

TOMKINSON.—W. Tomkinson, *The Diary of a Cavalry Officer in the Peninsular and Waterloo Campaigns*, 1894.

Two Duchesses.—V. Foster, *The Two Duchesses*, 1898.

VERE.—Vere, *Marches of the 4th Division*.

VERNER.—Col. Willoughby Verner, *History and Campaigns of the Rifle Brigade*, 1919.

VIVIAN.—C. Vivian, *Memoir of Richard, Lord Vivian*, 1897.

WARD.—S. G. P. Ward, *Wellington's Headquarters*, 1957.

WARRE.—Lt.-Gen. Sir William Warre, *Letters from the Peninsula*, 1909.

WELLER.—Jac Weller, *Wellington in the Peninsula*, 1962.

WELLER, *Waterloo.*—Jac Weller, *Wellington and Waterloo*, 1967.

Wellesley Papers.—*The Wellesley Papers*, 1914.

WELLESLEY-POLE.—*Some Letters of the Duke of Wellington to his Brother, William Wellesley-Pole* (ed. Sir C. Webster), Camden Miscellany, Royal Historical Society. Vol. XVIII, 1948.

Wellington and his Friends.—*Wellington and his Friends* (ed. 7th Duke of Wellington), 1965.

WELSH.—Col. James Welsh, *Military Reminiscences*, 1830.
WHEELER.—*The Letters of Private Wheeler* (ed. B. H. Liddell Hart), 1951.
WINDHAM.—*The Diary of William Windham* (ed. H. Baring), 1866.
Windham Papers.—*The Windham Papers*, 1913.

Index

INDEX

Wellington in the Pyrenees
From a watercolour by Thomas Heaphy 1813
National Portrait Gallery

By the same author and published by Collins

THE LION & THE UNICORN

The Story of England
MAKERS OF THE REALM B.C.-1272
THE AGE OF CHIVALRY 1272-1381

KING CHARLES II 1630-1685

RESTORATION ENGLAND

Samuel Pepys
THE MAN IN THE MAKING 1633-1669
THE YEARS OF PERIL 1670-1683
THE SAVIOUR OF THE NAVY 1683-1689

The Napoleonic Wars
THE YEARS OF ENDURANCE 1793-1802
YEARS OF VICTORY 1802-1812
THE AGE OF ELEGANCE 1812-1822

ENGLISH SAGA 1840-1940

The Alanbrooke Diaries
THE TURN OF THE TIDE 1939-1943
TRIUMPH IN THE WEST 1943-1946

THE FIRE AND THE ROSE

English Social History
THE MEDIEVAL FOUNDATION
PROTESTANT ISLAND

NELSON

JIMMY

THE GREAT DUKE